Globalization and Unemployment

Springer
Berlin
Heidelberg
New York
Barcelona
Hong Kong
London
Milan
Paris
Singapore
Tokyo

Helmut Wagner
Editor

Globalization and Unemployment

With 32 Figures
and 24 Tables

Springer

Prof. Dr. Helmut Wagner
University of Hagen
Chair of Macroeconomics
Feithstrasse 140
58084 Hagen

ISBN 3-540-66765-2 Springer-Verlag Berlin Heidelberg New York

Library of Congress Cataloging-in-Publication Data
Die Deutsche Bibliothek – CIP-Einheitsaufnahme
Globalization and unemployment: with 24 tables / Helmut Wagner (ed.). – Berlin; Heidelberg; New York; Barcelona; Hong Kong; London; Milan; Paris; Singapore; Tokyo: Springer, 2000
ISBN 3-540-66765-2

Printed in Germany

Hardcover-Design: Erich Kirchner, Heidelberg

SPIN 10724389 42/2202-5 4 3 2 1 0 – Printed on acid-free paper

Contents

Introduction

Helmut Wagner

University of Hagen,
Feithstr. 140, 58089 Hagen, Germany

Globalization and unemployment are two phenomena which are among the most widely discussed subjects in the economic debate today. In Europe in particular the tendency of unemployment to rise since the 1970s has become a center of political conflict which has had a seriously negative effect on the political confidence of the public in the ability of politicians and their advisors to act as crisis managers.

However, a view of the causes was very quickly developed which diverted responsibility from politicians and attributed it to an apparently exogenous factor. For example, many observers attributed the increase in unemployment above all to the worldwide trend towards globalization, i.e. to the increase in the world economic interdependence of markets and corporate activities, and the rapid spread of technologies, which has happened above all in the last two decades. However, this is countered by the success in many countries in combating unemployment in this period, above all in the USA, but also in Great Britain, the Netherlands and other smaller countries.

In principle, the correlation between globalization and unemployment has still not yet been fully clarified. Clarification of this correlation is not only of academic interest, but is also decisive for the drafting and designing of the fight against unemployment in terms of economic policy.

In this book experts examine fundamental questions on this subject, in particular the following:

What are the challenges of globalization in the advanced economies and how can they be met?

How did previous processes of globalization turn out, what economic consequences did they have (in particular on unemployment), and how were they stopped?

How has unemployment developed internationally? What common features were there, and what were the differences?

How can unemployment be explained? What are the different approaches for explaining it, and what are their common features and differences?

What impact does technical progress have on the structure of (un)employment and wages?

What influence does globalization have on the development of unemployment? What certain knowledge is available, and which questions are still open?

Will the EMU, which can be regarded as a specific characteristic or consequence of globalization, intensify or tend to weaken unemployment in Europe?

What role can national labor market policies play in an era of globalization?

What are the measures that a national fiscal policy can take to counter possible negative consequences of globalization for employment?

What are the effects of globalization on inflation, and beyond this on national stabilization policies and unemployment?

The following provides a brief overview of the contents of each article which is based on abstracts which were mainly drawn up by the authors themselves.

Most of the articles, including the accompanying commentary papers, were presented and discussed at a conference in Hagen in March 1999, and then revised. The purpose of the conference, and of this volume, was/is (as with the previous project: Wagner, H., Current Issues in Monetary Economics, Physica-Verlag 1998) to have recognized experts deal from different sides with a current, strictly delineated subject in accordance with a defined structure, which was developed and stipulated by the editor.[1]

Following this introduction, the book starts with the first part which contains two papers on globalization. The first article by **Daniel Citrin and Stanley Fischer** (the First Deputy Managing Director of the International Monetary Fund) explores the extent to which globalization has increased policy interdependence and reduced governments' ability to control their own economies. They ask: does globalization make it more difficult to achieve the legitimate and desirable aims of economic policy? Their answer is that globalization makes it easier to attain the ultimate goal of economic policy, which is higher incomes; redistributive policies and social safety nets, however, should be used to ensure that these gains are shared fairly. Even in a business cycle context, they argue, globalization is on the whole a force for greater stability—even though at times large short–term capital flows can adversely affect macroeconomic stability, and asset prices, including exchange rates, can as a result become misaligned. Globalization can act as a force for stability by limiting the scope for countries to pursue policies that are

[1] As the editor of the book, I would like to thank all authors for their cooperation during the long process of organizing this project, of conducting the preparatory conference and for revising their papers under consideration of the strict layout requirements set by the editor and the publisher.

incompatible with medium–term financial stability. The disciplining effect of global financial markets applies not only to policymakers, via financial market pressures, but also to the private sector, by making it more difficult to sustain unwarranted price markups and non-productivity driven wage increases.

They stress, however, that at the same time, it has to be recognized that overexuberant international capital flows can at times permit disequilibria to develop, and can require excessively large output adjustments in emerging market countries when flows reverse. These real possibilities reinforce the case for strengthening macroeconomic policies and financial systems in emerging market countries—and they also emphasize the urgency of strengthening the international financial architecture.

In the following paper, **Kevin O'Rourke** examines the role of globalization in a historical perspective. He makes clear that globalization has been an ongoing process for centuries and that history shows that globalization can and has often been reversed. This reversal can be linked to the distributional consequences of globalization, at least in the cases of commodity trade and labor migration, as O'Rourke illustrates in his paper.

He first provides a brief survey of broad trends in the integration and disintegration of the international economy. He then focuses more specifically on the impact of globalization on labor, concentrating on the last great wave of globalization which occurred a hundred years ago. Finally, he explores the political issues associated with international trade and factor flows, again mainly in the context of the late 19th century.

It is argued in the paper that the late 19th century resembled our own period in many respects, with rapid changes in the international division of labor due to declining costs of doing business across frontiers. The key differences between the two periods appear to have been (1) that many more international transactions take place within the firm today than was true a hundred years ago; and (2) that international flows of labor and capital were proportionately much larger then than now.

The distributional consequences of these shocks were much more clear cut for land than for labor, at least insofar as commodity trade was concerned. In labor-abundant Europe, left wing parties favored free trade more because they thought it would bring cheap food, than because they believed it would expand labor-intensive activities and promote employment. In the rich, labor-scarce New World, where globalization might have been expected to lower real wages rather than raise them, there were far more echoes of today's concerns about trade, inequality and unemployment in OECD economies.

O'Rourke illustrates that it was migration that had the greatest impact on workers' living standards, and when immigration led to unskilled wages lagging excessively behind average incomes, governments intervened to stem the migration flows. There are obvious parallels here with today's concerns that rising inequality will undermine the political support for globalization. However, as O'Rourke argues, there are important differences between the two epochs. The mass intercontinental migration which lowered New World living standards is absent today; while international institutions such as the WTO would make it much more difficult for politicians to dismantle today's international economy, should their constituents demand that they do so. Nonetheless, he emphasizes that the late 19th century experience does serve as a useful reminder that the political support for globalization cannot be taken for granted, and that the distributional consequences of a more tightly integrated international economy matter not just in their own right, but because of the policy responses which they can provoke.

The **second part** of the book contains three articles on empirical and theoretical aspects of unemployment. It starts with a paper by **Ronald Schettkat** who focuses on the definition and measurement of unemployment and establishes some facts about unemployment in an international comparative perspective. Schettkat emphasizes the difficulty of measuring unemployment because of the theoretical and empirical problem of distinguishing between unemployment, employment and leisure. He stresses that unemployment (i.e. involuntary unemployment) can only exist in models of imperfect labor markets, but that there is no clear dividing line between 'unemployment and employment' in a theoretical sense. Apart from theoretical problems there are more pragmatic problems about the way in which unemployment and employment are classified. Schettkat discusses these pragmatic problems and deals with questions such as the following: are workers in public work programs employed, or is this kind of work so artificial as to equal unemployment? He then proceeds to a comparison of different data series measuring employment and unemployment. He uses national definitions and compares them with internationally comparative data provided by the US Bureau of Labor Statistics (BLS). This analysis provides a basis on which to evaluate the sensitivity of labor market figures to national definitions.

Another issue is the choice of indicators used to represent employment and unemployment. Different indicators (unemployment rates, employment-population ratios, and working volume per head of population) are used and the relationships between them are investigated. Finally, Schettkat briefly investigates simple relationships between labor market indicators and other key economic variables, such as growth, wages, technological progress and inflation.

The main empirical findings of the paper are as follows. All G7 countries experienced a rise in the unemployment rate in the 1970s and 1980s, although the trend was less pronounced in Japan and the USA. These unemployment trends were accompanied by very different trends in the employment-population ratios. Countries with declining employment-population ratios also experienced a decline in average working hours. A comparison of unemployment rates and employment-population ratios as measured by national concepts and the approximated US concept shows that the difference is important for unemployment figures. Only the USA displays a strong positive trend in working hours per head of adult population, which is mainly caused by increasing participation. Employment growth and population growth are closely correlated. Differences in GDP growth rates cannot explain divergent employment trends, although economic growth, of course, affects employment positively. Countries with strong employment growth also show a high employment elasticity of GDP growth.

In the 1990s, inflation has been lower than in the 1960s, in all G7-countries, but at the same time, unemployment is higher everywhere, with the exception of the USA. This pattern is broadly consistent with the unemployment-inflation trade-off, but unemployment is much higher in the 1990s compared to the 1960s suggesting a rise in the NAIRU, which –except for the US- can be found in the data everywhere. The problem with NAIRU explanations is, however, that they do not fit institutional changes well.

The paper by **Thomas Beißinger and Joachim Möller** deals with the theoretical explanations of unemployment. In the 1970s and 1980s, various competing theories put forward by the classical and Keynesian camps tried to find a convincing explanation for the unemployment problem. The structuralist model emerged from these research efforts as the dominant approach of the nineties, combining both classical and Keynesian features. By generating a relationship between changes in inflation and deviations of unemployment from the long-run equilibrium, this approach carries on where the old Phillips curve debate left off.

In their contribution, Beißinger/Möller do not confine themselves to a review of the research from the last decade, but rather stress the implications of several extensions of the macroeconomic model as well. Whereas in the standard structuralist model the demand side has a negligible influence on unemployment in the medium term, they show that stabilization policies are of greater importance once unemployment persistence and/or the openness of economies are taken into account.

Furthermore, Beißinger/Möller build on the structuralist framework to address not only the macroeconomic aspects of the unemployment problem, but also the debate between trade theorists and labor economists about the impact of globalization and biased technical change on the employment performance of different skill groups. In the literature, contra-factual implications of the standard Heckscher-Ohlin model are often used as an argument against trade-based explanations of the unemployment problem. By relaxing the assumption of perfect competition, they show that major aspects of this critique can be overcome. On the other hand, conventional wisdom which favors the biased technical change hypothesis, can be questioned. Things are less obvious if the general equilibrium effects of biased technical change are taken into account. In contrast to results following from a simple partial framework, it has been shown that the unskilled could profit via indirect effects from biased technical change. To obtain the stylized fact that the unskilled lose employment shares, Beißinger/Möller stress that not only is a high elasticity of substitution needed, but also certain additional assumptions about the impact of biased productivity growth on the skill-specific wage formation process.

The following paper by **Winfried Vogt** analyzes the interaction between the changing structure of employment and wages and a biased technical progress. The analysis is based on a two-sector model. The two sectors can be interpreted in two different ways. In the first interpretation, there is an industrial and a service sector (or a country which mainly supplies industrial products, compared with a country in which the service sector dominates). In the second interpretation, there is a sector (or a country) with skilled labor and a sector (or a country) with unskilled labor. If there is a trade-off between sector-specific rates of technical progress, a mutual dependence exists between the structure of wages and employment on the one side, and a biased technical progress on the other side. This interdependence causes endogenous changes in the structure of employment and wages. The main conclusions are: firstly, as the elasticity of substitution between the industrial and the service sector is likely to be low, an industry-biased technical progress will eventually disappear. In the long run, the industrial and the service sector will grow at the same rate, and the structure of employment will remain constant. Secondly, as the elasticity of substitution between skilled and unskilled labor is likely to be high, skill-biased technical progress will gradually increase. This will lead to a rising inequality of earnings. If there is an appropriate wage floor (fixed by the state or the unions), which prevents inequality from growing, the increase in inequality will be replaced by a continuous increase in unemployment for unskilled workers. If unskilled workers have the option to become skilled, they may still be worse off, if they have to bear the training costs. Nevertheless, the rising relative supply of skilled workers could prevent the decline of the relative position.

The **third part** of the book is concerned with the effects on unemployment resulting on the one hand from globalization in general, and on the other hand from the introduction of the European Monetary Union which can itself be regarded as a consequence of the globalization process. The paper by **Oliver Landmann** examines the effects of globalization on unemployment. The recent debate about the labor market effects of globalization has been shaped by the coincidence of several major trends:

– The emerging economies' share in world exports of manufactured goods has sharply increased since 1970 and is due to increase further in the future.

– In most advanced countries, since 1980 at least changes in the structure of labor demand have clearly favored skilled labor at the expense of unskilled labor.

– Wage differentials have markedly widened in the United States (and to some extent in the United Kingdom), but have remained largely constant or have even narrowed in most continental European economies.

– At the same time, the growth rates of real wages and labor productivity have been substantially higher in Europe than in the USA.

– Europe has experienced stagnant employment and rising unemployment, in particular among the unskilled, whereas the United States has enjoyed brisk employment growth and thereby kept unemployment low.

Landmann's paper reviews some widely held views ('conventional wisdoms') concerning the causes of and the interrelation between these developments. One such view states that every economy faces a trade-off between real wage growth and unemployment. The United States, it appears, has opted for high employment growth and low real wage growth whereas most European countries, through the design of their labor market institutions and policies, have made the opposite choice. Landmann maintains that this view rests on weak foundations: there is no relationship between the extent of wage pressure and the productivity of jobs in the long run, once the induced adjustment of investment spending is taken into account. However, a high-wage policy can influence the composition of the jobs that are viable and thereby affect the aggregate wage and productivity statistics. A negative relation between employment and the average wage level thus reappears as a composite effect.

Another conventional wisdom investigated in the paper claims that the shift of labor demand towards high skills has created a trade-off between wage inequality and unemployment. If labor markets are flexible, and if the demand shift dominates any shifts in relative supplies (that may occur at the same time), the wage differential between skilled and unskilled labor widens, which is what happened on the US labor market. In contrast, if relative wages are rigid, which is largely the case in most continental European economies, the demand shift leads to an increase in unskilled unemployment. This proposition is built on theoretically more robust ground than the first. But this does not mean that relative demand shifts are necessarily the dominant force behind the rise in European unemployment, nor is the empirical picture quite as sharp as one might expect. The correlation between measures of relative wage rigidity and the unemployment rates of unskilled labor is somewhat fuzzy, as Landmann stresses. This is not entirely surprising once it is recognized that skilled labor can be adversely affected even if labor demand shocks are biased against unskilled labor, and that unskilled labor is disproportionately affected even by aggregate labor demand shocks.

A third proposition, examined in the paper, concerns the role of globalization. According to widely held views, which are often reinforced by the popular press and the infotainment industry, globalization is a major cause of labor market problems in general and of the deteriorating situation of the less-skilled in particular. Landmann maintains that mainstream academic research does not support this view so far. The volume of North-South trade is simply too small for competitive pressures from low-wage imports to become a major cause of labor market disruptions in the North. Instead, non-neutral technological change is seen by Landmann as the main driving force behind the structural changes on the demand side of the labor market. But, as he emphasizes, it would certainly be premature to regard the issue as resolved. Once channels of causation are considered that lie outside the focus of traditional HOS models of trade, the case for a major impact of globalization appears to grow stronger. On a more fundamental level, recent work questions the separability of technological change and globalization.

The following paper by **Ansgar Belke and Daniel Gros** deals with a special regional aspect of globalization, namely the European Monetary Union, and its consequences for unemployment. It finds that intra-European exchange rate variability had significant economic costs. Simple VAR causality tests show that higher short run variability of exchange rates was associated with higher unemployment, less employment and lower investment for most EU member countries (including France and Germany). The evidence is somewhat less consistent for dollar variability. Robustness tests show that this result holds up in the presence of a variety of policy instruments (e.g., interest rates) and cyclical variables (e.g., GDP growth) that might have also had an impact on exchange rate variability. The point estimates suggest that EMU could lower the German unemployment rate by about 0.5 to 0.75 percentage points. These statistical findings can be interpreted in the context of a simple model that incorporates the 'option value of waiting' and which suggests that even short-term spikes in volatility can have a strong impact on investment, one of the main determinants of the labor market stance. Moreover, given the high cost of firing workers in Europe, the same reasoning should apply to employment. The implications for the cost-benefits analysis of EMU are clear. Should these results also be confirmed for other countries there would also be implications for the desirability of floating exchange rates in general and the role of the Fund in the global monetary system.

Eliminating intra-European exchange rate variability is often portrayed as one major advantage of EMU (reducing it was already a goal of the creation of the EMS in 1979). But Belke/Gros ask: why should politicians and economists care about exchange rate variability? Up to now the answer has usually been that exchange rate variability discourages trade. Unfortunately, a large volume of empirical literature on this issue has not been able to document a strong link between exchange rate variability and the volume of trade. However, Belke/Gros argue that the absence of a strong impact of exchange rate variability on the volume of trade does not imply that there should be no link between exchange rate variability and (un-) employment and investment. They ask: why would an increase in exchange rate volatility lead quickly to a lower volume (flow) of trade? The theoretical models that are used in this context start typically from the idea that in order to export a sunk cost must be maintained. This sunk cost is meant to represent the need to build up a distribution system in foreign markets and that this is really a sunk cost like in the bare bones model used here. But in Europe most firms already have a very elaborate distribution network in all member countries. A German automobile manufacturer will typically not have to build up a new distribution system in order to increase sales in other European countries. Hence Belke/Gros argue that certainly for intra-European trade (the focus of their empirical work) market access costs cannot be the main reason why exchange rate volatility should affect trade.

Of course, an increase in volatility will lead firms to discount future profits from exports more heavily (as often assumed in the literature and also in the model they used, see below). But, as Belke/Gros stress, this implies only that firms will invest less in export (or in general in trade-) oriented activities. This might depress future export (trade) volumes but firms will not necessarily export less in the short run just because exchange rate variability has increased. The long-run response will be much more difficult to isolate in empirical work because there are other long-run trends (e.g. reductions in transport costs, shifts in tastes, etc.) and because variability changes so much over time. Trade volumes today might be a function of some average of the variability experienced over a number of years but this would be difficult to measure even with the annual data on volatility that is often used. Experience with large exchange rate swings in Europe during the 1990s has once again shown that there is a lot of 'pricing to market', i.e. firms keep local prices fixed even in the face of large exchange rate changes. This implies, as they point out, that quantities react little to exchange rates, but profits by much more. Firms simply keep producing and export more or less the same amount, but their domestic currency earnings become variable whereas their domestic cost remain stable. Exchange rate variability can thus certainly influence the variability of profits.

If firms react to an increase in exchange rate (and hence profit) variability in the first instance by reducing investment in trade related activities one would expect little impact on trade flows in the short run, but, potentially at least, a significant short-run impact on investment (as Belke/Gros find in their empirical investigations) and on (un-)employment because investment is an important component of demand. Moreover, they stress that in most continental European countries (and even in the UK until the 1980s) hiring workers represents also an investment in the sense that there are high costs involved in reversing this decision. This is an additional reason (independent of the demand effect) why exchange rate variability should affect (un-)employment. Moreover, if labor is de facto a semi-fixed factor of production, the short-run marginal costs of changing the volume of production should be very high. This fits well with the observed sluggish reaction of trade volumes to the exchange rate changes mentioned above. Belke/Gros therefore argue that exchange rate variability should have little impact on production and export sales in the short run. Firms will typically be reluctant to engage new labor (which involves a heavy sunk cost in most European countries) if the variability of the exchange rate is high so that the probability that this labor will not be used after all is also high.

The **fourth part** of the book deals with the economic policy consequences of globalization. It starts with a debate on the role of labor market policy in a globalized economy. First, the paper by **Norbert Berthold and Rainer Fehn** deals with the much discussed question of how to design labor market policy in a global economy. The starting point of the paper is the fact that national unemployment rates differ greatly, which implies that country-specific institutional factors are the most plausible culprits for increasing and lasting unemployment. Hence, identifying institutional setups which promote employment growth is seen as a prerequisite for successfully fighting unemployment. To this end the paper is divided into three main sections. The first section provides a non-technical synopsis of the main causes of persistently high unemployment which can be observed in particular in continental Europe. Special emphasis is put on the question of how the ongoing process of globalization of goods and factor markets relates to the rise in unemployment.

Berthold/Fehn argue that there can be little question that globalization opens greater exit possibilities for capital that has not yet been invested which, once invested, is threatened with appropriation by powerful insiders in certain countries. They maintain further that globalization increases the potential for specialization in production and the pressure to switch from a Taylorite to a holistic organization of production structures thus exacerbating appropriability problems; that it broadens the technological menu by facilitating international technology transfers, thus allowing a greater degree of substitution of labor by capital; and, finally, that it exposes firms and workers to greater volatilities, i.e. to a less stable macroeconomic environment. They show how these factors interact and how they conflict with important characteristics of the German economy in particular, which, however, is not too dissimilar to a number of other continental European countries. These characteristics are mainly generous and long-term transfer payments to the unemployed, high firing costs and centralized wage-setting.

The second section of Berthold/Fehn's paper discusses how labor market institutions should be reformed, and how labor market policy should be redesigned, in order to achieve better employment results. Under the premise that the above-mentioned factors are indeed important for explaining the severe unemployment problem, they argue that the thrust of such reforms must be in the direction of reducing aggregate wage pressure, of achieving greater flexibility in wage-setting and in employment contracts, of correcting the currently distorted incentive structures for the unemployed towards their acceptance of a greater variety of jobs, and of helping the unemployed to build the kind of human capital that is actually demanded by firms.

Finally, the third section of the paper discusses the positive economics of labor market policy in a global economy. Essentially all OECD countries are under pressure towards redesigning their labor market institutions and policies in a more efficient way. However, progress in this direction varies widely between countries not least due to difficulties in enforcing efficiency-enhancing reforms in the political decision-making process. However, it is shown that encompassing reform packages are more likely to be politically viable than piecemeal reforms.

In the following paper, **Jürgen Kromphardt** discusses an explanation of unemployment in a global economy which he proposes as an alternative to the traditional neoclassical explanation, which argues that real wages are too high. Kromphardt's explanation starts with the now "standard description" of the labor market development by Carlin/Soskice (1990) and used among others by Bean (1994) in his well-known survey article on European unemployment. Kromphardt stresses the importance of the "arrow of causation", which runs in this model from the rate of unemployment to the wage rate, contrary to the neoclassical tradition. He shows that the structure of the labor market is consistent with classical and with Keynesian unemployment.

On the empirical level, Kromphardt demonstrates in section two that in Germany (as in France) the real wage level has lagged behind productivity growth since 1982 (with very few exceptions, in particular in 1992 and 1993). Therefore, he argues, there is no empirical base to the claim that the growth of unemployment in the past two decades is due to real wage shocks as supposed, e.g. by Berthold/Fehn in this volume.

In section three, the implications for labor market and employment policies are discussed.

The next paper by **Clemens Fuest, Bernd Huber and Florian Wöhlbier** analyzes the employment effects and also, to a lesser extent, some distributive implications of various revenue-neutral reforms of the tax and transfer system. The analysis is carried out using the case of a small open economy with unemployment. Unemployment arises since wages are set via bargaining between trade unions and firms.

First, Fuest/Huber/Wöhlbier discuss the effects of a consumption tax reform. They show that a reduction of labor taxes financed by higher consumption taxes would increase employment. The reason is that the tax base of a consumption tax is broader than that of a labor tax. A tax reform of this nature therefore shifts part of the tax burden from employed workers to firm owners who receive profit income, and to the unemployed. That such a tax reform would also reduce the well-being of unemployed transfer recipients may be problematic from a distributional point of view. Fuest/Huber/Wöhlbier maintain that such a policy would be equivalent to a direct reduction in unemployment benefits, which would also increase employment but faces distributional objections. However, the positive employment effect of a consumption tax reform still holds if the unemployed are compensated for the higher consumption taxes by an increase in unemployment benefits.

Another tax reform strategy which is currently on the political agenda is the idea of financing labor tax reductions through higher environmental taxes. Fuest/Huber/Wöhlbier consider the case of an internationally tradable, polluting factor of production, such as petrol. They show that a reduction in labor taxes financed by higher taxes on internationally mobile factors of production increases employment. Moreover, they show that an environmental tax reform also leads to an increase in profits and, thus, to a Pareto-improvement in their model. This is due to the fact that such a tax reform reduces the factor price distortions relative to the situation where only labor is subject to taxation. If such a tax is available, however, it is argued that it is more effective to tax profits directly, because the burden of taxes on internationally mobile factors of production is borne by domestic immobile factors anyway. A critical implicit assumption underlying their analysis is that the wage rate emerging from the bargaining process is such that labor taxes are shifted entirely to firms. In bargaining models with different implications for tax incidence, different results may emerge.

As a third step, Fuest/Huber/Wöhlbier develop a proposal for a reform of the system of social security contributions that allows sufficient revenue to be raised but reduces the marginal cost of labor. This increases labor demand for a given net wage and induces the wage bargaining parties to agree on a lower wage rate.

They stress that such a reform can be implemented by making a firm's payroll tax payment contingent on the value of its tax base in the past or on changes in its tax base and, thus, on its employment history. By doing this, an increase in employment can be achieved without a redistribution of the tax burden to other agents in the economy as in the case of the two other reforms discussed. This proposal has similarities with the system of experience rating used, for instance, in the U.S. unemployment insurance system.

The book closes with a paper by **Helmut Wagner** who analyzes the effects of globalization on inflation and some of the consequences for stabilization policy. In this final contribution, globalization is understood as a development which increasingly exposes countries to international competition. This process or competition is regarded as being effective not only in the goods market, but also in the markets for mobile production factors (human and, in particular, real capital). The question is raised whether this tends to reduce inflation.

In section 2, the inflation problem is elaborated. In section 3, the question is analyzed of whether globalization may decrease inflation and through which channels. Firstly, the effects of globalization on the inflation bias motives are worked out, and secondly, the direct threat of losing capital and the resulting disciplinary mechanism induced by globalization (or international competition for portfolio capital and mobile production factors) are investigated. To sum up, globalization is interpreted here as a technological-institutional process that reduces the benefits of inflation and makes the production of inflation more costly for a society or country.

Section 4 analyzes three possible explanations of the recent decline in inflation. One explanation does not refer to globalization but explains the decline in inflation with different alteration speeds of employment aims and of the so-called “natural” employment rate following supply shocks. The other explanation refers to globalization as a process which makes the production of inflation more costly for a society or country. This cost-increasing effect of globalization is modeled alternatively as

1) a lower preferred inflation rate

2) a higher aversion to inflation

3) a lower output effect of a surprise inflation

4) an additional cost factor in the loss function of the central bank or of the government

5) an additional cost factor in the loss function of the society.

Furthermore, the paper points out an alternative interpretation which assumes that in the course of globalization more efficient communication and information technologies in connection with the introduction of financial innovations etc may lead to greater uncertainty in the transmission process of monetary policy. In all these cases, globalization is shown to reduce inflation.

Section 5 discusses possible institutional and policy consequences of such a reduction in inflation. First, it analyzes the effects of globalization on the optimal degree of central bank independence. It is shown that if central bank independence is measured against the degree of self-assertion of the central bank, it is possible to derive a decline in the degree of optimum central bank independence with ongoing globalization. Second, the hypothesis is established that, by exerting the above disciplinary mechanisms, globalization may reduce the frequency, duration and severity of recessions. In addition, it may increase the incentive to use international policy coordination and national coordination of monetary and fiscal policy.

Part 1 :

Globalization

I. Challenges

Meeting the Challenges of Globalization in the Advanced Economies*

Daniel Citrin and Stanley Fischer

International Monetary Fund,
Washington D.C., USA

Globalization refers to the growing economic interdependence of countries worldwide through the increasing volume and variety of cross-border transactions in goods and services and of international capital flows, and also through the more rapid and widespread diffusion of technology. On a broad level, the welfare benefits of globalization are essentially similar to those of specialization and the widening of markets through trade, emphasized by classical economists. By enabling a greater international division of labor and a more efficient allocation of capital, and by increasing the degree of competition faced by firms, globalization raises productivity and average living standards, while broader access to foreign products allows consumers to enjoy a wider range of goods and services at lower cost. On the capital account side, globalization can also confer benefits by allowing a country to mobilize a larger volume of financial savings and by spreading risks more effectively (in part because investors and savers have access to a wider range of financial instruments).

At the same time, globalization has been blamed for many undesirable developments. In particular, there have been concerns that globalization may erode the capacity of national authorities to manage economic activity, partly because mobile capital can avoid taxation, more importantly, because volatile capital flows have been associated with dramatic output declines. This paper explores the extent to which globalization has increased policy interdependence and reduced governments' ability to control their own economies. In Section 1 we document the growing integration of national financial markets and how that has altered the environment in which monetary and fiscal policy are conducted. Section 2 then examines some of the implications for national policy autonomy, including the implementation and transmission of monetary policy, the conduct of fiscal policy, and the implications for tax competition and tax systems. We conclude in Section 3.

---

* This paper draws heavily on Chapter IV of *World Economic Outlook*, May 1997, IMF.

1 Capital Market Integration: Capital Flows and Interest Rates

Current account convertibility among the industrial countries was achieved in the 1950s and 1960s. Starting mainly in the early 1970s, restrictions on international capital movements still in existence in many industrial countries began to be dismantled, but the process was gradual, stretching well into the 1990s. The dismantling of capital and exchange controls coincided with an intense period of deregulation of domestic financial markets and of extensive financial innovations. The liberalization of financial markets together with the decline in transactions costs and the emergence of new financial instruments resulted in a dramatic growth in cross-border financial transactions.[1] For instance, cross-border transactions in bonds and equities in the major advanced countries were less than 10 percent of GDP in 1980 but were generally well over 100 percent of GDP in 1995, and expanded markedly further in the subsequent three years (Table 1). Gross flows of portfolio investment and foreign direct investment among the advanced countries more than tripled between the first half of the 1980s and the first half of the 1990s (Table 2). Foreign direct investment flows resulted mainly from the expansion of the international activities of multinational enterprises, reflecting the globalization of business that has taken place in recent years. Finally, to single out one measure which is particularly relevant to the ability of monetary authorities to influence exchange rates through official intervention, average daily turnover in the foreign exchange market grew from about $200 billion in the mid-1980s (1.3% of global GDP) to around $1.5 trillion, (5.1% of world GDP), equivalent to over 85 percent of all countries' foreign exchange reserves in 1998 (Table 3). Thus, by any measure, the expansion of international financial transactions has been extraordinary.

However, it is interesting to note that net international capital flows among the industrialized countries do not show the explosive growth of gross flows. The current account imbalances of the advanced economies have remained rather small—in the 1990s, the absolute value of the advanced economies' current account imbalances relative to GDP has averaged around 2 percent, and the well-known Feldstein-Horioka finding is that domestic investment is financed mostly by domestic saving.[2] This has been interpreted by some as implying that international capital mobility is low. Others have argued, however, that the observed high correlation between domestic saving and investment rates need not

[1] See Goldstein and Mussa (1993), and Marston (1995).

[2] See Feldstein and Horioka (1980). A number of subsequent studies have found savings and investment rates highly correlated—for a review see Goldstein and Mussa (1993) and Taylor (1996).

be inconsistent with a high degree of capital mobility, if, for example, countries target current accounts.[3]

In any event, the extent of financial market integration cannot be inferred from the volume of capital flows alone. To assess the degree of financial market integration, it is also necessary to examine the extent to which asset returns are equalized across countries. This can be done at various levels. At one level, the integration of international financial markets requires that onshore and offshore yields on the same instruments, denominated in the same currency, are equalized. Since no currency risk is involved, yields can diverge only because of transaction and information costs and impediments to mobility, such as capital controls, political risk, and default risk. In keeping with the rapid decline in transactions costs and the dismantling of capital controls, onshore/offshore interest rate differentials have declined markedly during the past fifteen years and are now minuscule for most advanced economies, suggesting a very high degree of integration.

The trend toward closer integration is revealed also by the decline in deviations from covered interest parity (CIP).[4] With barriers between national markets greatly diminished, and not inhibiting potential arbitrage flows between national markets, and with currency risk eliminated by forward cover, departures from CIP have on average become much smaller.[5] Divergences from CIP for domestic short-term interest rates declined in the early 1980s in response to the financial deregulation and liberalization of capital movements undertaken by many countries (Chart 1). Since then the dispersion seems to have stabilized at a lower level, except for the temporary widenings associated with large disturbances, such as the 1992 European Monetary System (EMS) crisis.

Even with perfect capital mobility and no transaction costs, domestic nominal interest rates can of course still differ because of „currency premiums," comprising expected exchange rate changes and risk premiums. For countries maintaining fixed exchange rates, however, nominal interest rates can be expected to converge. For example, the dispersion of both short-term domestic interest rates and short-term Euromarket interest rates for European countries tended to decrease during the 1980s, a trend that was disrupted by the 1992 exchange market turbulence and the exit from the ERM of some major European currencies (Chart 2). Not surprisingly given the flexibility of their exchange rates, it is harder to detect a marked tendency for interest rates to converge among the three major industrial countries. Tests of uncovered interest parity (UIP) have—not

---

[3] See, for instance, Artis and Bayoumi (1989), and Frankel (1993, pp. 41-69).

[4] When CIP holds, the difference in interest rates on comparable instruments denominated in different currencies should equal the cost of cover in the forward exchange market.

[5] These departures, except for the wedge introduced by transactions costs, reflect „country premiums," that is, current capital controls or the expectation of future controls, and perceptions of default risk.

surprisingly—generally concluded that UIP does not hold and that assets denominated in different currencies are imperfect substitutes.[6] Both time-varying, exchange rate risk premiums and systematic exchange rate forecast errors have been found to underlie deviations from UIP.[7]

It is also of interest—though not a condition necessarily implied by full capital market integration—whether real interest rates are equalized among countries. Real interest rate parity is a more stringent condition than UIP because it requires in addition that expected changes in exchange rates equal anticipated inflation differentials. Given that UIP does not hold, real interest rate equalization is also unlikely to hold—and it does not. Nominal exchange rates have in fact departed considerably from the predictions of relative purchasing power parity (PPP), especially in the short run. It is only over long spans of years that there is more of a tendency for relative PPP to hold (Chart 3). The dispersion of real short-term interest rates declined in the 1980s but widened in the early 1990s in connection with various shocks, in particular, German unification and the EMS crises (Chart 4).

In summary, financial markets have become increasingly integrated, but they do not yet constitute a single global market. Still, the degree of integration is high enough to strongly affect the conduct and effects of macroeconomic, regulatory, and prudential policies of all countries integrated into the international financial system.

2 Implications for Macroeconomic Policy

One of the main implications of high capital mobility is that it has made adjustable exchange rate pegs more difficult to sustain in the absence of strict policy convergence and appropriate economic fundamentals.[8] Also, asymmetric real shocks that require real exchange rate adjustments may cause difficulties, especially in countries with rigid labor and product markets. That is why it may be preferable for countries to adopt either permanently fixed (as in a monetary union or currency board arrangement) or fully flexible exchange rates. The vulnerability of fixed-but-adjustable exchange rate systems to changes in investor sentiment has been illustrated by the 1992 and 1993 ERM crises, and the 1995 Mexican financial crisis, and most recently by the crises in Asia, Russia, and Brazil.

---

[6] UIP states that expected returns on investments in different currencies are equal when measured in a single currency. UIP is equivalent to the combination of CIP and the assumption that the forward exchange rate equals the expected future spot exchange rate.

[7] See Isard (1995).

[8] See Svensson (1994).

With floating exchange rates, national monetary authorities have greater independence in choosing their inflation objective. Although monetary policy is strongly influenced by international financial markets, increased financial market integration does not appear to have diminished its effectiveness. Closely linked capital markets have, however, changed the monetary transmission mechanism by enhancing the role of the exchange rate. Domestic interest rates may have to adjust less to achieve the monetary policy objective because more adjustment comes through the exchange rate. Further, international financial markets can also serve to discipline governments (either by raising default premiums or by forcing adjustments in exchange rates), encouraging the adoption of appropriate policies, and ultimately rewarding good policies.

However, internationally integrated financial markets can also produce unwarranted disturbances to economies if, as some believe, financial markets generate excessive volatility or excessive contagion. The evidence does not point to a rise in financial asset-price variability in recent decades.[9] Nor are there analytical grounds for believing that financial market integration increases volatility. However, the short-term volatility of asset prices, in particular exchange rates, has at times appeared excessive, when compared with the volatility of their fundamental determinants. Similarly, excessive contagion is hard to define precisely, but the contagion that moved from Russia to Latin America in 1998 is hard to reconcile with fundamental economic linkages.

Financial market prices can at times become misaligned, as exemplified by the overvaluation of the U.S. dollar in 1984–85, the rise in the U.S. stock market before the crash of 1987, the rise in Japanese asset prices in the late 1980s, and the appreciation of the yen in early 1995. Apart from the problems caused by the misalignments themselves, the eventual corrections can be disruptive and pose substantial risks for financial stability. Misalignments are often hard to identify because of the difficulty of assessing the level of asset prices consistent with macroeconomic fundamentals. And even when monetary authorities can identify a misalignment, say in the exchange market, the large volumes of private market flows may make it difficult for them to bring about a correction. Exchange market intervention by individual central banks may be insufficient for the task, and while coordinated intervention may be more effective, it may still be unable to match the resources of the private sector. Coordinated intervention may be far more effective, however, if it serves as a signal to markets of international macroeconomic policy cooperation and of a mutual commitment to the adoption of sustainable policies. The signal sent by a particular intervention may be far more important than the volume of intervention. This was illustrated in the summer of 1995, when coordinated intervention by the major central banks helped to bring about a correction of the yen/U.S. dollar rate from its excessively appreciated level.

---

[9] See, for example, Bank for International Settlements (1996).

The opposite may also occur. Markets may become convinced that a particular exchange rate is unsustainable, making it impossible for official exchange market intervention to support it effectively. The pressures against a parity may then be so intense that even extraordinarily large increases in interest rates may be ineffective, as experienced, for example, during the September 1992 ERM crisis.[10]

Another consequence of highly integrated financial markets is that shocks that occur in one market may be more easily transmitted to other markets. Shocks to asset prices in one country have at times spread quickly to similar assets in other countries, while generally they have not spilled over on a comparable scale into markets in other assets, so that the systemic consequences of disruptions in any one market have been limited. As the contagion in global markets following the August 1998 crisis in Russia vividly illustrated, the possibility cannot be dismissed that effects in different markets can interact to magnify shocks, thus creating macroprudential or systemic risk. Indeed, the experience of the last several years clearly demonstrates that the continuing globalization of financial markets demands a strong multilateral approach to maintaining a sound and efficient international financial system.[11]

The enormous growth of financial markets has also increased the tendency for countries with open capital markets to experience large inflows of foreign capital. While not uncommon in the advanced economies, in mid-1990s this was most marked in some rapidly growing emerging market economies with developing financial markets. Capital inflows can ease a country's external financing constraint; but large inflows can also adversely affect macroeconomic stability by fueling inflation and raising real exchange rates to unsustainably high levels. The latter is more likely to be the case when the inflows are temporary, driven, for instance, by international interest rate movements or by shifts in market sentiment not supported by changes in the host country's fundamentals, rather than by improved longer-term investment opportunities. In some cases, the capital inflows may be attracted by high domestic interest rates required for domestic stabilization and may pose difficulties when the capital inflows are too large to be sterilized. Depending on the nature and the cause of the capital inflows, and depending also on institutional factors such as the structure of prudential regulations and supervision and the robustness of the domestic banking system, authorities have various instruments in addition to sterilized intervention for dealing with large capital inflows. These include exchange rate, fiscal, and monetary adjustments, as

---

[10] The above discussion has focused on foreign exchange markets, the core of the international financial system, but similar considerations apply to other asset markets, in particular, equity and real estate markets. Recent examples include the run up and subsequent collapse of equity and real estate prices in several countries in the latter half of the 1980s and the 1994 drop in bond prices.

[11] See International Monetary Fund (1999), Chapter IV.

well as financial regulatory measures and price-based capital controls (i.e., various types of financial transactions taxes, stamp duties, and fees).

The increased integration of financial markets in recent years has made even more evident the well known proposition that of the three objectives of independent monetary policy, fixed exchange rates, and open capital markets, policymakers can simultaneously adopt no more than two. Recognition of this constraint has induced some to advocate throwing „sand in the wheels“ of the international financial market by taxing cross-border financial transactions.[12] The argument rests on the notion that a transactions tax will naturally tend to discourage short-term capital flows, which are assumed to be destabilizing and undesirable but not affect long-term capital flows, which are assumed to be desirable and based on fundamentals. The evidence is mixed on the effectiveness of such taxes, and from a practical perspective, unless the tax were implemented globally and across a broad range of financial instruments, its effect would simply be to shift the location of the trading and the instruments used. Nevertheless, they appear to have proved useful in certain countries, e.g. Chile.

While market-based measures to affect capital inflows have been useful in some emerging market countries, they should be regarded as a transition measure while countries strengthen their financial systems and macroeconomic policies. It is striking both that the most advanced countries have by and large renounced the use of capital controls, and that in the recent crisis, very few emerging market countries chose the capital controls route: rather virtually all chose to remain within the globalized world.

In addition to the implications for the conduct of stabilization policy, globalization also has implications for countries' tax systems. Present-day taxation is largely based on the „territoriality principle,“ that is, the right to tax incomes and activities within the territory of the jurisdiction. In an increasingly global environment, this principle loses efficiency and can prove to be a potential source of conflict.[13]

Globalization may be expected increasingly to constrain governments' choice of tax structures and tax rates, especially in smaller countries. Internationally mobile factors of production—financial capital and some highly trained segments of the labor market—can more easily avoid taxes levied in particular countries. The scope for tax evasion by individuals and corporations has also been enhanced. Indeed, many countries have experienced an erosion of the capital income tax base. Some governments have responded to the erosion by establishing favorable tax regimes. This „tax competition“ may affect the average tax level of some countries by obliging them to lower tax rates for certain taxes. To the extent that the allocation of capital will be driven by tax considerations rather than by pretax

---

[12] E.g., Tobin (1978, pp. 153-159).

[13] For a detailed discussion of these issues see Tanzi (1995, 1996).

rates of return, the allocation of capital will be less efficient. In a similar vein, personal income taxes and expenditure policies related to social spending are likely to become a more important factor in labor migration—but it is likely that tax competition will tend to reduce taxes on capital relative to those on less mobile factors of production. Presumably, globalization will in the longer run tend to cause tax systems to converge either through tax harmonization or via tax competition across jurisdictions.

Finally, the increased integration of national economies raises two other macroeconomic issues: Have output fluctuations become more synchronized across countries? And is globalization a force for lower inflation? Cyclical variations in output do not appear to have become more correlated internationally, as indicated by divergent movements in output gaps among the major advanced economies in recent years. The correlations were higher in the 1970s, because of the large supply shocks that affected all countries simultaneously. Also, although fluctuations in the growth of industrial production for the major advanced economies are strongly correlated with the „world business cycle“ (i.e., the common component of international fluctuations), there have been no systematic differences in these correlations over time.[14] Country-specific shocks and common shocks account for most of the variability in output in the major advanced economies—from 75 percent to 95 percent according to one recent estimate.[15] The transmission of country-specific shocks through trade links is rather limited, except for those originating in the United States, which, because of that country's economic size, are felt more strongly abroad than those of other countries. Thus, apart from the influence of common disturbances, such as commodity price shocks or technology shocks it is still mainly nonsynchronous domestic disturbances that drive business cycle fluctuations among the major economies.

As for inflation, its decline in recent years is mainly the result of determined policy actions to bring it under control. But the increased openness to trade and capital flows may also have played a role in some cases. Foreign competition, outsourcing, and the increased internationalization of production may have served to suppress wage demands or raise productivity growth, thereby reducing cost pressures. These effects of globalization will tend, however, to result in one–time downward shifts in the price level rather than ongoing restraints on the rate of inflation. An aspect of globalization that is more likely to have a long-lasting influence on inflation is the discipline on domestic financial policies imposed by increased financial market integration.

[14] See Lumsdaine and Prasad (1996).

[15] See Fabrizio and Lopez (1996).

3 Concluding Remarks

Does globalization make it more difficult to achieve the legitimate and desirable aims of economic policy? At a fundamental level, and assuming as we do that globalization is on balance a force for growth, the answer is that globalization makes it easier to attain the ultimate goal of economic policy, which is higher incomes; redistributive policies and social safety nets should be used to ensure that these gains are shared fairly. Even in a business cycle context, the answer is also that globalization is on the whole a force for greater stability—even though at times large short–term capital flows can adversely affect macroeconomic stability, and asset prices, including exchange rates, can as a result become misaligned. Globalization can act as a force for stability by limiting the scope for countries to pursue policies that are incompatible with medium–term financial stability. The disciplining effect of global financial markets applies not only to policymakers, via financial market pressures, but also to the private sector, by making it more difficult to sustain unwarranted price markups and non-productivity driven wage increases.

At the same time, it has to be recognized that overexuberant international capital flows can at times permit disequilibria to develop, and can require excessively large output adjustments in emerging market countries when flows reverse. These real possibilities reinforce the case for strengthening macroeconomic policies and financial systems in emerging market countries—and they also emphasize the urgency of strengthening the international financial architecture.

Table 1: *Cross-Border Transactions in Bonds and Equities*[1] *(In percent of GDP)*

	1970	1980	1985	1990	1995	1998
United States	3	9	35	89	135	230
Japan	...	8	62	119	65	91
Germany	3	7	33	57	172	334
France	...	5	21	54	187	415
Italy	...	1	4	27	253	640
Canada	6	9	27	65	187	331

Source: Bank for International Settlements (BIS)

[1]Gross purchases and sales of securities between residents and nonresidents.

Table 2 : *Gross Foreign Direct Investment Plus Portfolio Investment*[1]
(In percent of GDP)

	1975–79	1980–84	1985–89	1990–95	1996	1997
Belgium-Luxembourg	3.4	5.0	14.0	36.8	33.0	...
Canada	5.6	4.8	6.6	7.7	7.7	6.8
Denmark	1.0[2]	1.1[3]	4.1	9.9	7.3	11.3
France	1.3	2.1	4.1	7.3	7.3	12.5
Germany	1.4	1.7	5.2	6.0	6.8	10.1
Italy	0.5	0.7	1.9	5.5	9.3	12.4
Japan	0.6[5]	2.6	6.4	3.7	4.6	4.8
Netherlands	4.9	6.0	10.9	11.9	17.5	24.1
Norway	5.5	2.2	7.0	4.6	12.0	17.7
Portugal	0.5	1.1	3.6	7.3	10.8	15.6
Spain	0.8	1.2	3.0	7.6	3.0	7.7
Sweden	1.7	2.3	5.4	9.4	17.4	34.1
Switzerland	...	8.7[6]	14.4	12.2	16.2	...
United Kingdom	4.2	5.6	15.5	13.7	19.0	17.4
United States	2.0	1.6	3.3	4.2	8.4	8.5

[1] The sum of the absolute value of direct investment in reporting economy and abroad and portfolio investment assets and liabilities (including equity securities) as defined by the fifth edition of the *Balance of Payments Manual*
[2] The figure is for 1975 - 1978
[3] The figure is for 1981 - 1984
[4] The figure is for 1971 - 1974
[5] The figure is for 1977 - 1979
[6] The figure is for 1983 - 1984

Sources: *International Financial Statistics* for balance of payments data, *World Economic Outlook* for GDP data.

Table 3: *Foreign Exchange Trading (In billions of U.S. dollars and in percent)*

	1986	1989	1992	1995	1998
Global estimated turnover[1,2]	188	590	820	1190	1500
As a ratio of:					
World exports of goods and services	7.3	15.9	17.5	19.0	22.4
Total reserves minus gold (all countries)	36.7	76.0	82.8	81.0	85.8

[1]Daily average turnover, on spot, outright forward, and foreign exchange swap transactions, adjusted for local and cross-border double counting and for estimated gaps in reporting.

[2]Figures are based on surveys of activities in the three largest exchange market centers (London, New York, and Tokyo) in 1986, and markets in 21 countries in 1989, 26 countries in 1992 and 1995, and 43 countries in 1998. The London, New York, and Tokyo markets accounted for 57 percent of global turnover in 1989, 54 percent in 1992, 55 percent in 1995, and 57 percent in 1998.

Sources: Bank for International Settlements; and International Monetary Fund.

Chart 1: Divergences from Covered Interest Parity[1]
(In percent; three-month rates)

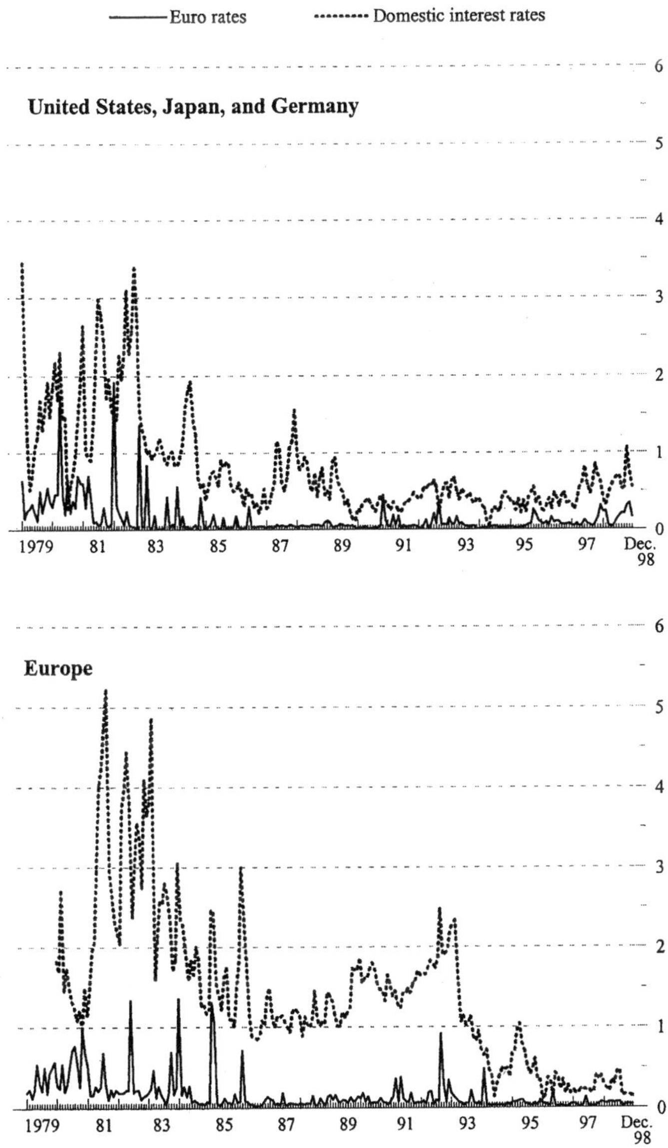

[1]Mean absolute deviations of covered interest differentials between U.S. three-month rates and corresponding rates whose dollar returns are covered in the forward exchange market. In the bottom panel, the differential is with respect to German three-month rates. Europe comprises Germany, France, the United Kingdom, the Netherlands, and Switzerland. Data are monthly averages.

Chart 2: Mean and Dispersion of Short-Term Interest Rates[1]
(In percent; three-month rates)

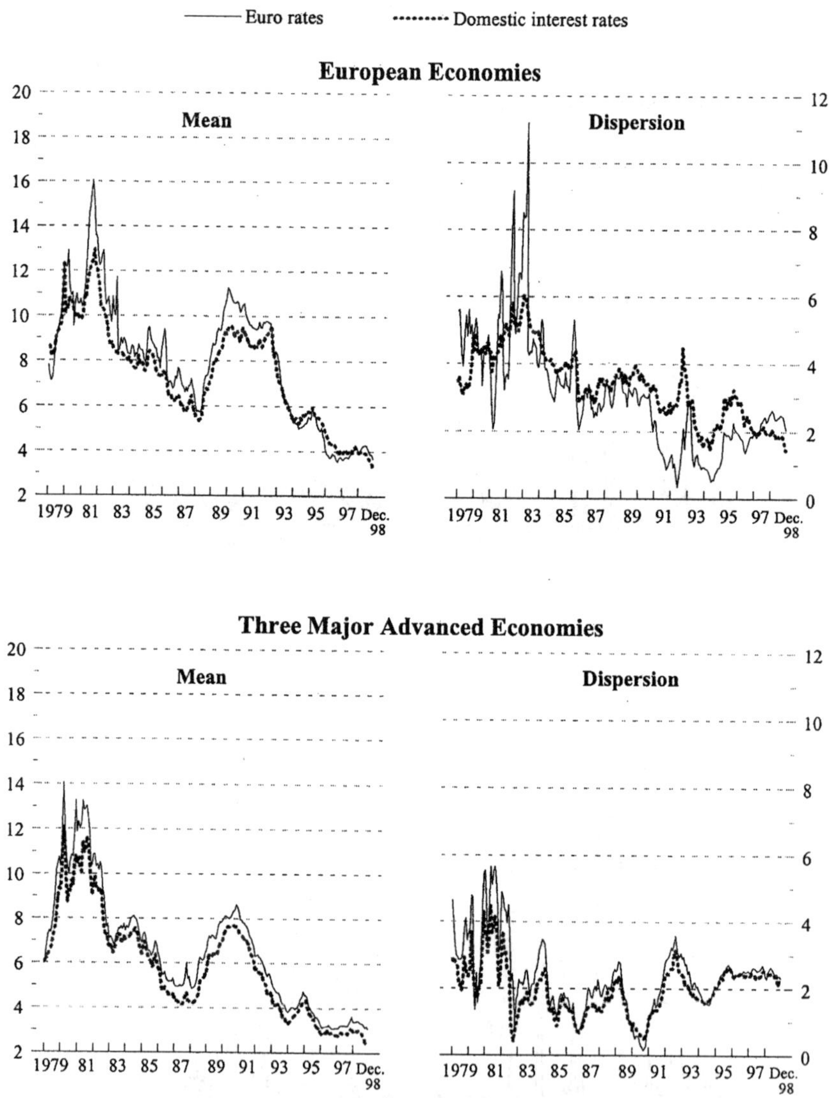

[1]Dispersion is defined as the standard deviation with respect to the appropriate cross-country mean. European economies comprise Germany, France, the United Kingdom, the Netherlands, and Switzerland; the three major advanced economies consist of the United States, Japan, and Germany. Data are monthly averages.

Chart 3: U.S. Dollar Exchange Rate Change and Inflation Differential

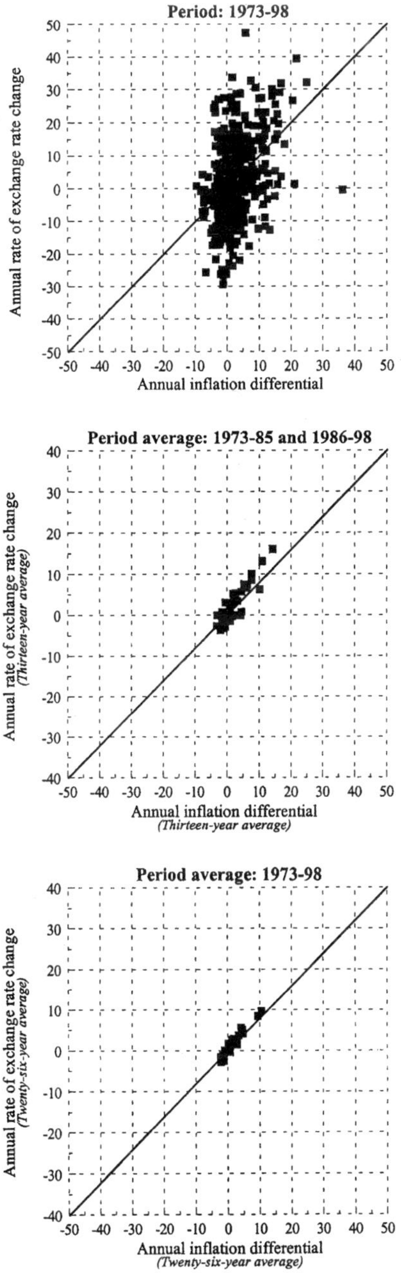

Chart 4: Mean and Dispersion of Real Short-Term Interest Rates[1]
(In percent; three-month rates)

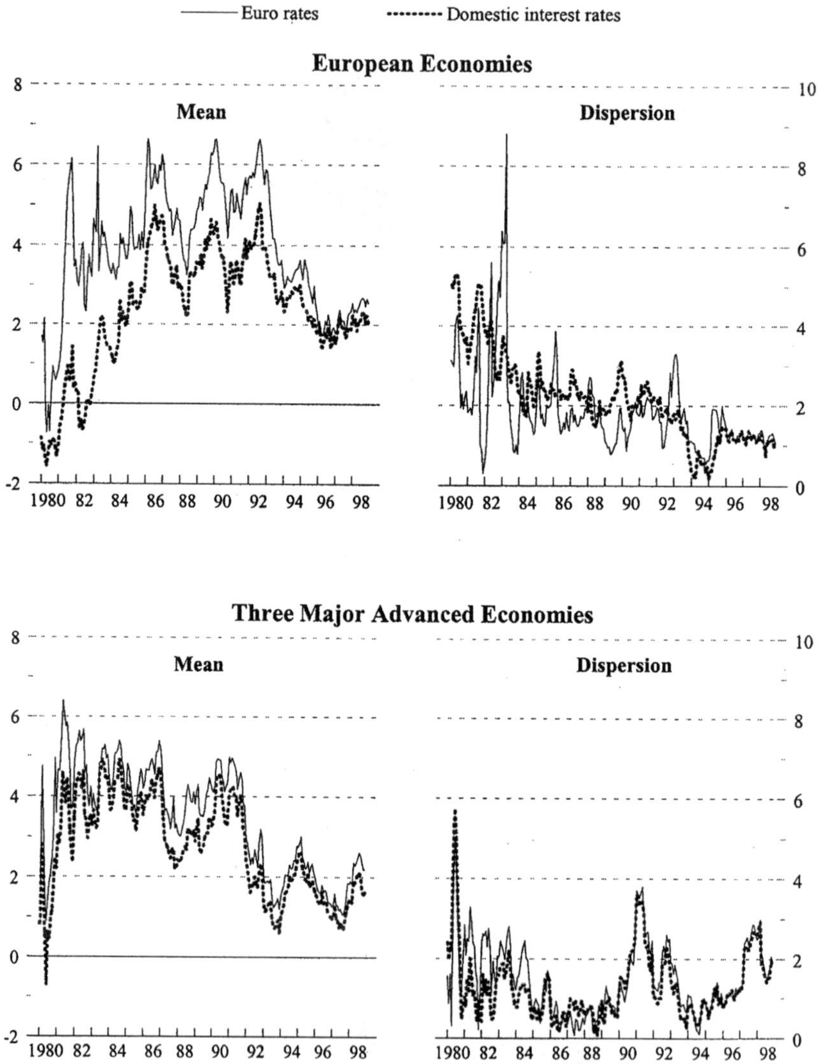

[1]Real interest rates are nominal rates deflated by the consumer prices index. Dispersion is defined as the standard deviation with respect to the appropriate cross-country mean. European economies comprise Germany, France, the United Kingdom, and the Netherlands; the three major advanced economies consist of the United States, Japan, and Germany.

References

Artis, M. and T. Bayoumi (1989), Saving, Investment, Financial Integration, and the Balance of Payments, IMF Working Paper 89/102, Washington, D.C.

Bank for International Settlements (1996), Financial Market Volatility: Measurement, Causes and Consequences, BIS Conference Papers 1, Basle.

Fabrizio, S. and J. H. Lopez (1996), Domestic, Foreign or Common Shocks?, IMF Working Paper 96/107 Washington, D.C.

Feldstein, M. and C. Horioka (1980), Domestic Saving and International Capital Flows, *Economic Journal* 90, 314–329.

Frankel, J.A. (1993), Quantifying International Capital Mobility in the 1980s, in : On Exchange Rates, Cambridge, Mass., 41–69.

Goldstein, M. and M. Mussa (1993), The Integration of World Capital Markets, IMF Working Paper 93/95, Washington, D.C. Also published in: Federal Reserve Bank of Kansas City (ed.), Changing Capital Markets: Implications for Monetary Policy, Kansas City, 295-313.

International Monetary Fund (1999), International Capital Markets: Developments, Prospects, and Key Policy Issues, Washington, D. C.

Isard, P. (1995), Exchange Rate Economics, Cambridge.

Lumsdaine, R. L. and E. S. Prasad (1996), Identifying the Common Component in International Economic Fluctuations (unpublished; IMF, December 1996).

Marston, R.C. (1995), International Financial Integration: A Study of Interest Differentials Between the Major Industrial Countries, Cambridge.

Svensson, L.E.O. (1994), Fixed Exchange Rates as a Means to Price Stability: What Have We Learned?, *European Economic Review* 38, 447–468.

Tanzi, V. (1995), Taxation in an Integrating World, Washington, D.C.

Tanzi, V. (1996), Globalization, Tax Competition and the Future of Tax Systems, IMF Working Paper 96/141, Washington, D.C.

Taylor, A.M. (1996), International Capital Mobility in History: The Saving-Investment Relationship, NBER Working Paper 5743, Cambridge, Mass.

Tobin, J. (1978), A Proposal for International Monetary Reform, *Eastern Economic Journal* 4, 153–159.

II. Historical Perspective

Globalization in Historical Perspective*

Kevin H. O'Rourke

University College, Dublin,
Belfield, Dublin 4, Ireland

1 Introduction

Together with the Internet, globalization has become the symbol of economic life in the 1990s, to the extent that both have become cliches in public discourse; but while the Internet is indisputably new, globalization has been an ongoing process for centuries. Indeed, as this chapter will show, globalization was further advanced along some (but by no means all) dimensions in the late 19th century than it is today. Further, while pundits, now as then, have tended to extrapolate the immediate past into the indefinite future, and have predicted the ever-increasing integration of the international economy, history shows that globalization can be reversed. All economic change produces losers as well as winners, and if the losers are not adequately compensated, and are sufficiently powerful politically, then they may use the political process to undo those changes which they dislike most. This is not just a theoretical concern. While the First World War was undoubtedly the key force dissolving the economic relationships which had linked nations and continents in the decades since 1850, a retreat from liberal economic policies had already begun, certainly by the 1880s or 1890s. This retreat can be clearly linked to the distributional consequences of globalization, at least in the cases of commodity trade (O'Rourke (1997); O'Rourke and Williamson (1999), Chapter 6) and labor migration (Timmer and Williamson (1998); O'Rourke and Williamson (1999), Chapter 10).

In this chapter, I first provide a brief survey of broad trends in the integration and disintegration of the international economy. I then focus more specifically on the impact of globalization on labor, which is the theme of this volume, concentrating on the last great wave of globalization which occurred a hundred years ago. Finally, I explore the political issues associated with international trade and factor flows, again mainly in the context of the late 19th century.

---

* This paper draws heavily on a recent collaboration with Jeffrey Williamson, *Globalization and History: The Evolution of a Nineteenth-Century Atlantic Economy* (MIT Press, 1999), and summarizes many of the arguments therein. I am grateful to Williamson for allowing me to make use of our shared work, and for many helpful conversations over the years.

2 Globalization and De-Globalization

Although Asian spices had been imported into Europe and Egypt for centuries (and, in the latter case, millennia), it was only between roughly 200BC and the birth of Christ that regular trade routes opened up between the eastern and western ends of the Eurasian landmass (Curtin (1984, pp. 90-91)). Security was the key concern for would-be traders, and the overland trade, in particular, was dependent on political stability; thus, the years around 0 AD were characterized by strong empires in both Europe and China. When empires fell, and wars erupted, the impact on trade could be catastrophic. One particularly dramatic episode of globalization, followed by de-globalization, was the period between 1250 and 1350, when the Mongols ruled from the Black Sea to China, and Europeans such as Marco Polo could venture overland to China in comparative safety. Famously, a Florentine banker, Francesco Balducci di Pegolotti, wrote around 1340 that the road to Peking was safe by day or night, and provided merchants with details as to how to get there, as well as information on local currencies and tariffs (Phillips (1998, p. 96)). But by then the 'pax Mongolica' was already beginning to wane, with Mongol rulers being overthrown in Iran in 1335, and China in 1368; in the words of R.S. Lopez, 'the eastern frontier of European trade gradually receded from the sea of China to the edge of the Mediterranean' (Lopez (1987, p. 383)). This left frustrated European traders once again at the mercy of the Muslims who controlled the routes to the Indian Ocean, and led to renewed dreams of a way to cut out the middlemen by circumnavigating Africa.

As we know, Europeans not only succeeded in sailing around Africa, but discovered the Americas as a byproduct of the effort to find a direct sea route to Asia. By the 18th century, the New World had become the focus of a complex international economy, linking Africa, America and Europe through the so-called triangular trade, which saw African slaves being shipped to America, American raw materials being shipped to Europe, and European manufactured goods being exported to the other two continents. While this may still have been the age of mercantilism, with numerous restrictions on trade and comparatively low volumes of trade for most countries, it remains true that these international links were of crucial significance for the most dynamic sectors of the European economy. In Britain, *the* most dynamic economy of the period, the ratio of exports to national output was 15% in 1760 (Crafts (1985, p. 131)), the same proportion as in 1913, or for that matter 1987 (O'Rourke and Williamson (1999, p. 30)). The leading industry of the British Industrial Revolution, cotton textiles, was not only dependent on a raw material shipped across the Atlantic (and produced by African slaves), but exported over 60% of its gross output in 1801 (O'Brien and Engerman (1991, p. 188)). On the European Continent, the great centers of industry were to be found on the Atlantic seaboard, where cities such as Bordeaux and Nantes produced products directly linked to shipping (such as rope, sails and ships), and processed colonial products such as sugar and tobacco. In the hinterland, and as far east as Germany, the dominant industrial activity was linen production, which again was a largely export-oriented activity (with linen being used to clothe New World slaves).

This dynamic and outward-looking Atlantic economy was to come to an abrupt end with the Napoleonic Wars, which saw the British blockading the Continent between 1807 and 1813; Napoleon imposing a counter-blockade which sought to prevent British goods being sold on the European mainland; and the United States banning trade with both belligerent parties in 1807. In a classic article, Crouzet (1964) documented how the focus of economic activity in France and other Continental economies shifted from the great seaports, whose populations in some cases declined, to interior regions such as Alsace, as import-substituting cotton textile factories born behind the protective barriers of the Continental System supplanted the Atlantic-oriented industries of the previous century. In an oft-repeated manner, these factories, developed in an artificial autarkic environment, would become a powerful lobby group for further protection, helping to explain, in Crouzet's eyes, the comparative strength of protectionism ever since in countries such as France. In a precisely similar manner, northeastern states such as Pennsylvania developed a range of manufacturing industries after 1807 (Frankel (1982)), and advocated tariffs for the remainder of the 19th century; while in the 20th century, the import-substitution policies adopted in the extreme conditions of the 1930s would prove very difficult to dismantle, both in the European periphery, and, more especially, in Latin America.

According to Paul Bairoch, European trade policy after Waterloo consisted of "an ocean of protectionism surrounding a few liberal islands" (Bairoch (1989, p. 7)).[1] In Britain, the symbol of protection was the Corn Laws, passed in 1815 in an attempt to maintain the high wartime grain prices which had enriched the powerful landowning class (yet another example of wartime shocks having long run effects via the political process). The act prohibited the sale of imported wheat unless the domestic price rose above 80 shillings per quarter; wheat prices had been 74s/4d in 1814, but were only 52s/10d in January 1816. The result was that domestic markets were closed to imported grain for most of the next seven years. However, the succeeding three decades saw a gradual liberalization in Britain, partly as a result of the growing power of urban and manufacturing interests, symbolized by the Reform Act of 1832, and partly as a result of the propagandistic activities of political economists. The ban on skilled workers emigrating was lifted in 1825; grain import prohibitions were replaced with sliding scale tariffs in 1828; various tariffs were lowered in 1833; the export of machinery was allowed in 1842, and in the same year the export tax on wool was abolished, and grain and other tariffs reduced. Finally, 1846 saw the symbolic beginning of Britain's unilateral commitment to free trade, when it abolished the Corn Laws altogether.

---

[1] This section draws heavily on O'Rourke and Williamson (1999, Chapter 3).

While some smaller European countries, such as the Netherlands, Portugal and Denmark, had also moved towards liberal trade policies, it was not until the 1860 Franco-British trade treaty that the major European powers embraced free trade principles. The treaty embodied the most-favored-nation principle, as did further bilateral treaties between various pairs of European countries, ensuring that concessions granted between two countries were swiftly and automatically generalized to all. France, Germany, Italy, Switzerland, Austria, Norway and Sweden all became involved in large-scale tariff-cutting; by 1877, a country such as Germany had moved all the way to free trade (Bairoch (1989, p. 41)).

The third quarter of the 19th century thus saw a decisive move towards free trade; but if the second half of the century was marked overall by a significant shift towards globalization, this was not due to policy, but to technology– a crucial difference, it turns out, from the late 20th century experience. Transport costs plummeted as steamships linked continents and railroads penetrated deep into their interiors. To take just one example from the grain market: in 1868 it cost 6s/11d to transport a quarter of wheat by lake and rail from Chicago to New York (O'Rourke and Williamson (1999, p. 41)). The cost using rail alone was 10s/2d; while the cost of shipping the same quarter of wheat from New York to Liverpool was 4s/7½d. In 1902, these costs had fallen to 1s/11d, 2s/11d and 11½d, respectively. Nor was commodity market integration limited to the grain market. O'Rourke and Williamson (1994) found that London-Cincinnati meat price gaps were 92.5% in 1870, but 17.9% in 1913; the Philadelphia-London iron bar price gap fell from 75% to 20.6%, while the pig iron price gap fell from 85.2% to 19.3% and the copper price gap fell from 32.7% to almost zero. Declining Anglo-American price gaps were also registered for cotton textiles, hides, wool, coal, tin and coffee. Moreover, this was a world-wide phenomenon, rather than one limited to the Atlantic economies alone. For example, cotton price gaps between London and Bombay fell from 57% in 1873 to 20% in 1913, while the rice price spread between London and Rangoon fell from 93% to 26% over the same period (Collins (1996), Table 4). This was in part due to the effects of the Suez Canal, which not only shortened the distance from Europe to Asia, but facilitated the switch from sail to steam (Fletcher (1958)).

These technological forces integrating international commodity markets were at work throughout the late 19th century, but in the four decades prior to 1914 political forces were working in the opposite direction, seeking to mute the distributional impact of cheaper trade, or in Paul Bairoch's memorable phrase, to substitute artificial oceans for the real thing (Bairoch (1989, pp. 55-58)). In the United States, the defeat of the Confederacy meant that northeastern protectionists were able to get high industrial tariffs passed, and other new world economies such as Canada, Victoria (and later Australia), and Brazil also adopted protection on infant industry grounds. The link between falling transport costs and protection is even clearer in Europe, where the grain invasion triggered agricultural tariffs in France, Germany, Sweden and most other major economies. In several countries, agricultural protection led to the reimposition of industrial tariffs as well. Thus, there were clear precedents for the widespread protectionism which followed the Great War, and the onset of the Great Depression: indeed, even the infamous Smoot-Hawley tariff of 1930 yielded an average tariff that was low, rather than high, by late 19th century American standards (De Long (1998, p. 358)).

The history of post-1945 trade liberalization, carried out under the auspices of such international organizations as the GATT, EPU, EEC and WTO, is too well known to need retelling here. Note that this episode differs from its late 19th century equivalent in a number of ways. First, shipping costs do not appear to have declined as significantly in the later episode as in the earlier. Douglass North's US export freight rate index dropped by more than 41% in real terms between 1870 and 1910, while Knick Harley's British import freight index fell by about 70% in real terms between 1840 and 1910. By contrast, recent research by David Hummels finds "no evidence that transportation costs have declined across a broad range of goods" during the postwar era (Hummels (1998, p. 19)). Second, this finding implies that trade liberalization since 1945 has been largely, or even mostly, due to political developments; before 1913, it was almost entirely due to transport innovations, with tariffs serving to offset their impact.

How much more globalized is the world economy today than in 1913? It is hard to say for sure, since no one has to my knowledge compiled the sort of information on international commodity price differentials in the late 20th century which have been collected by economic historians for the earlier period. All we can say is that, presumably, commodity markets are far better integrated today. But globalization can be thought of as a process, as well as an outcome, and when viewed in this light, the late 19th century experience emerges as comparable in scale. For example, the World Bank reports that tariffs on manufactures entering developed countries fell from 40 to 7% between the late 1940s and late 1970s, a 33 percentage point decline over a thirty year period (Wood (1994, p. 173)). By contrast, trade barriers fell by 45 percentage points between 1870 and 1913 due to transportation improvements.

When comparing the late 19th and 20th centuries, it is also important to remember that commodity trade is not the only relevant dimension of globalization. One dimension along which the earlier period was clearly more globalized is labor mobility. The late 19th century marks a liberal interlude between earlier periods, which saw barriers to emigration, and the 20th century, during which immigration restrictions became common. In addition, falling transport costs made travelling across the Atlantic more affordable, so much so that by the end of the period many Italian laborers commuted across the ocean on a seasonal basis, becoming known as "birds of passage" (Bailey (1912)). The net result was that roughly 60 million Europeans emigrated to the New World in the century following 1820 (Hatton and Williamson (1998); O'Rourke and Williamson (1999), Chapter 7). The only comparable intercontinental migration had been the forced migration of African slaves to the Caribbean and the Americas: 8 million or so had made the journey by 1820 (Eltis (1983, p. 252)), and no intercontinental migration has matched it since.

Comparing international capital market integration in the two periods is trickier (O'Rourke and Williamson (1999), Chapters 11 and 12). It is certainly true that in relative terms, the capital flows seen in the decades leading up to the First World War were larger than anything seen before or since, due to such factors as the lure of the resource-abundant frontier economies and a lack of New World savings, which opened up large incipient rate-of-return differentials between the Old and New Worlds; and the introduction of the telegraph, and adherence to the international gold standard, which helped integrate international capital markets. By 1913, the share of British wealth invested overseas was 33%, while foreigners owned almost half the Argentine capital stock (Edelstein (1982); Taylor (1992)). As a proportion of GDP, British capital exports were 6.9% in 1888, and 8.7% in 1911, dwarfing the magnitudes achieved by the key creditor nations of the 1980s, Japan and Germany, whose capital exports peaked at around 4 or 5% of GDP in the middle of the decade (IMF (1997, p. 165)). For a sample of 14 Atlantic economies (plus Australia), Obstfeld and Taylor (1998) show that the average share of the current account (absolute value) in GDP is still only half of what it was in the late 1880s.

However, international market integration cannot solely be measured by the volume of trade in commodities or capital, since high integration may coincide with small flows, and low integration may coincide with large flows. The most popular way of measuring capital market integration in recent years has been the Feldstein-Horioka (1980) methodology which looks at the extent to which savings and investment are correlated within individual countries. By this yardstick, international capital markets were better integrated between 1870 and 1924 than they were between 1970 and 1989 (Taylor (1996)). If global capital markets are on balance better integrated today, this is largely because of the enormous scale of direct foreign investment (DFI). True, the stock of US direct investments abroad in 1913 amounted to 7% of US GNP, the same share as in 1966, when Europeans fretted about *Le Défi Américain* (Servan-Schreiber (1968)); but today's flows are much larger, with the stock of DFI exceeding $3 trillion at the end of 1996. However, as has been understood by economists since Stephen Hymer wrote his dissertation in 1960 (published as Hymer (1976)), DFI is not solely, or even primarily, a matter of transferring capital across frontiers; rather, it is a means of transferring firm-specific intangible assets, such as goodwill, reputation and know-how. It is because of these activities, above all, that today's global economy is better integrated than that of 1913 (Bordo, Eichengreen and Kim (1998)).

3 Globalization and Labor in the Late 19th Century

What was the net effect of late 19th century globalization on the living standards of ordinary workers? Theory predicts that it had opposite effects in Europe and the New World. Europe at that time was labor-abundant and land scarce, while the New World was labor-scarce and land-abundant; thus wages were low in Europe and high in the New World, while land rents were high in Europe and low in the New World. Heckscher-Ohlin logic suggests that under these circumstances, globalization should have favored European labor and New World land, and hurt European landowners and New World workers.

Broadly speaking, these predictions are confirmed by the late 19th century evidence, although economic growth implied that New World workers certainly did not lose in absolute terms; however, they did lose relative to European workers, and relative to New World land-owners and capitalists. Williamson (1995) shows that there was international real wage convergence during this period, and that the bulk of this convergence was accounted for by European wages catching up on wages in the New World.[2] As for the position of unskilled New World workers relative to the rest of New World society, it deteriorated sharply, implying increasing inequality (Williamson (1997); O'Rourke and Williamson (1999), Chapter 9). For example, between 1870 and 1913 the ratio of unskilled wages to GDP per capita declined at an annual rate of 1.22% in Australia, and 1.45% in the United States, in a manner sharply reminiscent of the rising inequality levels which have been experienced recently throughout the OECD.

Turning to land prices, they increased by more than 400% in Australia between 1870 and 1910, and by over 250% in the United States, while they dropped in France, Sweden and Britain– in the latter case, by over 50%. Heckscher-Ohlin theory pays particular attention to factor price ratios, and suggests that wage-rental ratios should have declined in the New World, and increased in Europe: as predicted, the ratio of wages to land prices fell by around three quarters in Australia, and by half in the United States, while it increased by a factor of 2.7 in Britain, 5.6 in Ireland, 2.6 in Sweden, and 3.1 in Denmark. The increase was less pronounced in protectionist countries: the ratio increased by a factor of 2.0 in France, 1.4 in Germany, and not at all in Spain (O'Rourke, Taylor and Williamson (1996)).

All of these facts are consistent with the predictions of traditional trade theory, but correlation is not causation: these trends may have been due to factors other than globalization. Did commodity market integration affect factor prices by changing the commodity price ratios facing each country, as trade theory predicts? Using

[2] Williamson's real wage data base was updated in O'Rourke and Williamson (1997), and the evidence is summarized in O'Rourke and Williamson (1999), Chapter 2.

econometric evidence for a panel of late 19th century economies, O'Rourke, Taylor and Williamson (1996) found that the price of agricultural goods, relative to industrial goods, had the expected negative effect on wage-rental ratios in 5 of their seven countries, the exceptions being Australia and Denmark. Moreover, the Danish case was special, with Denmark switching from grain production to intensive grain-consuming animal husbandry, based partly on stall-feeding grain to cattle, and partly on organizational and technological innovation (O'Rourke (1999)).

Trade appears to have had important effects on factor price ratios during this period, but the impact of trade on wages was more subtle: trade changed the wage-rental ratio more by changing its denominator, land rents, than by changing its numerator, wages. Thus, O'Rourke (1997) finds a strong impact of agricultural and manufactured goods prices on land rents in the same panel of countries, in a manner consistent with theory, but systematic evidence of the impact of prices on wages is more elusive. This is not surprising. Land was specific to agriculture, and its fortunes were thus intimately connected with agricultural commodity markets, while labor was mobile between sectors. In the European context, cheap American grain might displace agricultural labor, and reduce nominal wages, but it also reduced the cost of living, with ambiguous implications for real wages highlighted in the textbook specific factors model of trade. O'Rourke and Williamson (1994) found that declining commodity price gaps (both agricultural and industrial) between Britain and the New World boosted British real wages by over 20% in the years between 1870 and 1913, accounting for over four-tenths of British real wage growth over the period. However, Britain appears to have been a special case: Anglo-American commodity market integration left American wages almost unchanged, rather than lowering them, while commodity price convergence relative to the United States only boosted Swedish real wages by some 6% (O'Rourke and Williamson (1995)). Considering the impact of cheap grain taken in isolation shows clearly how Britain was different from the rest of Europe. Only 23% of the British labor force was employed in agriculture in 1871, as opposed to 51% in a relatively developed Continental economy like France (O'Rourke (1997)). CGE exercises thus suggest that in Britain, lower agricultural employment due to the grain invasion had only a minor impact on economy-wide wages, and cheap food boosted living standards; while in France, by contrast, cheap grain lowered real wages.

Trade had ambiguous effects on European real wages, but globalization unambiguously raised European living standards, and lowered New World living standards: however, it was migration that did the bulk of the work (Hatton and Williamson (1998); O'Rourke and Williamson (1999), Chapter 8). Using econometric methods, Taylor and Williamson (1997) estimate that late 19th century emigration raised Irish real wages by 32%, Italian by 28%, and Norwegian by 10%; while immigration lowered Argentine real wages by 21%, Australian by 15%, Canadian by 16%, and American by 8%. CGE methods yield similar results; for example, Boyer, Hatton and O'Rourke (1994) find that Irish post-Famine emigration may have accounted for as much as a half of the real wage growth, and a quarter of the per capita GNP growth, observed in that country, which in fact converged on the economic leaders of the day, such as Britain and the United States, despite undergoing deindustrialization rather than industrialization.

It appears that labor flows had the impact on workers in both rich and poor countries that simple neoclassical theory predicts. What about the impact of capital flows? Did well-integrated international capital markets boost living standards in underdeveloped economies in a similar fashion? The answer, in general, is no, for the simple reason that capital sought out abundant resources rather than abundant labor during this period (O'Rourke and Williamson (1999), Chapter 12). Relatively poor, peripheral European economies such as Italy and Ireland may– the key word here is *may*– actually have exported capital during this period, while rich New World economies certainly imported it. On balance, international capital flows may have been a force for divergence during this period, rather than convergence.

4 The Politics of Globalization

International trade has always been a source of political tension, although the nature of those tensions has changed over time. For many centuries, intercontinental trade was so expensive that only very valuable commodities were profitably traded. Spices were a typical example, fetching exorbitant prices in Europe for the simple reason that they were not available there. The importation of such non-competing goods displaced no domestic production, and can have had virtually no impact on domestic income distribution via the reshuffling of domestic resources between alternative activities, in the manner emphasized by Heckscher-Ohlin theory. Their primary impact on economic welfare came through two mechanisms. First, they expanded consumer choice, by making available commodities which otherwise could not be procured at all. Second, insofar as trade in these goods could be monopolized, it offered traders or governments the chance to enrich themselves by earning substantial monopoly rents.

Before the exploits of Vasco da Gama, geography endowed the Muslims who controlled the Red Sea, the Persian Gulf, and the overland routes linking these waterways with the Mediterranean, with the ability to earn substantial middleman profits on the sale of Asian spices to Christian merchants. Once Europeans controlled the Indian Ocean, and bypassed Islam, their first thought was to reap such profits themselves; but Christians had to use violence in order to gain what had been granted to Islam by geography alone. Individual nations used force to control trade routes, or the ultimate sources of supply; one nation's gain was another's loss. Thus, the political tensions arising during this early phase of intercontinental trade were interstate in nature; mercantilist rivalries made sense when viewed in this perspective (Irwin (1991)).

As transport costs gradually declined, a broader range of products was traded between continents, with bulkier commodities of greater importance to the general economy being imported and exported. During the 18th century, Europe imported such commodities as tobacco and sugar from the New World, but also raw cotton, which substituted for, and eventually displaced, European wool and flax as the main fiber used in textile production. By the 19th century, the most basic commodities, such as grain, were being shipped across the Atlantic, directly displacing local production, with the effects on income distribution documented earlier. Globalization might benefit the economy as a whole, but now produced winners and losers within each country; trade-related conflict was now as much intra-state as inter-state, if not more so. Thus, a ferocious debate between the Anti-Corn Law League on the one hand, and the Tory representatives of the landed gentry on the other, preceded Robert Peel's decision to repeal the Corn Laws; while the 1890s saw an equally intense intellectual debate in Germany between agrarian protectionists such as Adolf Wagner, and free trade liberals such as Max Weber and Luigi Brentano, and a corresponding political debate between the Junkers on the one hand, and the Socialists on the other. In the New World too, trade policy became the subject of heated political debate, with the tariff issue persistently aggravating North-South relationships in the United States, to the extent that South Carolina actually threatened to withdraw from the Union after it declared null and void the highly protectionist 1828 "Act of Abominations" (Ashley (1905, pp. 171-172)).

As mentioned earlier, protectionists often succeeded in getting their way. There were three key shocks which produced a globalization backlash (Williamson (1998); O'Rourke and Williamson (1999), Chapters 6, 10): cheaper grain in Europe, which threatened European rents; European mass migration to the New World, which threatened New World wages; and competition from European manufacturers, which threatened the New World's infant industries and profit rates. There were four political responses to these three shocks. Continental Europe typically imposed tariffs on imports of grain. The United Kingdom and Denmark, by contrast, held firm to agricultural free trade. Within the New World, tariff barriers were erected to protect manufacturing; and finally, New World governments also gradually tightened immigration restrictions.

To make the connection between these globalization shocks and the policy responses outlined above in as convincing a manner as possible, it is necessary to show that the timing of these policies, and their variation across countries, can be explained by the variation in the distributional implications of globalization. After all, American immigration restrictions could also have been due to rising racism, or widening ethnicity gaps between current and previous immigrants; while the contrast between British and Danish free trade policies, and Franco-German protectionism, could be explained by such factors as the greater adherence to liberal economic doctrine in the homeland of Ricardo, than in that of Friedrich List; or by differences in political institutions across countries.

Take the latter issue first. The traditional view (e.g. Kindleberger (1951)) was that the European grain invasion was a classic example of a common shock producing different responses across countries; thus, those different responses must have been due to different political, sociological, or intellectual environments. However, O'Rourke (1997) shows that the grain invasion implied different price shocks in different countries, and that, since countries had different economic structures, even identical price shocks would have had different distributional implications in each. Thus the contrast in policies between France and Germany, on the one hand, and Britain and Denmark on the other, can be well explained by the size of the price shocks each country faced (grain prices declined by only 10% in Denmark, a traditional grain exporter, while they would have declined by 34% in France and Germany had those countries not imposed tariffs), and by the distributional consequences of those shocks (for example, cheap grain boosted British real wages, but lowered French real wages, as mentioned earlier). Thus, it makes sense to view late 19th century European tariff policies as endogenous responses to the distributional implications of globalization.

What about New World immigration restrictions, which had been on the increase for several decades prior to the Great War? Ashley Timmer and Jeffrey Williamson (1998) develop an index of immigration restrictions for Argentina, Australia, Brazil, Canada and the United States between 1860 and 1930, and then proceed to econometrically estimate the determinants of this policy index. It turns out that the most consistently significant variable in their regressions is the ratio of unskilled wages to GDP per capita, the index of inequality mentioned earlier: the higher was this index (i.e. the more equal was the distribution of income), the more open were a nation's frontiers. Rising inequality can explain a significant share of the trend towards tighter immigration restrictions over the period, and of course that rising inequality was itself largely a consequence of mass immigration, which as noted earlier lowered unskilled real wages, but raised the returns to complementary factors of production such as capital and land (Williamson (1997); O'Rourke and Williamson (1999), Chapter 9).

5 Conclusion

The late 19th century resembled our own period in many respects, with rapid changes in the international division of labor due to declining costs of doing business across frontiers. The key differences between the two periods appear to have been (1) that many more international transactions take place within the firm today than was true a hundred years ago; and (2) that international flows of labor and capital were proportionately much larger then than now.

The distributional consequences of these shocks were much more clear cut for land than for labor, at least insofar as commodity trade was concerned. In labor-abundant Europe, left wing parties favored free trade more because they thought it would bring cheap food, than because they believed it would expand labor-intensive activities and promote employment. In the rich, labor-scarce New World, where globalization might have been expected to lower real wages rather than raise them, there were far more echoes of today's concerns about trade, inequality and unemployment in OECD economies. Thus, around 1840 American protectionists began to argue that "high duties were necessary to shut out the competition of the ill-paid laborers of Europe, and to maintain the high wages of the laborers of the United States" (Taussig (1888, p. 66)), an argument which has a strikingly modern ring to it (with the obvious exception of the reference to low-paid European workers).

But it was migration that had the greatest impact on workers' living standards, and when immigration led to unskilled wages lagging excessively behind average incomes, governments intervened to stem the migration flows. There are obvious parallels here with today's concerns that rising inequality will undermine the political support for globalization, although in America the 'blue collar' challenge to free trade, associated with Pat Buchanan and Ross Perot, seems to have sharply declined over the course of the 1990s. Moreover, there are important differences between the two epochs. The mass intercontinental migration which lowered New World living standards is absent today; while international institutions such as the WTO would make it much more difficult for politicians to dismantle today's international economy, should their constituents demand that they do so. Nonetheless, the late 19th century experience does serve as a useful reminder that the political support for globalization cannot be taken for granted, and that the distributional consequences of a more tightly integrated international economy matter not just in their own right, but because of the policy responses which they can provoke.

References

Ashley, P. (1905), Modern Tariff History: Germany-United States-France, New York.

Bailey, W. B. (1912), The Birds of Passage, *American Journal of Sociology* 18, 391-397.

Bairoch, P. (1989), European Trade Policy, 1815-1914, in: Mathias, P. and S. Pollard (eds.), The Cambridge Economic History of Europe, Vol. VIII, Cambridge, 1-160.

Bordo, M. D., B. Eichengreen and J. Kim (1998), Was There Really an Earlier Period of International Financial Integration Comparable to Today? NBER Working Paper 6738, Cambridge, Mass.

Boyer, G. R., T. J. Hatton and K. H. O'Rourke (1994), Emigration and Economic Growth in Ireland, 1850-1914, in: Hatton, T. J. and J. G. Williamson (eds.), Migration and the International Labor Market, 1850-1939, London, 221-239.

Collins, W. J. (1996), Regional Labor Markets in British India, mimeo, Harvard University.

Crafts, N. F. R. (1985), British Economic Growth During the Industrial Revolution, Oxford.

Crouzet, F. (1964), Wars, Blockade, and Economic Change in Europe, 1792-1815, *Journal of Economic History* 24, 567-588.

Curtin, P. D. (1984), Cross-Cultural Trade in World History, Cambridge.

De Long, J. B. (1998), Trade Policy and America's Standard of Living: A Historical Perspective, in: Collins, S. M. (ed.), Imports, Exports, and the American Worker, Washington D. C., 349-388.

Edelstein, M. (1982), Overseas Investment in the Age of High Imperialism, New York.

Eltis, D. (1983), Free and Coerced Transatlantic Migrations: Some Comparisons, *American Historical Review* 88, 251-280.

Feldstein, M. and C. Horioka (1980), Domestic Saving and International Capital Flows, *Economic Journal* 90, 314-329.

Fletcher, M. E. (1958), The Suez Canal and World Shipping, 1869-1914, *Journal of Economic History* 18, 556-573.

Frankel, J. A. (1982), The 1807-1809 Embargo Against Great Britain, *Journal of Economic History* 52, 291-308.

Hatton, T. J. and J. G. Williamson (1998), The Age of Mass Migration: An Economic Analysis, New York.

Hummels, D. (1998), Transportation Costs and the Growth of World Trade, mimeo, University of Chicago.

Hymer, S. H. (1976), The International Operations of National Firms: A Study of Direct Foreign Investment, Cambridge, Mass.

IMF (1997), World Economic Outlook, Washington D.C.

Irwin, D. A. (1991), Mercantilism as Strategic Trade Policy: The Anglo-Dutch Rivalry for the East India Trade, *Journal of Political Economy* 99, 1296-1314.

Kindleberger, C. P. (1951), Group Behavior and International Trade, *Journal of Political Economy* 59, 30-46.

Lopez, R. S. (1987), The Trade of Medieval Europe: The South, in: Postan, M. M. and E. Miller (eds.), The Cambridge Economic History of Europe, Vol. II, 2nd edition, Cambridge, 306-401.

O'Brien, P. K. and S. L. Engerman (1991), Exports and the Growth of the British Economy from the Glorious Revolution to the Peace of Amiens, in: Solow, B. L. (ed.), Slavery and the Rise of the Atlantic System, Cambridge, 177-209.

Obstfeld, M. and A. M. Taylor (1998), The Great Depression as a Watershed: International Capital Mobility in the Long Run, in: Bordo, M. D., C. D. Goldin and E. N. White (eds.), The Defining Moment: The Great Depression and the American Economy in the Twentieth Century, Chicago, 353-402.

O'Rourke, K. H. (1997), The European Grain Invasion, 1870-1913, *Journal of Economic History* 57, 775-801.

O'Rourke, K. H. (1999), Culture, Politics and Innovation: Creamery Diffusion in Late 19th Century Denmark and Ireland, mimeo, Harvard University.

O'Rourke, K. H., A. M. Taylor and J. G. Williamson (1996), Factor Price Convergence in the Late Nineteenth Century, *International Economic Review* 37, 499-530.

O'Rourke, K. H. and J. G. Williamson (1994), Late 19th Century Anglo-American Factor Price Convergence: Were Heckscher and Ohlin Right?, *Journal of Economic History* 54, 892-916.

O'Rourke, K. H. and J. G. Williamson (1995), Open Economy Forces and Late 19th Century Swedish Catch-Up: A Quantitative Accounting, *Scandinavian Economic History Review* 43, 171-203.

O'Rourke, K. H. and J. G. Williamson (1997), Around the European Periphery 1870-1913: Globalization, Schooling and Growth, *European Review of Economic History* 1, 153-191.

O'Rourke, K. H. and J. G. Williamson (1999), Globalization and History: The Evolution of a Nineteenth-Century Atlantic Economy, Cambridge, Mass.

Phillips, J. R. S. (1998), The Medieval Expansion of Europe, 2nd edition, Oxford.

Servan-Schreiber, J. J. (1968), The American Challenge, New York.

Taussig, F. W. (1888), The Tariff History of the United States: A Series of Essays, New York.

Taylor, A. M. (1992), External Dependence, Demographic Burdens, and Argentine Economic Decline After the Belle Epoque, *Journal of Economic History* 52, 907-936.

Taylor, A. M. (1996), International Capital Mobility in History: The Saving-Investment Relationship, NBER Working Paper 5743, Cambridge, Mass.

Taylor, A. M., and J. G. Williamson (1997), Convergence in the Age of Mass Migration, *European Review of Economic History* 1, 27-63.

Timmer, A. and J. G. Williamson (1998), Immigration Policy Prior to the Thirties: Labor Markets, Policy Interactions and Globalization Backlash, *Population and Development Review* 24, 739-771.

Williamson, J. G. (1995), The Evolution of Global Labor Markets Since 1830: Background Evidence and Hypotheses, *Explorations in Economic History* 32, 141-196.

Williamson, J. G. (1997), Globalization and Inequality, Past and Present, *World Bank Research Observer* 12, 117-135.

Williamson, J. G. (1998), Globalization, Labor Markets and Policy Backlash in the Past, *Journal of Economic Perspectives* 12, 51-72.

Wood, A. (1994), North-South Trade, Employment and Inequality: Changing Fortunes in a Skill-Driven World, Oxford.

Part 2 :

Unemployment

I. Empirical Trends

International Unemployment Trends: Measurement and Stylized Facts*

Ronald Schettkat, Marinus Verhagen

Utrecht University,
P.O. Box 80.140 3508 EC Utrecht, The Netherlands

1 Introduction and Summary

According to Alan Blinder (1989, p. 143), unemployment poses two challenges to economics: (1) definition and (2) theoretical explanation. This paper is almost entirely about the first challenge, i.e. it focuses on definition and measurement issues and establishes some facts about unemployment in an international comparative perspective. However, there can be no definition and no facts without theory and hopefully no economic theory independent of facts. Definition and measurement are particularly important where international comparative analysis is used to investigate the impact of institutional arrangements on economic performance. A good example is the European (German) view that the US has performed better in terms of unemployment than the German economy, a contention true only of the late 1980s and the 1990s. In all other periods, Germany's unemployment performance emerges as clearly superior, provided that unemployment is measured in a comparable way and the unemployment rate is computed using the same formula (see section 3).

'There is a fact, a big unmistakable unsubtle fact: essentially, everywhere in the modern industrial capitalist world, unemployment rates are much higher than they used to be two or three decades ago.' (Solow (1986, p. 23)) Although Solow stated this fact more than 10 years ago, figure 1 shows that since then the aggregate G7 unemployment rate (US, Canada, Japan, UK, France, Germany and Italy) has increased even further.[1] The aggregate in figure 1 hides substantial national variations. The national minimum and maximum (broken lines in figure 1) diverge substantially from the average. Measured unemployment rose with country-specific variations in the industrialized world from very low levels of less than 1% in the 1960s to more than 10% in some countries in the 1990s (see figure 1, upper panel).

---

* We are grateful to Hilla Dotan for research assistance.

[1] Computations are based on the BLS international comparative database.

From today's perspective, the lowest unemployment rates in the 1960s (see figure 1, upper panel, lower broken line) seem simply to reflect measurement error. Indeed, it is difficult to measure unemployment because of the theoretical and empirical problem of distinguishing between unemployment, employment and leisure. It is a recurrent question whether unemployment is voluntary or involuntary, i.e. whether unemployment is real or whether it constitutes a measurement error deeply rooted in economic theory. Involuntary unemployment simply cannot exist in the Walrasian system of perfect markets and therefore cannot be an economic problem. However, no professional economist takes the Walrasian system as a description of the real world and hardly anybody would deny that it is a real phenomenon, in the sense that unemployment can be involuntary at least at the individual level. Nevertheless, the extent to which involuntary unemployment is accepted as a real phenomenon varies substantially,

Figure 1: *Unemployment rates, Employment Population Rates and Working Volume per adult Population in the G7 Countries*

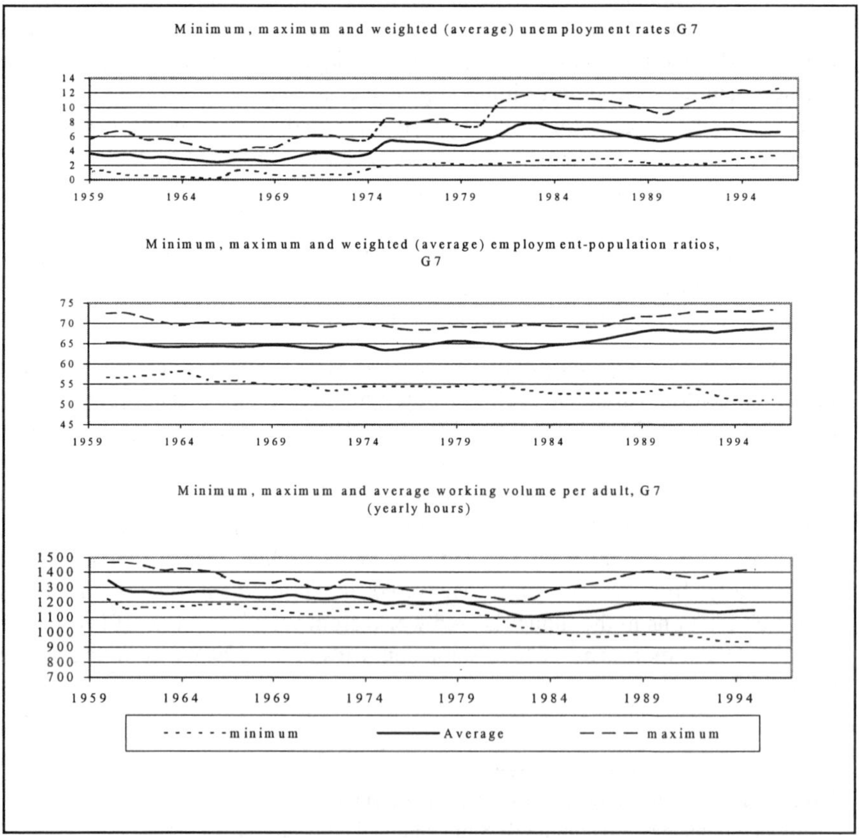

as does the identification of the side of the market that is most important to explain unemployment.

Aside from fundamental theoretical distinctions between employment, unemployment and leisure, there are more pragmatic problems about the way in which we classify unemployment and employment. Are workers in public work programs employed or is this kind of work so artificial as to equate to unemployment? How do we treat early retirement programs, which are often designed to reduce unemployment? Should we count those workers who receive unemployment benefits but who are not available for work as unemployed? Is low-paid work or part-time work employment or not? Is imprisonment a specific solution to employment problems and should the prison population be counted as unemployed (Freeman (1995))?

National unemployment figures are not only influenced by measurement conventions in the narrow sense, but also by a multitude of other variables which limit the information that unemployment rates can provide on labor market performance. Unemployment rates are not therefore in themselves a sufficient basis for the evaluation of labor market performance. For this reason, we shall include in our analysis employment-population ratios (the share of employment in the adult population) and the ratio of working volume to adult population (figure 1, middle and lower panel). Judged on the basis of the employment-population ratio, the G7 aggregate does not seem to indicate a labor market problem, since the ratio is rising in line with the unemployment rate. Again, however, the aggregate hides substantial differences between countries (broken lines for minimum and maximum values). A reverse trend is revealed if the working volume to adult population ratio is used as an indicator for employment performance. Although the number of persons in employment has increased, especially in the 1980s, the hours worked per adult have declined (lower panel of figure 1).

Are pure labor market quantity measures a sufficient basis on which to evaluate economic performance? Without a possible trade-off between wages and employment, or between productivity growth (income) and employment, the answer is yes. However, if such a trade-off exists, it will not be sufficient to analyze the labor market variables in isolation and it will be necessary to control for other variables, such as income. This feeds back into the issue of definition and measurement, particularly because it raises the question of whether the quality of work needs to be taken into account.

This paper will begin by discussing theoretical issues concerning the definition of unemployment and employment and then proceed to a comparison of different data series measuring employment and unemployment. We will use national definitions and compare them with internationally comparative data provided by the US Bureau of Labor Statistics (BLS). This analysis will provide a basis on which to evaluate the sensitivity of labor market figures to national definitions. Another issue is the choice of indicators used to represent employment and unemployment. Different indicators (unemployment rates, employment-population ratios, and working volume per head of population) will be used and the relationships between them will be investigated. Finally, we shall briefly investigate simple relationships between labor market indicators and other key economic variables, such as growth, wages, technological progress and inflation.

Our main conclusions are:

1. Unemployment (i.e. involuntary unemployment) can only exist in models of imperfect labor markets but there is no clear dividing line between 'unemployment and employment' in a theoretical sense.
2. If there is a potential trade-off between employment creation and efficiency (productivity), it will be insufficient to evaluate economic policy on the basis of labor market performance alone.
3. The unemployment rate is only one indicator of labor market performance. Other important indicators - focusing on quantitative measures only - are employment-population ratios and trends in working volume.
4. All G7 countries experienced a rise in the unemployment rate in the 1970s and 1980s, although the trend was less pronounced in Japan (which had a low unemployment rate of less than 4% even in the 1990s) and the US (which achieved in the 1990s a return to the unemployment level of the early 1970s).
5. These unemployment trends were accompanied by very different trends in the employment-population ratios.

Employment-Population ratio	*Unemployment rate (trends from 1960 to 1996)*	
	Constant (with variations)	*Upward trend*
Upward trend	US	Canada
Downward or constant trend	Japan	UK, France, Germany, Italy

6. In those countries for which data is available, it is clear that it is not the reduction in average working hours, which led the employment-population ratios to increase, but rather the reverse. Countries with declining employment-population ratios also experienced a decline in average working hours.

7. The comparison of unemployment rates and employment-population ratios as measured by national concepts and approximated US concept shows that the difference is important for unemployment figures. German national definition of unemployment overstates unemployment especially since the 1980s.
8. Only the US experiences a strong positive trend in working hours per head of adult population, which is mainly caused by increasing participation.
9. Employment growth and population growth is closely correlated. About 70% of the expansion in US employment can be explained by reference to population growth. Population grew less in Europe and thus absolute employment was lower.
10. Employment growth and population growth is closely correlated. About 70% of the expansion in US employment can be explained by reference to population growth. Population grew less in Europe and thus absolute employment was lower.
11. Differences in GDP growth rates cannot explain divergent employment trend, although economic growth, of course, affects employment positively.
12. Countries with strong employment growth also show high employment elasticity of GDP growth.
13. In the 1990s inflation is lower than in the 1960s in every G7-country but at the same time unemployment is higher everywhere except in the US.
14. This pattern is broadly consist with the unemployment-inflation trade-off but unemployment is much higher in the 1990s compared to the 1960s suggesting a rise in the NAIRU, which –except for the US- can be found in the data everywhere.
15. The problem with NAIRU explanations is, however, that they do not fit institutional changes. These would suggest a decline in the NAIRU rather than an increase. Similarly in the US where the NAIRU estimates decline one cannot identify the institutional changes, which may have caused this trend.

2 Employment, Unemployment, and Leisure

2.1 Theoretical Definitions

Within the Walrasian system of perfect markets and universal maximizing behavior, workers are assumed to be on their supply curve (i.e. to choose their optimal combination of work (income) and leisure and thus maximize their utility). Within this framework, unemployment is difficult to define because it is always the result of overly high wages and wage adjustments can therefore always reduce unemployment. Should someone be classified as unemployed because his optimum is higher than the equilibrium real wage? In the Walrasian system, unemployment can only be voluntary, so measured unemployment must be an error. It takes a more complex model presupposing heterogeneous labor demand and supply, imperfect information or simply wage rigidity to give unemployment a meaning, although even then it may still be voluntary, as in some models of search unemployment (Rothschild (1978), Schettkat (1992)). Labor supply is elastic with respect to the real wage.[2]

In contrast, the Keynesian labor supply function is inelastic with respect to the real wage (i.e. it is a vertical in the real wage-employment diagram) and workers are concerned about relative nominal wages rather than absolute levels of real wages. Workers can be constrained by labor demand. Whenever there is unused labor, involuntary unemployment can occur as a phenomenon of aggregate demand rather than of individual optimizing behavior. The Keynesian model allowed for involuntary unemployment but was not a structural model in the sense that it could explain the workings of the labor market. It remained at the aggregate level and failed to provide much insight into the functioning of complex labor markets. In this sense it was no better than the classical model. With respect to labor market mechanisms it had as little to say as the classical model; the difference is the shift of the possible adjustment mechanism from the supply to the demand side.

Andrew Oswald and Danny Blanchflower have researched whether the unemployed are happier than, or at least as happy as, their employed counterparts. All their analyses produce the same result: that the unemployed are less happy than the employed. In other words, periods of high unemployment represent a loss rather than a gain; they are not the result of individual maximizing behavior, but rather imply substantial social costs (Oswald (1997)).

Robert Solow suggests a definition of involuntary unemployment from the "economist's point of view" in which involuntary unemployment exists whenever "the marginal (consumption) value of leisure is less than the going real wage in occupations for which they [i.e. the individuals involved] are qualified. That definition covers underemployment as well as total unemployment, and it covers both the skilled mechanic who does not take work as a sweeper and the one who does" (Solow (1985, p. 33)). This last definition of involuntary unemployment - not identified in unemployment statistics - is particularly relevant where the quality of employment growth is under discussion. Are workers in jobs paying wages substantially below the average actually employed or unemployed? George Akerlof and Janet Yellen (1986, p. 11) define involuntary unemployment against

---

[2] This issue is well illustrated in Richard Freeman's explanation of the reduced availability of low-skilled workers in the US. Robert Topel explains it as a supply reaction to falling real wages, whereas Richard Freeman argues that low-skilled workers are a labor demand constraint (Freeman (1995)).

the background of a dual labor market: "And although it is true that every unemployed worker might be able to get a secondary job (so that in one sense there is not involuntary unemployment), it is also true that unemployed workers would be more than willing to work in primary sector jobs at prevailing wage rates. In that sense such workers are involuntary unemployed."[3]

Less abstract models allow excess labor supply and labor demand to coexist in equilibrium. The most prominent of these is the Hansen model, which distinguishes notional and actual market exchange curves from which the Beveridge curve can be derived, and the Layard-Nickell model of wage and price setting in imperfectly competitive markets (see Beißinger/Moeller (1999)). The upshot of these models is the natural rate of unemployment and the NAIRU. What is new and valuable about natural rate or NAIRU models is that both kinds depend heavily on institutions' facilitating or impeding the labor market mechanism (Schettkat (1992, 1996) for an overview of dynamic labor market analysis).

The important question, however, is to what extent the natural rate or the NAIRU are endogenous to economic development. Is the natural rate a constant or is it a fiction? Serious doubts have been cast on the validity of the "natural rate" concept by the great variations in the estimated rates both between and within countries. Solow (1985, p. 32) mentions that "natural rate" estimates for Germany increased from 1.6% to 8% within a period of ten years and asks whether these dramatic changes in the estimates can be rationalized in a satisfactory way. Such questions have prompted the search for features able to explain variations in the natural rate between countries and within individual countries over time. The cross-country evidence is quite plausible but usually fails in the longitudinal, single-country perspective (Nickell (1998), Schettkat (1992), Fuchs/Schettkat (1999), Esping-Andersen/Regini (1999)).

It is not surprising therefore that the "natural rate" has been set in relation to the actual rate (hysteresis, Blanchard/Summers (1986)). In particular, the development in the US over the last four years is forcing natural rate proponents to develop explanations for the fact that falling unemployment has not led to accelerating inflation, given their belief that unemployment was at its natural level four years ago (compare the discussion in the American Economic Review, Papers and Proceedings, 1999). Robert Solow has concluded that "A natural rate that hops around from one triennium to another under the influence of unspecified forces

---

[3] With respect to the possibility that skilled workers could accept lower-skilled, lower-paid jobs than they used to have and that their unemployment should therefore be classified as voluntary, Robert Solow (1985, p. 33) writes: "by this standard, all American soldiers who were killed in Vietnam could be counted as suicides since they could have deserted, emigrated to Canada or shot themselves in the foot, but did not". Similarly, Rothschild argues that individuals cannot be blamed for acting under current laws and institutional arrangements (Rothschild (1978, p. 31)).

including past unemployment rates, is not `natural' at all. `Epiphenomenal` would be a better adjective; look it up" (Solow (1985, p. 33)).

Is rising employment always desirable? If one assumes the economy to be in equilibrium and markets to be perfect, then the answer is yes, because by definition any change in such a model must lead to a situation representing higher utility. Thus, a fall in employment could also be positive. In less perfect systems there may be a productivity-employment trade-off and improvement in the one variable may be compensated by deterioration in the other. By this token, job expansion may be paid for by slower growth in real wages and productivity, and some additional employment may reflect a deterioration rather than an improvement in economic well-being (Freeman (1988, p. 299)).

To summarize, there are arguments to suggest that actual unemployment is lower than measured unemployment but there are also arguments to suggest the reverse. Some countries include 'discouraged workers' in their surveys but the authors know of no statistics that attempt to implement the theoretically sophisticated definition of unemployment put forward by Robert Solow. The argument of entirely voluntary unemployment has been laid to rest, since the unemployed are clearly not as happy as one would expect them to be if they enjoyed unemployment (Oswald (1997)). In practice, it proves to be difficult to adjust for pure measurement variation as it occurs not only between countries but also within individual countries over time.

2.2 Measurement

International comparisons of labor markets in different countries require a common definition of employment and unemployment. The development of this definition has been a lengthy process because countries have often collected unemployment data for specific purposes. For example, most European countries have needed to collect information in relation to their compulsory unemployment insurance systems. For this purpose, they have needed to identify the number of workers insured against unemployment, the number of people on unemployment benefits, and the total amount of benefits paid during the year. In other countries, especially in the United States after the great depression, the main concern has been to measure the number of people actively and currently seeking work, so as to obtain up-to-date information on the minimum number of jobs required. This has resulted in the development of the labor force framework and the joint measurement of employment and unemployment in household sample surveys (the Current Population Survey, CPS).

The first international standards for the measurement of employment and unemployment based on the labor force framework were introduced in 1947. Successive revisions finally led to the 'ILO resolution concerning statistics on the economically active population, employment and underemployment' adopted by the Thirteenth International Conference of Labor Statisticians in October 1982. This international standard definition makes no reference to institutional or legal provisions, such as receipt of unemployment insurance benefits or registration at a public employment exchange. The criteria are intended to refer exclusively to the person's activities during a specified reference period.

According to this definition, the 'unemployed' are all persons above a certain specified age who are during the reference period:

(a) 'without work': i.e. not in paid employment or self-employment

(b) 'currently available for work': i.e. available for paid employment or self-employment

(c) 'Seeking work': i.e. have taken specific steps within a specified recent period to seek paid employment or self-employment. (These steps may include registering at a public or private employment exchange, applying to possible employers, answering newspaper advertisements, seeking the assistance of friends or relatives, etc.)

The active population (labor force) comprises all persons of either sex who contribute or want to contribute to economic activity.[4] Excluded are by this definition unpaid activities such as unpaid domestic activities and volunteer community services (ILO (1985, pp. 14-15)). Employed is everybody, who works at least one hour during the survey week (ILO (1985, p. 71)).[5]

The implementation of the 1982 standards poses specific requirements for the collection of data. In particular, the need on information for those 'seeking work' without reference to unemployment benefits makes the labor force survey the most appropriate method for collecting data. It is also an appropriate method with which to address the fact that the dividing line between the labor force and the economically inactive population has become increasingly blurred due to the increasing incidence of part-time and temporary work and the ease with which large numbers of persons move in and out of the labor force.

Administrative data from social welfare and other schemes has been an important source of unemployment and employment statistics in many European countries. However, these sources have some important disadvantages. First, the underlying

---

[4] Economic activity covers aside from gainful employment also certain types of non-market production, including production and processing of primary products for own consumption, production for own consumption of other commodities if they are also produced for the market by the same households and all production of fixed assets for own use.

[5] The international standards while recommending the one hour criterion, specify that the reference period to which this criterion should be applied could be either one week or one day (ILO (1985, p. 71)).

systems are based on social welfare or other administrative provisions, which may not necessarily accord with the accepted conventions for defining employment and unemployment. Secondly, experience shows that these arrangements frequently change, creating discontinuities in the data. Thirdly, given the variations between insurance systems in different countries, international comparison of data based on such sources is very difficult.

A recent empirical study in which unemployment figures based on administrative sources are compared to figures based on labor force statistics shows large differences between these two sources (Chernyshev (1998)). In twelve out of 36 countries, including the United States and Sweden, the Labor Force Survey unemployment figures are always higher than those collected by administrative records in the period 1975-1996. In eight countries, including Italy, the administrative records figures always remain higher than the Labor Force Survey figures. The other 16 countries show an irregular pattern. In none of the countries the gap between the two sources remains stable over a sustainable period. The largest differences may be found in the United States (245%), Canada (142%), Sweden (119%), Netherlands (54%), Italy (53%), Relative small differences may be found in France, Germany and the United Kingdom. Since administrative has been a major for labor market data of the 1960 and 1970s is not fully comparable with later data based mainly on surveys.

However, as discussed above, no measurement of employment and unemployment will satisfy all the theoretical requirements and there must always be compromise. For example, the current definition may significantly underestimate the under-utilization of labor, since part-time work may be involuntary and discouraged workers may withdraw from the labor market. International comparisons of unemployment rates including these two forms of unmeasured unemployment show important differences from those examining conventional measures. For example, the two countries with the lowest unemployment rates in 1989 (Sweden and Japan) have the largest proportionate rates of increase in unemployment as measured by the new indicators (Sorrentino (1993, 1995)).[6]

---

[6] The 'under-utilization of labor' concept shifts the emphasis to working volume or 'unused time capacity'. It is therefore necessarily difficult to establish and, of course, involves subjective elements.

Figure 2: *Comparison of different unemployment definitions (source: Sorrentino (1995))*

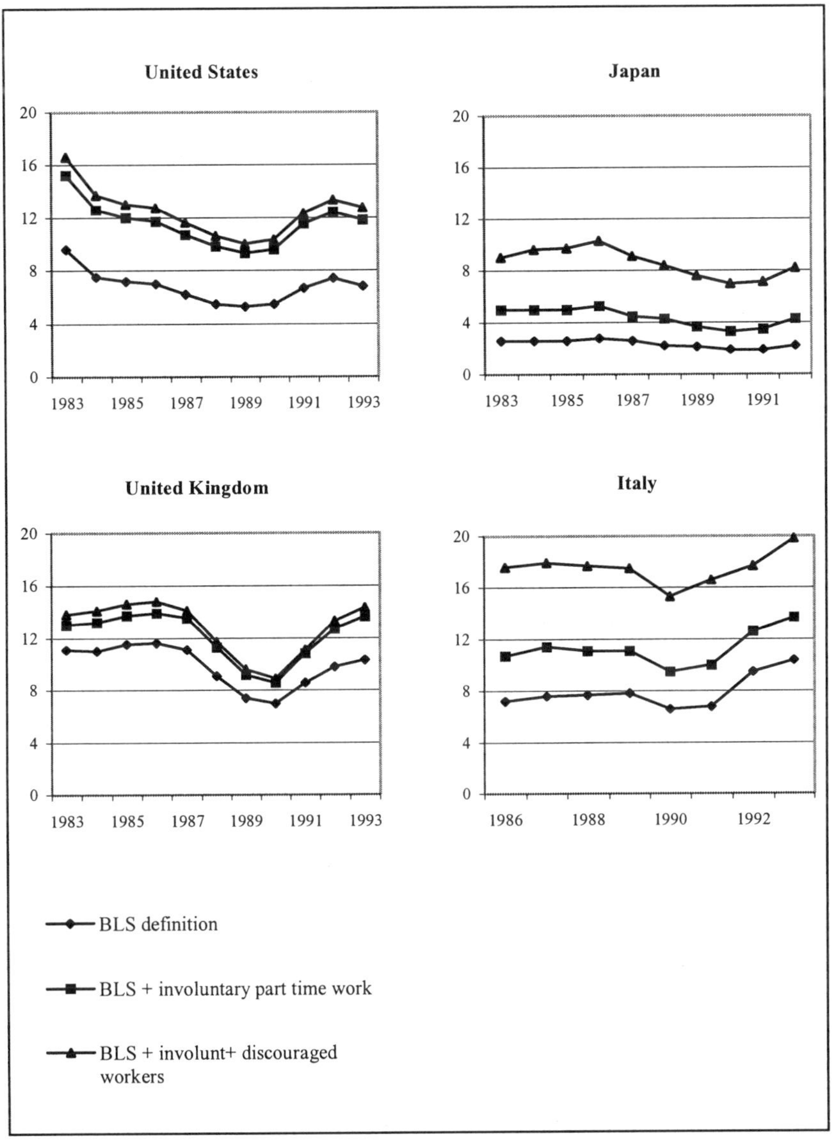

The ILO definition of unemployment does not prevent particular national policies or circumstances influencing the unemployment rate. For example, active labor market policies in Sweden have had a moderating effect on the unemployment rate (Sorrentino (1995)). Similarly, Freeman (1995) has shown that the unemployment rate in the United States is depressed because large numbers of people are in prison and are not therefore considered as part of the labor force because they are unavailable for work. Finally, the under-utilization of labor may be influenced by policies promoting early retirement or encouraging employed workers in poor health to apply for disability benefits.

Unemployment statistics by themselves do not, therefore, provide a sufficient basis for the evaluation of labor market performance. Employment-population ratios also need to be included, as do working volume estimates (in order to control for working time trends). The American Bureau of Labor Statistics attempts to make international labor market statistics comparable, using US concepts as their reference point. Likewise, the OECD provides data for international comparisons, although its series are not always strictly comparable. In the following, we use data from the BLS internationally comparative database, since this provides the best internationally comparable aggregate data. In addition, we construct working volume figures and standardize these for the working age population (15-65). This controls for differences in working time trends, such as part-time work, holidays, parental leave and standardized working weeks.

3 Unemployment and Employment Trends: Different Concepts Compared

Figure 3 shows employment and unemployment trends for the individual G7 countries as measured by the national concepts and by the (approximated) US concept, which fits the ILO definition best. In addition we include working-hours per head of adult population for those countries where hours of work are available.

Compared to the US concept national measures deviate mainly in the unemployment figures but much less in employment data. Major differences between the two data series occur in Germany, the UK and Italy. Italian unemployment is up to the mid-1990s severely overstated by the Italian concept as compared to the US concept. Also in Germany the unemployment is overstated by the national concept especially since the early 1980s and here the difference is rising rather than diminishing as in the case of Italy and the UK. However, there is less reason to worry about the unemployment statistics than it is often claimed. For policy purposes the comparison of trends between countries is probably more important than the comparison of level (for reasons discussed above). The good news is that independent of the underlying concept each measure captures the unemployment trends well.

Employment-population ratios differ much less by the underlying concept. Another reason to prefer employment-population ratios over unemployment rates in international comparative studies of labor market performance. Most interesting, however, are the diverging trends in employment population ratios. The US and Canada show a clear upward trend but the European countries experience stagnating or falling trends although average hours worked are declining in Europe but not in America. Consequently the time spent in economic activities per head of the adult population declines in Europe but rises substantially in the US. Even if one takes into account that hours worked are poorly measured, the trends seem to be to clear as being classified as measurement error only.

Most remarkable is the fact that in the 1960s and early 1970s employment population ratios and hours worked per head of adult population were higher in Europe than in the US. The differences developed over the late 1970s and 1980s for reasons, which are still not well understood (for some efforts to clarify the 'miracle' Freeman/Schettkat (1998, 1999a and b), Krueger/Pischke (1999)).

Figure 3: *Unemployment, Employment-Population, and Working Time Volume Trends: National Figures and US-Concepts Compared*

National concept	US concept	Working volume
Unemployment rate(%) Employment-population rate (%)	Unemployment rate(%) Employment-population rate (%)	(yearly hours / Adult)

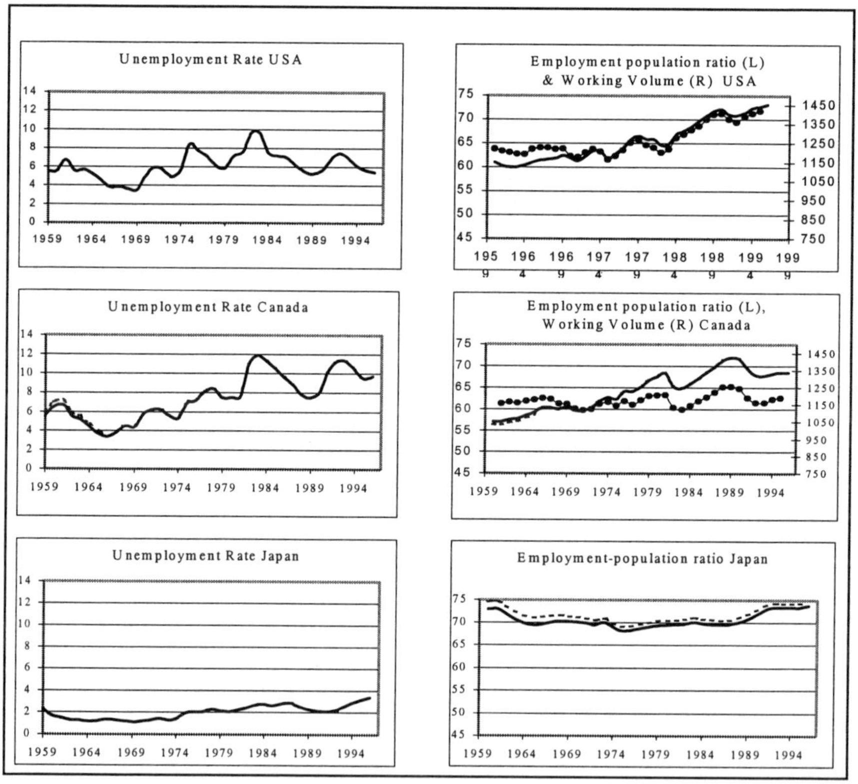

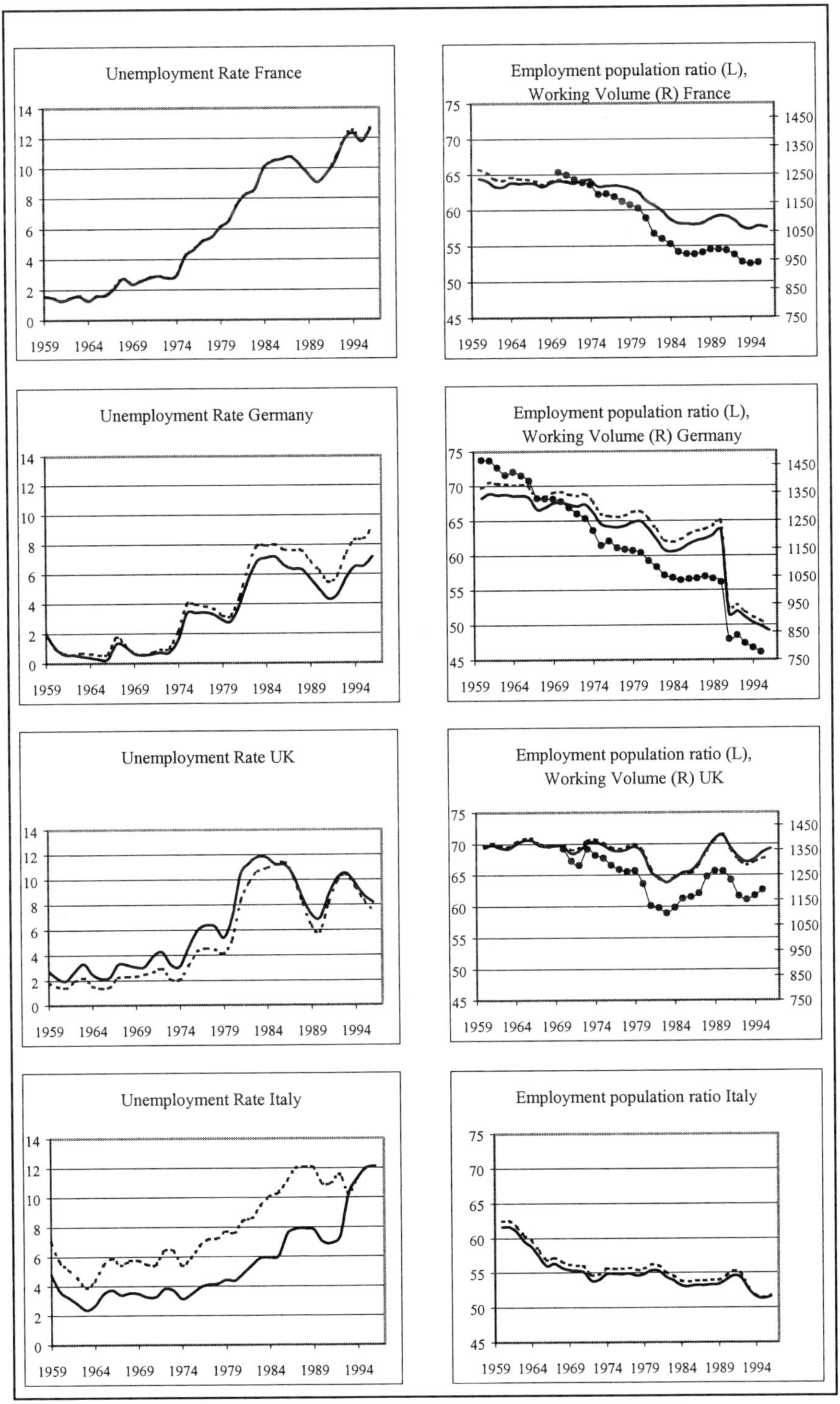
Unemployment Rate France
14
12
10
8
6
4
2
0
1959 1964 1969 1974 1979 1984 1989 1994
Employment population ratio (L), Working Volume (R) France
75
70
65
60
55
50
45
1450
1350
1250
1150
1050
950
850
750
1959 1964 1969 1974 1979 1984 1989 1994
Unemployment Rate Germany
14
12
10
8
6
4
2
0
1959 1964 1969 1974 1979 1984 1989 1994
Employment population ratio (L), Working Volume (R) Germany
75
70
65
60
55
50
45
1450
1350
1250
1150
1050
950
850
750
1959 1964 1969 1974 1979 1984 1989 1994
Unemployment Rate UK
14
12
10
8
6
4
2
0
1959 1964 1969 1974 1979 1984 1989 1994
Employment population ratio (L), Working Volume (R) UK
75
70
65
60
55
50
45
1450
1350
1250
1150
1050
950
850
750
1959 1964 1969 1974 1979 1984 1989 1994
Unemployment Rate Italy
14
12
10
8
6
4
2
0
1959 1964 1969 1974 1979 1984 1989 1994
Employment population ratio Italy
75
70
65
60
55
50
45
1959 1964 1969 1974 1979 1984 1989 1994

4 Some Stylized Facts

4.1 Employment Growth and Population Growth

In the G7 as a whole, civilian employment grew over the long period from 1960 to 1995 by .9% a year, as the regression estimate of the coefficient for the linear time trend in table 1 (equation 1) indicates. The overall trend hides diverse national patterns: the US experienced employment growth 1% above this average, and Canadian employment growth was even stronger. Japan's employment growth roughly equals the average of the G7, but the European countries are all substantially below US employment growth (see table 1, equation 2). Employment growth is substantially influenced by population growth, and the overall trend growth of .9% is the net result of population growth combined with a slightly negative trend in the employment-population ratio. Per head of adult population (aged 15 to 65 years), employment actually declined (equation 3 in table 1).

Again, the picture is diverse. The US (the country omitted from the regression estimates) derives almost 70% of its employment growth from population growth and thus only 30% from increasing participation. In Canada, population growth affects employment in a similar way but in all other countries – again, especially in the European countries – employment is less strongly affected by population than in the US. Even so, the effect remains positive in all countries (equation 4 of table 1). However, population growth obviously translates into employment growth at very different rates.

Table 1: *Employment Growth*

	Equation			
	1	2	3	4
Log population	-	-	1.34 (21.4)	1.34 (30.5)
Trend	.92 (16.2)	1.94 (46.0)	-.41 (5.8)	-.01 (1.8)
Interaction terms (countries with)	**Trend**		**Log population**	
Canada	-	.49 (8.2)	-	-.03 (.99)
UK	-	-1.78 (29.9)	-	-1.14 (6.9)
Japan	-	-.88 (14.8)	-	-.44 (10.1)
France	-	-1.51 (25.2)	-	-.93 (17.4)
Germany	-	-1.74 (29.2)	-	-1.21 (31.5)
Italy	-	-1.75 (29.4)	-	-1.13 (14.1)
R2 (adjusted)	98.02	99,84	99.3	99.89
N	259	259	259	259

t-values in parentheses, omitted country: US, all equations include country dummies for intercept, civilian employment approximated US concept, population 15-65 years.

4.2 Employment Elasticity of Economic Growth

The fact that in many European countries employment has stagnated at a time when there are positive rates of GDP growth has been interpreted as 'jobless growth'. As a description of such a situation this seems adequate, but it is a mistake to interpret it as indicating a causal relationship. To do so, productivity growth would have to be endogenous to economic growth with a coefficient of at least one. Under this condition, economic growth would raise productivity at least proportionally and employment would indeed stagnate or shrink despite rising GDP growth rates. However, this is hardly the situation in the highly industrialized countries. Productivity growth has slowed since the early 1970s and has not risen as it would be expected to do under 'jobless growth' scenarios.

Furthermore, the relation between economic growth and productivity growth – the so-called Kaldor-Verdoorn relationship – has become weaker rather than stronger, as the following analysis suggests. An entirely different question, however, is whether GDP growth rates are high enough to increase employment – so-called employment thresholds or normal growth rates, which are essentially the productivity growth rates - and whether such growth rates can be achieved given the relatively high rates of productivity growth in most European countries.

It is well known that the US employment miracle is strongly related to a high employment elasticity of economic growth rather than to high rates of economic growth as such (Schettkat (1992), Freeman (1988), Buttler et al. (1995)). Therefore, it is important to analyze the relationship between employment growth and economic growth and to investigate whether lower employment elasticity distinguishes the European countries from the other G7 economies and whether changes in this elasticity have occurred over time.

There are a number of reasons why the elasticity of economic growth may vary between countries and over time. As mentioned above, a weaker impact of economic growth on productivity growth would increase employment elasticity. This may happen because service industries come to outweigh manufacturing industries in which economic growth may have induced more investment and thus endogenous productivity growth (Kaldor's engine of growth). If labor markets become more flexible (i.e., if labor input can be adjusted more easily to match demand variations), the relationship between employment and economic growth will get stronger. A decline in average hours worked may have different effects on the employment elasticity of economic growth. With rising employment and positive GDP growth rates, the employment elasticity of GDP will rise, assuming that shorter working hours require more persons to be employed. However, with falling employment, a reduction of hours worked will reduce the employment elasticity of GDP growth (again assuming that a reduction in hours worked has a positive effect on the number of employed persons). Any evaluation of the impact of working hours on employment elasticity will therefore have to include a check for potential asymmetries.

This section contains an analysis of differences in employment elasticity over time and between countries. The coefficients in regressions of changes in employment on GDP growth may differ, depending on the definition of employment. Different results may be obtained if employment is measured in overall hours worked (working volume) rather than in terms of persons employed. The real world, however, places many restrictions on researchers: information on hours worked is not regarded as very reliable (see the warnings below the table on hours worked in the Employment Outlook) and is anyway only available for the US, Canada, the UK, Germany and France (and then only with some limitations).

Trends in average working hours vary remarkably between countries yet have no obvious impact on numbers of persons employed. Working hours have remained roughly constant in the US and Canada (with a recent increase), but have declined in Europe. Yet employment-population ratios have not increased in Europe as might have been expected. Instead, higher employment-population ratios have gone hand in hand with constant, or even rising, average hours of work in the US. Working volume per head of population (15-65 years) has declined in the European economies, in stark contrast to the US where it has grown. These trends seem to support the skepticism of many economists towards the view that 'working less' can bring more people into production. Hardly anybody will contest that shorter working hours will increase employment, given a set GDP growth rate, but GDP is endogenous and not exogenous. The positive effect of shorter working hours on employment may be compensated or even over-compensated by counter-effects such as higher wage costs, increasing non-wage costs, increases in productivity (through higher capital intensity), reductions in flexibility, increasing labor supply, etc. To analyze these effects in depth obviously requires a structural model which is not available for this paper.

Table 2 shows estimates of employment elasticity. The figures in the upper panels give coefficients for employment elasticity where the dependent variable is the deviation of employment growth from the mean growth rate and the independent variable is the deviation of GDP growth from the mean growth rate. Employment is measured in persons employed (top panel) and in overall hours worked (second panel from the top). The regression analysis clearly shows that there is no jobless growth. Above-average GDP growth leads to higher employment growth and vice versa. However, the strength of the relationship varies substantially between countries and over time.

Very high coefficients (for persons in employment but also for working volume[7]) occur in the US. One explanation may be easier hiring and firing procedures and therefore a more exact match between labor input and output. This would also be in line with the high coefficients in Canada and the UK, where firing constraints are low and labor turnover seems to be affected (Schettkat (1996)). Dismissal laws may be a hiring constraint, but the US experienced only 3 years of declining employment in the course of the 36 years covered by the analysis. For this reason, another interpretation of the high US coefficients could be that employment elasticity is high when employment is growing, especially if it continues to grow over long periods. Because of the lack of data, this hypothesis cannot be tested.

High employment elasticity of economic growth is a good thing if there is unemployment which can be more easily absorbed with a high elasticity. With respect to business cycles, however, high elasticity is not necessarily preferable to low elasticity in this respect. If measures like subsidized short-hours working

---

[7] Coefficients close to one or even above in the equations for working volume should not be taken at face value but rather as a warning signal, given that the working volume figures are rough estimates only and data on working hours is unreliable.

reduce firms' turnover and thus employment elasticity, this may prevent the loss of human capital investments which would result if workers were laid off in recessions (Abraham/Houseman (1993)). However, higher GDP growth has a positive effect on employment, whether measured in persons or in working hours.

4.3 Unemployment and Economic Growth: Okun's Law

The impact of economic growth (here measured on the basis of growth rates in GDP) on unemployment rates is usually called Okun's law. Arthur Okun related changes in deviations in GDP growth from the average growth rate (or from the 'normal rate of growth') to changes in the unemployment rate. In general, we expect the relationship between economic growth and the unemployment rate to be negative (i.e. higher rates of economic growth will reduce the unemployment rate and vice versa). This is true for every country in all periods (see table 3, top panel). Again, there are substantial inter-country variations: a GDP growth rate 1 point above the average reduces the unemployment rate by .3 to .45 percentage points in the US, Canada and the UK, but only by .1 to .2% in Japan and Europe (although France and Italy seem to have closed the gap with the US).

There may be various reasons for the rising Okun coefficients. For example, unemployment may become a more usual point of departure for entry into the labor market, other labor reserves (hidden unemployment) may be exhausted or economic growth may have a stronger impact on employment creation (compare the last subsection). In Germany, the low Okun coefficient may relate to the dual education system: if firms use their apprentices as a hiring pool, unemployment will be less affected and thus the Okun coefficient will be low. We cannot investigate this hypothesis here, but it is consistent with the falling coefficient over recent years, when apprentices have become a more important hiring pool.

Table 2: *Employment Elasticity of Economic Growth*

	USA	Canada	Japan	UK	France	Germany	Italy
	Employment elasticity, persons employed, civilian employment						
1961-1996	.72	.84	.21	.77	.58	.51	.50
1975-1996	.71	.79	.34	.94	.65	.37	.70
1983-1996	.71	.78	.48	1.0	.65	.30	1.05
	Employment elasticity, working volume						
1961-1996	.99	1.06	n.a.	.96	.52	.43	n.a.
1975-1996	1.02	.98	n.a.	1.15	.61	.20	n.a.
1983-1996	1.13	1.29	n.a.	1.35	.57	.11	n.a.
	Mean employment growth (log difference * 100)						
1961-1996	1.82	2.30	1.06	0.23	0.46	0.17	0.03
1975-1996	1.72	1.84	0.97	0.17	0.18	0.17	0.13
1983-1996	1.72	1.53	1.00	0.67	0.17	0.30	0.14
	Mean working volume growth (log difference * 100)						
1961-1996	1.76	2.26		0.14	0.40	0.13	
1975-1996	1.86	1.99		0.27	0.32	0.35	
1983-1996	2.11	1.92		1.02	0.56	0.76	
	Mean GDP growth (log difference *100)						
1961-1996	3.08	3.66	5.13	2.29	3.21	3.08	3.20
1975-1996	2.62	2.75	3.30	2.00	2.11	2.56	2.12
1983-1996	2.85	2.74	3.04	2.46	1.98	2.97	1.89

Source: Regressions based on BLS and OECD data (International Structural Database for working hours); working volume is average hours worked times civilian employment. The reported employment elasticity is based on the model: $(\Delta \ln E_t - \text{mean}(\Delta \ln E)) = \alpha + \beta 1(\Delta \ln Y_t - \text{mean}(\Delta \ln Y)) + \beta 2\ (\Delta \ln Y_{t-1} - \text{mean}\ (\Delta \ln Y)) + \gamma$ trend, reported coefficients are $\beta 1 + \beta 2$. $\Delta\ln$ = first difference in logs, E = civilian employment, and working volume respectively; Y = GDP.

In welfare states with generous unemployment benefit systems, a closer link between economic growth and unemployment will free substantial resources otherwise used for transfers once employment starts growing. Just as rising unemployment creates additional costs, which may further harm employment, so declining unemployment lowers labor costs and may support employment growth.

Okun's law is often associated with so-called 'normal growth rates'. These are the GDP growth rates necessary to keep employment and unemployment rates constant. In other words, GDP must grow in line with productivity and the labor force in order to achieve a constant unemployment rate. The normal growth rate and its components are displayed in the lower panels of table 3.

The decomposition of the 'normal growth rates' into productivity growth and growth in the labor force shows the major difference between economic trends in Europe and the US. In Europe, 'normal growth' is dominated by productivity growth, whereas in the US labor force growth dominates.

Long-term unemployment (for periods of 12 months or more) is a major problem in the European countries but hardly figures in the US (table 3). This comes as no surprise, since the US is experiencing rising employment and thus has plenty of scope to absorb the unemployed. In addition, it is difficult for individuals to continue in long-term unemployment without support through transfers and the relative lack of such support forces workers into jobs in the US. However, there have always been discouraged workers and it must be remembered that the extraordinarily large prison population in the US may reduce the figures for long-term unemployment (Freeman (1995)).

4.4 Unemployment and Inflation

Table 4 summarizes the inflation and unemployment rates for the entire 1961-1996 and for sub-periods. In the 1990s inflation is below the rate of the 1960s without any exception. For unemployment rates the reverse applies. Except for the US all countries experienced a substantial increase in unemployment. Inflation is down to about 60% of the 1960s levels but unemployment is about twice as high, and in some countries – those countries, which experienced very low rates of unemployment in the 1960s - it increased even more.

Table 3: *Okun's law*

	USA	Canada	Japan	UK	France	Germany	Italy
	Okun coefficients						
1961-1996	-.36	-.28	-.03	-.32	-.16	-.17	-.13
1975-1996	-.45	-.36	-.09	-.44	-.27	-.17	-.11
1983-1996	-.38	-.36	-.11	-.35	-.36	-.12	-.33
	Normal growth rates						
1961-1996	3.13	3.8	5.35	2.56	3.37	2.79	3.58
1975-1996	2.65	3.13	3.43	2.35	2.58	2.07	2.68
1983-1996	2.54	2.62	3.17	2.39	2.33	1.94	2.49
	Mean productivity growth rates						
1961-1996	1.29	1.40	4.20	2.08	2.52	2.43	3.32
1975-1996	0.92	1.05	2.35	1.82	1.91	1.59	2.05
1983-1996	1.14	1.18	2.06	1.85	1.81	1.47	2.03
	Mean labor force growth rates						
1961-1996	1.84	2.40	1.15	0.48	0.85	0.36	0.26
1975-1996	1.73	2.08	1.08	0.53	0.67	0.48	0.63
1983-1996	1.40	1.44	1.11	0.54	0.52	0.47	0.46
	Mean population growth rates (15-65 years)						
1961-1996	1.33	1.78	1.06	0.31	0.80	0.50	0.50
1975-1996	1.09	1.45	0.68	0.36	0.66	0.46	0.46
1983-1996	0.85	1.18	0.62	0.29	0.52	0.31	0.31

Source: Computations are based on BLS internationally comparable data. Productivity and population figures are from OECD, Economic Outlook, CD-ROM.

Okun's law is estimated as: $(uer_t - uer_{t-1}) = \beta(\Delta gdp_t - \text{average}(\Delta gdp))$, where Δ is the annual percentage change.

Table 4: *Inflation Rates and Unemployment Rates (Annual Average)*

Periode	**US**	**C**	**J**	**UK**	**F**	**G**	**I**	**US**	**C**	**J**	**UK**	**F**	**G**	**I**
	Inflation rate							**Unemployment rates**						
1961-96	4.3	4.5	4.6	6.9	5.8	3.3	8.5	6.1	7.6	2.0	6.5	6.3	3.5	5.4
	2.5	*3.1*	*4.1*	*5.0*	*3.8*	*1.7*	*5.9*	*1.5*	*2.5*	*0.7*	*3.3*	*3.9*	*2.5*	*2.7*
1961-74	3.4	3.7	7.2	5.7	5.5	3.7	6.1	5.0	5.0	1.3	3.0	2.1	0.7	3.3
	2.4	*2.5*	*4.4*	*3.8*	*3.1*	*1.8*	*5.4*	*1.0*	*1.0*	*0.1*	*0.6*	*0.6*	*0.4*	*0.4*
1975-82	8.0	9.3	8.1	14.5	11.5	4.9	17.3	7.2	7.7	2.0	6.7	5.6	3.4	4.2
	1.8	*1.6*	*5.6*	*4.5*	*1.9*	*1.5*	*2.5*	*1.3*	*1.5*	*0.3*	*2.6*	*1.7*	*1.1*	*0.7*
1983-92	4.0	4.1	1.8	5.2	4.3	2.3	7.9	6.8	9.7	2.5	9.8	9.9	6.0	7.0
	0.7	*1.3*	*0.9*	*1.0*	*2.5*	*1.6*	*3.1*	*1.3*	*1.6*	*0.3*	*1.8*	*0.7*	*1.1*	*0.8*
1993+	2.4	1.3	0.7	2.7	1.8	2.4	3.9	6.0	10.2	3.0	9.3	12.1	6.5	11.4
	0.2	*0.4*	*0.7*	*0.4*	*0.3*	*0.9*	*1.6*	*0.7*	*0.8*	*0.4*	*1.0*	*0.4*	*0.6*	*0.9*
	Change in inflation rates							**Change in unemployment rates**						
1961-96	0.0	0.0	-0.1	0.0	-0.1	0.0	0.0	0.0	0.1	0.0	0.2	0.3	0.2	0.2
	1.4	*1.5*	*2.9*	*3.0*	*1.9*	*1.1*	*2.7*	*1.0*	*1.0*	*0.2*	*1.0*	*0.5*	*0.6*	*0.6*
1961-74	0.7	0.8	1.1	1.1	0.9	0.3	1.5	0.0	-0.1	0.0	0.1	0.1	0.0	0.0
	1.4	*1.4*	*3.5*	*2.8*	*2.4*	*1.0*	*3.1*	*0.8*	*0.7*	*0.1*	*0.6*	*0.3*	*0.4*	*0.4*
1975-82	0.0	0.4	-0.9	0.0	0.5	-0.2	0.3	0.5	0.6	0.1	0.9	0.6	0.5	0.2
	2.6	*2.0*	*5.3*	*5.7*	*3.1*	*1.2*	*4.1*	*1.3*	*1.3*	*0.2*	*1.3*	*0.4*	*0.8*	*0.3*
1983-92	-0.2	-0.9	-0.1	-0.4	-0.9	0.0	-1.1	-0.2	0.0	0.0	-0.1	0.2	-0.1	0.2
	0.8	*1.7*	*0.8*	*1.7*	*1.3*	*1.4*	*1.5*	*0.9*	*1.1*	*0.2*	*1.1*	*0.6*	*0.6*	*0.6*
1993+	-0.1	0.0	-0.1	-0.5	-0.2	-0.5	-0.6	-0.5	-0.4	0.3	-0.5	0.5	0.7	1.2
	0.3	*0.7*	*0.9*	*0.7*	*0.2*	*0.5*	*1.1*	*0.3*	*0.5*	*0.1*	*0.6*	*0.8*	*0.5*	*1.2*

Source: Computations based on BLS data and OECD. Rate of inflation: CPI.

This pattern broadly fits the Phillips trade-off between unemployment and inflation. But unemployment increased more over the entire period than inflation declined and therefore the NAIRU estimates are higher in the 1990s than in the 1960s. In many countries one can also see the stagflation periods, i.e. the joint increase of inflation and unemployment. In the 1980s and 1990s the reverse of stagflation occurs in the US. Inflation and unemployment are now falling simultaneously. These trends in the 1990s caused again doubts on the natural rate hypothesis because both inflation and unemployment were falling substantially in the US (see the papers in the American Economic Review, papers and proceeding, forthcoming). Why does the NAIRU fall in the US although there are hardly any substantial changes in the institutional frameworks, which may explain the fall in the NAIRU. Many US economists think it is Greenspan rather than natural.

Figure 4: *NAIRU Estimates*

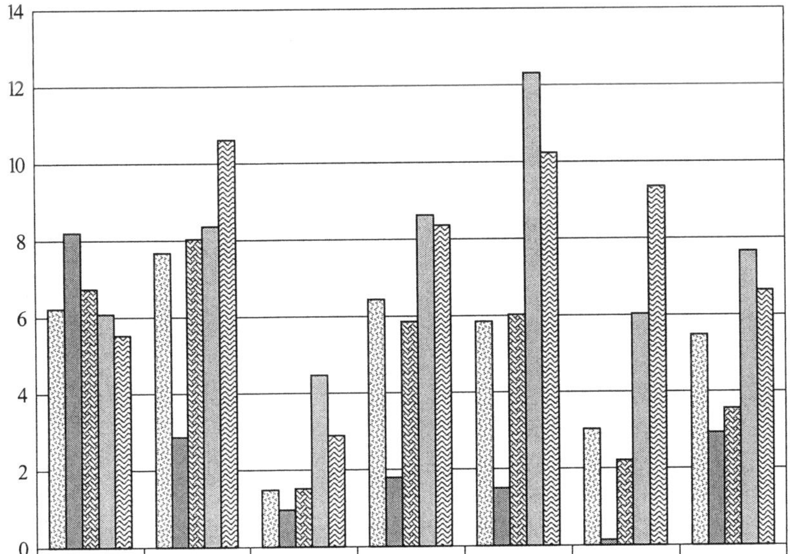

	US	Canada	Japan	UK	France	Germany	Italy
1961-96	6,22	7,67	1,48	6,45	5,84	3,02	5,48
1961-74	8,20	2,87	0,96	1,79	1,49	0,14	2,92
1975-82	6,74	8,04	1,52	5,85	6,02	2,21	3,55
1983-92	6,07	8,35	4,46	8,62	12,31	6,03	7,66
1993+	5,52	10,61	2,88	8,35	10,23	9,36	6,64

Source: Computations based on BLS data.
The estimated relation is:
$\Delta P_t - \Delta P_{t-1} = \alpha + \alpha_2 u_{t-1} + e_t$, where ΔP is inflation rate and u is the unemployment rate.

References

Abraham, K.G. and S.N. Houseman (1993), Job Security in America: Lessons from Germany, Washington, D.C.

Beißinger, T. and J. Moeller (1999), *contribution in this volume.*

Blanchard, O. and L. Summers (1986), Hysteresis and the European Unemployment Problem, in: Fischer, S. (ed.), NBER Macroeconomics Annual 1986, Cambridge, Mass, 15-78.

Blinder, A. (1988), The Fall and Rise of Keynesian Economics, *Economic Record* 64, 278-294.

Blinder, A. (1989), Macroeconomics under Debate, Ann Arbor.

BLS (1997), Comparative Civilian Labor Force Statistics, Ten Countries 1959-1996, Washington, Bureau of Labor Statistics, U.S. Department of Labor.

Buttler, F., W. Franz, R. Schettkat and D. Soskice (1995), Institutional Frameworks and Labor Market Performance, London, 1-19.

Chernyshev, I. (1998), Integration of Data from Different Sources: Unemployment, *Bulletin of Labour Statistics* 1998-2, xi-xxiii.

Esping-Andersen, G. and M. Regini (1999), Introduction, in: Esping-Andersen, G. and M. Regini (eds.), The Impact of Labor Market Deregulation, Oxford.

Freeman, R. (1988), Evaluating the European View that the United States Has No Unemployment Problem, *American Economic Review* 78, 294-299.

Freeman, R. (1995), The Limits of Wage Flexibility to Curing Unemployment, *Oxford Review of Economic Policy* 11, 63-72.

Freeman, R. B. and R. Schettkat (1998), From McDonalds to McKinsey: Comparing German and US Employment and Wage Structures, Leverhulme II Conference, September 1998, Institute of Economics and Statistics, Oxford.

Freeman, R. B. and R. Schettkat (1999a), The Role of Wage and Skill Differences in US-German Employment Differences, *Jahrbuecher fuer Nationaloekonomie und Statistik* (forthcoming).

Freeman, R. B. and R. Schettkat (1999b), Zwischen Fastfood und Excellence: Die Beschaeftigungsluecke in Deutschland im Vergleich zu den USA, *Hamburger Jahrbuch fuer Wirtschafts- und Gesellschaftspolitik.*

Fuchs, S. and R. Schettkat (1999), Germany, in: Esping-Andersen, G. and M. Regini (eds.), The Impact of Labor Market Deregulation, Oxford.

Hofer, H., K. Pichelmann and A. U. Schuh (1998), Price and Quantity Adjustments in the Austrian Labour Market, Institute for Advanced Studies: Working Paper 57, Vienna.

ILO, (1990), Surveys of Economically, Active Population, Employment, Unemployment and Underemployment. An ILO manual on concepts and methods, Geneva.

Kromphardt, J. (1987), Arbeitslosigkeit und Inflation, Goettingen.

Krueger, A. and S. Pischke (1999), Observations and Conjectures on the U.S. Employment Miracle, American Economic Association Meetings, New York.

Nickell, S. (1998), Unemployment: Questions and Some Answers, *Economic Journal* 108, 802-816.

OECD (1998), Employment Outlook, Paris.

Oswald, A. (1997), Happiness and Economic Performance, Working Paper 18, Department of Economics, University of Warwick.

Pichelmann, K. (1999), A Few Stylized Facts about Euroland's Labour Market(s), mimeo, Brussels, European Union.

Rothschild, K. W. (1978), Arbeitslose: Gibt's Die?, *Kyklos* 31, 21-35.

Schettkat, R. (1992), The Labor Market Dynamics of Economic Restructuring, New York.

Schettkat, R. (ed.) (1996), The Flow Analysis of Labour Markets, London.

Schettkat, R. (1997), Employment Protection and Labor Mobility in Europe: an Empircal Analysis Using The EU's Labor Force Survey, *International Review of Applied Economics* 11, 105-18.

Schettkat, R. (1998), Small Economy Macroeconomics: Economics Trends in Austria, Denmark, Ireland, and The Netherlands, Employment Conference, Geneva.

Solow, R. (1985), Unemployment: Getting the Questions Right, *Economica* 53, 23-34.

Sorrentino, C. (1993), International Comparisons of Unemployment Indicators, *Monthly Labor Review* 1993 (March), 3-24.

Sorrentino, C. (1995), International Unemployment Indicators, 1983-93, *Monthly Labor Review* 1995 (August), 31-50.

II. Theoretical Explanations

Unemployment: Theoretical Explanations*

Thomas Beißinger, Joachim Möller

University of Regensburg,
Universitätsstr. 31, 93053 Regensburg, Germany

1 Introduction

> The European unemployment problem is becoming so severe and prolonged that the influence of that event will almost certainly change theories of unemployment in the next few years. Dornbusch, Fischer (1987)

The European unemployment problem today is still at least as relevant as it was in the late eighties. Has the persistence and even aggravation of the phenomenon led to the creation of substantial new theoretical concepts? Have we a better understanding of stubborn mass unemployment compared to the state-of-the-art theories a dozen years ago? Do we know more about the presumably endogenous causes of shifts in the equilibrium unemployment rate? Can we sufficiently explain the striking differences in the labor market performance of different countries? Is there a consensus about the major causes of unemployment and are there generally accepted policy measures for fighting it? More than ten years after the prophecy of Dornbusch and Fischer it seems worthwhile to scrutinize the major theoretical developments which have taken place since then.

Most modern macroeconomic textbooks are still dominated by an aggregate demand/aggregate supply framework which implies a unique natural output or unemployment level. However, this clearly conflicts with the stylized fact that European unemployment has followed a marked positive trend since the mid-seventies. According to theoretical concepts that were developed during the seventies, periods of rising unemployment are interpreted as deviations from the natural rate due to expectation errors. Unfortunately, since the adjustment of expectations can be considered to be short-lived, the model is at odds with the evidence. Moreover, the error correction process is unlikely to differ so substantially across countries that this factor could explain the significant international differences in absorbing shocks. In this sense, Phelps (1994, p. vii) argues that long swings in unemployment "... are an equilibrium phenomenon, not a matter of misperceptions or misforecasts and consequent wage-price misalignments...".

---

* We thank Jürgen Antony, Oliver Büsse, Susanne Koch, Karen Thompson and the participants of the workshop "Globalization and Unemployment" at Hagen for helpful comments.

Other theoretical concepts for the explanation of stubborn unemployment, that were *en vogue* during the seventies and eighties, have more or less disappeared from sight. Among these is the quantity rationing theory as developed by Malinvaud (1977, 1980) and others. Today many economists still concede that market disequilibria may be relevant in the short run. Yet at the same time it is argued that rationing phenomena, especially on the goods market, are not likely to persist over a longer time horizon (cf. Zimmermann (1997)). A further approach, known as real wage-gap analysis, claims that "too high" real wages can be blamed for aggregate unemployment (cf. Bruno, Sachs (1985)). However, this approach can be criticized since the wage formation process is not modeled explicitly. Moreover, the real wage-gap analysis is too partial in nature, since it neglects the interaction between wage and price-setting agents.

The attempt to develop a more convincing framework for explaining high unemployment *as an equilibrium phenomenon* has led to at least three major trends in macroeconomics since the mid-eighties. First, the micro-foundation of macroeconomic theory has been strengthened. The modern analysis of the behavior of firms, households and unions is based on rational decisions. Second, the theoretical models increasingly leave behind partial analysis and move on to a general-equilibrium framework. Third, Walrasian-type models which assume perfect markets have become more and more obsolete.

Today, the dominant explanation of aggregate unemployment, the so-called "structuralist" approach[1], starts with imperfect competition on labor and goods markets. In the basic scenario firms exert some influence on the prices for their products and wages are determined in a bargaining process between unions and employers or by efficiency wage considerations. This implies that the interdependence of wage and price formation is explicitly taken into account. The unemployment rate is the key variable that equilibrates the conflicting claims of wage and price-setting agents. This approach allows the influence of a variety of factors determining changes in equilibrium unemployment to be studied.

Since we do not intend to summarize *all* theoretical developments since the mid-eighties, our contribution starts with a description of the standard structuralist model. Although several reviews of this approach exist in the literature[2], the basic framework is recapitulated in section 2. It is well known that in this model equilibrium unemployment is not affected by stabilization policies, but rather only depends on the institutional setup. Since this implication does not correspond with the empirical facts, we consider two extensions of the basic model. The first stresses the importance of persistence and hysteresis effects on unemployment, the

---

[1] This notion was coined by Phelps (1994).

[2] The most influential contributions are Layard *et al.* (1991) and Phelps (1994). Excellent surveys can be found in Nickell (1990), Lindbeck (1992), Bean (1994a, 1994b), Manning (1995), Franz (1996) and Blanchard, Katz (1997).

second focuses on open-economy aspects. It can be shown that through both extensions the demand side once again comes into play.

Building on the structuralist framework, we then turn to a two-sector economy differentiated by the skill intensity of their products in section 4. By using such an approach it is possible to create a link between macroeconomic theory and the recent literature dealing with the impacts of globalization and biased technical change on the employment performance of different skill groups. Our aim is to introduce some new aspects to this important debate. The paper ends with a summary and conclusions in section 5.

2 Unemployment as a Structural Labor Market Problem

2.1 The Structuralist Model

Rejecting the unrealistic construction of a Walrasian auctioneer, the structuralist model takes the assumption of imperfect competition on goods and labor markets as a starting point instead. The different variants of this approach can, in principle, be condensed into two central equations for real wages and unemployment which serve as substitutes for the supply and demand relationships in traditional labor market analysis.

The first relationship, called the price-setting equation, stems from firm behavior on the goods markets and is usually derived under the assumption of monopolistic competition using a variant of the influential Blanchard, Kiyotaki (1987) model. This approach offers the great advantage that strategic interactions among firms can be neglected as the single firm is small compared to the economy. A sensible, but rarely used, alternative to this type of modeling rests on the assumption of "conditional monopolies" whose market power is constrained by the (higher) marginal costs of potential competitors (cf. Vogt (1996)). However, both approaches share the assumption of identical firms and individuals and of a symmetric demand for commodities, which, in principle, leads to the same price-setting equation in the correct-expectation equilibrium.

Profit maximizing firms set prices as a mark-up μ on marginal costs, the latter depending on wages and employment. This price-setting equation can be solved for real wages, thus determining the real wage the firms are willing to pay at each level of employment. We use the term "price-setting equation" for this transformed expression as well. Assuming the labor force, L, to be given, the level of employment, N, can also be expressed as $(1-u)L$, where u is the unemployment rate. Hence the price-setting equation can be written as

(1) $\frac{W}{P} = \frac{A}{\mu} G\big((1-u)L\big), \qquad \mu > 1, G_u > 0, G_L < 0,$

where W is the wage including non-wage labor costs, P the producer price level and A productivity. The sign of the partial derivatives of G, denoted by subscripts, is due to the declining marginal product of labor given by $A \cdot G(N)$. In the special case of perfect competition on the goods market ($\mu = 1$), the price-setting equation can be solved for employment as a function of the predetermined real wage, which leads to a standard labor demand function. In accordance with the static nature of most models, the capital stock is assumed to be given and therefore only implicitly included in G.

In a real wage/unemployment diagram the price-setting schedule is upward sloping. However, some authors argue that a horizontal price-setting curve would be more relevant empirically, since it could explain why there is no strong pattern in the movement of the real wage over the business cycle. There are several possibilities for justifying such an assumption which implies that $G_u = G_L = 0$. For instance, Carlin, Soskice (1990) point out that the assumption of normal-cost pricing as well as the combination of increasing marginal costs and a counter-cyclical mark-up would both lead to a flat price-setting curve. This would also result in the case of flexible capital stock and constant returns to scale (cf. Bean (1989) and Landmann, Jerger (1993)).

It is important to stress that eq. (1) implies market-clearing for the goods markets. Also note that for the medium run the assumption of correct expectations is reasonable. Hence only the actual and not the corresponding expected variables appear in eq. (1) and the following equations.

We now turn to the second relationship between real wages and unemployment, the wage-setting equation. Several alternative theoretical foundations have been proposed for this relationship, all leading, in principle, to an equation of the form[3]

(2) $\frac{W}{P} = AH(u, \mu, \mathbf{z}), \qquad H_u < 0, \quad H_\mu > 0, \quad H_{z_i} > 0 \ \forall\, i,$

where $\mathbf{z} := (z_1, \ldots, z_n)$ is a vector of institutional variables comprising, for instance, of the level of unemployment benefits and the tax wedge.[4] The variables contained in $\mathbf{z}$ are defined in such a way that a rise in any of these variables leads to a rise of H, i.e. they generate wage pressure. Eq. (2) can be justified, for instance, by bargaining or efficiency wage models. According to these models

---

[3] The equivalence of different microfoundations of the wage-setting curve is shown by Layard *et al.* (1991), chap. 2 and 3. For a further discussion see also Beißinger (1996).

[4] An increase in the tax wedge, i.e. in the difference between labor costs and take-home pay, leads to higher wage pressure as long as employees show consumption wage resistance.

wages at the firm (or sector) level are set as a mark-up on the income that workers can expect outside their firm (or industry), the so-called outside option. The wage mark-up is, among other things, a positive function of the price mark-up μ of firms on marginal costs.[5] The value of the outside option does not only depend on wage rates elsewhere in the economy but also on unemployment benefits and the unemployment rate. Policy measures extending the generosity of the welfare system raise the alternative income and lead to a higher wage pressure. Rising unemployment, on the other hand, decreases the re-employment probability, thereby depressing the expected alternative income and moderating wage aspiration levels.

Depending on the chosen micro-model, other indicators for the state of the labor market can be considered instead of the unemployment rate. For example, following the matching approach as formalized by Diamond (1982) and Pissarides (1990), a preferable labor-market indicator would be the exit rate from unemployment, defined as the number of hires divided by the number of unemployed (cf. Blanchard, Katz (1997)). However, in the following analysis we decided to use the unemployment rate as indicator for labor market slackness.

Although we do not intend to consider the microfoundations in detail, we will assume that the wage-setting equation represents the outcome of a wage bargain between firms and labor unions when interpreting the results of the model. This is only for ease of exposition and does not mean that other types of explanations, such as efficiency wages, are less relevant.

Given the set of exogenous variables, the wage-setting and price-setting equation suffice to determine equilibrium real wages $(W/P)^*$ and the equilibrium, "natural" or "structural" rate of unemployment u^*.[6] At u^* the real wage the firms are willing to concede is consistent with the real wage as claimed by labor unions. Using eq. (1) and eq. (2), equilibrium unemployment is implicitly given as

$$(3) \quad \frac{1}{\mu} G\left(\left(1-u^*\right)L\right) = H(u^*, \mu, \mathbf{z}) .$$

It is clear from eq. (3) that productivity growth does not influence equilibrium unemployment. Several authors have convincingly argued that this is a desirable property of the model because otherwise the unemployment rate would exhibit a long-run trend, which is not plausible. The same argument applies with regard to the stock of capital.[7] If the stock of capital or a productivity variable were explic-

---

[5] At least this is the case for bargaining models as shown by Nickell *et al.* (1994) and Nickell (1998). If the effort of workers is also a function of μ, then efficiency wages depend on the market power of firms as well (Nickell (1998)).

[6] Some authors prefer the notation *Quasi-Equilibrium Rate of Unemployment* (QERU). See Lindbeck (1992) and Franz (1996, 1998).

[7] See, for example, Layard *et al.* (1991), Lindbeck (1992) and Bean (1994a).

itly considered in the price-setting equation, they should be included in the wage-setting equation in a identical way. In this case changes in the capital stock and productivity growth will shift the price and wage-setting curve by the same amount so that there is no effect on equilibrium unemployment. But how can these specifications be justified theoretically? If a bargaining approach lies behind the wage equation, it is relatively simple to construct a model that leads to the desired neutrality results. The reason is that in a bargaining model all variables influencing labor demand will also appear in the wage equation (cf. Manning (1993)). On the other hand, obtaining corresponding results from efficiency wage models is no trivial task. In the standard models, changes in productivity or the stock of capital only shift the price-setting curve, leaving the wage-setting curve unchanged. Hence the special case of a vertical wage-setting curve is often considered in the literature.[8] Phelps (1994) shows in an intertemporal general equilibrium model that it is not necessary to assume a vertical wage-setting curve if real wealth or real non-wage income are incorporated into the wage equation. With productivity growth raising profits, i.e. non-wage income, the wage-setting curve will shift by the same amount as the price-setting curve leaving equilibrium unemployment unchanged.

A similar problem arises with respect to a growing work force. According to eq. (3), this would also generate a trend in the unemployment rate. Analogous to the discussion of productivity and capital stock changes we will assume that the underlying micro-model is specified in such a way that L has no influence on u^*. In this case, the solution to eq. (3) can be written as

$$(4) \quad u^* = u^*(\mathbf{z}, \mu) \ .$$

Substituting eq. (4) for u in eq. (2), equilibrium real wages can be determined as a function of productivity and the exogenous wage and price pressure variables. Since the labor force L is given, equilibrium employment is $N^* = (1 - u^*) L$ and the corresponding output can then be obtained by the production function. To determine the aggregate price level, an equation linking the demand for goods and the real money supply is required. Theoretically this equation can be derived from the underlying microeconomic model by considering cash-in-advance constraints or incorporating money into the consumer's utility function. In the aggregate this leads to nominal demand being proportional to the money supply as in the simple quantity theory of money. With constant velocity of money and output growing at the same rate as productivity, $\hat{Y} = \hat{A}$, it follows that $\hat{P} = \hat{M} - \hat{A}$. In equilibrium, inflation $\hat{P}$ is equal to the growth rate of the money supply $\hat{M}$ minus the rate of productivity growth $\hat{A}$. If money grows at a constant rate, so does inflation at the

---

[8] See Manning (1993, 1995) and Beißinger, Büsse (1999) for a discussion of the necessary assumptions required in this special case.

equilibrium unemployment rate u^*. For this reason, u^* is also well-known as the Non-Accelerating Inflation Rate of Unemployment or NAIRU.

2.2 Policy Implications

The model can be used to identify the factors that may have contributed to the rise in European unemployment and are responsible for international differences in unemployment. With this aim we refer to eq. (4) stating that a rise in equilibrium unemployment in the medium run is due to factors affecting wage and price pressure, or more precisely

$$\frac{\partial u^*}{\partial \mu} = -\frac{(1/\mu^2)G(N) + H_\mu}{(L/\mu)G_N + H_u} = \frac{A\left[(1/\mu^2)G(N) + H_\mu\right]}{\Omega} > 0$$

and

$$(5) \quad \frac{\partial u^*}{\partial z_i} = -\frac{H_{z_i}}{(L/\mu)G_N + H_u} = \frac{AH_{z_i}}{\Omega} > 0 \qquad \forall i,$$

where Ω is the sum of the absolute value of the slope of the price-setting (PS) and the wage-setting (WS) curve, i.e.

$$(6) \quad \Omega := \frac{\partial(W/P)}{\partial u}\bigg|_{PS} + \left|\frac{\partial(W/P)}{\partial u}\bigg|_{WS}\right|.$$

For a better understanding of eq. (5), the effects of an increase in one of the wage pressure variables z_i on equilibrium unemployment and real wages are depicted by the solid lines in *figure 1*. For ease of exposition, productivity growth is neglected. The PS line represents price-setting (eq. (1)) and the WS_0 line wage-setting (eq. (2)). At the (initial) equilibrium unemployment rate u_0^* the real wage claims of firms and labor unions are mutually consistent. Therefore, inflation will be equal to the constant growth rate of money supply. Now assume, for example, that the generosity of the welfare state is extended. This leads to higher wage pressure, i.e. an upward shift of the wage-setting curve to WS_1. At u_0^* the real wage claims of labor unions are now higher (point B) than the real wage the firms are willing to concede (point A). Labor unions and firms try to obtain their desired real wage by pushing up nominal wages and prices respectively. With a constant money growth rate the increasing inflation reduces the real money supply and therefore also the demand for goods. The consequence is a decline in output and a rise in unemployment. This process eventually comes to an end at the unemployment rate u_1^*, where the real wage claimed by labor unions is equal to the real wage acceptable to the firms under the new conditions. At point C, inflation corresponds to the growth rate of money supply again.

In *figure 1* rising wage pressure leads to a higher real wage due to the upward sloping price-setting curve. However, if the price-setting curve is horizontal higher wage pressure will cause higher unemployment *without* increasing real wages. Hence in such a situation it would be quite misleading to blame too high real wages for unemployment (as done in the real wage-gap literature).

Figure 1: *The consequences of an increase in wage pressure for countries with different degrees of real wage rigidity*

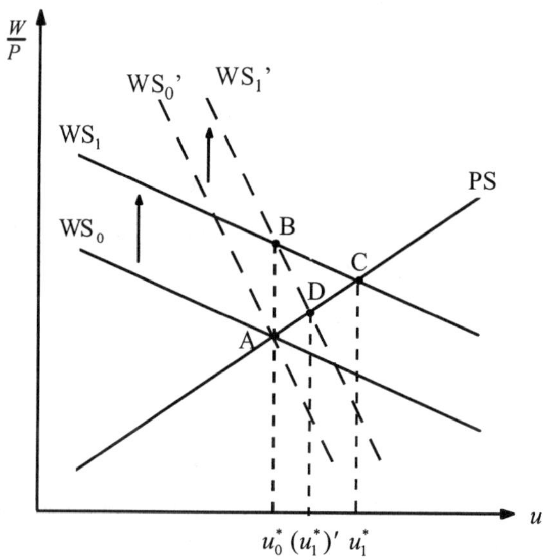

In the light of the graphical analysis and eq. (5) it can be argued that the *increase* in European unemployment is due to a rise of factors contained in **z**, such as non-wage labor costs, firing restrictions and the generosity of the welfare state (cf. Siebert (1997)). Alternatively, an increase in the monopoly power of firms, μ, may serve as an explanation. It should be stressed that changes in **z** or μ affect the supply side of the economy and therefore belong to the class of supply shocks. Note that in this stylized model, a higher μ could also represent an adverse oil price shock which leads to firms only being willing to concede lower real wages as well as to higher product wage demands by labor unions. This would result in a downward shift of the price-setting and an upward shift of the wage-setting curve, thus increasing equilibrium unemployment.

To explain cross-country *differences* in unemployment two different routes can be followed. First, it could be argued that national economies were either hit by different *types* of supply shocks (expressed by μ or $\mathbf{z}$) or, in the case of the same types of shocks, that the *size* of the shock was country-specific. As a further possibility, it could be postulated that countries were affected by similar shocks, but the *transmission* of the shocks was country-specific. At least for the oil-price shocks, the second line of reasoning is often considered to be more plausible. As implied by eq. (5), the transmission of the shocks depends on the slopes of the wage-setting and price-setting curve. The slopes indicate the degree to which the behavior of wage and price-setting agents leads to real wage changes in the face of rising unemployment. This is why Layard *et al.* (1991) define the degree of *real wage rigidity* (RWR) prevailing in an economy as

$$(7)\quad \mathrm{RWR} = \frac{1}{\Omega}.$$

The higher the degree of real wage rigidity, the greater is the response of the NAIRU to a given supply shock. This result can also be seen in *figure 1*, where the WS_0 and WS'_0 curves represent wage setting in two countries with different degrees of real wage rigidity. Note that in this figure both countries share the same price-setting curve. This can be justified by arguing that the slopes of the price-setting curves will not differ much across countries, because production technologies and price mark-ups are rather similar. Therefore, differences in the degree of real wage rigidity have to be mainly attributed to the wage-setting process. In *figure 1* both countries are hit by the same supply shock shifting the wage-setting curve from point A to point B. The impact on unemployment, however, is different. In the country with higher real wage rigidity, i.e. a flatter wage-setting curve, the increase in equilibrium unemployment is more pronounced (point C) than in the country with lower real wage rigidity (point D).

According to the literature, real wage rigidity is much higher in most European countries than, for instance, in Japan or the USA.[9] This might explain why the medium-run consequences of the oil price shocks on European unemployment in the seventies and eighties were worse than in the other OECD countries.

Layard *et al.* (1991) attribute the extent of real wage rigidity prevailing in an economy to institutional factors. According to their analysis, the real wage rigidity is influenced, for instance, by the duration of unemployment benefits. Another important factor affecting the shape and position of the wage-setting curve is the level of wage negotiations. Consider a bargaining framework where wages are negotiated at the national level instead of being set at the industry or firm level. In this case, the wage pressure may *ceteris paribus* be lower since rational behavior of unions implies that the effect of a wage increase on the aggregate price level

[9] See Bruno, Sachs (1985), Layard *et al.* (1991), Bean (1994a).

will be taken into account. At national level, the union also takes the fiscal budget constraint relating the financing of unemployment benefits and income taxes into consideration. Furthermore, lower wage pressure also results from a lower alternative income which, in this case, is equal to unemployment benefits. Hence economy-wide wage negotiations have the advantage of internalizing the costs of excessive wage pressure, thus moderating aspiration levels and leading to stronger wage reaction when unemployment changes. This analysis suggests that wage pressure is lower, the more centralized the level of wage bargaining is. Calmfors, Driffill (1988), however, argue in favor of a hump-shaped relationship between wage pressure and the level of wage negotiations. Wage bargaining at the firm level may also lead to lower wage demands compared to the outcome of negotiations at the industry level. The reason for this is that the elasticity of the demand for goods, and hence also the elasticity of labor demand, is higher at firm level.[10]

It is no coincidence that we have not mentioned the role of demand in explaining unemployment so far. Since the structuralist model exhibits classical features, *equilibrium* unemployment is solely determined by exogenous supply-side variables. Expansionary demand policies have no effect on equilibrium unemployment. Any increase in the growth rate of money supply eventually leads to higher inflation without any impact on the real economy in the medium or long run. Provided that the specifications of the above model are correct, one has to conclude that the fight against unemployment can not be conducted from the demand side.

However, there is a consensus among macroeconomists that changes in the demand for goods may have an impact on the unemployment rate *in the short run*. This fact is usually explained by nominal rigidities which are analyzed in great detail in the New Keynesian Economics literature.[11] In the structuralist model nominal rigidities can be incorporated by replacing actual variables by their expected counterparts in the labor market equations. By causing expectation errors, shifts in demand may then lead to temporary deviations from the NAIRU.[12]

The problem with the short-run analysis is that the European unemployment phenomenon in particular can not be explained by temporary deviations from an unchanged equilibrium unemployment rate, or as Phelps (1994, p. 245) puts it: "We need models showing how shifts in real supplies and demands disturb the equilibrium employment path." Only such an approach can give a convincing answer to the question, why unemployment in Europe has *persistently* risen to a higher level and why the labor market performance over the last few decades has been so different between countries. As we summarized in the above paragraphs,

[10] A review of the literature is found in Calmfors (1993a). See also Beißinger (1996), chap. 4 and Layard *et al.* (1991), chap. 2 for a more detailed analysis of the different impacts of centralized and decentralized bargaining on the wage-setting curve.

[11] See, for instance, Mankiw, Romer (1991) and Benassy *et al.* (1994).

[12] See Vogt (1996) for a detailed analysis of temporary equilibria besides the NAIRU.

most of the literature in this context points to supply factors using a variant of the structuralist model. Therefore, it comes as no surprise that nearly all proposals for a *reduction* of equilibrium unemployment concentrate on μ and the factors contained in the vector $\mathbf{z}$. According to the structuralist model, the fight against unemployment requires a reform of the welfare system aimed, for instance, at a reduction of the level and duration of unemployment benefits, a reduction of non-wage labor costs, deregulation of labor and product markets and other supply-side oriented measures.[13]

2.3 A Critical Assessment

According to the structuralist model, inflation will increase or decrease depending on whether unemployment is above or below the NAIRU, but corresponds to money growth minus productivity growth if unemployment is at the natural rate. Based on this analysis the inflation rate is left as a discretionary variable for central bankers who usually prefer an inflation rate close to zero. This view has already been questioned by Tobin (1972) who argued that inflation greases the wheels of the labor market by allowing real wages to fall even when nominal wages are sticky downwards. It took more than two decades, however, before economists captured Tobin's idea in a formal model and attempted to quantify the "benefits of inflation" (cf. Akerlof *et al.* (1996)). Knowing that economists are rather reluctant to accept the assumption of downward nominal wage rigidity which implies money illusion on the part of the workers, Akerlof *et al.* (1996) present a bulk of empirical evidence demonstrating that downward rigidity is an important feature of wage behavior. They use a modification of the formal model sketched in section 2 that allows for downward wage rigidity. Being corroborated by simulation and estimation methods, the basic message is that zero inflation would imply higher *equilibrium* unemployment compared to a situation with positive inflation.

Several objections have been raised against this analysis. For instance, Knoppik (1999) criticizes that the empirical model in Akerlof *et al.* (1996) exhibits several undesirable long-run properties which are not discussed in their paper. Others, like Gordon (1996) and Mankiw (1996), argue that it is not possible to transfer the evidence for nominal wage rigidity in situations with rapid nominal wage changes to a hypothetical situation of zero wage inflation. They point out that the analysis of Akerlof *et al.* (1996) is open to the Lucas critique. It is possible that in times of low inflation the money illusion which stands behind the nominal wage rigidity might vanish. Despite these objections, the contribution of Akerlof *et al.* (1996)

[13] For an evaluation of different policy proposals see, for instance, Snower (1995). Berthold, Fehn (1996) scrutinize the political problems that arise by implementing supply-side reforms.

raises an interesting question which points to the possibility that low inflation is not as innocuous as is commonly believed.

Other critics of the structuralist model refer to the result that demand may generate short-run fluctuations around the NAIRU but exerts no influence on the NAIRU itself. In their opinion, the (equilibrium) path of unemployment can only be explained by looking at the demand for goods as well. To justify this view theoretically, the model has to be modified in such a way that the demand for goods plays a role in determining unemployment beyond the short run. In a technical sense, this requires that also in the medium run the real variables of the model can not be determined by the supply-side equations alone, i.e. the recursivity of the model has to be abandoned. Of course, a convincing explanation has to be given for such a modification of the model. In section 3 we will discuss several alternatives.

It should be stressed, however, that the emphasis put on the supply side in the previous paragraphs is not mistaken. As we will argue in section 3, there are strong limitations to reducing unemployment by demand management alone. However, solely relying on supply side policies in the fight against unemployment may be equally ill-advised. Supply-side reforms will only indirectly affect production and employment after the effects of downward adjustment of wages and prices have worked through the economic system, decreased real interest rates and eventually increased demand. To shorten the time lag for the decline in unemployment, an accompanying demand expansion may be a useful policy instrument. In this sense, we share the view of Bean (1997, 1998) and others, that the fight against unemployment is best conducted by a "two-handed" approach encompassing measures on both the supply *and* demand side.

Other economists attack the conclusions drawn in the last section by pointing to the weak empirical support for the structuralist model. Since in our review we are concentrating on the theoretical aspects of the above framework, we leave the detailed discussion of the empirical research to others and only pick out some conclusions drawn in the literature. For instance, Blanchard and Katz (1997, p.52), after stressing the theoretical progress made in explaining unemployment, come to the conclusion that "... empirical knowledge sadly lags behind. Economists are a long way from having a good quantitative understanding of the determinants of the natural rate, either across time or across countries." And Bean (1994a, p. 614) in his empirically oriented survey poses the rhetorical question: "So what have we learned from this decade-long research effort? A cynic might reply: Not that much." The puzzling fact is that the time pattern observed for the NAIRU is at odds with the change in the underlying explanatory variables μ or $\mathbf{z}$ of the theoretical model (cf. Nickell (1997)). The crucial point is that institutional settings did not alter as rapidly as would be necessary to explain the path of the NAIRU, even worse: they sometimes changed in the wrong direction.

However, as we pointed out already, it would be possible to defend the conclusions of section 2.2 by stressing the dependence of the *transmission mechanisms* on the institutional setup. Hence it is not necessary to look for *changes* in the institutions. It is argued that the European unemployment problem resulted from the inability of the generous European welfare states to cope with the economic turbulences since the mid-seventies.[14] This is ascribed to the higher real wage rigidity prevailing in the European economies. It has to be stressed, however, that the assertion of a higher European real wage rigidity still lacks an empirical validation. Layard *et al.* (1991) present estimates for the slopes of the wage- and price-setting curves for different countries, thus providing a measure for the extent of real wage rigidity. However, serious objections can be raised against their method, making the results not very credible. From a theoretical perspective, it can be argued that it is generally impossible to identify the parameters of the wage-setting curve without relying on *ad hoc* restrictions (cf. Manning (1993)). It is also puzzling that the results of the extensive study by Blanchflower, Oswald (1994), based on large regional data sets, imply rather uniform parameters for the wage curve across countries, thus contradicting the results of Layard *et al.* (1991). Using micro data sets, the studies of Card *et al.* (1996) and Beißinger, Möller (1998) also raise some doubts as to whether the real wage-rigidity story is correct.

Notwithstanding these objections, in section 4 the hypothesis of a higher real wage rigidity in most European countries is taken as a starting point. We will then look in more detail at various types of turbulences that may have caused problems for the European countries. As has already been stressed above, shifts in the institutional variables contained in $\mathbf{z}$ can not serve as plausible candidates. The adverse oil price shocks, that changed the variable μ, have also faded away a long time ago and should have contributed to a *decline* in unemployment in recent years. Therefore, in the last decade the focus has been on other types of turbulences, the most prominent being globalization and biased technical change. Before discussing these issues in more detail in section 4, we first turn to variants of the structuralist model that allow for a greater role of demand.

3 Extensions of the Structuralist Model

3.1 Unemployment Persistence

There is a general agreement that a satisfactory explanation of the European unemployment path has to include the mechanisms that have generated the stubbornness of the phenomenon. Persistence mechanisms lead today's equilibrium

[14] For a formal theoretical analysis along these lines, see Ljungquist, Sargent (1998).

rate of unemployment to be positively related to yesterday's realization of unemployment. In a technical sense, persistence effects are usually introduced into the macroeconomic model by adding a term in first differences beside the level of unemployment into the Phillips curve or wage equation (cf. Franz, Gordon (1993)). In the special case of hysteresis the level term disappears, making the *long-run* equilibrium dependent on the history of unemployment.

Various sorts of persistence or hysteresis mechanisms have been suggested in the literature.[15] A prominent explanation, put forward by Solow (1985), Blanchard, Summers (1986) and Lindbeck, Snower (1988), relies on insider membership dynamics. In these models, the bargaining power of the incumbent workforce (i.e. the "insiders") is explained by turnover costs such as hiring and firing as well as training costs. These costs enable insiders to push wages above market-clearing levels without being replaced by the "outsiders". To see the implications of this approach, consider an adverse demand shock that was not expected by the insiders. Since wages are not immediately adjusted downwards, firms will react to this shock by reducing employment. If the displaced workers loose their insider status, the subsequent recovery will be used by the remaining insiders to demand higher wages. Thus they prevent employment from expanding in the upswing. As a result, equilibrium employment today depends on lagged employment. Lindbeck (1996) argues that it is difficult to show empirically whether the path of real wages in the European economies has contributed to the persistence of unemployment. Despite these empirical problems, the insider-outsider approach provides a useful framework for explaining how the wage-formation process reduces employment.

Labor-turnover costs also contribute directly to employment/unemployment persistence by rendering employment adjustments more costly for firms. Hiring and firing costs create a "zone of inaction" within which firms will not increase employment even if demand conditions start to improve.[16] The reason is that the presence of hiring and firing costs makes the employment decision similar to an ordinary investment decision that implies sunk costs.[17] Given the uncertainty about the future demand conditions, it may be worthwhile for firms to wait and see whether the upswing will be sustained or interrupted by, for example, a restrictive monetary policy.

Another persistence mechanism, that is regarded to be empirically relevant, focuses on long-term unemployment. If unemployment erodes skills and working habits, as already suggested by Phelps (1972), firms may use the employment record of applicants as a signal for their productivity. Blanchard, Diamond (1994) show that wages tend to be higher when a ranking of applicants occurs because

---

[15] See the reviews of Bean (1994a, 1997), Franz (1996) and Lindbeck (1996).

[16] See Bentolila, Bertola (1990), Bertola (1990) and Lazear (1990).

[17] For a general theory of the investment decision under uncertainty see Dixit, Pindyck (1994).

the newly unemployed will have a better chance of being re-employed than the long-term unemployed. A similar effect on wages results from the fact that job-seeking of the long-term unemployed is usually less intensive due to the demoralization caused by the prolonged failure of getting a job. Both these arguments imply that wage pressure at a given rate of unemployment increases with the proportion of the long-term unemployed.[18]

The implications of a heterogeneous pool of unemployed workers for inflation and unemployment can be analyzed by using the stylized model presented in the foregoing sections. To capture the special influence of long-term unemployment, the wage relation (eq. (2)) has to be modified to

$$(2') \quad \frac{W}{P} = AH(u, u^{\mathrm{LT}}, \mu, \mathbf{z}), \qquad H_u < 0, \quad H_{u^{\mathrm{LT}}} > 0, \quad H_\mu > 0, \quad H_{z_i} > 0 \ \forall i.$$

Note that in eq. (2') the actual rather than the expected price level is used. We will therefore only consider perfect-foresight equilibria. Eq. (2') describes the effect of the long-term unemployed on wage pressure. At a given unemployment rate u, a higher proportion of long-term unemployed in total unemployment (u^{LT}) increases wage pressure because the number of "effectively unemployed" individuals is reduced. Of course, the share of the long-term unemployed is itself an endogenous variable. When unemployment rises, i.e. $\Delta u \equiv u - u_{-1} > 0$, the inflow of new entrants lowers u^{LT}. In the long-run flow equilibrium, however, higher unemployment is associated with a higher proportion of long-term unemployed. Thus a typical specification similar to the one suggested by Layard *et al.* (1991) would be

$$(8) \quad u^{\mathrm{LT}} = u^{\mathrm{LT}}(u, \Delta u), \qquad u^{\mathrm{LT}}_{\mathrm{u}} > 0, \ u^{\mathrm{LT}}_{\Delta\mathrm{u}} < 0, \ u^{\mathrm{LT}}_{\mathrm{u}} < \left|u^{\mathrm{LT}}_{\Delta\mathrm{u}}\right| .$$

The last condition is necessary to guarantee that a rise in actual unemployment u leads to a decline of u^{LT} in the short run. The incorporation of eq. (8) in the wage equation eq. (2') might seem straight-forward, but the consequences are far-reaching. Hitherto the modeling implied a unique unemployment rate u^* with constant inflation. In what follows, we will call u^* the long-run NAIRU. Additional to u^*, a whole range of short-run constant-inflation unemployment rates u_S^* exists. Bearing in mind that inflation will be constant whenever the real wage implied by price setting corresponds to the bargained real wage, this can easily be verified. Equating the price- and wage-setting relation (eq. (1) and eq. (2') respectively) yields an equation that implicitly defines u_S^*:

$$(3') \quad \frac{1}{\mu} G\left(\left(1 - u_S^*\right)L\right) = H\left(u_S^*, u^{\mathrm{LT}}\left(u_S^*, \Delta u\right), \mu, \mathbf{z}\right) .$$

[18] This view is corroborated by empirical studies such as Layard, Nickell (1987), Nickell (1987) and Franz (1987).

Note that u_{-1} enters eq. (3') via Δu as an additional variable. Hence u_S* depends on unemployment history which is also influenced by demand shocks. The long-run NAIRU, however, is again independent of the level of demand. It can be obtained from eq. (3') for $\Delta u = 0$, i.e. for constant unemployment.

The implications of eq. (3') on the path of inflation and unemployment are explained in *figure 2*. The line WS depicts the long-run wage-setting curve with Δu set equal to zero, whereas the wage-setting curve, given u_{-1}, is represented by the line $\overline{\text{WS}}$.[19] The WS and $\overline{\text{WS}}$ lines will cross when $u = u_{-1}$, i.e. $\Delta u = 0$. The long-run NAIRU u^* corresponds to point A, where the long-run wage-setting curve and the price-setting curve intersect. Assume that unemployment in the last period was equal to u^*. Then, the $\overline{\text{WS}}$ line cuts the WS line at point A. Note that the long-run WS curve will be flatter compared to the wage-setting curve of the previous sections. Therefore, the persistence effects caused by long-term unemployment contribute to the real wage rigidity prevailing in an economy. The short-run $\overline{\text{WS}}$ curves will, however, be steeper. As a result, an increase in unemployment has a strong negative effect on real wages in the short run, but not in the long run.

Now consider the implications of an adverse demand shock. Assume, for instance, that in the (very) short run only nominal wages are rigid. In this case, the adverse demand shock will lead to higher unemployment $\tilde{u}$ and to temporary higher real wages (point F). Note that in the above formal analysis, we do not explicitly consider the "very short run" with expectation errors. For ease of exposition, we do not incorporate the wage-setting curve with false price expectations that would pass through point F in *figure 2* either.

In the period after the shock, expectations will be revised. This will lead to lower real-wage claims (point E) compared to real wages the firms are ready to pay (point F), thereby initiating wage and price deflation. The consequence is an increase in aggregate demand and a reduction of unemployment below $\tilde{u}$. However, the deflationary process will temporarily be interrupted *before* the long-run NAIRU u^* is reached. This can be seen in *figure 2* by noting that the increase in unemployment will shift the $\overline{\text{WS}}$ curve in the period after the shock through point E. Since real wage demands at point D are temporarily compatible to the real wages firms are willing to concede, the deflationary spiral already breaks off when unemployment reaches the short-run NAIRU u_S*. Of course, the $\overline{\text{WS}}$ curve will shift again in the next period, then cutting the WS curve at u_S*. This leads to a lower short-run NAIRU. The process continues until actual unemployment eventually reaches the long-run NAIRU u^*. Since this adjustment process is more

[19] For the long-run WS curve to be downward sloping, it has to be assumed that $|H_u| > H_{u^{LT}} \cdot u_u^{LT}$, where subscripts again denote partial derivatives.

time-consuming than in the models discussed so far, the inclusion of long-term unemployment in the wage equation offers an explanation for persistence.

Figure 2: *The distinction between short-term and long-term NAIRU due to unemployment persistence*

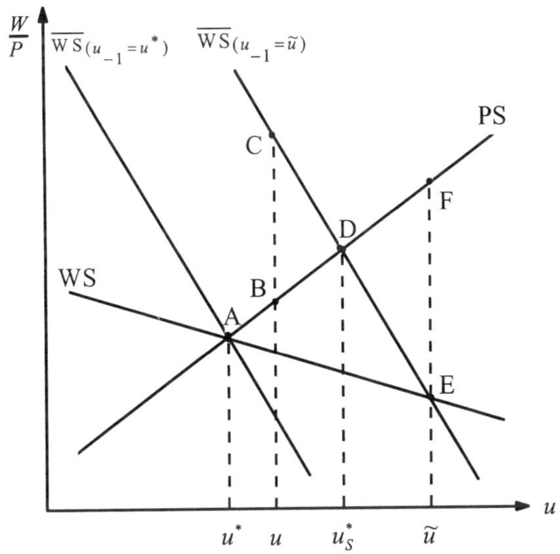

This analysis could have important consequences for monetary policy. Assume, for instance, that demand recovery is supported by fiscal expansion. Starting from $\tilde{u}$, this may lead to the unemployment rate u instead of u_S* in the period after the shock (see *figure 2*). At the unemployment rate u, real-wage claims are higher (point C) than the real wage the firms are willing to concede (point B). Hence inflation will already start rising although unemployment is still *above* the long-run NAIRU u*. Assume further, that the central bank concentrates on keeping the inflation rate constant. The rise in inflation at the unemployment rate u may therefore induce the central bank to switch to a restrictive monetary policy which leads again to an increase in unemployment. Due to such behavior of monetary authorities, it is possible that unemployment will not reach u* and, in the worst case, even begin to deviate more and more from the long-run NAIRU.[20]

This theoretical analysis shows that a too restrictive demand policy may well have contributed to the persistence of unemployment in Western Europe. This view is

[20] This possibility is discussed in Schlicht (1995), Vogt (1996), and Beißinger (1996).

also supported by Lindbeck (1996, p. 617) who raises the question why unemployment has been so prolonged in Europe. He concludes: "*Restrictive demand management* is certainly one important factor often motivated to bring down inflation, limit budget deficits and support a fixed exchange rate. Thus restrictive demand management policies have often contributed to keeping the actual unemployment rate above the long-term equilibrium rate." And Calmfors (1993b, p. 58), after discussing the Swedish experience, states with respect to the European economies: "General macro policy may after all be more important than seems to have been believed in recent years."

3.2 Open Economy Aspects

With the exception of the hysteresis case, the model presented so far implies the unemployment rate to be nailed to the NAIRU u^* in the long run. This result has to be altered once the openness of economies is taken into account. Unfortunately, the analysis with imperfect competition on goods and labor markets is seldom extended to the open economy.[21] In what follows, we will show how the structuralist model has to be modified in the case of an open economy that is too small to influence output and prices abroad. For simplicity, taxes and productivity growth are neglected in the analysis.

In the open economy, the real exchange rate c enters the wage and price equation as an additional endogenous variable. The variable c can be interpreted as describing the competitiveness of the economy, and is defined as

$$(9) \quad c \equiv \frac{P^f E}{P},$$

where P and P^f denote domestic and foreign prices for consumer goods and E the nominal exchange rate. There are several explanations why c may have an impact on price setting. Since firms import raw materials from abroad, their costs are influenced by the nominal exchange rate and raw material prices denoted in foreign currency. Beißinger (1996) shows that the resulting price-setting equation can be transformed in such a way that it depends on c and the wedge between world prices of raw materials and consumer goods. Another argument, put forward by Layard *et al.* (1991), suggests that a rise in international competitiveness renders the demand for domestic firms less elastic. Since both arguments qualita-

[21] One of the rare exceptions is the textbook by Carlin, Soskice (1990). However, for ease of exposition their analysis employs several *ad hoc* assumptions. In the work of Layard *et al.* (1991), only a small part is dedicated to the open economy. Moreover, as shown by Harrigan *et al.* (1993), this part of the analysis is flawed. In Beißinger (1996), a model for the small open economy is developed which explicitly takes the consequences of oil price shocks on price setting into account.

tively imply the same price-setting equation, we will follow the second line of reasoning here and replace the price-setting equation (1) by

$$(10)\quad \frac{W}{P}=\frac{1}{\mu(c)}G\big((1-u)L\big), \qquad \mu_c>0,\, G_u>0,\, G_L<0,$$

where productivity A is set equal to unity. Wage setting depends on real consumption wages $W/\widetilde{P}$, where the consumer price level $\widetilde{P}$ is defined as

$$(11)\quad \widetilde{P}=P^{1-\beta}\left(P^f E\right)^{\beta}.$$

The parameter β represents the fraction of foreign goods in the domestic consumer basket. With the definition of c and eq. (11) the wage equation can be written as

$$(12)\quad \frac{W}{P}=\frac{\widetilde{P}}{P}H(u,\mu,\mathbf{z})=c^{\beta}H(u,\mu,\mathbf{z}).$$

As pointed out above, inflation will be constant whenever the real wage claims of labor unions (eq. (12)) are consistent with the real wage the firms are willing to concede (eq. (10)). This condition is fulfilled if

$$(13)\quad \frac{1}{\mu(c)}G\left(\left(1-u^{*}\right)L\right)=c^{\beta}H(u^{*},\mu,\mathbf{z}).$$

It becomes evident that depending on the real exchange rate, a whole range of unemployment rates associated with constant inflation exists. Using the terminology of Carlin, Soskice (1990) the *Competing-Claims Equilibrium* (CCE) relation can be derived from eq. (13) as

$$(14)\quad u^{*}=u^{*}(\mu,\mathbf{z},c), \qquad u^{*}_{\mu}>0,\, u^{*}_{z_i}>0,\, u^{*}_{c}>0.$$

If the real exchange rate c rises, higher unemployment is necessary for inflation to remain constant. Since the real exchange rate itself is an endogenous variable, a second relation stemming from the demand side has to be derived to pin down both unemployment and competitiveness. In order to do this we have to specify the demand side in more detail than in the previous sections. We assume that aggregate demand for goods can be described as

$$(15)\quad Y=D(Y,r)+GE+T(c,Y), \qquad 0<D_Y<1,\quad D_r<0,\quad T_c>0,\quad T_Y<0,$$

where D is private domestic demand depending on aggregate income Y and the real interest rate r, GE denotes government spending and T the (real) trade balance. The partial derivatives exhibit the usual signs, with $T_c>0$ following from the Marshall-Lerner condition. To also determine the nominal variables, money market equilibrium has to be taken into account. Let i denote the nominal interest rate. Then in the usual way $M/P = f(Y, i)$ with $f_Y > 0$, $f_i < 0$. The nominal interest rate is equal to the real interest rate plus the expected inflation rate. As the analysis is restricted to the medium run, it is assumed that expectations are fulfilled. It follows that $i = r + \hat{P}$ and $i^f = r^f + \hat{P}^f$, where the second relation refers to the world economy and a hat over a variable denotes the respective growth rate. The model is closed with the uncovered interest parity condition $i \approx i^f + \hat{E} = r^f + \hat{P}^f + \hat{E}$, again assuming correct expectations.

In the steady state the *real* exchange rate remains constant, thus in the case of flexible exchange rates it must hold that $\hat{P} = \hat{P}^f + \hat{E}$. If the nominal exchange rate is fixed, domestic inflation is pinned to world inflation, i.e. $\hat{P} = \hat{P}^f$. In both cases it can be deduced from the interest parity condition and the equation for nominal interest rates that the domestic real interest rate is tied to the interest rate abroad, i.e. $r = r^f$. Using this result, the demand equation (15) implies a relation between competitiveness and output. Alternatively, eq. (15) can be written as

$$(15') \quad Y\big((1-u)L\big) = D\Big(Y\big((1-u)L\big), r^f\Big) + GE + T\Big(c, Y\big((1-u)L\big)\Big),$$

where the production function $Y(N)$ is substituted for output Y and the transformation $N = (1 - u)\,L$ is used. The aggregate demand (AD) equation (15') and the CCE relation (14) together determine the real exchange rate and unemployment.

This result is depicted in *figure 3*, where unemployment and competitiveness are jointly given by the intersection of the CCE and the AD line. Additionally, the BT line represents all u-c combinations where trade is balanced, i.e. $T\Big(c, Y\big((1-u)L\big)\Big) = 0$.[22] Points below the BT curve represent a trade deficit, since at a given unemployment rate the real exchange rate and therefore net exports are too low. Conversely, points above the BT curve correspond to a trade surplus.

In *figure 3*, the initial equilibrium (with balanced trade) is determined by the intersection of the AD_0 line and the CCE line, leading to the unemployment rate u_0 and the real exchange rate c_0. Now consider an expansionary fiscal policy. In the standard NAIRU model of the closed economy, the fall in unemployment will be completely offset by the initiated wage-price spiral and the implied real balance effect. In the open economy, however, the demand expansion leads to lower unemployment even in the medium run (with correct expectations). This can be seen in *figure 3*, where an increase in government spending shifts the AD curve to the left to AD_1. However, the lower unemployment rate u_1 is accompanied by an ap-

[22] Simple calculations reveal that the BT curve is flatter than the AD curve.

preciation of the real exchange rate which curbs net exports.[23] Hence the costs of this policy would be a trade deficit. It is clear that such a deficit can not be sustained in the long run.

Figure 3: *Expansionary fiscal policy in the small open economy*

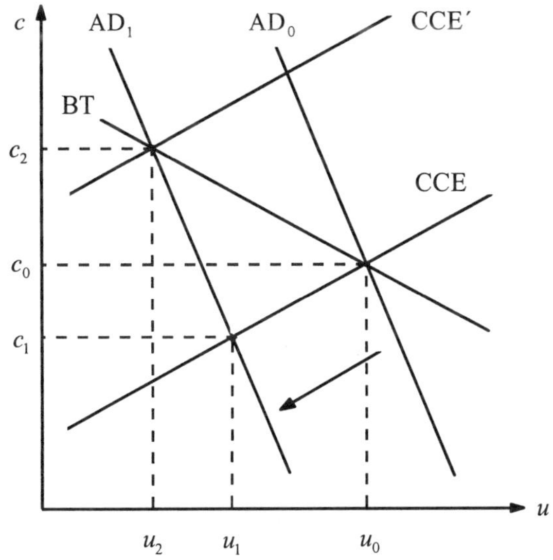

The size of the deficit will also depend on the reaction of other countries. If the main trading partners are unwilling to pursue an expansionary policy in their own country the domestic trade deficit will be more pronounced. Consequently, it could be argued that a fiscal expansion is only a useful policy instrument if it is also pursued by other countries. In the face of a coordinated demand expansion, however, the world interest rate may rise. Phelps (1994) shows that this will directly reduce firms' investment in the stock of employees, since in an intertemporal general equilibrium model the real wage acceptable to the firms is also a negative function of the real interest rate.[24] This argument is perhaps less of a problem, if the coordinated demand expansion is thought to counteract a worldwide recession that should be expected to be accompanied by declining real interest rates. In any case, the adverse impact of the fiscal expansion on the trade balance may be avoided or at least mitigated by supply-side reforms aimed at lowering wage pressure. According to eq. (14) this will shift the CCE curve to the left. The shift may

---

[23] Note that results for c and u are independent of the exchange-rate system. For the nominal variables, however, different results are obtained. These are deduced by taking the equation for money market equilibrium into account. For details see Beißinger (1996).

[24] See also the reviews of Phelps' book by Woodford (1994), van Ees, Garretsen (1996) and Malinvaud (1997).

be strong enough to reach the unemployment rate u_2 where trade is balanced again.

From the above objections, it follows that a policy only relying on a demand expansion will hardly be sustainable in the longer run. On the other hand, focusing solely on the supply side may be equally unwise. As already pointed out, supply-side reforms will reduce unemployment only after a considerable time-lag, whereas a demand expansion has direct effects on production and employment. In our view, the most reasonable policy recommendation is therefore a two-handed approach, encompassing measures on both the demand and supply side. In this case, the adverse effects of the demand expansion on inflation and deficits are mitigated by supply-side reforms which will reduce wage pressure and increase the competitiveness of firms.

4 Globalization and Biased Technical Change

The model considered so far is monolithic in the sense that it analyses the effects of aggregate demand and supply shocks in a one-sector economy with homogeneous labor. It does not take into account that labor market problems may be caused to a substantial extent by shifts in demand between different groups of workers and between sectors of the economy. Overwhelming empirical evidence in the developed countries points, however, to the fact that particularly the labor market performance of low-skilled workers has deteriorated. The facts suggest that the low-skilled have either suffered from a serious blow to their wages or from high increases in unemployment. Consequently, the famous "two-sides-of-the-same-coin" hypothesis (Krugman (1994)) establishes a link between the relative wage losses of these persons in countries with apparently highly flexible labor markets like the U.S. on the one hand and their poor employment performance in typical European economies with a relative rigid wage structure on the other.[25]

Although the basic evidence can not be disputed, there is a debate on the relative magnitude of group-specific labor demand shocks as opposed to neutral shocks. Some authors argue that the apparently clear-cut conclusions from the empirical evidence might be misleading. For example, Blanchard (1995) points out that the change in the distribution of unemployment rates would also be exactly what one would expect to happen in response to a shift in aggregate rather than relative demand for labor. First, this result may be due to "ladder" and "ranking" effects, i.e. the fact that the skilled can do many of the unskilled jobs and during recessions firms may therefore "hoard" skilled workers. This labor hoarding occurs

[25] In a theoretical model, Vogt (1999b) argues that the trade-off between unemployment and inequality in the economic policy debate has to be extended by a further dimension, namely the stance of monetary policy.

because the human capital of skilled workers, particularly of the specific type, increases their attachment to firms. A second argument relies on the observation that unemployment of low-skilled workers is higher in general. Due to the convexity of the skill-specific wage-setting curves, the wage elasticity of the unskilled is lower than for skilled workers. Therefore a neutral adverse shock is likely to increase the unemployment rate of the unskilled to a greater extent.[26] Hence the relative magnitude of specific versus neutral labor demand shocks is likely to be over-estimated by just comparing changes in unemployment rates for different groups.

Despite the plausibility of these arguments, it can hardly be denied that, at least to some extent, shifts in the relative demand for different types of labor have contributed to the rise in aggregate unemployment in Europe as well as to the rise in U.S. wage inequality. The monolithic model considered in section 2 is not adequate for explaining these developments. We, therefore, extend our framework by considering a stylized two-sector economy with two types of labor in order to obtain an enhanced resolution picture of the labor market. The aim of the analysis is to contribute to the debate on the underlying causes of the shifts in relative labor demand.

In recent literature the focus has been on the specific labor market consequences of mainly two factors, technical change and/or international trade (globalization). Intuition as well as casual evidence both suggest that these factors are the driving forces behind the observed changes in the structure of wages and employment. Differences with respect to skill play a most prominent role in this context. Despite its theoretical appeal, the literature tackling the interactions between technology and/or globalization on the one hand, and skill-specific labor market performance on the other, mainly concentrates on empirical aspects, whereas stringent analytical contributions are rare. This is probably due to the complexity which arises from the necessity to consider different sectors producing goods with different types of labor in a model with market imperfections.

In the following sections we first investigate the labor market consequences of the increased openness of the economy and then turn to a technology-based approach.

4.1 Trade-Based Explanations

Of all the trade-based explanations, the famous Heckscher-Ohlin theory of international trade has attracted most attention, both from economists and the general public. This approach predicts that reductions in barriers to trade would affect the

---

[26] This argument has been stressed by Nickell, Bell (1995, 1996). These authors show that if the wage curve can be approximated by a log-linear relation, the unemployment effects of a neutral adverse shock would tend to be *equiproportionate*, rather then equal percentage-point increases.

factor content of production in the trading countries. The relative scarcity of factors determines the direction of specialization. On the one hand, developing or newly industrializing countries ("the South") are abundant in low-skilled labor. These countries consequently have a comparative advantage in the production of goods which use this factor intensively. On the other hand, developed countries would be expected to specialize in products with a relatively high content of skilled labor. As a result, the relative demand for the abundant factor rises. Hence the change in the industry mix will increase the demand for high-skilled labor and reduce the demand for the low-skilled in the North (and *vice versa* in the South). Under conditions of wage flexibility this should have consequences for relative factor prices. According to the factor price equalization and Stolper-Samuelson theorems, the skill premium in the North will tend to rise while shrinking in the South. Although there are overall gains from trade, low-skilled workers in the North are hurt and the formerly favorable market position of high-skilled workers in the South deteriorates. According to the theory, negative effects for these groups are inevitable. If – as in some Northern countries it can be expected to be the case – a rigid wage structure hinders the relative wage to adjust, higher unemployment of low-skilled workers will result. Hence the developed countries face a devil's choice between higher inequality and/or higher unemployment in the low-skill segment of the labor force.

Despite its theoretical foundations and its general plausibility, the Heckscher-Ohlin and Stolper-Samuelson story of the unemployment/inequality dilemma is far from being widely accepted as a satisfactory explanation of the empirical evidence in the discipline. The following assertion given by Krugman stands for many in this context:

> All in all, the proposition that globalization explains the simultaneous growth in inequality and unemployment makes a nice, intellectually appealing package; it is not surprising that it should command wide acceptance.
>
> Unfortunately, empirical research is nearly unanimous in rejecting the idea that imports from the Third World have been a major factor in reducing the demand for less-skilled workers. (Krugman (1994, p. 35))

This rather harsh critique relies on three major arguments. First, the sheer quantity of trade with the Third World or newly industrializing countries is fairly small for the U.S. or the European Union as a whole. It is well-known that the bulk of trade is intra-North, not North-South. Since the latter appears to be a periphery rather than a core phenomenon in the Northern countries, the case for trade-based theories in general is weakened. Second, changes in the skill premium resulting from greater exposure to trade should, in general equilibrium, be reflected in the relative prices of goods with different "skill content". The argument that trade with unskilled-labor abundant countries has led to an "immiseration of the unskilled" also requires falling prices for goods with a high content of low-skilled labor (cf. Bhagwati (1995)). Although empirical studies come to different conclusions in this respect, some evidence seems to suggest "... that the goods prices had actually gone the other way from that required by the assertion." (Bhagwati (1995, p. 43)).[27] Third, under the assumption of perfect competition the trade story would imply a specific change of relative factor use. Since an extension of the skill premium implies that the relative price of low-skilled labor falls, this factor should consequently be used more intensively in all sectors of the economy. Unfortunately, this is at odds with the evidence in developed countries. As has been documented by many studies, the trend to employ a *more* qualified workforce is observed across all industries.[28] However, several authors point out that the theoretical basis of the last two objections can be questioned. It is well known that the Heckscher-Ohlin theory as well as the Stolper-Samuelson and related theorems rely on several assumptions, many of which are likely to be violated in reality. The most prominent one is the assumption of perfect competition not only on goods but also on factor markets. Deardorff, Haikura (1994) cite studies based on computable general equilibrium models showing that effects on relative factor prices are by no means clear-cut if this critical assumption is relaxed. It seems even possible, that real wages of the unskilled in the developed countries increase as barriers of trade are reduced. Given these doubts concerning the theoretical implications of the trade-based explanation of the unemployment/inequality dilemma, it is useful to re-investigate the effects on wage inequality and skill intensity within the framework of the model developed in section 2.

4.1.1 An Analytical Framework

Assume that the economy is divided into two sectors with different skill requirements in production. The first sector (b) employs workers with basic skills, while the second (s) needs highly-skilled labor only. Since the assumption of perfect competition seems less problematic for goods markets than for labor markets, we give up the assumption of imperfect competition on product markets by setting μ_i equal to unity for ease of exposition. Domestic product prices are exogenously determined by world prices. We neglect the influence of productivity in the labor demand and wage-setting functions. In analogy to eq. (1) the labor demand of the firms in the two sectors is then characterized by

$$(16) \quad \frac{W_i}{P_i} = G_i(N_i) = G_i\left(\left(1-u_i\right)L_i\right), \qquad i = \{b,s\} .$$

[27] Bhagwati refers to the Lawrence, Slaughter (1993) study that supports his view and critically reviews the contradictory evidence presented by Sachs, Shatz (1994). In a recent paper, Wood (1998) concedes that the movements of goods prices are not in line with the factor price equalization argument. For a critical review of the methodology of these studies as well as of recent extensions, see Slaughter (1998).

[28] See, for example, Levy, Murnane (1996), Berman, Bound, Griliches (1994) and Berman, Bound, Machin (1998).

Up to a negligible constant factor, the aggregate price level in the economy under Cobb-Douglas preferences is $P = P_b^{\alpha} P_s^{1-\alpha}$, or,

$$(17) \quad \frac{P}{P_b} = \left(\frac{P_s}{P_b}\right)^{1-\alpha} \quad \text{and} \quad \frac{P}{P_s} = \left(\frac{P_b}{P_s}\right)^{\alpha}.$$

When solved for the consumer's real wage, the labor demand equations can be written as

$$(18) \quad \frac{W_b}{P} = \left(\frac{P_s}{P_b}\right)^{-(1-\alpha)} G_b\big((1-u_b)L_b\big) \quad \text{and} \quad \frac{W_s}{P} = \left(\frac{P_s}{P_b}\right)^{\alpha} G_s\big((1-u_s)L_s\big).$$

The sector specific wage-setting relationships are

$$(19) \quad \frac{W_i}{P} = H_i(u_i, \mathbf{z}_i), \qquad i = \{b, s\}.$$

Equating eq. (18) and eq. (19) yields equilibrium unemployment for low and high-skilled workers

$$(20) \quad u_b^* = u_b^*\left(\frac{P_s}{P_b}, L_b, \mathbf{z}_b\right) \quad \text{and} \quad u_s^* = u_s^*\left(\frac{P_b}{P_s}, L_s, \mathbf{z}_s\right),$$

where all partial derivatives are positive.

If relative prices P_s/P_b change in favor of high-skilled labor intensive goods because low-skill labor abundant countries get increasingly access to world markets, the unemployment rate of low-skilled workers rises, whereas that of high-skilled workers is reduced. Of course, the adverse effect for the former can be mitigated by dampening the institutional wage-push factors contained in the vector $\mathbf{z}_b$.

Figure 4 gives a graphical representation of the situation. With the *consumer's real wage* drawn on the vertical axis, an exogenous increase of relative prices in favor of skill-intensive goods moves the equilibrium from point A to point B in both sectors. In the sector employing low-skilled workers (left-hand graph) the labor demand (LD) curve shifts downwards (see eq. (18)). With constant wage-setting behavior (WS), this leads to a rise in the unemployment rate from u_b^0 to u_b^1 and to a fall in the worker's consumption wage. The situation is exactly mirrored in the sector employing high-skilled labor (see the right-hand graph). If P_s/P_b goes up, the consumption wage W_s/P acceptable to the firm increases, or equivalently, the LD-curve shifts upwards. With no changes in wage-setting behavior, unemployment for skilled workers shrinks ($u_s^1 < u_s^0$). Comparing the situation in the two sectors, it becomes evident that the skill premium widens (implying more wage inequality) while the relative unemployment situation deteriorates for the unskilled. With constant labor supply, this implies an *increasing* skill intensity in the economy.

Figure 4: *The effects of globalization on unskilled and skilled workers*

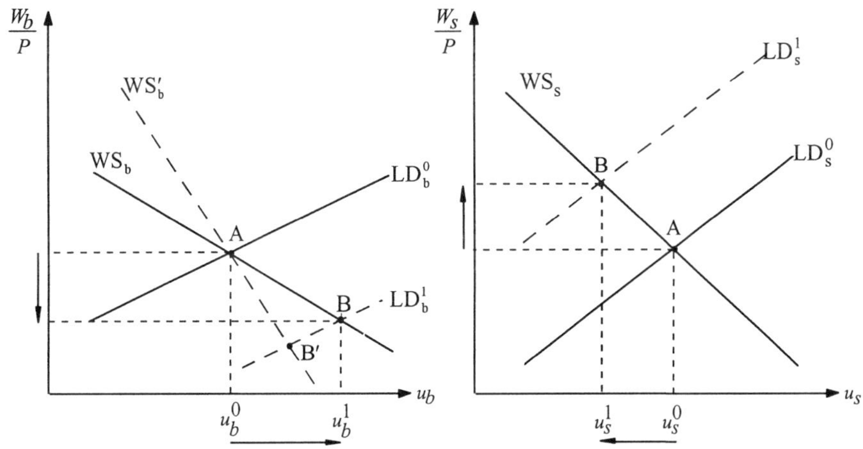

As discussed in section 2, the response of the unemployment rates crucially depends on the slope of the wage-setting curves which reflects the extent of real wage rigidity in the wage-setting process. As indicated by the dashed line WS_b, the figure shows that with more real wage flexibility, or a steeper WS-curve, the harmful unemployment effects of globalization on the unskilled in the low-skilled segment would be mitigated. Hence the model predicts that countries with less restrictions on the labor markets (like the U.S.) would more easily overcome the possible adverse consequences of globalization on the unemployment of unskilled workers. In this case, however, the consumption wage for this group would fall even more. Hence the typical trade-off between higher unemployment and a higher skill premium (or higher wage inequality) becomes visible. Reducing the unemployment effects of globalization comes along with increasing wage differentials between skill groups. Note that we did not draw a corresponding alternative wage-setting curve for skilled workers because cross-country evidence suggests that international differences in high-wage flexibility are not substantial (cf. Blau, Kahn (1996)).

4.1.2 A Critical Assessment of the Trade-Based Explanation

In the stylized two-sector model presented above we have analyzed the labor markets effects of globalization by relaxing the assumption of perfect competition on that market. If increasing trade affects the relative price of goods with high and low skill content as postulated, the implications of the model correspond well to the stylized facts. However, the minor quantitative importance of North-South trade remains as a major objection against the relevance of the globalization-based explanation of higher structural unemployment.

Although the evidence seems quite clear at first glance, the issue is still open to debate since the protagonists of a trade-based approach have partly reformulated and sharpened their arguments after the first line of criticism. Adrian Wood (1994, 1995) points out that statistical information indicating that North-South trade is of minor importance for the North could be quite misleading. Given the large wage differentials between Northern and Southern workers, a dollar of imported goods embodies a much higher amount of labor than the same amount of domestically produced goods. While the argument is accepted by most economists in principle, the magnitude of the understatement is unclear. Hard evidence is lacking because the results heavily depend on the assumptions made in the analysis. Some calculations based on plausible settings indicate that the total effect of North/South trade on the relative factor demand of the North might be quite substantial.[29]

Wood also stresses the need to take a dynamic rather than a comparative-static perspective as in the early work of the same author. Hence he proposes to look at the data "... in terms of acceleration or deceleration of secular upward trends in both the relative demand for and supply of skilled labor" (Wood (1998, p. 1464)). Wood's reading of the U.S. data is that the trend in relative demand in favor of a more qualified workforce has been accelerating in the last two decades or so, exceeding the secular trends in labor supply working in the same direction. Globalization, in his view, is the major factor behind the *acceleration* in the relative demand for more qualified labor while other factors (especially biased technical change) are responsible for long-run shifts in the relative demand.

In recent contributions, Feenstra (1998a,b) points to some new aspects in the debate. His main argument rests on the observation that "... an increasing amount of international trade takes the form of trade in intermediate inputs." (Feenstra (1998a, p. 139)) *Global sourcing* or outsourcing across borders has been significantly increasing in the last decades. There is also strong evidence for "vertical specialization", i.e. economies specialize in particular segments of the value chain (cf. Hummels *et al.* (1997)). Merely focusing on trade with final goods might be quite misleading. More specifically, one can question the Lawrence, Slaughter (1993) investigation of differences in price inflation for skill-intensive and non skill-intensive industries. Even with inflation rates in the latter exceeding those in the former, this would not rule out the basic argument of adherents of the trade-

[29] After correcting for the statistical bias mentioned above and taking several other influences into account, Wood (1998) concludes that North/South trade has raised the relative demand for skilled labor in the North by about 20 percent.

based view, because under a regime of vertical specialization relative inflation rates between industries are of minor importance for the hypothesis. Given that developed countries concentrate on the most skill-intensive segments of the value chain *within* each industry, one should rather look at the difference between value-added prices in the trade-exposed industries and the corresponding import prices. Empirical evidence tends to confirm the view that prices for domestically produced value added have risen significantly more than those of imported goods.

This reasoning shows that the key arguments against the trade-based explanation of the unemployment-inequality dilemma appear to be substantially weakened. Consequently, the trade story is still in the game. Taking into account the growing importance of outsourcing which has been fostered by improvements in communication and monitoring technologies in the last one or two decades, it can be argued that the trade-versus technology rivalry should be settled, because both approaches could support each other. This is also one of the conclusions drawn by Feenstra who states that: "... trade (through outsourcing) and technology (through computerized communication and inventories) are complementary rather than competing explanations..." (Feenstra (1998a, p. 152)).

Before a final assessment is given, we would like to investigate the skilled-biased technical change approach in more detail. This is done in the next section.

4.2 Technology-Based Explanations

For many authors skill-biased technical change gives the most promising explanation of rising inequality in the U.S. and especially high unemployment rates among the unskilled in typical European countries.[30] The approach seems to be especially attractive to labor economists. Hence Berman, Bound, Machin (1998, p. 1246) state that, despite the unsettled debate between protagonists of trade or technology based theories, "... labor economists generally believe that skilled-biased technological change is the principal culprit." The reason for this belief is not so much an overwhelming evidence in favor of the technology-based explanation but rather the alleged weakness of the alternative trade-based hypothesis. It is often argued that trade theory can not explain the fact that the share of the highly qualified workforce continues to rise in many industries even though the skill premium has expanded considerably (cf. Lawrence, Slaughter (1993), Slaughter (1998)). However, as we have shown above, these trends are not contradictory to a trade-based model if imperfect competition on the labor market is taken into account. A further argument against trade-based explanations relies on intra-sectoral developments. As shown by Machin, van Reenen (1998) among others, the higher relative demand for skilled workers is to a large extent due to intra-industry not inter-industry changes. This is at odds with the standard Heck-

---

30 See, among others, Bound, Johnson (1992), Krugman (1994).

scher-Ohlin theory that explains changes in relative labor demand by intersectoral shifts. However, if one takes account of the phenomenon of vertical specialization which leads to outsourcing *within* industries (cf. Feenstra (1998a,b)), the trade-based approach is reconciled with the stylized facts.

These arguments weaken the critique of protagonists of the technology-based explanation on the trade-based approach. This does not mean that biased technical change is of minor importance. In recent contributions, several attempts have been made to find direct empirical evidence for the relevance of this hypothesis. Since the influential micro-data study of Krueger (1993), it has become increasingly popular to identify the computer revolution as the driving force behind the unemployment/inequality dilemma. At the present state of technology, computers and other high-tech equipment appear to be relative complements to skilled or highly skilled workers.[31] Given these developments, the marginal product of the skilled relative to the unskilled has increased. But again, the implications of this are not immediately obvious. One *caveat* in this respect stems from Leamer (1994). Leamer argues that in a Heckscher-Ohlin model of a small open economy and two factors of production the skill-bias argument is not convincing. In such a setting, technical change in a single country is irrelevant to the wage structure. This is why Berman, Bound, Machin (1998) stress the fact that skill-biased technical change is a phenomenon in *all* developed countries (because of modern communication, new technologies are quickly adopted world wide). Hence, "*pervasive* skill-biased technical change *will* affect relative wages, since an integrated world economy will respond to such technological change as a closed economy would." (Berman, Bound, Machin (1998, p. 1247)).

Unfortunately most adherents of the technology-based hypothesis derive their results from a partial analysis. For instance, the general equilibrium income effects of skill-specific productivity growth are seldom taken into account. Furthermore, the impact of productivity growth on the wage-bargaining process is usually neglected. This might be due to the complexity of general equilibrium models with imperfect competition. Moreover, as Gregg, Manning (1997) point out, the structuralist framework makes it difficult to deal with skilled-biased technical change because this framework is designed to reflect the long-run neutrality of technical change on the unemployment rate (see section 2). These authors propose a modification by formulating the wage-setting curve as a function of *relative* wages. They conclude that a link between the reservation wages of both groups is required to obtain the result that "a shift in the relative demand curve towards skilled labor tends to raise the relative wage and tends to reduce skilled unemployment and raise unskilled unemployment." (Gregg, Manning (1997, p. 1187)). Their model, however, only allows the analysis of relative and not absolute changes in the labor market performance of the different skill groups. Therefore, it

[31] Cf. Krueger (1993), Levy, Murnane (1996) and Autor, Katz, Krueger (1998).

seems worthwhile, to re-examine the theoretical argument for the relevance of skill-based technical change in the framework presented in section 2.[32]

4.2.1 An Analytical Framework

For convenience, perfect competition is again assumed on the goods markets. We consider a closed economy that consists of two sectors each operating under constant returns with basic and high skilled labor, respectively. In contrast to the trade-based model of section 4.1, the prices of goods are now endogenous. The price of the good in the first sector is taken as *numéraire*. The efficiency of skilled labor is described by a variable $A_s \geq 1$. Under these assumptions the production functions are simply $Y_b = N_b$ and $Y_s = A_s N_s$. In equilibrium, the following relation between wages and prices must hold

$$(21) \quad W_b = 1 \qquad \text{and} \qquad \frac{W_s}{P_s} = A_s .$$

For the wage-setting relations one obtains[33]

$$(22) \quad \frac{W_b}{P} = \tilde{A}_b H_b(u_b) \qquad \text{and} \qquad \frac{W_s}{P} = \tilde{A}_s H_s(u_s) ,$$

where $\tilde{A}_i$ describes the group-specific effect of technical progress on wage setting and arguments other than the unemployment rate in the functions H_i have been neglected. P denotes the aggregate price level. For modeling consumer's choice we use a CES-utility function[34] $U=(\alpha Y_b^{-\rho}+(1-\alpha)Y_s^{-\rho})^{-1/\rho}$. Let I stand for nominal income. Utility maximization of a representative household under the budget constraint $Y_b + P_s Y_s = I$ yields a relation for the relative demand of goods. Since demand is equal to supply in equilibrium, one gets a relation for relative production depending on goods prices in the s-sector:

$$(23) \quad \frac{Y_b}{Y_s} = \left(\frac{\alpha}{1-\alpha}\right)^{\sigma} P_s^{\sigma} ,$$

where α denotes a preference parameter for b-sector goods and $\sigma = 1/(1+\rho)$ is the elasticity of substitution. Equating eq. (21) and eq. (22) leads to

---

[32] General equilibrium models in the context of skill-biased technical change are analyzed by Davis (1998) and Agénor, Aizenman (1997).

[33] For simplicity these equations rely on the assumption that there are separate labor unions for each skill group. Fitzenberger (1998) develops a theoretical model in which one union acts in the interest of several skill groups.

[34] Note that in the Cobb-Douglas case ($p = 0$) the ratio of the payrolls in the two sector is constant and therefore independent of A_s, which seems to be overly restrictive.

(24) $P\tilde{A}_b H_b(u_b) - 1 = 0$

and

(25) $\frac{P_s}{P} A_s - \tilde{A}_s H_s(u_s) = 0$.

Note that this two-equation system contains four unknowns (u_b, u_s, P, P_s). To determine the model solution we eliminate P and P_s. Corresponding to the CES-utility function as given above, the aggregate price level P is defined as:

(26) $P = \left(\alpha^{\sigma} + (1-\alpha)^{\sigma} P_s^{1-\sigma}\right)^{1/(1-\sigma)}$.

The relation between s-sector prices and the general price level is

(27) $\frac{P_s}{P} = \left(\alpha^{\sigma} P_s^{-(1-\sigma)} + (1-\alpha)^{\sigma}\right)^{-1/(1-\sigma)}$.

Solving eq. (23) for P_s, using the production functions and the definition of unemployment yields

(28) $P_s = \left(\frac{(1-u_b)L_b}{\beta A_s (1-u_s) L_s}\right)^{1/\sigma}$,

where $\beta := \alpha^{\sigma}(1-\alpha)^{-\sigma}$. More generally, the price of s-sector goods is a function of the unemployment rates of both skill groups, technical efficiency in the s-sector and labor supply variables (which are neglected here):

(29) $P_s = P_s(u_b, u_s, A_s)$ with $P_{s,1} < 0$, $P_{s,2} > 0$, $P_{s,3} < 0$,

where $P_{s,i}$ stands for the partial derivative with respect to the i-th argument of the function. Since P and P_s/P are positive functions of sector s prices they can be expressed as

(30) $P = \pi(u_b, u_s, A_s)$ and $\frac{P_s}{P} = \bar{\pi}(u_b, u_s, A_s)$,

with the sign of the partial derivatives π_i and $\bar{\pi}_i$ as in eq. (29). Substituting P and P_s/P in eq. (24) and eq. (25) by these relations, one obtains

(31) $\pi(u_b, u_s, A_s)\, \tilde{A}_b H_b(u_b) - 1 = 0$

and

$$(32)\quad \bar{\pi}\left(u_b, u_s, A_s\right) A_s - \tilde{A}_s H_s(u_s) = 0 .$$

This system of equations can be solved for the unemployment rates u_b and u_s. We will use this system to study the effects of biased technical progress on wages and unemployment for the two skill groups. Different assumptions for the productivity related wage-pressure variables A_i are possible.

4.2.2 Variants of the Model

In order to understand the model, note that several effects are caused by sector-specific productivity growth. First, relative prices will change and will affect the relative demand for goods. Second, real income in the economy will increase generating a higher demand for products of both sectors. Third, given the level of demand, productivity growth leads to labor saving. Fourth, the wage claims in terms of the production wage will change in both sectors because wage-setters are oriented towards the real wage in terms of the overall price index. Fifth, the labor market outcome also depends on the direct impact of productivity growth on wage pressure.

In the first variant of the model it is assumed that efficiency gains in the s-sector do not affect the wage-setting functions in either sector ($A_b = A_s = 1$).[35] We start with the effect of skill-biased technical change on unemployment of the unskilled. Analytically, one obtains in this variant of the model:

$$(33)\quad \frac{\mathrm{d}u_b}{\mathrm{d}A_s} = \frac{1}{|\mathbf{J}|}\left(H_b(H_s'\ \pi_3 + \bar{\pi}\pi_2)\right) < 0 ,$$

where $|\mathbf{J}| < 0$ is the determinant of the Jacobi matrix. Hence it turns out that the unemployment rate in sector b unambiguously *falls*. To understand this result, it is useful to look at the development of the price variables. From eq. (24) it can be deduced that u_b and the general price level P must move in the same direction, i.e. P also declines. As eq. (26) shows, this requires P_s to fall. Hence conflicting forces are at work. On the one hand, changes in relative prices are unfavorable for the *relative* demand of goods produced with low-skilled labor. On the other hand, wage pressure in terms of the *producer's* real wage is reduced in sector b due to the decline of P. Furthermore, total demand for goods increases because of higher real income. The analytical result reveals that the positive effects dominate the negative one so that the employment situation of the unskilled improves. Moreo-

[35] For the moment we neglect the unrealistic implications this has in the long run. Note that the assumption $A_b = A_s = 1$ does not imply that real wages of the two skill groups are equal. To guarantee that the wages of skilled workers exceed those of the unskilled in the initial equilibrium it is sufficient that $H_s(x) > H_b(x)$ for all x and $u_b \geq u_s$.

ver, it follows from eq. (22) that the real consumption wage of the unskilled also increases.

For the unemployment response to productivity changes in sector s one gets

$$(34)\quad \frac{\mathrm{d}u_s}{\mathrm{d}A_s} = \frac{1}{|\mathbf{J}|}\left(-\pi_1 H_b \bar{\pi} - H_b' P_s\left(1 - \frac{1}{\sigma}\left(1 - (1-\alpha)^{\sigma} \bar{\pi}^{1-\sigma}\right)\right)\right).$$

If the elasticity of substitution σ is equal or greater unity, the unemployment rate of the skilled unambiguously declines. However, with σ being sufficiently small, the opposite result would occur. To clarify the result one has to bear in mind that beside the labor-saving productivity growth a second adverse effect occurs in sector s. Since P_s declines more than P, wage claims in terms of the *producer's* real wage are rising. With a sufficiently high elasticity of substitution, these adverse effects are out-weighed by higher demand for s-sector goods triggered by lower relative prices and higher real income. In this case, with no additional wage pressure generated by higher productivity, employment in the respective sector rises and, if not neutralized by increases in labor supply, the unemployment rate falls. With a low elasticity of substitution, the relative demand for goods of the skill-intensive sector does not increase enough to compensate for the aforementioned adverse effects.[36] This would imply that unemployment of the skilled even rises.

Similar to the ambiguous result for unemployment in sector s, also the change in real wages depends on the elasticity of substitution. Only if σ is sufficiently large, can the implications of the model be reconciled with the stylized fact that the real wage of skilled workers has increased. Note that the relative magnitude of the employment/real-wage effect depends on the extent of real wage rigidity in both sectors.

In the second variant of the model, it is assumed that workers in the s-sector adjust the productivity-related wage-pressure variable A_s such that their unemployment rate remains constant, while workers in the b-sector keep still ($A_b = 1$). In this case, the solution for the response of b-sector unemployment can easily be computed from eq. (31):

$$(35)\quad \left.\frac{\mathrm{d}u_b}{\mathrm{d}A_s}\right|_{\mathrm{d}u_s=0} = -\frac{\pi_3 H_b}{\pi_1 H_b + \pi H_b'} < 0.$$

Hence the unskilled can improve their employment situation under this setting as well. It can be seen from eq. (22) that the general price level must have declined

[36] In a different context, Appelbaum, Schettkat (1995) argue that the decline in the price elasticity of demand for goods in the high-productivity sector of the economy is one of the main causes of today's unemployment problem.

leading to an increase in the real consumption wage of the unskilled. The decline in P is only possible if P_s has fallen as well. As in the first variant of the model, the change in the real consumption wage of skilled workers depends on the elasticity of substitution.

In the third variant, wage-setting institutions are solidaristic, i.e. it is intended that each group gains equally from efficiency growth $\mathrm{d}\tilde{A}_b = \mathrm{d}\tilde{A}_s = \mathrm{d}\tilde{A}$. To determine the model solution, a further restriction is required. A reasonable assumption in this context is that $\mathrm{d}\tilde{A}$ is chosen such that it is compatible with constant aggregate employment. If employment in both sectors is approximately equal in the initial situation, this can be implemented by setting the condition $\mathrm{d}u_b + \mathrm{d}u_s = 0$. After some simple, but tedious, algebra one can show that

$$\text{(36)} \quad \operatorname{sign}\left(\frac{\mathrm{d}u_b}{\mathrm{d}A_s}\right) = \operatorname{sign}\left(1 - \frac{1}{\sigma}\right).$$

Again, the results crucially depend on the elasticity of substitution. We only consider the case where σ exceeds unity. Then $\mathrm{d}u_b / \mathrm{d}A_s$ is positive, and, correspondingly, $\mathrm{d}u_s / \mathrm{d}A_s < 0$. From eq. (28) and eq. (26) it can be seen that the price variables P_s and P are both decreasing. Since W_b is constant, the real consumption wage of the unskilled increases. From the wage-setting equation for the unskilled (eq. (22)) it follows that $\tilde{A}$ must have risen. Therefore, also the real wage of skilled workers is higher in the new equilibrium.

To obtain the result for relative wages one can divide the two wage-setting equations (22). This yields

$$\text{(37)} \quad \frac{W_s}{W_b} = \frac{H_s(u_s)}{H_b(u_b)}.$$

Since unemployment of unskilled (skilled) workers has increased (decreased, respectively), it is obvious that the changes in the relative wage are in favor of the skilled. Hence in this special case of the model, the "typical" results are obtained. Biased technical change deteriorates the employment chances of the unskilled and improves that of skilled workers. At the same time, wage inequality increases.

4.2.3 Critical Assessment

Our analysis reveals that the conventional wisdom with regard to biased technical change needs some qualifications. Things are less obvious if general equilibrium effects are taken into account. In contrast to results following from a simple partial framework, it has been shown that the unskilled could profit via indirect effects from biased technical change. Productivity growth for the skilled means higher real income in the economy, *ceteris paribus* affecting demand for all products positively. Typically, the relative price for *s*-sector products declines, leading also to a lower aggregate price level.[37] The latter effect reduces wage pressure of unskilled workers in terms of the producer's real wage. If, as assumed in the first two variants, no additional wage pressure is generated, these positive effects on employment of the unskilled dominate the negative relative price effect that triggers the substitution of *b*-sector goods.

These results contradict the assertion that the unskilled are hurt by biased technical change *per se*, which is often taken as granted in the literature. To obtain the stylized fact that the unskilled *loose* employment shares, it is required that the elasticity of substitution exceeds unity. This presumption is confirmed by most empirical studies[38]. However, one also has to introduce the assumption that the unskilled try to participate in productivity gains of sector *s* through higher wage claims. For this case, we have additionally shown that wage inequality rises. With respect to the *level* of the real consumption wage, the low-skilled are better off when skilled workers exhibit higher productivity growth. If our model gives a reasonable description of the effects of skill-biased technical change, the well-documented real-wage *decline* for low-skilled U.S. workers can not be attributed to this cause.

It has become clear that the technology-based explanation of the unemployment/inequality dilemma is not so self-evident as might seem at first glance. However, if one accepts this hypothesis as the main cause of the shifts in the relative demand for labor, the question remains how cross-country differences can be explained by the pervasive phenomenon of skill-biased technical change. A possible answer lies in the fact that the relative magnitude of the unemployment/wage response depends on the degree of real wage rigidity, i.e. the slopes of the wage and price-setting curves. This is where the institutional framework may come into play again. In a recent paper, Mortensen, Pissarides (1999) claim that differences in the system of unemployment insurance as well as in employment protection legislation are sufficient to explain the contrasting performance of European and U.S. labor markets in face of skill-specific technical shocks.[39] A quite different position in this respect is expressed by Falkinger, Grossmann (1999) who argue that biased productivity growth may deteriorate the employment chances of the unskilled even in the absence of real wage rigidity. Their model relies on the assumption that changes in the techniques and organization of production have also affected the required quality of work. Given that low-skilled workers are trained and supervised by high-skilled workers, it is possible that profit-maximizing firms have a limited demand for unskilled workers even if wages are perfectly flexible.

---

[37] Only in the third variant of the model is a different result possible if the elasticity of substitution is quite below unity.

[38] See, for instance, Bound, Johnson (1992), Fitzenberger (1998) and Möller (1996).

[39] Marimon, Zilibotti (1999) also stress the important role of the unemployment compensation system.

Since the basic argument applies to all developed countries, there should be no significant international differences in the employment situation of the unskilled. This is indeed what some empirical studies seem to suggest (cf. Nickell, Bell (1995, 1997)).

Given that the knowledge of economists about the driving forces lying behind technical change is still rather limited, it can also be asked whether the phenomenon of skill-biased technical change will continue to be relevant in the future. As economic history shows, there are many examples of new technologies replacing rather than complementing skilled workers. Hence several authors have pointed out that the complementarity of skills and technology is not a natural law. The question arises whether biased productivity growth is the result of a rational decision process about the choice of technology. In a recent paper, Acemoglu (1998) develops a model in which new technologies are *designed* to be skill-complementary. This is so because the unprecedented increase in highly skilled labor during the sixties and seventies has increased the market for skill-complementary capital goods. Vogt (1999a) follows a different approach for endogenising the choice of technology. He shows that there is a mutual dependence between the structure of wages and employment on the one side, and biased-technical progress on the other. The results crucially depend on the elasticity of substitution between unskilled and skilled workers as well as between the products with different skill-intensity. Vogt argues that with a plausible order of magnitude for these parameters, skill-biased technical change is likely to continue in the future.

5 Summary and Conclusions

In the seventies and eighties various competing theories put forward by the classical and Keynesian camps tried to find a convincing explanation for the unemployment problem. The structuralist model emerged from these research efforts as the dominant approach of the nineties, combining both classical and Keynesian features. Moreover, by generating a relationship between changes in inflation and deviations of unemployment from the long-run equilibrium, this approach carries on where the old Phillips curve debate left off.

In our contribution we do not confine ourselves to a review of the research of the last decade, but rather stress the implications of several extensions of the macroeconomic model as well. Whereas in the standard structuralist model the demand side has a negligible influence on unemployment in the medium run, we show that stabilization policies are of greater importance once unemployment persistence and/or the openness of economies are taken into account.

Furthermore, we build on the structuralist framework to not only address the macroeconomic aspects of the unemployment problem, but also the debate between trade theorists and labor economists about the impact of globalization and biased technical change on the employment performance of different skill groups. In the literature, contra-factual implications of the standard Heckscher-Ohlin model are often used as an argument against trade-based explanations of the unemployment problem. By relaxing the assumption of perfect competition, we show that major aspects of this critique can be overcome. On the other hand, conventional wisdom which favors the biased technical change hypothesis can be questioned. Things are less obvious if the general equilibrium effects of biased technical change are taken into account. In contrast to results following from a simple partial framework, it has been shown that the unskilled could profit via indirect effects from biased technical change. To obtain the stylized fact that the unskilled *loose* employment shares, one not only needs a high elasticity of substitution, but also certain additional assumptions about the impact of biased productivity growth on the skill-specific wage formation process.

From the analysis of the different variants of the structuralist model, several conclusions can be derived. First, the impact of aggregate demand on employment and output is not limited to the short run as often claimed in the literature. This is most clearly seen in the open-economy model of section 3.2. Even in the closed economy, the demand side exerts an influence on the path of actual employment due to unemployment persistence.

Second, given the various persistence (or hysteresis) mechanisms, it seems reasonable to advise governments to counteract demand and supply shocks *immediately*, before higher hard-core unemployment emerges. Of course, it can be argued, that the persistence mechanisms are a consequence of the institutional setup. Instead of relying on demand management, one could also avoid persistence effects by institutional reforms, as, for instance, a reduction of the level and duration of unemployment benefits. However, if society has opted for the welfare state due to equity considerations, demand management has a greater responsibility. If economic policy does not prevent unemployment from rising in the face of adverse shocks, long-term unemployment builds up and the welfare state inevitably runs into budget problems. As a consequence, the welfare state itself would be at risk. Certainly, “fine-tuning” demand management policies exhibit the problem of possibly destabilizing rather than stabilizing the economy due to various time lags inherent in policy actions. Therefore, demand management should be confined to “coarse tuning” in the case of either deep recessions or overheated booms. Unfortunately, in many European countries economic policy did not steer against the rise in unemployment during the deep recessions since the mid-seventies. Given the persistence mechanisms, a monetary policy merely focusing on inflation, perhaps accompanied by a fiscal policy primarily looking at budget deficits, may have contributed to today's high unemployment level in Europe. Things may have been worsened by monetary policies striving for zero inflation. As we pointed out in section 2.3, too low an inflation rate may have caused a higher long-run equilibrium unemployment rate in the face of downward nominal wage rigidity.

Third, even if economic policy was partly responsible for the increase in unemployment in the past, it can not be concluded that expansionary demand policies alone would be a suitable remedy against unemployment today. Due to the presence of unemployment persistence, a demand expansion will quickly lead to increasing inflation although the unemployment rate is well above the long-run NAIRU. Additionally, as outlined in section 3.2, a fiscal expansion will cause a trade deficit besides the higher budget deficit, especially if the main trading partners will not pursue a similar demand expansion. In this case, demand management would have to tolerate huge deficits if the aim is a significant reduction in unemployment. In the case of a coordinated demand expansion in a group of countries this problem would be mitigated, but then new problems may arise because of an increase in the world interest rate. In the long run this will eventually reduce investment of firms in the employment stock, as is discussed in section 3.2.

From the above objections, it follows that a policy only relying on a demand expansion will hardly be sustainable in the longer run. The problems of a purely demand-oriented strategy are aggravated if the deep structural changes caused by globalization and/or skilled biased technical change are taken into account. Although one has to concede that during a general upswing all groups of workers are likely to have employment gains, it can hardly be denied that a specific policy designed to foster the labor market chances of problem groups is necessary. The reason is that these structural shifts are long-term phenomena which can not be neutralized by a temporary demand expansion. Hence there are valid reasons to check the adequacy of the institutional framework as well as of the stance of wage policy in face of the above-mentioned world-wide challenges.

On the other hand, focusing solely on the supply side may be equally unwise. Supply-side reforms will reduce unemployment only after a considerable time-lag, whereas a demand expansion has direct effects on production and employment. In our view, the most reasonable policy recommendation is therefore a two-handed approach, encompassing measures on both the demand and supply side. In this case, the adverse effects of the demand expansion on inflation and deficits are mitigated by supply-side reforms which reduce wage pressure and increase the competitiveness of firms.

References

Acemoglu, D. (1998), Why Do New Technologies Complement Skills? Directed Technical Change and Wage Inequality, *Quarterly Journal of Economics* 113, 1055-1089.

Agénor, P. R. and J. Aizenman (1997), Technological Change, Relative Wages, and Unemployment, *European Economic Review* 41, 187-205.

Akerlof, G. A., W.T. Dickens and G.L. Perry (1996), The Macroeconomics of Low Inflation, *Brookings Papers on Economic Activity* 1, 1-76.

Appelbaum, E. and R. Schettkat (1995), Employment and Productivity in Industrialized Economies, *International Labour Review* 134, 605-623.

Autor, D. H., L. F. Katz and A. B. Krueger (1998), Computing Inequality: Have Computers Changed the Labor Market?, *Quarterly Journal of Economics* 113, 1169-1213.

Bean, C.R. (1989), Capital Shortages and Persistent Unemployment, *Economic Policy* 8, 11-53.

Bean, C.R. (1994a), European Unemployment: A Survey, *Journal of Economic Literature* 32, 573-619.

Bean, C.R. (1994b), European Unemployment: A Retrospective, *European Economic Review* 38, 523-534.

Bean, C.R. (1997), The Role of Demand-Management Policies in Reducing Unemployment, in: Snower, D. J., G. De la Dehesa, (eds.), Unemployment Policy: Government Options for the Labor Market, Cambridge, 83-115.

Bean, C.R. (1998), The Interaction of Aggregate-Demand Policies and Labor Market Reform, *Swedish Economic Policy Review* 5, 353-382.

Beißinger, T. (1996), Inflation und Arbeitslosigkeit in der Bundesrepublik Deutschland. Eine Analyse anhand von Modellen mit unvollkommenem Wettbewerb, Marburg.

Beißinger, T. and O. Büsse (1999), Wages and Unemployment in a Monetary Union, Discussion Paper 323, University of Regensburg, Regensburg.

Beißinger, T. and J. Möller (1998), Wage Flexibility and Employment Performance: A Microdata Analysis of Different Age-Education Groups for Germany, Discussion Paper 307, University of Regensburg, Regensburg.

Benassy, C., A. Chirco and C. Colombo (1994), The New Keynesian Economics, Oxford and Cambridge, Mass.

Bentolila, S. and G. Bertola (1990), Firing Costs and Labor Demand: How Bad is Eurosclerosis?, *Review of Economic Studies* 57, 381-402.

Berman, E., J. Bound and Z. Griliches (1994), Changes in the Demand for Skilled Labor Within U.S. Manufacturing: Evidence From the Annual Survey of Manufactures, *Quarterly Journal of Economics* 109, 367-397.

Berman, E., J. Bound and S. Machin (1998), Implications of Skill-Biased Technological Change: International Evidence, *Quarterly Journal of Economics* 113, 1245-1279.

Berthold, N. and R. Fehn (1996), The Positive Economics of Unemployment and Labour Market Inflexibility, *Kyklos* 49(4), 583-613.

Bertola, G. (1990), Job Security, Employment and Wages, *European Economic Review* 34, 851-879.

Bhagwati, J. (1995), Trade and Wages: Choosing Among Alternative Explanations, *Federal Reserve Bank of New York Economic Policy Review* 1, 42-47.

Blanchard, O. (1995), Macroeconomic Implications of Shifts in the Relative Demand for Skills, *Federal Reserve Bank of New York Economic Policy Review* 1, 48-53.

Blanchard, O. and P.A. Diamond (1994), Ranking, Unemployment Duration and Wages, *Review of Economic Studies* 61, 417-434.

Blanchard, O. and L. F. Katz (1997), What We Know and Do Not Know About the Natural Rate of Unemployment, *Journal of Economic Perspectives* 11, 51-72.

Blanchard, O. and N. Kiyotaki (1987), Monopolistic Competition and the Effects of Aggregate Demand, *American Economic Review* 77, 647-666.

Blanchard, O. and L. H. Summers (1986), Hysteresis and the European Unemployment Problem, in: Fischer, S. (ed.), NBER Macroeconomics Annual, Cambridge, Mass., 15-78.

Blanchflower, D. G. and A. J. Oswald (1994), The Wage Curve, Cambridge, Mass. and London.

Blau, F. D. and L. M. Kahn (1996), International Differences in Male Wage Inequality: Institutions versus Market Forces, *Journal of Political Economy* 104, 791-837.

Bound, J. and G. Johnson (1992), Changes in the Structure of Wages in the 1980's: An Evaluation of Alternative Explanations, *American Economic Review* 82, 371-392.

Bruno, M. and J. D. Sachs (1985), The Economics of Worldwide Stagflation, Cambridge, Mass.

Calmfors, L. (1993a), Centralisation of Wage Bargaining and Macroeconomic Performance: A Survey, OECD Economics Department Working Papers 131, Paris.

Calmfors, L. (1993b), Lessons From the Macroeconomic Experience of Sweden, *European Journal of Political Economy* 9, 25-72.

Calmfors, L. and J. Driffill (1988), Bargaining Structure, Corporatism and Macroeconomic Performance, *Economic Policy* 6, 14-61.

Card, D., F. Kramarz and T. Lemieux (1996), Changes in the Relative Structure of Wages and Employment: A Comparison of the United States, Canada, and France, NBER Working Paper 5487, Cambridge, Mass.

Carlin, W. and D. Soskice (1990), Macroeconomics and the Wage Bargain, Oxford.

Davis, D. R. (1998), Technology, Unemployment, and Relative Wages in a Global Economy, *European Economic Review* 42, 1613-1633.

Deardorff, A. V. and D. S. Haikura (1994), Trade and Wages - What Are the Questions? in: Bhagwati, J. and M. H. Kosters, (eds.), Trade and Wages. Leveling Wages Down?, Washington, D.C., 76-107.

Diamond, P. (1982), Wage Determination and Efficiency in Search Equilibrium, *Review of Economic Studies* 49, 217-227.

Dixit, A. K. and R. S. Pindyck (1994), Investment under Uncertainty, Princeton, New Jersey.

van Ees, H. and H. Garretsen (1996), The Natural Rate Moves, *De Economist* 144, 23-44.

Falkinger, J. and V. Grossmann (1999), Skills, Unemployment and the Costs of Organizing Jobs, University of Regensburg, mimeo, Regensburg.

Feenstra, R. C. (1998a), New Technology and Trade: A Threat to Low-Skilled Workers?, *Swedish Economic Policy Review* 1, 137-163.

Feenstra, R. C. (1998b), Integration of Trade and Disintegration of Production in the Global Economy, *Journal of Economic Perspectives* 12, 31-50.

Fitzenberger, B. (1998), Wages and Employment Across Skill Groups in West Germany During the 1970's and 1980's, Habilitationsschrift, University of Konstanz, Konstanz.

Franz, W. (1987), Hysteresis, Persistence, and the NAIRU: An Empirical Analysis for the Federal Republic of Germany, in: Layard, R. and L. Calmfors, (eds.), The Fight against Unemployment, Cambridge, Mass., 93-122.

Franz, W. (1996), Theoretische Ansätze zur Erklärung der Arbeitslosigkeit: Wo stehen wir 1995?, in: Gahlen, B., H. Hesse, and H.J. Ramser, (eds.), Arbeitslosigkeit und Möglichkeiten ihrer Überwindung, Wirtschaftswissenschaftliches Seminar Ottobeuren, Band 25, Tübingen, 3-45.

Franz, W. (1998), The German Unemployment Problem: What We Know and Do Not Know, Publications of the German-American Academic Council, Symposia, 5, Labor Markets in the USA and Germany, Baden-Baden, 25-46.

Franz, W. and R. J. Gordon (1993), German and American Wage and Price Dynamics: Differences and Common Themes, *European Economic Review* 37, 719-762.

Francois, J. F. and D. Nelson (1998), Trade, Technology, and Wages: General Equilibrium Mechanics, *Economic Journal* 108, 1483-1499.

Gordon, R. J. (1996), Comment on Akerlof et al. (1996), The Macroeconomics of Low Inflation, *Brookings Papers on Economic Activity* 1, 60-66.

Gregg, P. and A. Manning (1997), Skill-biased Change, Unemployment and Wage Inequality, *European Economic Review* 41, 1173-1200.

Harrigan, F., P. G. McGregor, K. Swales and Y. P. Yin (1993), Openness, Imperfect Competition and the NAIRU, *Journal of Economic Studies* 20, 52-72.

Hummels, D., D. Rapoport and K.-M. Yi (1997), The Changing Nature of World Trade, University of Chicago and the Federal Reserve Bank of New York.

Knoppik, C. (1999), Empirical Macroeconomics of Low Inflation and the Role of Limits to Nominal Wage Rigidity, University of Regensburg, mimeo, Regensburg.

Krueger, A. B. (1993), How Computers Have Changed the Wage Structure: Evidence From Micro Data, *Quarterly Journal of Economics* 108, 33-60.

Krugman, P. (1994), Past and Prospective Causes of High Unemployment, *Economic Review* 79, 23-41.

Landmann, O. and J. Jerger (1993), Unemployment and the Real Wage Gap: A Reappraisal of the German Experience, *Weltwirtschaftliches Archiv* 129, 689-717.

Lawrence, R. and M. Slaughter (1993), Trade and U.S. Wages in the 1980s: Giant Sucking Sound or Small Hiccup?, *Brookings Papers on Economic Activity* 2, 161-226.

Layard, R. and S. Nickell (1987), The Labour Market, in: Dornbusch, R. and R. Layard (eds.), The Performance of the British Economy, Oxford, 131-179.

Layard, R., S. Nickell and R. Jackman (1991), Unemployment, Oxford.

Lazear, E. P. (1990), Job Security Provisions and Employment, *Quarterly Journal of Economics* 105, 699-726.

Leamer, E. E. (1994), Trade, Wages, And Revolving Door Ideas, NBER Working Paper 4716, Cambridge, Mass.

Levy, F. and R. J. Murnane (1996), With What Skills Are Computers a Complement? *American Economic Review* 86, 258-262.

Lindbeck, A. (1992), Macroeconomic Theory and the Labour Market, *European Economic Review* 36, 209-235.

Lindbeck, A. (1996), The West European Employment Problem, *Weltwirtschaftliches Archiv* 132, 609-637.

Lindbeck, A. and D. Snower (1988), The Insider-Outsider Theory of Employment and Unemployment, Cambridge, Mass.

Ljungquist, L. and T.J. Sargent (1998), The European Unemployment Dilemma, *Journal of Political Economy* 106(3), 514-550.

Machin, S. and J. Van Reenen (1998), Technology and Changes in Skill Structure: Evidence from Seven OECD Countries, *Quarterly Journal of Economics* 113, 1215-1244.

Malinvaud, E. (1977), The Theory of Unemployment Reconsidered, Oxford.

Malinvaud, E. (1980), Profitability and Unemployment, Cambridge.

Malinvaud, E. (1997), Edmund Phelps' Theory of Structural Slumps and its Policy Implications, in: Snower, D. J. and G. de la Dehesa (eds.), Unemployment Policy: Government Options for the Labour Market, Cambridge, 116-141.

Mankiw, N. G. (1996), Comment on Akerlof et al. (1996), The Macroeconomics of Low Inflation, *Brookings Papers on Economic Activity* 1, 66-70.

Mankiw, N. G. and D. Romer (eds.), (1991), New Keynesian Economics, Cambridge, Mass. and London.

Manning, A. (1993), Wage Bargaining and the Phillips Curve: The Identification and Specification of Aggregate Wage Equations, *Economic Journal* 103, 98-118.

Manning, A. (1995), Developments in Labour Market Theory and Their Implications for Macroeconomic Policy, *Scottish Journal of Political Economy* 42, 250-266.

Marimon, R. and F. Zilibotti (1999), Unemployment vs. Mismatch of Talents: Reconsidering Unemployment Benefits, *Economic Journal* 109, 266-291.

Möller, J. (1996), Technological Change, Unemployment, and Recent Trends in Human Capital Formation - Did the German Wage Structure Respond to These Impulses?, Discussion Paper 280, University of Regensburg, Regensburg.

Mortensen, D. T. and C. A. Pissarides (1999), Unemployment Responses to `Skill-Biased' Technology Shocks: The Role of Labour Market Policy, *Economic Journal* 109, 242-265.

Nickell, S. (1987), Why is Wage Inflation in Britain so High?, *Oxford Bulletin of Economics and Statistics* 49, 103-129.

Nickell, S. (1990), Unemployment: A Survey, *Economic Journal* 100, 391-439.

Nickell, S. (1997), Unemployment and Labor Market Rigidities: Europe versus North America, *Journal of Economic Perspectives* 11, 55-74.

Nickell, S. (1998), Product Markets and Labour Markets, Institute of Economics and Statistics, University of Oxford, Adam Smith Lecture at the Tenth Annual Conference of the European Association of Labour Economists (EALE), 19th September 1998 at Blankenberge, Belgium.

Nickell, S., J. Vainiomaki and S. Wadhwani (1994), Wages and Product Market Power, *Economica* 61, 457-473.

Nickell, S. and B. Bell (1995), The Collapse in Demand for the Unskilled and Unemployment Across the OECD, *Oxford Review of Economic Policy* 11, 40-62.

Nickell, S. and B. Bell (1996), Changes in the Distribution of Wages and Unemployment in OECD Countries, *American Economic Review* 86, 302-308.

Nickell, S. and B. Bell (1997), Would Cutting Payroll Taxes on the Unskilled Have a Significant Impact on Unemployment?, in : Snower, D. J. and G. de la Dehesa, (eds.), Unemployment Policy: Government Options for the Labour Market, Cambridge, 296-328.

Phelps, E. S. (1972), Inflation Policy and Unemployment Theory, London.

Phelps, E. S. (1994), Structural Slumps - The Modern Equilibrium Theory of Unemployment, Interest, and Assets, Cambridge, Mass. and London.

Pissarides, C. (1990), Equilibrium Unemployment Theory, Oxford.

Rowthorn, R., R. Kozul-Wright and Y. Akyüz (1997), Adapting to North-South Trade: A General Equilibrium Approach to Policy Options, *Oxford Economic Papers* 49, 483-503.

Sachs, J. D. and H. Shatz (1994), Trade and Jobs in US Manufacturing, *Brookings Papers on Economic Activity* 1, 1-84.

Schlicht, E. (1995), Autonomous Wage Inflation, in: Gerlach, K. and R. Schettkat (eds.), Determinanten der Lohnbildung. Theoretische und empirische Untersuchungen. Belin, 187-201.

Siebert, H. (1997), Labour Market Rigidities: At the Root of Unemployment in Europe, *Journal of Economic Perspectives* 11, 37-57.

Slaughter, M. J. (1998), International Trade and Labour-Market Outcomes: Results, Questions, and Policy Options, *Economic Journal* 108, 1452-1462

Snower, D. J. (1995), Evaluating Unemployment Policies: What Do The Underlying Theories Tell Us?, *Oxford Review of Economic Policy* 11, 110-135.

Solow, R. M. (1985), Insiders and Outsiders in Wage Determination, *Scandinavian Journal of Economics* 87, 411-428.

Tobin, J. (1972), Inflation and Unemployment, *American Economic Review* 62, 1-18.

Vogt, W. (1996), Accelerating Inflation or Rising Unemployment - Is There An Alternative?, *Metroeconomica* 47, 197-230.

Vogt, W. (1999a), Endogenously Biased Technical Progress and the Macroeconomic Structure of Employment and Wages, *contribution in this volume.*

Vogt, W. (1999b), Inequality, Unemployment and Inflation, University of Regensburg, mimeo, Regensburg.

Wood, A. (1994), North-South Trade, Employment and Inequality: Changing Fortunes in a Skill-Driven World, Oxford.

Wood, A. (1995), How Trade Hurt Unskilled Workers, *Journal of Economic Perspectives* 9, 57-80.

Wood, A. (1998), Globalisation and the Rise in Labour Market Inequalities, *Economic Journal* 108, 1463-1482.

Woodford, M. (1994), Structural Slumps, *Journal of Economic Literature* 32, 1784-1815.

Zimmermann, K. F. (1997), Discussion [to: Edmund Phelps' Theory of Structural Slumps and its Policy Implications], in: Snower, D.J. and G. de la Dehesa, (eds.), Unemployment Policy: Government Options for the Labour Market, Cambridge, 151-160.

Comment on Beißinger and Möller : "Unemployment: Theoretical Explanations"

Bernd Fitzenberger

Dresden University of Technology,
01062 Dresden, Germany

Beißinger and Möller (BM) provide a survey on macroeconomic theories of unemployment using the structuralist model. This model reduces to a system of a price and a wage setting equation both relating to the level of unemployment in the economy (and therefore employment in the economy when labor supply is fixed). The framework allows to discuss various causes for unemployment and it is viewed by BM as dealing with a not-too-short-term situation of the macroeconomy when expectation errors are overcome but the capital stock and the technology are given. The standard structuralist model with one homogeneous type of labor has been discussed extensively in the literature (see the references given in the paper) and its main features are nicely presented in section 2 of the paper. Here, there is not that much to add considering the survey character of the paper. Then, section 3 introduces two extensions to the standard model for homogeneous labor, namely the issues of unemployment persistence and open economy aspects. BM show how these issues can be integrated easily into the structuralist model and that they give a particular role for the demand side of the economy. Finally, section 4 incorporates the much disputed issue of the skill bias in labor demand and as to whether it can be attributed to trade or technology effects. The structuralist analysis is extended to two types of labor and the economy consists of two sectors. Providing a comprehensive discussion of the literature and augmenting the analysis by original work in section 4, the authors obtain a very balanced view of the relevance of trade and technology effects on the skill bias. In the light of their theoretical analysis, BM recommend a balanced two-handed-approach of supply and demand policies to fight unemployment.

Because of its survey character and because of my comparative advantage, my comments on section 2 are very brief. My discussion focuses on the contribution of sections 3 and 4 to the debate on the causes of unemployment. A lot more than space permits could be said about this paper which surveys such a large body of literature and which, at the same time, presents original theoretical work.

Structured along a comprehensive framework, the survey is very clearly presented. Evaluating the strengths and weaknesses of the structuralist framework and identifying various deficits, BM also attempt to fill these gaps. My subsequent detailed comments are mainly concerned with these original aspects of the paper. Overall, I view the paper as a useful survey which provides some thought provoking original work. At the theoretical level of the paper, there can be little dispute as to whether a balanced two-handed-approach of supply and demand policies is appropriate to fight unemployment. However, it would be beyond the scope of this discussion to analyze different concrete policy options which are mentioned at various places in the paper.

Detailed Comments

1. The empirical relevance of the comparative static results obtained in the structuralist model, which are used to "identify the factors that have contributed to the rise of unemployment" (section 2.2 of the paper), depends upon the stability of the wage and price setting equation in response to an exogenous shock. Later in the paper, BM discuss various sources for instability. In my opinion, the basic structuralist model can be a reasonable assumption in the short run (say for a period of some years). However, it seems difficult to imagine that such stable relationship holds for a period of 20 to 25 years if one tries to apply these ideas to the unemployment history since the oil price shocks during the 70's. Even though there exists some evidence in the literature (see Blanchflower and Oswald (1994)) that the wage setting relationship ("wage curve") proves quite stable across time and countries, I would be quite surprised, if stable aggregate wage and price setting relationships were not refuted empirically. Clearly, this is a very general critique of the relevance of macroeconomic modeling which extends upon the formation of expectations as emphasized by the rational expectations school (Lucas-Critique). Technical progress, the investment behavior of firms, the increasing openness of the economy, effects of long-term unemployment or demographic trends could change the wage and price setting equations. Just to be clear, BM discuss most of these issues in one way or another in sections 3 and 4.

2. Being related to the first remark, it is an open issue whether in the two-factor-case (section 4) of the paper, wage setting behavior can be modeled as a stable function of the unemployment rate of the respective skill type of labor. Such a simplified approach is often used in the literature on wage setting with heterogeneous labor (see the references given by BM). A general union utility function (see Fitzenberger, 1998, chapter 6) can be expressed as

$$(1) \quad \Gamma(w_b, w_s, L_b, L_s, \overline{L}_b, \overline{L}_s)\ 1$$

where L_i is employment of skill group i and the bar indicates the respective supply.

In the monopoly union case, this utility function is maximized subject to a system of factor demand equations

$$(2) \quad L_j = L_j^d(w_b, w_s, Y, K) \text{ for } j = b, s, 2$$

where Y denotes output and K capital. When an industry-level union bargains over wages, the variables represent industry-level values and it is possible that aggregate conditions have an impact. This model reduces to the wage setting equation used in the paper only under very special conditions. A necessary condition would be that union utility depends only upon wages and employment rates. In addition, factor demand would have to accommodate any changes in labor supply for given wages. The latter seems extremely unlikely with a constant capital stock, which is a maintained assumption in the paper. Hence, the wage setting relationships used in the papers seem appropriate to analyze changes in the short run but not for a period of up to 20 years during which the formal skill level of the labor force has increased considerably.

All this is in contrast to the Stolper-Samuelson effect for a small open economy with given goods prices on the world market. Under these assumptions, domestic factor supply does not matter for relative factor prices due to the possibility of between industry reallocation. However, if wage setting depends upon factor supplies, this property is lost for the case of a small open economy.

3. Section 3.2 introduces open economy aspects with competitiveness being defined as the real exchange rate. It is unfortunate that this discussion omits the issue of technical progress. Since productivity increases can result in lower prices or higher wages in a closed economy, it is conceivable that the equilibrium unemployment rate does not depend upon the productivity parameter A in section 2. However, cross country differences in technical progress could have an effect on this neutrality result since the consumer wage now depends upon a weighted average of domestic and foreign prices. Thus, even if consumer wages are set in proportion to productivity gains for a given rate of unemployment, the neutrality result of section 2 might not apply any more. This argument parallels the discussion of technology effects in section 4.2, which shows that technology effects depend strongly upon the assumed reaction of wage setters. Concluding this point, I would prefer that the issue of competitiveness in section 3.2 were not treated completely separately from the trade-based explanations in section 4.1. This critique is not specific to this paper but rather general. One rarely finds papers which integrate issues in international macroeconomics and trade theory.

4. Unfortunately, section 4 omits the possibility of goods market imperfections. Among others, Borjas and Ramey (1995) discuss for the case of the U.S. whether increasing international competition can foster an erosion of rents in Manufacturing to the detriment of blue-collar workers' wages in this part of the economy. The argument builds on the observation that in contrast to a one-sector-closed economy model (equation (1) in the paper), it is possible that both firms and workers in one industry benefit from the less elastic goods demand in that industry ("rent sharing"). Analogously, increasing capital mobility might have similar effects.

5. A somewhat neglected result in standard trade theory, see e.g. Leamer (1996, section 1), states that, if countries are sufficiently dissimilar in their factor supply ratios, it can be the case that skill abundant countries specialize completely on skill intensive goods. In such a situation, also the real wages of the unskilled in the skill abundant countries can even increase when the barriers of trade are reduced. Thus, relating to the discussion right before section 4.1.1, it is not necessary to invoke market imperfections to obtain such a result.

6. The assessment of the trade-based explanation in section 4.1.2 of the paper points to the issue of increasing trade in intermediate inputs, see Feenstra (1998). Within an industry, outsourcing occurs such that those segments in the value added chain are imported which can be produced more cheaply abroad. This effect questions evidence on trade effects based on relative price trends in skill-intensive and non skill-intensive industries. The trade effect via outsourcing changes the skill mix within all industries thus resulting in within-industry upgrading of skills (the latter refutes standard trade theory when the relative wage of skilled labor increases). When a full-fledged input-output analysis is lacking, one should look as to whether the difference between value-added prices (or export prices) and import prices has increased over time. In fact, my empirical results confirm this implication for West Germany during the time period from 1970 to 1990, see Fitzenberger (1998, chapter 4).

7. The discussion before section 4.1.1 refers to the issue of within-industry substitution of factor usage. Unfortunately, this effect is defined away in the analytical treatment by dividing the economy in into two sectors among which one uses only low-skilled workers and the other only high-skilled workers (by this assumption also outsourcing, as discussed in the previous point, cannot play a role). Substitution between the two skill groups is introduced indirectly via the substitution between the two goods in consumer demand. In fact, section 4.2.3 makes this direct analogy when arguing that empirically the substitution elasticity is above unity. However, it is important to distinguish the two substitution effects, in particular, since they differ empirically. The substitution in consumption between the final

products from highly aggregated industries is fairly limited, see e.g. the argument in the theoretical appendix of Calmfors and Driffill (1988), while the substitution between different skill types of labor in production appears to be fairly high. However, in Fitzenberger (1998), I only find for Non-Manufacturing, but not for Manufacturing, that the elasticity of substitution in production is significantly larger than unity. When discussing technology effects in section 4.2, it seems necessary to allow for the possibility of within-industry substitution in reaction to skill-biased technical change in order to obtain the "typical" result since one cannot rely on the substitution elasticity in consumer demand to lie above unity.

8. Section 4 assumes homothetic utility functions to determine the relative demand for goods. This implies that there exist no income effects on the interindustry structure of demand. If one considers the Manufacturing versus Services distinction, it is often argued that technical progress is stronger in Manufacturing compared to Service Industries and that, at the same time, the income elasticity of the demand for Manufacturing goods is less than unity implying a declining share of Manufacturing (="well paid jobs for blue-collar workers") in the economy, see Sachs and Shatz (1994).

References

Blanchflower, D.G. and A.H. Oswald (1994), The Wage Curve, Cambridge, Mass.

Borjas, G. J. and V. A. Ramey (1995), Foreign Competition, Market Power, and Wage Inequality, *Quarterly Journal of Economics* 110, 1075-1110.

Calmfors, L. and J. Driffill (1988), Bargaining Structure, Corporatism and Macroeconomic Performance, *Economic Policy* 6, 14-61.

Feenstra, R. C. (1998), Integration of Trade and Disintegration of Production in the Global Economy, *Journal of Economic Perspectives* 12(4), 31-50.

Fitzenberger, B. (1999), Wages and Employment Across Skill Groups: An Analysis for West Germany, Heidelberg.

Leamer, E. E. (1996), In Search of Stolper-Samuelson Effects on U.S. Wages, in: Collins, S. (ed.), Imports, Exports and the American Worker, Washington, D.C.

Sachs, J. D. and H. J. Shatz (1994), Trade and Jobs in U.S. Manufacturing, *Brookings Papers on Economic Activity* 1, 1-84.

Endogenously Biased Technical Progress and the Macroeconomic Structure of Employment and Wages*

Winfried Vogt

University of Regensburg,
Universitätsstr. 31, 93053 Regensburg, Germany

1 Observations and Problems

This paper analyses the interaction between the changing structure of employment and wages, and a biased technical progress. The fact that there have been large changes in the macroeconomic structure of employment and wages has been widely documented.

First, there has been a continuous shift of employment from the manufacturing (industrial, non-service) sector to the service sector. In contrast, the accumulation of capital has been faster in the industrial sector than in the service sector. Consequently, the capital intensity and the productivity of labor have grown faster in the industrial sector. This transformation is particularly noticeable when the service sector is confined to the supply of labor services which are based on a personal relationship.

Second, wages for skilled workers have risen faster than wages for unskilled workers. Indeed, it seems that unskilled labor can only be fully employed when the evolution of its real wage lags behind the real wage of skilled labor. Otherwise, more and more unskilled workers are made redundant. In any case, the capital intensity of skilled labor has risen faster than the capital intensity of unskilled labor.

An explanation, which has received special attention, attributes these structural changes to a specifically biased technical progress. It has been argued that a labor-saving technical progress has been biased in favor of the industrial sector and of skilled labor. It is plausible that an "industry-biased" technical progress can be

---

* Earlier versions of this paper were presented at a summer workshop at the University of Regensburg and at a meeting of the German Association of Political Economy. I am grateful for comments from participants. I also thank Thomas Beißinger, Joachim Grosser and Bernhard Rauch for valuable comments. Special thanks go to Joachim Grosser for suggesting the basic idea of the paper. All remaining errors and omissions are my own.

favorable to a high capital accumulation in the industrial sector and to an outflow of labor to the service sector. It is equally plausible that a "skill-biased" technical progress can contribute to a faster growth of the real wage and the capital intensity of skilled labor.

Changes in the structure of manufacturing and services have long been observed and analyzed. Early contributions are Clark (1951) and Kuznets (1966). A first theoretical analysis of the role of a biased technical progress was offered by Baumol (1967). More recent contributions include Bhagwati (1984), Inman (1985), and Klodt, Maurer and Schimmelpfennig (1997). The growing inequality of skilled and unskilled workers has been observed, documented and analyzed especially in the last decade. Important contributions are Bound and Johnson (1992), Juhn, Murphy and Pierce (1993), Organisation for Economic Cooperation and Development (1994), Krugman (1994), Berman, Bound and Griliches (1994), Topel (1994), Agénor and Aizenman (1997), Gregg and Manning (1997), Machin and Van Reenen (1998), and Caselli (1999). In most of these contributions, a skill-biased technical progress is seen as an important source of the widening wage gap.

The purpose of the following analysis is to study the relationship between the structure of employment and wages on the one side, and a biased technical progress on the other side. The analysis is based on a two-sector model, in which the sectors are interpreted either as an industrial and a service sector, or as one sector with skilled labor and one with unskilled labor. The paper will first examine the impact of a biased technical progress on the structure of wages and employment. Here, the analysis follows some well-known patterns. However, it will also tackle the question, whether a changing structure of employment and wages might, in turn, influence the bias of technical progress. This can be the case if there is a trade-off between sector-specific rates of technical progress. Firms can then choose a profit maximizing bias of technical progress. It is plausible that such a choice may depend on the relative wage costs of the two sectors. This is, indeed, confirmed by the model. In this way the model shows that a mutual dependence exists between the structure of wages and employment on the one side, and a biased technical progress on the other side. This interdependence gives rise to an endogenous dynamic change in the structure of employment and wages. It turns out that the direction of this change is crucially dependent on two elasticities of substitution. The first one is the elasticity of substitution of labor and capital, which concerns the production of commodities. The second one is the demand elasticity of substitution, which concerns the demand for the products of different sectors. The following analysis outlines the likely future development of the structure of employment and wages for empirically plausible values of these elasticities.

The main conclusions can be summarized as follows. First, the development of the industrial sector and of the service sector depends on the possible substitution of personal services by capital or by industrial products. If the corresponding elasticities of substitution are low, an industry-biased technical progress will eventually disappear. As a consequence, the re-allocation of labor from the industrial sector to the service sector will gradually diminish and come to an end. In the long run, both sectors will grow at the same rate, and the structure of employment will remain constant. Second, the divergence in earnings between skilled and unskilled workers depends on the possibility of substituting unskilled workers by skilled workers and their products. If the corresponding elasticities of substitution are high, a skill-biased technical progress will gradually increase. Consequently, the inequality of earnings and capital endowments will also increase. This could be prevented by linking the real wage of unskilled labor to that of skilled labor. However, such a policy would cause an increase in unemployment for unskilled workers. Therefore, it could be preferable to reduce the share of unskilled workers by appropriate training and education programs, especially as such a policy could also reduce or even eliminate the growth of the wage gap.[1]

2 A Two-Sector Model

Consider an economy with two sectors of production indicated by i=1,2. The production function of a representative firm of a sector is given by

(1) $Y_i = F_i\,(T_i\,N_i\,,\,K_i) = K_i f_i\,(x_i), \qquad x_i := T_i\,N_i\,/K_i\,, \qquad i=1,2.$

The quantity of production, Y_i, depends on the input of labor, N_i, and of capital, K_i. The capital stock $K = K_1 + K_2$ consists of units of the first commodity. Returns to scale are constant, and $f_i' > 0$, $f_i'' < 0$. The production elasticity of labor is defined as $\eta_i := x_i f_i' / f_i$, $0 < \eta_i < 1$. T_i indicates the level of technology. Its rate of growth is a labor-saving technical progress.

There is perfect competition. In each sector, capital and labor are paid according to their marginal products. The demand for labor is given by

(2) $w_i = p_i\,T_i f_i'(x_i) \qquad i=1,2.$

Here, p_i is the market price of the commodity that is produced in sector i. If commodity 1 is used as a numéraire, $p_1 \equiv 1$, and $p := p_2$ by definition. Then w_i is the wage expressed in units of commodity 1.

As capital has the same price as commodity 1, the demand for capital is given by

[1] However, in Acemoglu (1998), a rise in the supply of skilled labor raises the wage ratio. It encourages a skill-biased technical change because it provides a large market for skill-complementary technologies.

(3) $r = p_i\,(f_i - x_i f_i'),$ $\qquad i=1,2,$

where r is the real rate of interest.

It simplifies the following analysis considerably, if the rate of interest is constant. This is the case, if it is given by the world market or determined by the time preference of the households.

The structure of demand is generally derived from optimal intertemporal decisions of households. The usual assumption is that a representative household maximizes the intertemporal utility function

$$\sum_{t=0}^{\infty} (1+\rho)^{-1}\, U(C_{1t},C_{2t}) \quad \text{,subject to } C_{1t} + p_t C_{2t} = (1+r_t)\,K_t - K_{t+1} + \text{wage income.}$$

Here, C_{it} is the consumption of commodity i in period t, and ρ is a utility discount rate. This gives a static optimality condition for the structure of consumption in each period, $U_2(t)/U_1(t) = p_t$, and, together with a transversality condition, a dynamic condition for the accumulation of capital, $U_1(t\text{-}1)/U_1(t) = (1+r_t)/(1+\rho)$. The only tractable solution to this general dynamic problem is the steady state solution. As the following analysis deals with structural changes outside a steady state, some simplifying assumptions are necessary. They can be justified by observing that households would be unable, anyway, to solve the full dynamic problem (which also implies a correct forecast of a variable rate of interest). The assumption is that households split their utility maximization in two separate problems. First, they solve the intertemporal optimization problem. They allocate their income from capital and labor to consumption and savings in such a way that they maximize a linear intertemporal utility function,

$\sum_{t=0}^{\infty} (1+\rho)^{-t}\, C_t$, s.t. $C_t = (1 + r_t)\, K_t - K_{t+1}$ + wage income. Here, C_t is the expenditure for consumption in period t (in units of the first commodity). Second, they choose C_1 and C_2 in each period, given $C_1 + pC_2 = C$. Maximizing a linear intertemporal utility function facilitates the analysis considerably, because it leads to a completely elastic supply of capital at $r_t = \rho$. In this way, the rate of interest is given by the utility discount rate. The choice of the structure of consumption follows from the static optimality condition mentioned above. This condition is simplified if the utility function is homothetic, i.e.

$U = U(C_1,C_2) = C_2\, u(C_1 / C_2)$. Then the static optimality condition is

$$(4) \qquad \frac{u(y) - u'(y)y}{u'(y)} = p,$$

where $y = C_1/C_2$. Generally, one cannot express the structure of total demand, Y_1/Y_2, so straightforwardly, because it depends not only on the structure of consumption but also on the demand for investment goods. To simplify the analysis further, assume that the investment I, which consists of units of the first good, is produced by a separate technology $I = V(I_1,I_2) = I_2\, v(I_1/I_2)$, which uses both commodities in the amounts I_1 and I_2. These amounts are chosen by minimizing the investment expenditure $I_1 + pI_2$ for each level of I. The corresponding optimality condition is analogous to (4). If one assumes V = U, the structure of the demand for investment goods is the same as the structure of consumption. Then, equilibrium in the commodity markets implies $y = C_1/C_2 = I_1/I_2 = Y_1/Y_2$.[2]

The advantage of these admittedly strong assumptions is that they make the analysis tractable. (4) gives a simple relationship between the ratio of the two commodities and their relative price. Furthermore, if the real rate of interest is given, (3) yields a constant value of x_1, and this, together with (2), implies a constant value of w_1/T_1.[3]

Within the framework of this two-sector model, two different structural problems can be identified and analyzed: first, the structure of employment, when the two sectors are the industrial and the service sector, and second, the ratio of real wages, when the first sector uses skilled labor and the second sector uses unskilled labor.

2.1 Interpretation A: Industrial Sector and Service Sector

In this interpretation, sector 1 is an industrial sector that produces material commodities. Sector 2 supplies services, which depend on some personal relationship between the producer and the customer. It is assumed that the work force employed in the two sectors is homogeneous. Hence, under competitive conditions, the wages of the two sectors must be equal. Furthermore, it is assumed that the supply of labor is given, N = N°, and that there is full employment:

(5A) $$w_1 = w_2 = w, \qquad N_1 + N_2 = N^\circ .$$

The 9 equations (1), (2), (3), (4) and (5A) determine the 9 variables Y_1, Y_2, N_1, N_2, K_1, K_2, w_1, w_2 and p, given the rate of interest and the technology levels T_1 and T_2. In particular, one can show that the employment ratio N_1 / N_2 depends on the technology ratio T_1/T_2. A change in this ratio indicates a bias of technical progress. Hence, it is the evolution of this bias that changes the structure of employment. This relationship will be explored in greater detail in the next section.

---

[2] In the case of a small country with an exogenously given rate of interest, the same result is obtained, if one assumes that traded goods have the same structure as domestic consumption.

[3] This result does not depend on the choice of the numéraire. It is due to the assumption that the capital stock has the same price as the first commodity, because it consists of the same units as the first commodity.

2.2 Interpretation B: Skilled and Unskilled Labor

In this interpretation, labor is heterogeneous. Sector 1 uses skilled labor and capital to produce commodity 1, and sector 2 uses unskilled labor and capital to produce a different commodity 2. It is assumed that the supply of skilled labor is given by $N_1°$, and the supply of unskilled labor by $N_2°$. It is obvious that the two sectors can also be understood as two different regions, with skilled labor in the first one and unskilled labor in the second one. For example, one could think of a developed and a less developed country.

In the first case, full employment is secured by flexible wages at the equilibrium values w_1* and w_2*:

$$(5B) \quad N_1 = N_1°, \; N_2 = N_2°, \qquad w_1=w_1* > w_2=w_2*.$$

$w_2* > w_1*$ can be ruled out, if skilled labor can also be used in the production of commodity 2, and the special case $w_2* = w_1*$ can be eliminated by an adequate choice of the parameters of the model.[4] A second case arises, when - by some intervention - the wage of unskilled labor is set above its equilibrium value. This would cause a corresponding amount of unemployment of unskilled workers:

$$(5B') \quad w_2 > w_2* \Rightarrow \qquad N_2 < N_2°.$$

The 9 equations (1), (2), (3), (4) and (5B) or (5B'), determine the 9 variables Y_1, Y_2, N_1, N_2, K_1, K_2, w_1, w_2 (or $N_2 \neq N_2°$), given the rate of interest and the technology levels T_1 and T_2. In particular, one can show that either (at full employment) the wage ratio w_1/w_2 or (at an administered wage w_2) the employment ratio N_1/N_2 depends on the technology ratio T_1/T_2. Again, a change in this ratio indicates a bias of technical progress. Hence, it is the evolution of this bias that changes the structure of wages or employment. This relationship will also be explored more closely in the next section.

3 The Impact of a Biased Technical Progress on the Structure of Wages and Employment

Technical progress is defined as the rate of growth of the technology variables T_1 or T_2. In the following analysis, the sign ^ over a variable indicates the rate of growth of this variable. Accordingly, the rates of technical progress are denoted by $\hat{T}_1$ and $\hat{T}_2$. A bias of technical progress is defined as the difference between

4 The wage ratio w_2/w_1 falls with rising values of x_2. One can choose a function $f_2(x_2)$ in such a way that $w_2/w_1<1$ even for $x_2=0$. An example would be $f_2(x_2)=(ax_2+b)^\alpha$, $0<\alpha<1$, and a sufficiently small value of $\alpha a/b$.

these rates, $\hat{T}_1 - \hat{T}_2$. Of special interest is a positive difference indicating either an industry-biased or a skill-biased-technical progress.

The following equations show the impact of the rates of technical progress and of their bias on the main variables of the model, especially on the structure of employment and wages.

At a given rate of interest, the real wage of the first sector rises with the corresponding rate of technical progress:

(6) $\hat{w}_1 = \hat{T}_1$.

For the second sector, (2) and (3) imply a relationship between the labor intensity x_2 and the factor price ratio rT_2 / w_2:

$$\frac{r}{w_2 / T_2} = \frac{f_2(x_2) - x_2 f_2'(x_2)}{f_2'(x_2)}.$$

It can be expressed in growth rates by introducing the elasticity of substitution σ_2, which specifies the proportionate rate of change of the labor intensity caused by a changing factor price ratio:

(7) $\hat{x}_2 = \sigma_2 (\hat{T}_2 - \hat{w}_2)$ or $\hat{w}_2 = \hat{T}_2 - \hat{x}_2 / \sigma_2$.

The proportionate rate of change of the relative price can be deduced from equation (3) for $i = 2$. One gets

(8) $\hat{p} = - \eta_2 \hat{x}_2 / \sigma_2$,

where η_2 is the elasticity of f_2 defined above.

As (4) shows, the structure of demand depends on the relative price of the second commodity. Expressed in growth rates one gets $\hat{Y}_1 - \hat{Y}_2 = \varepsilon \hat{p}$. Here, ε is the elasticity of substitution, which indicates the substitution of commodity 2 by commodity 1 caused by a changing relative price. Deriving $\hat{Y}_1 - \hat{Y}_2$ from (1) and inserting $\hat{p}$ from (8) gives

(9) $(\hat{N}_1 + \hat{T}_1) - (\hat{N}_2 + \hat{T}_2) = - \beta \hat{x}_2 / \sigma_2$.

Here, the parameter β is defined as $\beta := \eta_2 \varepsilon + (1 - \eta_2) \sigma_2$.[5] It is a weighted average of the elasticities of substitution ε and σ_2. This parameter is of crucial importance for the development of the structure of the economy. In particular, its value determines the rate of change of the wage cost ratio λ, defined as $\lambda := w_1 N_1 / w_2 N_2$. (6), (7) and (9) yield:

---

[5] Readers might wonder why only σ_2 (and not σ_1) is important. This is due to the assumption that the capital stock consists of the same goods as the first commodity.

(10) $\hat{\lambda} = (1-\beta)\hat{x}_2/\sigma_2$.

Finally, it is interesting to look at the rate of growth of each sector's capital intensity, which follows directly from the definitions of x_1 and x_2:

(11) $\hat{K}_1 - \hat{N}_1 = \hat{T}_1, \quad \hat{K}_2 - \hat{N}_2 = \hat{T}_2 - \hat{x}_2$.

These results can now be supplemented by the assumptions characterizing the two interpretations of the basic model.

3.1 Interpretation A: Industrial Sector and Service Sector

In this interpretation, the real wages of both sectors are equal. (5A) is valid, and one gets

(12A) $\hat{x}_2 = \sigma_2(\hat{T}_2 - \hat{T}_1)$.

According to (11), the capital intensity of the first sector rises at the rate of this sector's technical progress. The rate of growth of the capital intensity of the second sector can be derived from (11) and (12A). It is a weighted average of the two rates of technical progress:

(11A) $\hat{K}_2 - \hat{N}_2 = \sigma_2\hat{T}_1 + (1-\sigma_2)\hat{T}_2, \; (\hat{K}_1 - \hat{N}_1) - (\hat{K}_2 - \hat{N}_2) = (1-\sigma_2)(\hat{T}_1 - \hat{T}_2)$.

(10) together with (12A) yields the rate of change of the employment ratio N_1 / N_2:

(10A) $\hat{\lambda} = \hat{N}_1 - \hat{N}_2 = (1-\beta)(\hat{T}_2 - \hat{T}_1)$.

This result shows that the employment ratio is affected by a biased technical progress, if $\beta \neq 1$. Here, β is a weighted average of the elasticity of substitution of labor and capital in the service sector, σ_2, and of the elasticity of substitution of industrial goods and services, ε. Services which depend on a personal relationship between the producer and customer cannot be easily substituted either by capital or by industrial products. Hence, the elasticities of substitution, ε and σ_2, will be small. This is expressed by

Assumption I: The average elasticity of substitution of the service sector is low, i.e. $\beta < 1$.

In this case, the employment ratio λ falls when the technical progress is industry-biased, i.e. $\hat{T}_1 > \hat{T}_2$. Hence, the continuous shift of labor from manufacturing to services can be explained by an industry-biased technical progress and a low average elasticity of substitution of the service sector.

It may be interesting to add some further results. The rate of growth of the relative price is given by $\hat{p} = \eta_2(\hat{T}_1 - \hat{T}_2)$, see (9). This also confirms a well-known result: an industry-biased technical progress raises the relative price of the service sector, i.e. it makes services increasingly more expensive. As $\hat{Y}_1 - \hat{Y}_2 = \varepsilon\hat{p}$, a rising price of services implies a gradual substitution of services by industrial commodities. Even if this substitution were only weak because ε is small, the result might contradict some empirical observations and reflections. It has been claimed that the real demand for services has risen faster than the real demand for industrial goods, because the income elasticity of services is greater than one. It is doubtful whether this assertion applies to the more narrowly defined service sector of the present model. It is true, however, that the model's utility function implies an income elasticity of one for both sectors. This could be corrected by a more general utility function.[6]

3.2 Interpretation B: Skilled and Unskilled Labor

In this interpretation, one must distinguish between two cases: First, the case of full employment, and second, the case of a given wage rate for unskilled labor, which implies unemployment.

(5B) describes the first case. All skilled and unskilled workers are employed. As the employment ratio N_1 / N_2 remains constant, (9) gives:

$$\text{(12B)} \quad \hat{x}_2 = \frac{\sigma_2}{\beta}(\hat{T}_2 - \hat{T}_1).$$

Then, the rate of growth of the relative price is given by $\hat{p} = (\hat{T}_1 - \hat{T}_2)\eta_2/\beta$, see (8). Furthermore, $\hat{Y}_1 - \hat{Y}_2 = \varepsilon\hat{p}$. Hence, a skill-biased technical progress raises the relative price of the products of unskilled labor. Accordingly, those products are substituted by products of skilled labor.

For each sector, the accumulation of capital can be derived from (11), (5B) and (12B):

$$\text{(11B)} \quad \hat{K}_1 = \hat{T}_1, \; \hat{K}_2 = \frac{\sigma_2}{\beta}\hat{T}_1 + (1 - \frac{\sigma_2}{\beta})\hat{T}_2, \; \hat{K}_1 - \hat{K}_2 = (1 - \frac{\sigma_2}{\beta})(\hat{T}_1 - \hat{T}_2).$$

---

[6] For this discussion, see Gundlach (1994 and 1996), Quibria and Harrigan (1996) and Beißinger (1999).
A more general utility function could be $U(T_1Y_1, T_2Y_2) = T_2Y_2u(T_1Y_1 / T_2Y_2)$. Then the optimality condition (4) would determine T_1Y_1 / T_2Y_2 as a function of pT_1 / T_2. One would then get $\hat{Y}_1 - \hat{Y}_2 = (\varepsilon\eta_2 + \varepsilon - 1)(\hat{T}_1 - \hat{T}_2)$. One can see that this expression could be negative without changing the sign of $\hat{\lambda} = -[(1-\beta) + (1-\varepsilon)](\hat{T}_1 - \hat{T}_2) < 0$.

In the sector with skilled labor, the accumulation of capital is equal to this sector's technical progress. In the sector with unskilled labor, it is determined as a weighted average of both rates of technical progress.

The real wage of skilled labor rises with the sector-specific technical progress. One can deduce from (7) that the real wage of unskilled labor rises with a weighted average of both rates of technical progress:

(7B) $$\hat{w}_2 = \frac{1}{\beta}\hat{T}_1 + (1 - \frac{1}{\beta})\hat{T}_2.$$

The development of the wage ratio follows from (10):

(10B) $$\hat{\lambda} = \hat{w}_1 - \hat{w}_2 = (\frac{1}{\beta} - 1)(\hat{T}_2 - \hat{T}_1)$$

With a constant supply of labor of each type, a bias of technical progress changes the wage ratio of skilled and unskilled labor. Once more it is important whether the average elasticity of substitution β is greater or smaller than one. The crucial factors are the elasticity of substitution of capital and unskilled labor, σ_2, and the elasticity of substitution of the products of skilled and unskilled labor, ε. The empirical evidence supports the assumption that it is rather easy to substitute unskilled labor by capital, and also to replace the products of unskilled labor by products of skilled labor. These observations can be summarized by

Assumption II: The average elasticity of substitution of skilled and unskilled labor is high, i.e., $\beta > 1$.

In this case, a skill-biased technical progress raises the wage ratio of skilled and unskilled labor. This confirms the common assumption that the rising gap between the wages of skilled and unskilled labor is due to a skill-biased technical progress in connection with a high elasticity of substitution of skilled and unskilled labor.

(5B') describes the second case. A growing gap between the wages of skilled and unskilled labor is prevented by some intervention, which links the real wage of unskilled labor to the real wage of skilled labor. The wage ratio remains constant if the real wage of unskilled labor is adjusted in such a way that $\hat{w}_2 = \hat{w}_1 = \hat{T}_1$. In this case, (7) yields

(12B') $$\hat{x}_2 = \sigma_2(\hat{T}_2 - \hat{T}_1).$$

The rate of growth of the relative price is then given by $\hat{p} = \eta_2(\hat{T}_1 - \hat{T}_2)$, see (8). Furthermore, $\hat{Y}_1 - \hat{Y}_2 = \varepsilon\hat{p}$. Again, a skill-biased technical progress raises the relative price of the products of unskilled labor, and hence these products are substituted by products of skilled labor.

For each sector, the accumulation of capital can be derived from (11), (5B') and (12B'). The capital intensities of the two sectors diverge according to

(11B') $(\hat{K}_1 - \hat{N}_1) - (\hat{K}_2 - \hat{N}_2) = (1 - \sigma_2)(\hat{T}_1 - \hat{T}_2).$

A skill-biased technical progress induces a faster rise of the capital intensity of the first sector.

The most important consequence of a constant wage ratio is a reduction of the demand for unskilled labor. The extent of the reduction follows from (9) (with $\hat{N}_1 = 0$), (7), and $\hat{w}_2 = \hat{w}_1 = \hat{T}_1$:

(10B') $-\hat{N}_2 = \hat{\lambda} = (\beta - 1)(\hat{T}_1 - \hat{T}_2).$

The attempt to avoid a rising wage gap leads to a rising rate of unemployment of unskilled workers. Hence, a skill-biased technical progress raises the wage cost ratio λ in spite of a constant ratio w_1/w_2.

4 An Endogenous Bias of Technical Progress

1. The comparative analysis has shown that the structural development of the economy crucially depends on the bias of technical progress. This insight provokes the question as to whether the bias itself can be explained by economic forces. A possible clue for an answer may be found in the treatment of different kinds of technical progress in the "old" growth theory of the sixties. There one used to distinguish between labor saving and capital saving technical progress. In this context it was suggested that a trade-off between these two types of technical progress might exist, and that firms could use this opportunity to select a certain combination (see Samuelson (1965)).

An analogous choice between different kinds of technical progress may also exist with respect to the rates of technical progress in the two-sector model. A trade-off of the following kind is suggested:

$$T_{1s} = c_s\, T_{1,s-1} \qquad\qquad T_{2s} = \varphi(c_s) T_{2,s-1}\,, \quad c_s,\ \varphi \geq 1.$$

Here, s is a time index. c_s-1 is the rate of growth of technical progress in the first sector, φ-1 is the rate of growth of technical progress in the second sector. The trade-off is characterized by φ', $\varphi'' < 0$. It can be summarized by $T_{2s} / T_{2,s-1} = \varphi(T_{1s} / T_{1.s-1})$, or, in terms of the rates of technical progress, $\hat{T}_1$ and $\hat{T}_2$:

(13) $\hat{T}_2 + 1 = \varphi(\hat{T}_1 + 1), \quad \varphi' < 0, \ \varphi'' < 0, \quad \hat{T}_1,\ \hat{T}_2 \geq 0.$

A corresponding trade-off is illustrated in the following figure. It shows the possible combinations of the two rates of technical progress. When both rates are equal, their value is $\hat{T}_i = \theta$. The maximum rate of growth of the first sector is $\hat{T}_1 = \gamma$ at $\hat{T}_2 = 0$.

2. One could imagine a separate research sector, in which this trade-off is generated by the input of capital and labor. This sector would sell each type of technical progress to the corresponding production sector in separate markets. In each market, the selected rate of technical progress would result as the equilibrium outcome of supply and demand. The demand for technical progress would depend on its productivity and on its price. The supply of each type would depend on the trade-off and the price ratio of the two types. However, the introduction of a separate research sector would require a more complicated model. Firms could no longer operate in a perfectly competitive environment without a surplus that is necessary to purchase a superior technology. Furthermore, one would have to specify the technology by which the trade-off itself is produced, and its influence on the allocation of capital and labor.

Figure 1: *The Technological Trade-Off*

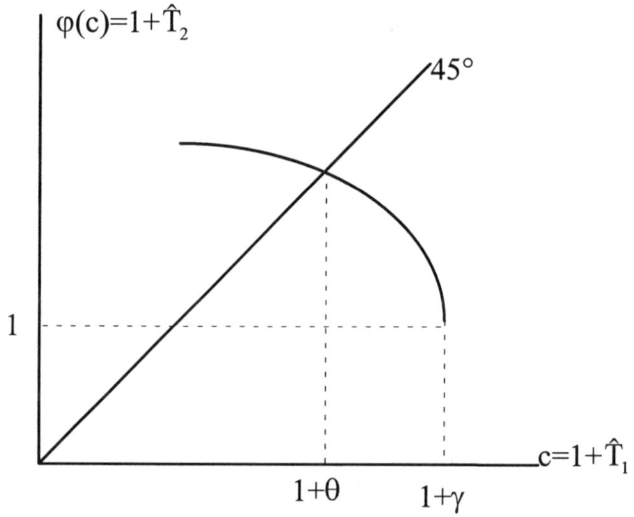

To avoid these complications, it is assumed that each entrepreneur can use the trade-off without incurring costs. This only makes sense if an entrepreneur can produce in both sectors. Hence, the assumption is that s/he has a firm in both sectors, or that s/he is going to set up, with equal probability, a firm in one of both sectors after having selected an optimal technology.

3. The combination of the rates of technical progress is then selected in the following way. In a period s-1, the entrepreneur chooses the technology parameters to maximize the present value of the future profits:

$$\max \sum_{\tau=s}^{\infty} (1+r)^{-\tau} [F_1(T_{1\tau}N_{1\tau},K_{1\tau})-w_{1\tau}N_{1\tau}-rK_{1\tau} + p_\tau F_2(T_{2\tau}N_{2\tau})-w_{2\tau}N_{2\tau}-rK_{2\tau}]$$

$$\text{s.t.} \qquad T_{1\tau} = c_\tau T_{1,\tau-1} = c_\tau c_{\tau-1} c_{\tau-2} \ldots c_s T_{1,s-1}$$

$$T_{2\tau} = \varphi(c_\tau) T_{2,\tau-1} = \varphi(c_\tau)\varphi(c_{\tau-1})\varphi(c_{\tau-2})\ldots\varphi(c_s) T_{2,s-1} \,.$$

The optimal choice of c_t yields the condition[7]

$$\sum_{\tau=t}^{\infty} (1+r)^{-\tau} \left[\frac{\partial F_1(\tau)}{\partial T_1 N_1} N_{1\tau}T_{1\tau}/c_t + p_\tau \frac{\partial F_2(\tau)}{\partial T_2 N_2} N_{2\tau}T_{2\tau}\varphi'(c_t)/\varphi(c_t)\right] = 0.$$

If one uses the first-order conditions for the optimal choice of labor, $\partial F_1(\tau) / \partial T_1 N_1 = w_{1\tau} / T_{1\tau}$ and $p_\tau\, \partial F_2(\tau) / \partial T_2 N_2 = w_{2\tau} / T_{2\tau}$, one gets

$\sum_{\tau=t}^{\infty} (1+r)^{-\tau} [w_{1\tau}N_{1\tau}/c_t + w_{2\tau}N_{2\tau}\varphi'(c_t)/\varphi(c_t)] = 0$. From this equation one can derive the result:

$$(14) \quad E(c_t) := -\, c_t\varphi'(c_t)/\varphi(c_t) = \sum_{\tau=t}^{\infty} a_\tau \lambda_\tau / \sum_{\tau=t}^{\infty} a_\tau =: \Lambda_t \,,$$

$$t \geq s, \qquad a_\tau := (1+r)^{-\tau} w_{2\tau} N_{2\tau}.$$

Here, E denotes the (positive) elasticity of the trade-off φ. $\lambda = w_1N_1 / w_2N_2$ is the wage cost ratio of the two sectors, as defined above, and Λ_t is a weighted average of the future values of λ_τ, $\tau \geq t$.

(14) shows that the choice of c_t depends on the (correct) expectation of the future development of wages and employment. In turn, wages and employment of a given period depend on the technology levels of the same period, which can be expressed by the corresponding value of c. In this way, (14) describes the evolution of c_τ in a perfect foresight equilibrium.

The computation of this solution would have to proceed by backward induction. For a given finite time horizon H, it is easy to verify that $E(c_{s+H}) = \lambda_{s+H}$ would be used as the starting point. It is obvious that an explicit computation would be extremely difficult, if not impossible. A suitable approximation is the myopic solution $E(c_s) = \lambda_s$, which neglects the impact of the optimal choice on future periods. It was shown that λ_s can be expressed as a function of T_{1s} / T_{2s}. Moreover,

---

[7] The second-order conditions are satisfied, if there are sufficient concavity conditions on the functions F_i (with respect to labor) and on φ.

$T_{2s} = \varphi(c_s)T_{2,s-1}$ and $c_s = T_{1s} / T_{1,s-1}$. Hence, given the technology values of the planning period $T_{1,s-1}$ and $T_{2,s-1}$, the myopic solution yields optimal values of T_{1s} and T_{2s} for each planning period s.

5 The Dynamics of a Biased Technical Progress and the Structure of Employment and Wages

The transformation of the macroeconomic structure of employment and wages is driven by two dynamic relations. On the one hand, (14) reveals that the development of a bias of technical progress depends on the expected evolution of the wage ratio λ. On the other hand, this evolution depends on the existing bias of technical progress, as the various forms of (10) show. Hence, there is a dynamic interdependence between the development of the bias of technical progress and of the structure of employment and wages. This interdependency is explored in this final section.

First, one can verify that the expected average wage ratio Λ_t will rise (fall) in the course of time, if λ_τ $(\tau > t)$ rises (falls), because

$$\Lambda_{t+1} - \Lambda_t = \frac{a_t}{\sum_{\tau=t}^{\infty} a_\tau \left(\sum_{\tau=t}^{\infty} a_\tau - a_t \right)} \sum_{\tau=t}^{\infty} a_\tau (\lambda_\tau - \lambda_t)$$

is positive (negative), if $\lambda_\tau > (<) \lambda_t$, $\tau > t$.

Second, the elasticity of the trade-off, E(c), rises with increasing values of c, i.e. with downward movements on the trade-off, because $E'(c) = c(\varphi' / \varphi)^2 - \varphi' / \varphi - c\varphi'' / \varphi > 0$.

Therefore, (14) implies that c rises (falls) with rising (falling) values of Λ, and hence with rising (falling) expected future values of λ. In this way, the expected evolution of λ affects the bias of technical progress. For example, if λ is expected to rise, firms will increase the first sector's technical progress at the expense of the second sector's technical progress. Thus, an already existing bias of technical progress in favor of the first sector will be reinforced.

On the other hand, the comparative analysis has revealed that the development of λ itself depends on the bias of technical progress. The diverse equations (10) show that λ rises (falls) in the course of time, if the technical progress is biased in favor of the first sector, and if $\beta > 1$ $(\beta < 1)$.

Altogether, the analysis reveals an interesting dynamic interdependence. In each period, the expected average wage cost ratio determines a certain bias of technical progress, which changes the current wage cost ratio. If the technical progress is already biased in favor of the first sector, and if $\beta < 1$, the bias will be reduced, because the wage cost ratio will fall. If $\beta > 1$, it will be raised, because the wage ratio will rise. It was assumed above that $\beta > 1$ in the first interpretation and $\beta < 1$ in the second interpretation of the two-sector model. The following analysis shows the consequences for each of the two interpretations.

5.1 Interpretation A: Industrial Sector and Service Sector

In this case, λ denotes the employment ratio N_1 / N_2. Its evolution is given by (10A), which explains the continuous re-allocation of labor from the industrial sector to the service sector. However, falling values of λ gradually reduce the expected average employment ratio Λ. This leads to a falling value of c in favor of an increasing value of $\varphi(c)$, i.e. there will be an upward movement on the corresponding trade-off (see the figure). If firms observe and correctly expect that wage costs rise faster in the service sector than in the industrial sector, they will prefer more labor saving inventions in the service sector and less in the industrial sector, i.e. they will reduce the industry-biased technical progress. This process will continue as long as such a bias exists, because it will further depress λ. The reduction of the bias will slow down the transfer of labor from the industrial sector to the service sector. In the long run the bias will gradually diminish and cease to exist. A steady state will be reached, in which $\hat{T}_1 = \hat{T}_2 = \theta$. Then both sectors will expand at the same rate of growth. The structure of employment ($\lambda = N_1 / N_2$) and of capital (K_1 / K_2), will remain constant. Thus, the main prediction of the model is that in the long run an industry-biased technical progress will disappear and the economic structure will become stable.

5.2 Interpretation B: Skilled and Unskilled Labor

Here, two cases must be distinguished. In the first case, flexible wages secure full employment of each type of labor. The proportionate rate of change of the wage ratio λ is given by (10B), which explains a widening gap between the wages of skilled and unskilled labor. As λ rises, firms will expect a gradual increase of the future average wage ratio Λ. This will lead to a rising value of c and a falling value of $\varphi(c)$, i.e. there will be a downward movement on the corresponding trade-off (see equation (14) and the figure). Firms invest more in labor saving innovations for skilled labor in order to reduce the corresponding wage pressure. However, since $\beta > 1$, this endeavor has the opposite effect: it further increases the wage ratio λ.[8] The dynamic interaction of relative wages and the bias of technical progress is unstable. The bias rises until $\hat{T}_1$ reaches its maximum at $\hat{T}_1 = \gamma$ and

[8] $\lambda = w_1 / w_2 = T_1 f_1' / T_2 p f_2'$. Both p and f_2' rise with rising values of T_1 / T_2. However, the rate of growth of pf_2' is only $1 / \beta$ times the rate of growth of T_1 / T_2.

$\hat{T}_2$ has fallen to zero (see the figure). In this state, the capital intensity of skilled labor will continue to rise faster than the capital intensity of unskilled labor, see (11B). Even without technical progress, the real wage of unskilled labor will still continue to rise, see (7B), but less than that of skilled labor. So the wage gap will continue to widen.

The second case considers the possibility of preventing a widening wage gap by linking the real wage of unskilled labor to that of skilled labor, for example by setting $\hat{w}_2 = \hat{w}_1 = \hat{T}_1$. However, as (10B') has already shown, this would cause a rising rate of unemployment of unskilled labor. It would also raise the wage cost ratio $\lambda = w_1N_1 / w_2N_2$, because w_1N_1 / w_2 is constant and N_2 would fall. Hence, the dynamic development would also lead to the final state that was described above, in which the technological state of unskilled labor is stagnant, whereas the technology of skilled labor expands at its maximum speed. Thus, a rising inequality at full employment can only be avoided by the gradual displacement of unskilled labor.

All in all, the main prediction of the model is that in the long run a skill-biased technical progress will reach a maximum, and unskilled labor will continually fall behind. This is a gloomy prediction, which underlines the importance of reducing the share of unskilled workers by adequate education and training programs. It is interesting to study the impact of a rising employment ratio N_1 / N_2 on the wage ratio w_1 / w_2 and on the long run development of the skill-bias. If the supply of skilled and unskilled labor changes, (7) and (9) yield

$$\hat{w}_1 - \hat{w}_2 = (1-\frac{1}{\beta})(\hat{T}_1 - \hat{T}_2) - \frac{1}{\beta}(\hat{N}_1 - \hat{N}_2), \quad \hat{\lambda} = (1-\frac{1}{\beta})(\hat{T}_1 - \hat{T}_2) + (1-\frac{1}{\beta})(\hat{N}_1 - \hat{N}_2).$$

One can see that the increase in λ, caused by a skill-biased technical progress, will accelerate if N_1 / N_2 rises ($\hat{N}_1 - \hat{N}_2 > 0$). Thus, the economy will still settle down at $\hat{T}_1 = \gamma$ and $\hat{T}_2 = 0$, i.e. the technical progress of unskilled labor will still disappear. Yet, a rising employment ratio reduces the difference between $\hat{w}_1$ and $\hat{w}_2$. The wage ratio w_1/w_2 will actually remain constant, if $\hat{N}_1 - \hat{N}_2 = (\beta - 1)(\hat{T}_1 - \hat{T}_2)$. For example, assume that the supply of unskilled labor falls at a constant rate $\nu > 0$. If the total supply of labor, $N_1 + N_2$, is constant, the supply of skilled labor rises at the corresponding rate $\nu N_2 / N_1$. In the long run, $\hat{N}_1$ tends to zero. As the same is true for $\hat{T}_2$, one arrives at $\hat{\lambda} = (1-\frac{1}{\beta})(\gamma + \nu)$, and $\hat{w}_1 - \hat{w}_2 = \beta^{-1}[(\beta - 1)\gamma - \nu]$. The wage ratio w_1 / w_2 could be kept constant if it were possible to reduce the supply of unskilled labor at the rate $\nu = (\beta - 1)\gamma$. The wage cost ratio λ would also rise at this rate, but only because the employment ratio N_1 / N_2 increases. Thus, a gradual change of the skill structure might, indeed, prevent a permanently widening wage gap.[9]

[9] See, however, the different result in Acemoglu (1998).

References

Acemoglu, D. (1998), Why do New Technologies Complement Skills? Directed Technical Change and Wage Inequality, *Quarterly Journal of Economics* 113, 1055-1089.

Agénor, P.-R. and J. Aizenman (1997), Technical Change, Relative Wages, and Unemployment, *European Economic Review* 41, 187-205.

Baumol, W. J. (1967), Macroeconomics of Unbalanced Growth: The Anatomy of Urban Crises, *American Economic Review* 57, 415-426.

Beißinger, T. (1999), Technischer Fortschritt als Ursache sektoralen Wandels, mimeo, Regensburg.

Berman, E., J. Bound and Z. Griliches (1994), Changes in the Demand for Skilled Labor within U.S. Manufacturing: Evidence form the Annual Survey of Manufacturers, *Quarterly Journal of Economics* 109, 367-397.

Bhagwati, J.N. (1984), Why are Services Cheaper in the Poor Countries?, *Economic Journal* 94, 279-286.

Bound, J. and G. Johnson (1992), Changes in the Structure of Wages in the 1980's: An Evaluation of Alternative Explanations, *American Economic Review* 82, 371-392.

Caselli, F. (1999), Technological Revolutions, *American Economic Review* 89, 78-102.

Clark, C. (1951), The Conditions of Economic Progress, 2nd ed., London.

Gregg, P. and A. Manning (1997), Skill-biassed Change, Unemployment and Wage Inequality, *European Economic Review* 41, 1173-1200.

Gundlach, E. (1994), Demand Bias as an Explanation for Structural Change, *Kyklos* 47, 249-267.

Gundlach, E. (1996), Demand Bias and Structural Change: Reply, *Kyklos* 49, 215-217.

Inman, R. P. (1985), Introduction and Overview, in: Inman (ed.), Managing the Service Sector. Prospects and Problems, Cambridge, 1-24.

Juhn, D., K. M. Murphy and B. Pierce (1993), Wage Inequality and the Rise in Returns to Skill, *Journal of Political Economy* 101, 410-442.

Klodt, H., R. Maurer and A. Schimmelpfennig (1997), Tertiarisierung in der deutschen Wirtschaft, Tübingen.

Krugman, P. (1994), Past and Prospective Causes of High Unemployment, in: Federal Reserve Bank of Kansas City (ed.), Reducing Unemployment: Current Issues and Policy Options, Kansas City, 49-80.

Kuznets, S. (1966), Modern Economic Growth. Rate, Structure, and Spread, New Haven.

Machin, S. and J. Van Reenen (1998), Technology and Changes in Skill Structure: Evidence from Seven OECD Countries, *Quarterly Journal of Economics* 113, 1215-1244.

Organisation for Economic Cooperation and Development (1994), Job Study, Paris, OECD.

Quiriba, M. G. and F. Harrigan (1996), Demand Bias and Structural Change, *Kyklos* 49, 205-213.

Samuelson, P.A. (1965), A Theory of Induced Innovations along Kennedy-Weizsäcker Lines, *Review of Economics and Statistics* 47.

Topel, R. H. (1994), Regional Labor Markets and the Determinants of Wage Inequality, *American Economic Review, Papers and Proceedings* 84, 17-22.

Part 3 :

Globalization and Unemployment

I. Effects of Globalization on Unemployment

Wages, Unemployment, and Globalization: a Tale of Conventional Wisdoms*

Oliver Landmann

University of Freiburg,
79085 Freiburg, Germany

1 Introduction

The widespread fear of globalization – "globaphobia" as Burtless et al. (1998) have termed it – may have several sources. But the most immediate concern of most people surely is what globalization has done or will do to their prospects on the labor market. Interestingly, this is true even for the United States where unemployment has steadily been falling over the past years to its lowest level in decades. But at the same time, US real wages have increased very slowly for more than two decades, and at the bottom end of the wage ladder, the rate of change of real incomes has even been negative. In Europe, in contrast, it is the intractable problem of high and persistent unemployment that forms the backdrop to the globalization debate. Here too, the least skilled workers are hit worst. The common concern on both sides of the Atlantic is that globalization might depress labor incomes, increase income inequality and thus eventually turn out to be a social time bomb.

Why did suddenly these worries emerge after several decades of steady trade liberalization and increasing global integration that are generally hailed as a major force sustaining the historically high growth rates of the post-war era? True, there was a marked slowdown of economic growth in the early 1970s, i.e. around the time that is often identified with the beginning of the modern globalization era. If something began to change at that time, it was the structure of world trade and the scope for global movements of capital. Whereas the spectacular expansion of world trade in the immediate post-war period was largely confined to intra-industry trade among the advanced industrial economies, the early 1970s marked the beginning of the equally spectacular rise of some newly industrializing, mostly Asian economies as significant producers and exporters of manufactured goods.

---

* Valuable comments by my discussant Arne Heise and other conference participants as well as by Michael Pflüger are gratefully acknowledged. Klaus Veigel helped with the figures and the layout.

Soon, these economies also attracted relatively large amounts of foreign direct investments and other forms of capital.

This emerging North-South trade differed from the still dominant North-North trade in that it was largely inter-industry trade, based on differential factor endowments – the South deriving its comparative advantage from its large supplies of cheap, but potentially efficient labor. This explains the worries that give rise to „globaphobia": If globalization means that producers and workers worldwide are increasingly required to compete on globally integrated markets, how can it be that the abundant supply of cheap labor in low-wage countries does not pose a major threat to jobs and wages in the advanced countries? Among many politicians and in the public at large, perceptions of globalization are strongly shaped by concerns of such immediate intuitive appeal.

The globalization debate has sparked an outburst of academic research as well, again with a heavy emphasis on the implications for the labor market. This new research blended with and added to the earlier research efforts devoted to the explanation of wage behavior and employment in the industrial economies. In particular, the globalization issue heightened the challenge of providing a convincing and coherent account of the sharp differences between labor market developments in the USA and in Europe. These differences are the subject of popular views so widely shared that they attained the status of conventional wisdoms. In particular, they involve propositions concerning, on the one hand, a trade-off between real wage growth and employment growth and, on the other hand, a trade-off between inequality and unemployment.

The present paper cannot attempt to do justice to the huge theoretical and empirical literature dealing with the effects of globalization on wages and employment. A few remarks in section 5 will have to suffice. Rather, its aim is to place the current concerns about globalization into the context of the earlier conventional wisdoms. To this purpose, section 2 briefly summarizes the substance and factual background of the conventional wisdoms while the subsequent sections take up the underlying theoretical ideas: Sections 3 addresses the alleged trade-off between the wage level and unemployment, section 4 explains how globalization could pose a trade-off between wage inequality and unemployment and how the two trade-offs could be related. Section 6 concludes.

2 Conventional Wisdoms: New and Old

Much research has recently been devoted to the labor market effects of globalization. If there is anything like a mainstream view emanating from this research, it does not support the notion that globalization is a major factor behind OECD labor market developments. However, it is also fair to say that this mainstream view, and the theoretical and empirical results on which it is based, leave quite a few questions unanswered and, therefore, leave ample room for dissenting views.[1] While it may be hard to agree on a common interpretation and explanation of the facts, there is little disagreement as to what the facts are. The major stylized facts that frame the debate can be summarized by the following four observations:

1. The share of emerging economies in world exports of manufactured goods has sharply increased since 1970 and is due to increase further in the future.[2]

2. In most advanced countries, changes in the structure of labor demand since at least 1980 have clearly favored skilled labor at the expense of unskilled labor.[3]

3. Wage differentials have markedly widened in the United States and the United Kingdom, but remained largely constant or even narrowed in most continental European economies.[4] As figure 1 suggests, this is true irrespective of the specific measure of wage dispersion considered.[5]

4. Countries that have avoided the increase in wage inequality have typically experienced rising unemployment rates, in particular among the unskilled (cf. figure 2[6]).

Observations 2-4 suggest an interpretation which is so intuitively appealing that it is almost universally accepted as a "Conventional Wisdom" (Krugman (1994)): Where labor market institutions are designed to pursue egalitarian goals, they collide with market forces that pull in the opposite direction. This inevitably results in high unemployment rates. Where the determination of the wage structure is left to market forces, in contrast, unemployment can be kept low. The price to be paid for avoiding high unemployment, it seems, is the creation of an underclass of "working poor". In short, there appears to be an unpleasant trade-off between unemployment and wage inequality.

---

[1] For recent surveys and debates, see the symposia in the *Journal of Economic Perspectives*, Vol. 9, No. 3, 1995, and Vol. 12, No. 4, 1998, in *The Economic Journal*, September 1998, as well as IMF (1997), Collins (1998) and Siebert (1999).

[2] Cf. World Bank (1997).

[3] Cf. Nickell/Bell (1995), Drèze/Sneesens (1997), Blanchard (1997b).

[4] Cf. IMF (1997) and the studies in Freeman/Katz (1995).

[5] Figure 1 is reproduced from Hesse (1998), p. 160

[6] Figure 2 is reproduced from Phelps (1997).

Figure 1: *Wage differentials in international perspective*

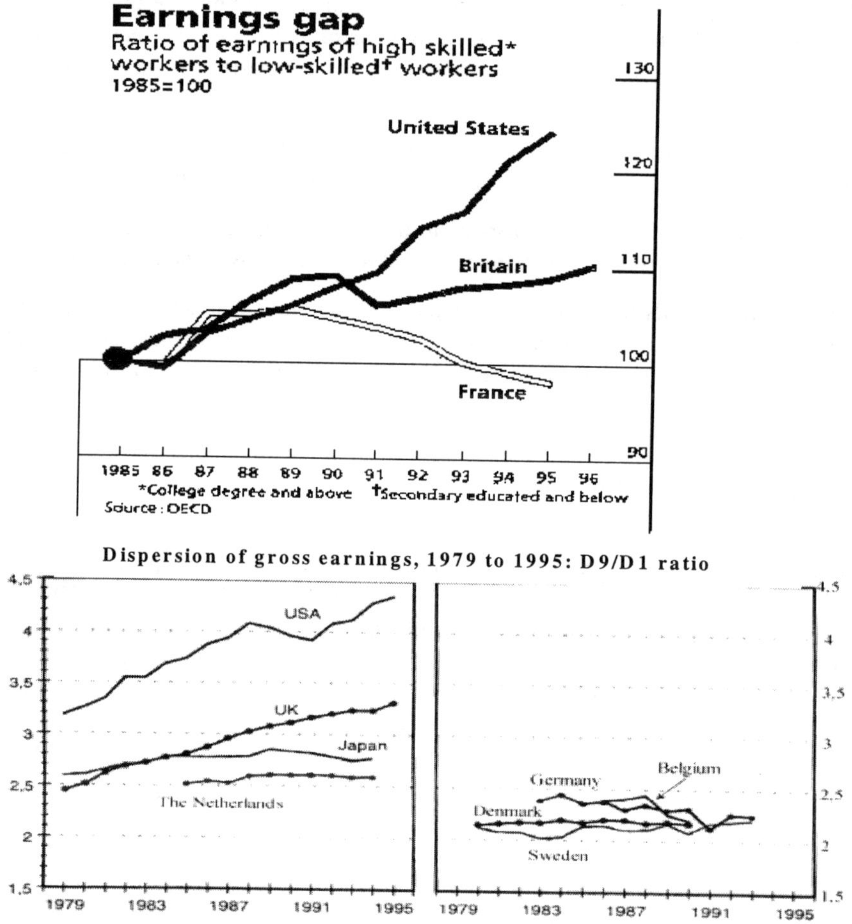

The D1/D9 ratio is the ratio of the lower boundary of the top income decile and the upper boundary of the bottom income decile.

Source: Hesse (1998), p. 160

Figure 2: *Unskilled wages and employment*

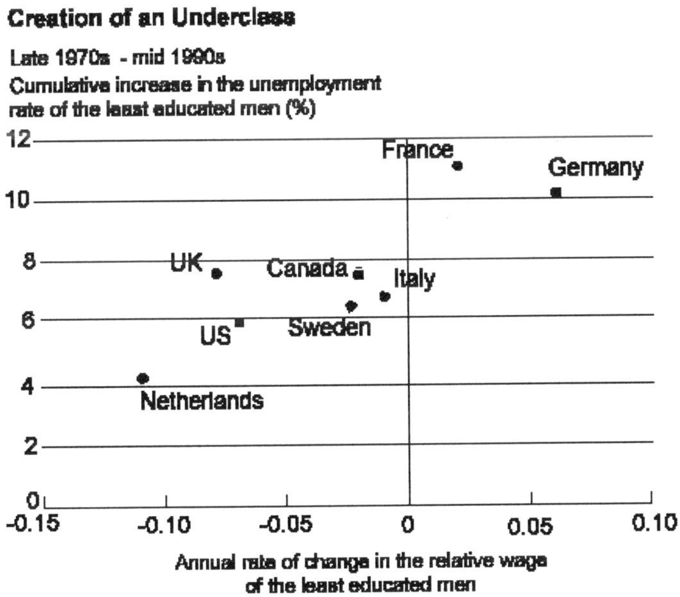

Source: Phelps (1997)

Not too long ago, there used to be another and somewhat different conventional wisdom which was concerned less with the *structure* of wages than with the absolute *level* of wages. This older story dates back to the 1970s when the oil price shocks confronted the advanced industrialized economies with yet another dark side of globalization. The sudden increase of the oil price not only imposed a real income loss on oil-importing countries, but also reduced the marginal product of their labor in proportion to their dependency on foreign energy sources. If this exogenous shock was to be absorbed without serious damage to employment, real wages needed to display a fair amount of flexibility. The worldwide productivity slowdown that occurred at about the same time for partly independent reasons placed an additional burden of adjustment on labor markets. As the story goes, the United States was relatively well prepared for this kind of adjustment. To be sure, the supply shocks, the ensuing inflation, and the efforts of macroeconomic policymakers to deal with these unexpected disturbances, exposed the US economy to quite some cyclical instability;[7] but this did not visibly affect the unemployment rate in the longer term.

---

[7] This instability shows up quite clearly in the unemployment series displayed in figure 3.

Not so in Europe. In most European countries, the stagflationary effects of the external supply shock were exacerbated by the refusal of wage setters to share the burden of higher oil prices and to adjust their wage demands sufficiently downwards in response to the productivity slowdown. This *real wage resistance*, as it came to be called by Sachs (1979) and Bruno/Sachs (1985), translated the adverse shift of the labor demand schedule into higher unemployment. Worse, the external supply shock coincided with a wage explosion which had its roots in the labor unrest of the late 1960s. The resulting cumulation of external and internal cost push provided a ready case study for the concept of *classical unemployment* which was much en vogue among Europe's academics at that time (cf. Malinvaud (1977)).

As it turned out, the insufficient responsiveness of wage setting process to unemployment was a deep-seated feature of European labor markets that continued to prevent a return to full employment ever since – notwithstanding the more than complete reversal of the external supply shocks later on. Looking back on the entire time span since 1970, it is apparent that Europe and the United States experienced sharply differing evolutions of their respective real wage and employment levels. The middle and the bottom panels in figure 3 convey this well known picture.

In its May 1995 World Economic Outlook, from which figure 3 is reproduced, the International Monetary Fund succinctly summarized the conventional wisdom regarding these sharply contrasting labor market experiences in two propositions.[8] The first proposition is about the factors that are *not* to blame for Europe's dismal employment performance: Obviously, insufficient demand growth and too low a rate of capital formation are unlikely causes of the unemployment problem. After all, as the two top panels of figure 3 demonstrate, the average growth rates of real GDP and the capital stock have been nearly equal in the United States and in Europe. The second proposition offers an alternative explanation placing less emphasis on the *volume* of investment than on the *type* of investment that occurred: Rigid labor markets and excessive wage claims in Europe have encouraged capital-labor substitution (capital deepening) whereas the more flexible US labor market favored employment-generating capacity expansion (capital widening). As a consequence, Europe experienced relatively strong increases in the capital-labor ratio and in labor productivity which in turn supported the relatively strong real wage performance. However, as the IMF puts it, "the higher real wages benefited a declining share of the European labor force."

[8] See IMF (1995) and the summary in the IMF Survey, July 3, 1995, pp. 212-13.

Figure 3: *Europe vs. The United States, 1970-94*

The European Union and the United States: Output, Capital, Employment, and Wages
(1970 = 100, unless noted otherwise)

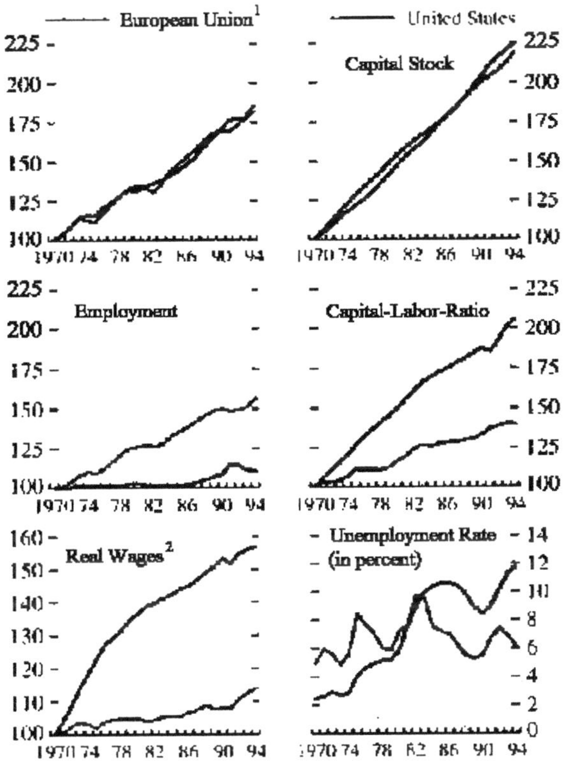

Sources: OECD, analytical data base; and IMF staff estimates.

[1]Excluding Luxembourg and Portugal. Real GDP, capital stocks, and real wages are calculated using PPP-based weights.

[2]National accounts compensation per employee deflated by the GDP deflator.

Source: IMF (1995), p. 32

The two conventional wisdoms do not tell the same story. The more recent conventional wisdom is about the skill intensity of production and the skill premium. It portrays the choice between the American model and the European model as a choice between wage inequality and unemployment. The earlier conventional wisdom is a more traditional story about aggregate employment, the capital-labor ratio, labor productivity, and the general wage level. Here the trade-off appears to be between extensive and intensive growth or, by implication, between strong employment growth and strong real wage growth. Both conventional wisdoms obviously fit the stylized facts to which they refer. But what are their theoretical foundations? How do they fit together? And how do they relate to globalization? These are the questions to which we turn next.

3 A Trade-Off Between Unemployment and Real Wages?

This section takes a closer look at the alleged trade-off between the real wage level and the volume of employment. The notion of such a trade-off is immediately appealing to basic economic intuition since this is essentially the trade-off suggested by the neoclassical labor demand curve of our textbooks. Similarly, it seems plausible that this trade-off is reinforced in the medium run by the response of capital investment to wage behavior. Aggressive wage increases push firms into capital-intensive modes of production and thus make it harder to recover the lost jobs at a later point. It is a trade-off that the United States and Europe, according to the old conventional wisdom, have solved in different ways. Also, it is indisputable that the terms of this trade-off are very much on the mind of politicians as they debate employment and labor market policies. If the only way back to full employment is the creation of US-style wage and productivity stagnation, many Europeans argue, it may not be worth it.

There is just one problem with this point of view: It is in conflict with standard macroeconomic unemployment theory. According to the textbook model of long-term employment determination, there is no such thing as a trade-off between jobs and wages over any extended period of time. The trade-off may exist in a short run for any given production capacity, but as time passes and investment responds, labor demand becomes very elastic. With a constant-returns-to-scale technology and a fully endogenous capital stock, the long-run labor demand curve in fact becomes horizontal.[9] This is not the place to develop the argument in full detail.

---

[9] See Bean (1989) and Blanchard (1990). Burda (1988) and Landmann/Jerger (1993) develop fully dynamic models of employment and capital stock adjustment. For a textbook treatment, see Landmann/Jerger (1999), Ch. 6. The relevant model is also sketched by Berthold/Fehn (1999) in this volume.

The important point to realize is that the real wage cannot in a meaningful way be regarded as an exogenous variable in long-run general equilibrium. Hence, it is misleading to treat it as a major determinant of the aggregate capital-labor ratio. If anything, the causation runs the other way round. In the most elementary model of long-run equilibrium, the structure of the relationships that determine employment, the capital stock and the wage level is fully recursive: The long-run capital-labor ratio is uniquely determined by technology and the cost of capital. The real wage, in turn, is a single-valued function of the capital-labor ratio and thus independent of wage-setting behavior. It is in this sense that labor demand is perfectly elastic with respect to the real wage level. All that is left for wage-setting to do is the determination of the equilibrium employment level along the horizontal labor demand function.[10] Given the capital-labor ratio, the absolute capital stock can then be derived as well.

A crucial implication of this account is, of course, that it debunks the notion of a long-run trade-off between the level of real wages and the level of employment. Simple as it may be, the standard model is strongly supported by the observation that European unemployment has remained high or even increased in the face of slowing real wage growth and a declining labor share throughout the 1980s and 1990s.[11] While it is true that the supply shocks of the 1970s initially pushed up both real wages and unemployment, thus pointing to a wage-employment trade-off, the picture changed as the response of investment to the job losses made itself felt. In an attempt to bring back their capital-labor ratios into line with the requirements of cost minimization, firms cut back their investment spending and thus diminished the scope for further productivity and wage growth. This adjustment was reinforced by the steep rise of real interest rates which occurred worldwide around the year 1980 and warranted a further downward revision of optimal capital-labor ratios.[12] It is not altogether surprising, therefore, that real wages appear to have been pushed even below their pre-supply-shock baseline path in the process.

One might be tempted to dismiss this account of events on the grounds that it is inconsistent with the observed behavior of capital-labor ratios which continued to rise throughout Europe even though the relevant theory says they should have

---

[10] In general, with imperfect competition on the goods market, it is more appropriate to speak of a price-setting function instead of a labor demand function.

[11] Landmann, Jerger (1993) analyze the experience of Germany along these lines. Caballero, Hammour (1997) study the effects of changing labor relations on factor substitution in France. Blanchard (1997a) looks at the recent slide of the labor share throughout continental Europe.

[12] This rise of global interest rates plays a major part in Phelps's (1994) account of what he terms "structural slumps".

been revised downwards in the course of the adjustment process.[13] However, this observation can seem puzzling only if one neglects the trend increase of capital-labor ratios due to (the labor augmenting component of) technical progress. Having estimated this trend component and after adjusting the time path of Germany's capital-labor ratio accordingly, Landmann/Jerger (1993) find clear evidence for the expected fall of the adjusted capital intensity from 1977 onwards, which accounts for the further slowdown of productivity and real wage growth during the 1980s as compared to the already low post-1973 rates.

In short, the notion of a long-run trade-off between unemployment and real wages does not stand up to careful theoretical and empirical analysis. Aggressive wage-setting behavior does not accelerate capital-deepening for long nor can it secure sustainable real wage gains for workers. It does set in motion, though, a vicious circle of job losses and capacity destruction feeding upon each other. In the process, the equilibrium unemployment rate is pushed up.

This account might prompt the question of why wage setters push for higher wages at all if they have to be aware that, in the final analysis, all they get is fewer jobs instead of higher wages. There are two answers to this: First, to the extent that wage bargaining takes place in a decentralized way, wage setters play a non-cooperative game in which they do not only have a stake in their sector's relative wage, but also, since the aggregate price level is a public good, in their individual real wages. This will become quite clear in the relative wage model of the next section. Second, workers benefit from lags. The horizontal labor demand function is a long-run concept. It takes time for the capital stock to adjust to lower employment and, in the shorter run, it also takes time for the price level to catch up with higher wages. Under these circumstances, simple dynamic optimization principles suggest that it is worthwhile to exploit the trade-off while it lasts.

All of which leaves yet another question unanswered: if we indeed believe that differences in wage-setting behavior can explain differences in the long-term evolution of unemployment, and if we also believe that these differences are unrelated to the long-term growth of real wages and capital-labor ratios, how do we explain the picture conveyed by figure 3 which seems to suggest that the relatively strong real wage growth in Europe is the mirror image of her weak employment performance?

---

[13] This observation prompted Caballero/Hammour (1997) to construct a model which reconciles sustained capital-deepening in the face of rising unemployment by the assumption that firms switch to more labor-saving technologies in order to protect themselves from the appropriation attempts of labor. This model has the remarkable property that a wage-setting shock may even lower the real wage level in the long run. However, the model would thereby seem to imply an acceleration of labor-saving technical change, which is the opposite of what is generally found in studies of the well-known 'productivity slowdown'.

This question is addressed in a recent paper by Gordon (1997) who has couched the trade-off issue in terms of the relationship between unemployment and productivity growth. Of course, long-run real wage growth is closely related to the growth of labor productivity even though the shifts in the labor share indicate that the correlation is not perfect. Gordon's findings strongly support the theoretical presumption that the contrasting unemployment experiences of the USA and Europe have little to do with the differential productivity and real wage patterns. Rather, his productivity growth regressions confirm the insights of the voluminous convergence literature according to which a substantial fraction of the more rapid productivity growth in Europe as compared to the United States is due to catch-up.

It is well known that this convergence of productivity levels, and hence real wage levels, among the advanced industrial nations has been going on over the entire post-war period. In fact, the US-European differential with respect to capital accumulation, productivity growth and real wage growth was significantly larger before 1970 than after. In other words, Europe has experienced a much sharper productivity slowdown than the USA. These already diminished differentials are what we see in the real wage and capital-labor ratio panels of figure 3.

Also, Gordon's decomposition of labor productivity growth into the respective contributions of capital deepening and total factor productivity growth shows that labor productivity grew more slowly in all major European countries in the 1979-92 period than during 1973-79 and that slowing capital deepening played a major part in almost every case whereas exactly the opposite happened in the USA.[14] This finding directly contradicts the IMF's (1995) interpretation of the relative capital-intensity and real wage developments cited in the last section, but it is perfectly consistent with the disinvestment story sketched in this section. The downward revision of European capacity expansion plans in response to sluggish employment growth thus contributed to a further narrowing of the US-European productivity and real wage growth differential throughout the 1980s – in spite of (or rather in line with) the further build-up of the unemployment differential.

In the light of these results, it is hardly surprising that Gordon was unable to detect any significant effect of the change in unemployment in his productivity growth regressions. What he did find, though, were significant coefficients on various sector dummies, indicating substantial productivity growth differentials across sectors. This implies that the aggregate productivity and real wage figures can be strongly affected by changes in the sectoral output mix of an economy. Of course, the sectoral structure of production is at the very core of the theory that underlies the more recent conventional wisdom about the trade-off between unemployment and the dispersion of wages. As the next section takes a closer look at that theory, it will be natural to ask, therefore, whether the effects of *relative* labor demand

[14] Cf. Gordon (1997, Table 14.2, p. 455).

shifts that result under alternative assumptions about *relative* wages can add to our understanding of *aggregate* wages and *aggregate* employment.

4 Globalization, the Structure of Labor Demand, and Relative Wages [15]

The interaction of unemployment, productivity, the real wage and capital formation is an inherently macroeconomic story. Apart from external supply shocks and perhaps global interest-rate shocks, this story does not prominently feature international economic linkages, trade and globalization. In contrast, the analysis of relative labor demand shifts, relative wages and the structure of employment requires an explicitly microeconomic framework. And since globalization is a prime suspect in this plot, the natural place to start with is standard general equilibrium trade theory. Much of the theoretical and empirical work on the labor market effects of globalization has indeed been placed into the framework of the HOS (Heckscher-Ohlin-Samuelson) model. As will become clear below, though, there are legitimate concerns that this paradigm might narrow down the issues more than is warranted.

Since the popular concern is with developing or newly industrializing countries that are abundantly endowed with cheap labor and, hence, are positioned to flood the markets of advanced economies with low-wage exports, the standard approach in this literature is to build models of inter-industry North-South trade with two factors of production, skilled labor and unskilled labor. Physical capital is typically left out of the picture. This specification is sometimes justified by reference to perfect international capital mobility which removes rate-of-return differentials as a source of comparative advantage (Wood (1991)). With fully endogenous adjustment of capital stocks, the overall capital-labor ratios are determined by exactly the same logic as in the long-run macro model of the preceding section. As a consequence, capital can be lumped together with total factor productivity and relegated to the back-stage as the analysis of relative skill intensities proceeds.

Even if one hesitates to apply the extreme assumption of perfect international capital mobility to real capital, it can legitimately be argued that wage and per-capita income disparities between North and South are not easily explained by differences in physical capital-labor ratios. Indeed, if human capital formation is the driving force of economic development, as the work of Lucas (1988) and Romer/Mankiw/Weil (1992) suggests, it appears not too far-fetched to use a skill-based trade model for the analysis of North-South trade.

---

[15] This section draws freely on Landmann/Pflüger (1996 and 1998).

It is straightforward to derive the implications of such trade for relative labor demand and the structure of employment in the North, depending on whether relative wages are assumed flexible or rigid. The essence of what the HOS model predicts under either assumption is captured by figure 4.[16] The North produces two goods, a high-tech good F and a low-tech good M. The factors of production, skilled labor K and unskilled labor L, earn wages r and w, respectively. High-tech production is assumed to be more skill-intensive than low-tech production. The North is depicted as a large, initially closed economy. The pre-globalization state of the world is thus represented by the simplifying assumption that there is no North-South trade at all. As the South enters world trade in manufactured goods, the effects on the North are conditioned by the relative scarcity of skilled labor in the South.

The upper-right panel of figure 4 depicts the goods market equilibrium, with the relative price and the relative quantity of the two goods being shown on the axes. *RD* is the ratio of Northern consumers' demand for the high-tech good and their demand for the low-tech good. This relative demand curve slopes downward reflecting the usual response of the consumption pattern to changes in the relative price p_F / p_M.[17] The supply schedule *RS*, in contrast, shows how the production pattern changes as Northern producers move along their production possibilities frontier in response to a relative price change. This schedule is thus derived under the assumption of fully employed factors.[18] The intersection of *RS* and *RD* at point *A* establishes the autarky equilibrium of the North. The autarky price ratio is given by $(p_F / p_M)_N$.

The factor market implications of the goods market equilibrium are evident from the upper-left and the lower-left panels. The *S-S* schedule in the upper-left panel represents the relationship between the relative goods price p_F / p_M and the relative factor price w / r spelled out by the Stolper - Samuelson theorem. The factor price ratio, in turn, determines factor intensities in both industries. The factor intensity functions in the lower-left panel reflect the assumption about the comparative factor intensity of the two industries stated above. Evidently, the North remains incompletely specialized as long as its overall factor endowment ratio *No* remains in the range between $(K / L)_F$ and $(K / L)_M$ – which is simply assumed here. Finally, the lower-right panel depicts the relationship between F / M and K / L as implied by the Rybczynski theorem for any given factor price ratio.

---

[16] The figure is reproduced here with minor modifications from Landmann/Pflüger (1998) where all the equations underlying the particular schedules are given in full detail.

[17] Strictly speaking, the unique relationship between relative demand and relative prices requires homothetic utility.

[18] The full employment condition is actually stronger than what is needed. *Constant* employment rates of both factors would do as well.

Figure 4: *Globalization as seen through the lens of the HOS model*

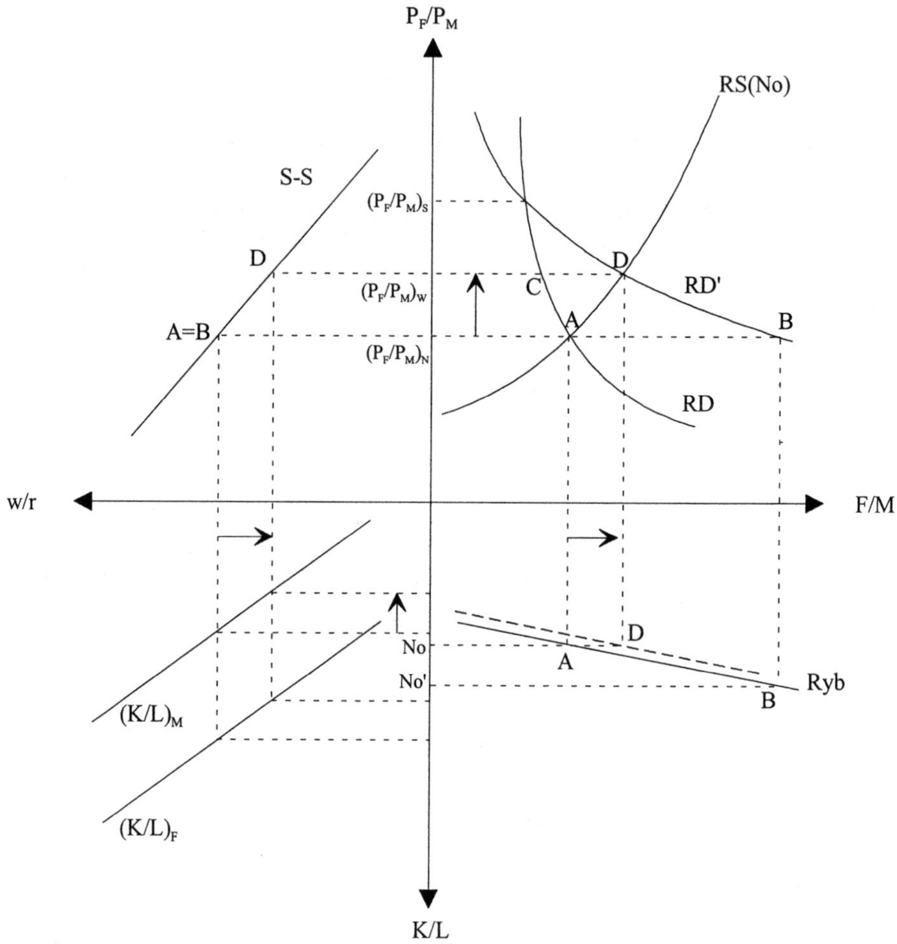

Source: Landmann/Pflüger (1998), p. 134

What happens when the South enters the market? Being abundantly endowed with unskilled labor, it should be expected to have a comparative advantage in the production of the low-tech good. Northern producers of the low-tech good are thus confronted with a fall in demand due to increasing import penetration, whereas the market for Northern producers of the high-tech good expands. These changes can be summarized by a shift of the relative demand curve from *RD* to *RD'*. With $(p_F / p_M)_S$ denoting autarky prices in the South, the horizontal distance from *RD* to *RD'* is a measure of the net trade volumes implied by the Southern offer curve at any given price ratio.

If markets are open and prices flexible, a new equilibrium is established at point *D*. Northern producers and consumers face a higher relative price of the high-tech good as the world market price settles at $(p_F / p_M)_W$. High-tech production in the North expands at the expense of low-tech production while consumers choose the new consumption point *C* where they demand relatively more of the now cheaper low-tech-good. The distance $\overline{CD}$ is related to the volume of North-South trade obtaining in the new situation. It is straightforward to derive the further implications of this trade: According to the Stolper-Samuelson logic, the skill premium goes up, i.e. the factor price ratio w / r falls. As a consequence, the skill intensity in both industries falls as well. The Rybczynski relationship in the lower-right panel shifts to the right so as to reconcile the change in the output mix with the unchanged factor endowment.

The same apparatus can be used to analyze the rigid wage case.[19] The early literature on the implications of rigid wages in trade models has tended to stipulate some type of real wage rigidity.[20] However, in view of the ample evidence for rigid wage structures in continental Europe, the assumption of rigid *relative* wages appears more appropriate to our present purpose.

How does the entry of labor-abundant emerging economies affect a rigid North? If the factor price ratio w / r is not allowed to fall in the face of changing supply and demand conditions, the first immediate implication is that the relative price of the two goods cannot change either. That is, the Samuelson-Stolper theorem cuts both ways – as a mere corollary of profit maximization conditions, it does not require any assumption of flexible factor prices. The economic intuition behind this result is that, for any given c.r.s technology, a constant factor price ratio implies unchanged factor intensities and, therefore, unchanged factor productivities in both industries. Hence, producers face constant marginal costs and are ready to accommodate any demand changes along horizontal supply curves. A first conclusion immediately follows: The factor market rigidity, by suppressing the response of the goods prices, represents a free gift of the North to the South in the sense that the latter gets more favorable terms of trade than would be obtainable with flexible markets.

Under these circumstances, and again assuming open markets, the goods market equilibrium in the upper-right panel of figure 4 moves horizontally from A to B. It is evident from the figure that the rigidity of relative prices amplifies both the extent of structural change, i.e. the adjustment of the output mix F / M, and the volume of North-South trade. The latter is determined by the offer curve of the South, given the terms of trade implied by factor prices in the North. Assuming a normally sloped offer curve, the volume of trade is increasing in the relative price

---

19 The application of the HOS apparatus to the analysis of North-South trade when factor prices are rigid in the North was pioneered by Krugman (1995).

20 See, in particular, Brecher (1974a,b).

of the low-tech good. Also, being pushed by market forces to point B, producers in the North are obviously thrown off their flexible-price supply curve *RS*. This is tantamount to saying that the economy is pushed off its production possibilities frontier. In fact, due to the rigid factor prices, the structure of production does not adjust simply through sectoral reallocation of the factors, but also through adjustments in overall factor use. Instead of moving along its bowed out production possibilities frontier, the economy moves inside the frontier along a straight Rybczynski line (cf. Krugman (1995), Srinivasan (1995)).

Just as the factor price rigidity gives rise to a peculiar causal interpretation of the Stolper-Samuelson theorem, the Rybczynski theorem is put to some uncommon use in the present context: Normally seen as a statement about the effect of changing factor supplies on the sectoral structure of output, it serves here to highlight the repercussions of the trade-induced adjustment in the sectoral output mix on effective factor use. This effect is expressed in figure 4 by the movement from A to B along the "Ryb"-schedule in the lower-right panel. Because of the fixed factor price ratio, the position of this schedule is unchanged. As a consequence, the overall K / L-ratio of the economy must increase. If we assume that skilled labor is initially fully employed or, more generally, that its employment rate cannot be raised any further, the only way to achieve the required adjustment in K / L is by shedding unskilled labor. The change in K / L from *No* to *No'* thus indicates the amount of unemployment that arises among the unskilled. It is easy to see that the unemployment generated by North-South trade is directly proportional to the volume of that trade, and it is equally straightforward to show (though not immediately within the panels of figure 4) that the factor market distortion turns the potential mutual gains from trade into an absolute real income loss for the North.

As will become clear in the next section, there is considerable controversy about the empirical relevance and importance of these labor market effects of globalization, particularly in comparison to technical change. But regardless of how this controversy might eventually be resolved, there is a lesson in the above analysis that is more general than the specific shock at work: Whatever it is that causes the structure of labor demand to change, if relative wages are not allowed to reflect these changes, employment levels will have to carry the burden of adjustment.

There is also scope for disagreement about the relative importance of shocks to the structure of labor demand and shocks to the aggregate level of labor demand. For example, Blanchard (1997b) argues that changes in the composition of unemployment cannot be regarded as discriminating evidence in favor of relative labor demand shifts as opposed to aggregate labor demand shifts or wage-setting shocks. For various reasons – 'ladder' effects, 'ranking' effects, and so on –, even fully symmetric adverse shocks tend to increase unemployment among unskilled workers by much more than among the skilled. But again, there is a more general point worth making: Whatever it is that causes unemployment disproportionally to affect unskilled labor, the asymmetric incidence has important implications for the aggregate summary statistics that are typically used to describe labor market developments. In particular, as low-wage jobs are destroyed (or prevented from being created), the aggregate wage bill suffers less than the aggregate volume of employment. As a consequence, the aggregate real wage level, defined as the ratio of the aggregate wage bill and aggregate employment, rises along with the unemployment rate. Although no individual wage rate needs to have changed, the trade-off between the real wage level and the unemployment rate reappears as an aggregation phenomenon.

The model in figure 4 is well suited to illustrate the point. We only need to compare the two scenarios for the behavior of the North. With flexible wages, the Stolper-Samuelson theorem tells us that the emergence of the South raises the wage of skilled labor and lowers the wage of unskilled labor, not only relative to each other, but also in real terms. The aggregate real income of the two factors must rise due to the gains from trade while their employment rates remain unchanged. With rigid relative wages, both real wage rates are constant, but unskilled employment falls. Hence, per capita income must fall, but if the wage differential between the two types of labor is big enough, the average income per employed can easily rise by much more than it does in the flexible wage scenario.

The relevance of this phenomenon extends beyond the structural adjustments that the model of this section can capture. In particular, the employment prospects of the less-skilled does not just depend on what globalization and technological change do to high-tech and low-tech manufacturing industries, but also very much on the pace of job creation in the nontradables sector. Wage rigidities and regulations can have strong effects on the capacity of the service sector to expand so as to make up for job losses elsewhere in the economy. Clearly, this is an important part of the explanation for the employment growth differential between the United States and Europe.

It is a popular, though misleading caricature of the American 'employment miracle' to portray it as consisting mainly of low-wage, hamburger-flipping jobs. It is true, however, that the flexibility of the wage structure in the USA has facilitated the absorption of large numbers of low-skilled workers into the employment system[21] whereas in Europe, high minimum wages and rigid relative wages have kept the number of low-paying jobs low. Again, the macro statistics suggest that the rigidities buy higher average wages and productivity at the cost of lower employment (the trade-off notion of section 3). But again, this does not mean that existing jobs are necessarily better paid on average than they would be in the absence of the rigidities. All it means is that there are fewer poorly paid low-productivity jobs.

---

[21] Cf. Ochel (1998).

This interpretation of the role of the service sector as a potential 'employer of last resort' for unskilled labor is vividly illustrated by Gordon's (1997) comparison of French and US productivity growth in the 1979-92 period. In France, where the minimum wage was set as a high and rising fraction of average hourly compensation, output per hour grew with an annual rate of 2.55%, more than double as fast as in the USA where the minimum wage was a low and rapidly falling fraction of average hourly compensation. But remarkably, productivity growth hardly differed between the two countries in manufacturing: 2.85% in France as compared to 2.50% in the USA. The difference rather arises in the non-manufacturing, non-farm, non-mining sector (i.e. essentially in services and construction) where output per hour grew by a mere 0.63% p.a. in the USA, less than a third of the French rate. In the same vein, Corrado/Slifman (1999) demonstrate that aggregate productivity statistics for the USA are heavily colored by compositional effects, with measured (mismeasured?) construction and service sector productivities acting as a drag on the overall productivity performance in the 1977-1997 period.

5 Open Questions about the Impact of Globalization

The HOS model presented in the previous section has served as a point of reference for much of the debate on the impact of globalization. But the availability of a neat, well-known model does not mean that globalization is an important factor behind recent labor market developments, or if it is an important factor, it cannot be taken for granted that its effects make themselves felt mainly along the lines suggested by the model. The relevant literature is large and rapidly growing and this is not the place for a survey.[22] A few remarks shall suffice in this section.

Generally speaking, the literature has proceeded from simple judgements that were based on simple observations to more sophisticated approaches covering a wide array of transmission channels. Much attention has been attracted by disputes over methodology.

As an example of a simple observation cited as support for far-reaching claims about the impact of globalization, figure 5 shows a seemingly strong correlation between the decline in the share of manufacturing employment and the increase in manufactured imports from developing countries for a sample of advanced industrialized countries. This correlation was presented by Wood (1995, p. 63) as evidence that North-South trade hurts unskilled labor. To him, the cross-country evidence looks so strong as to "make it hard to believe that trade had only small

[22] Again, the reader is referred to the sources cited in footnote 1, above.

effects, for if this were so, the association would surely be disguised by other influences."

Figure 5: *Declining manufacturing employment and import penetration*

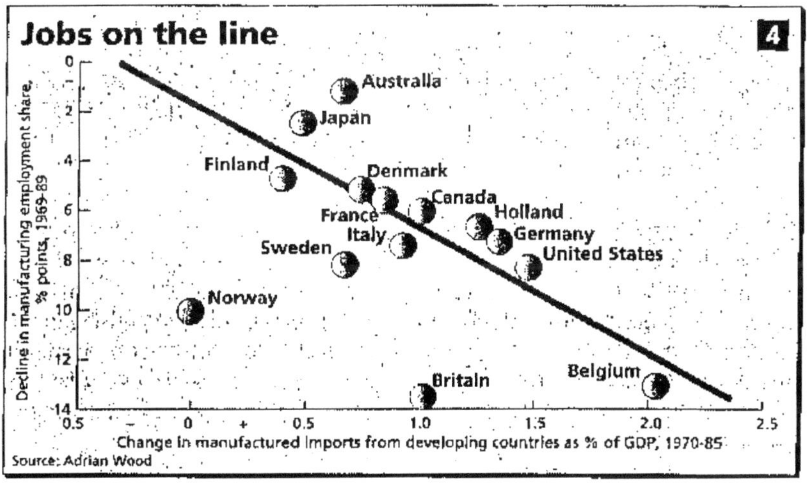

Source: The Economist, April 2, 1994

Apart from the fact that the absolute magnitudes along the horizontal axis are extremely small, such correlations always raise questions about causality. While it may be that trade is the forcing variable and manufacturing employment the effect, reverse causation is also possible as Wood himself acknowledges. The model of figure 4, above, can easily be used to show how this could happen. Suppose relative wages are rigid and the gap between skilled and unskilled wages is narrowed, say by a hike in the minimum wage. Obviously, this would force the production of the low-tech good to contract, its relative price to rise and, hence, import penetration to rise as well.

Wood dismisses the possibility of such reverse causation on the grounds that it would imply a positive cross-country correlation between import penetration and the relative wage of the unskilled, which he says is not what we observe. But even this clever argument does not really close the case. Suppose, for example, that there is non-neutral technical change, biased against unskilled labor. This would, by itself, tend to lower the relative wage of unskilled workers. If the political system leans against this tendency by increasing the minimum wage, however, we may well get a (mitigated) fall of the relative wage associated with increasing import penetration and falling employment. All of which only serves to illustrate the point that bivariate correlations are hard to interpret if various exogenous forces can vary at the same time.

The non-neutral technical change just mentioned is in fact the most-cited alternative to globalization as a cause of the deteriorating labor market position of unskilled workers. That it must be an important factor – in fact, a more important factor than globalization – has been argued by Krugman and Lawrence (1994) on the basis of yet another simple observation. If globalization caused the rising skill premium on the US labor market along the lines of the HOS model, the corollaries of the implied chain of transmission should also be observable. According to that model, as the relative price of skilled labor rises due to the forces of globalization, one should see the skill-intensity of production fall across industries as producers turn towards the factor which is getting cheaper. But in fact, the skill-intensity of production has strongly risen in the USA across the board, even in the nontradables sector, and in spite of the rising relative price of skilled labor. One is thus forced to conclude that factor demand functions have shifted for technological reasons. Whether the terms of trade have turned against import competing sectors as the HOS-globalization story would also imply, is a hotly disputed matter. The evidence on goods prices is hard to read because of numerous measurement problems.[23]

Apart from the obvious importance and likely non-neutrality of technological change, the most persuasive evidence against the globalization hypothesis is related to the volume of North-South trade which, despite its growth in recent years, is indeed very small compared to the size of the North – below 2% of the combined GDP of all industrial economies (cf. Krugman 1995). The significance of such figures has been questioned on the grounds that the relevant variable on which all further effects depend is relative prices, not volumes. But of course, from a general equilibrium perspective, even if it is as simple as the one in figure 4, above, prices and quantities are jointly determined by exogenous forces acting through supply or demand. And simulations of calibrated general equilibrium models such as those by Krugman (1995) and Cline (1997) find it hard to attribute a major part of observed wage and employment changes to globalization.

If there is anything like a conventional wisdom regarding the effects of globalization on wages and unemployment, it can thus be characterized as saying that globalization is an indisputable force which makes itself felt on the labor markets of the advanced industrial economies, but that it cannot account for more than a minor part of the shifts in the wage distribution or of the increase in unemployment. Slaughter and Swagel (1997) dare to put a summary figure on this

[23] On this issue, see the studies in Part II of the Collins (1998) volume.

conventional wisdom and speak of 10-20 percent of the changes in wages and income distribution in the advanced economies that are due to imports from developing countries. The impact on unemployment in the rigid European economies could be somewhat larger.[24]

It may nevertheless be too early to conclude with reasonable confidence that this conventional wisdom is correct. Research has begun increasingly to explore effects and mechanisms that are beyond the reach of the simple trade models which have largely dominated the literature so far. The findings do not all point the same way, but they open up new perspectives and lead to sometimes surprising insights. An interesting point in case is the trade in intermediates that has resulted from the fragmentation of the value chain as a consequence of low transportation costs and efficient information processing. Of course, such trade has long been recognized as an important aspect of globalization. The ease with which various parts of the production chain can be moved from one place to another introduces considerable instability into factor markets and increases the demands that are placed on the flexibility of workers and markets.

Apart from the volatility issue, however, the 'footloose' character of globalized production processes also suggests a different assessment of the relative labor market effects of trade and technology. Feenstra (1998), in particular, argues that existing studies could be seriously biased against the quantitative importance of trade by their neglect of trade in intermediates. The point is very simple: If outsourcing is most likely to affect the least skill-intensive activities, the average skill-intensity of production must rise regardless of changes in the skill-intensity of those activities that remain. Therefore, as Feenstra puts it, "globalization has an impact on employment and wages that is *observationally equivalent* to the changes induced by technological innovation."[25] This compositional effect is similar in spirit to the one invoked above to explain the US-European differential with respect to average productivity growth in the service sector.

The significance of Feenstra's point extends far beyond the specifics of quantifying the impact of globalization. What it does on a more fundamental level is to demonstrate the conceptual difficulty of trying to discriminate between technological shocks and globalization in the first place. Time and again, authors contributing to the debate on trade and wages have observed that technological

---

[24] Bhagwati (1998) sharply criticizes such estimates that result from averaging the available empirical studies since this procedure ignores "the fact that, in science, the average of good and bad is bad." His own estimate is an outlier in that he argues that globalization has actually favored labor-intensive manufacturing industries in the North.

[25] Feenstra (1998), p. 32 (italics in the original). The interdependence of technology and globalization that arises through the fragmentation of the production process is also emphasized by Burda/Dluhosch (1998) and Deardorff (1998).

innovations have fostered globalization and that globalization in turn facilitates the development and diffusion of new technologies. Nevertheless, the literature has gone on debating the relative importance of globalization and technology as if economists did not learn early in their careers that there are only two truly exogenous forces in economics: tastes and technology. In fact, as classical trade theory has always emphasized, trade is just another technology for turning resources into the goods consumers value most. It is indeed no accident that the effects of technological progress and expanding trade are similar in many respects and that they encounter much the same sort of resistance along the way.

6 Summary and Conclusion

This paper has considered three conventional wisdoms concerning the relationships between wages, unemployment and globalization:

1. It is widely believed that economies face a trade-off between real wage growth and unemployment. The United States, it appears, has opted for high employment growth and low real wage growth whereas most European countries, by the design of their labor market institutions and policies, have chosen the opposite. This view needs to be qualified: A high-wage policy cannot, in the long run, raise the productivity of jobs, but it can influence the composition of the jobs that are viable and thereby affect the aggregate picture.

2. Another conventional wisdom maintains that the shift of labor demand towards high skills has created a trade-off between wage inequality and unemployment. If labor markets are flexible (and if the demand shift dominates any shifts in relative supplies that may occur at the same time), the wage differential between skilled and unskilled labor widens, which is what happened on the US labor market. If relative wages are rigid, in contrast, which is largely the case in most continental European economies, the demand shift leads to an increase in unskilled unemployment. This proposition is built on theoretically more robust ground than the first. But this does not mean that relative demand shifts are the dominant force behind European unemployment, nor is the empirical picture quite as sharp as one might expect. The correlation between measures of relative wage rigidity and the unemployment rates of unskilled labor is somewhat fuzzy. This is not entirely surprising once it is recognized that skilled labor can be adversely affected even if labor demand shocks are biased against unskilled labor (cf. Burda/Dluhosch 1998), and that unskilled labor is disproportionately affected even by aggregate labor demand shocks (cf. Blanchard (1997b)).

3. A third proposition concerns the role of globalization. According to widely held views, often reinforced by the popular press and the infotainment industry, globalization is a major cause of labor market problems in general and of the deteriorating situation of the less-skilled in particular. Mainstream academic research does not support this view so far. The volume of North-South trade is simply too small for competitive pressures from low-wage imports to become a major cause of labor market disruptions in the North. Instead, non-neutral technological change is seen as the main driving force behind the structural changes on the demand side of the labor market. But it would certainly be premature to regard the issue as resolved. As channels of causation are considered that lie outside the focus of traditional HOS models of trade, the case for a major impact of globalization appears to grow stronger. On a more fundamental level, recent work questions the separability of technological change and globalization.

Globalization is not an entirely new phenomenon. Recent historical research has uncovered many parallels between today's globalized economy and the world economy of the late 19th century. Distributional effects were a serious concern then as much as today. According to Williamson (1998), they contributed to the backlash against globalization which eventually caused the world to drift away from its previous liberal international order. As we know today, the real threat to jobs, wages and economic prosperity did not originate from globalization, but from the backlash against it. That is why the current widespread obsession with globalization as a threat to jobs and wages is fundamentally misplaced. But for the very same reason, it must be taken seriously.

Of course, globalization also means that far-away events can sometimes have adverse effects on individuals, businesses and entire economies. The oil price shocks of the 1970s were a reminder of this obvious truth. They also exposed the labor market rigidities that are the subject of conventional wisdom No. 1, above. But at the same time, globalization is just one of the many forces that make for permanent structural change. And as Schumpeter has famously remarked, such change involves a fair amount of 'creative destruction', which includes the destruction of existing jobs. The challenge is to make sure that the destruction is in fact creative, i.e. that there are no impediments to the creation of new jobs. This is a general challenge to the design of the economic order and labor market institutions, not a challenge posed by globalization in particular.

Whether or not the forces that generate a trade-off between inequality and unemployment are the dominant causes of the European unemployment problem, they demonstrate how labor market institutions that are designed to protect the stakes of job holders reduce the adjustment capacity of the system as a whole and thereby reveal the essence of the underlying labor market malfunctioning. On the political level, therefore, the challenge is to redesign the social safety measures for the losers of the creative destruction process so as to minimize their interference with the allocation function of the labor market. There is no lack of promising ideas. But these are beyond the scope of this paper.[26]

---

[26] The issue of labor market policies is taken up by Berthold/Fehn (1999, contribution in this volume).

References

Bean, Ch. (1989), Capital Shortages and Persistent Unemployment, *Economic Policy* 8, 12-53.

Berthold, N. and R. Fehn (1999), Labor Market Policy in a Global Economy, *contribution in this volume*.

Bhagwati, J. (1998), Play it Again, Sam: A New Look at Trade and Wages, mimeo, Columbia University.

Blanchard, O. (1990), Unemployment: Getting the Questions Right – and Some of the Answers, in: Drèze, J. and Ch. Bean (eds.), Europe's Unemployment Problem, Cambridge, 66-89.

Blanchard, O. (1997a), The Medium Run, *Brookings Papers on Economic Activity* 2, 89-141.

Blanchard, O. (1997b), Macroeconomic and Policy Implications of Shifts in the Relative Demand for Skills, in: Snower, D. and G. de la Dehesa (eds.), Unemployment Policy, Cambridge, 282-290.

Brecher, R. (1974a), Optimal Commercial Policy for a Minimum-Wage Economy, *Journal of International Economics* 4, 139-149.

Brecher, R. (1974b), Minimum Wage Rates and the Pure Theory of International Trade, *Quarterly Journal of Economics* 88, 98-116.

Bruno, M. and J. Sachs (1985), Economics of Worldwide Stagflation, Cambridge.

Burda, M. (1988), Is There a Capital Shortage in Europe?, *Weltwirtschaftliches Archiv* 124, 38-57.

Burda, M. and B. Dluhosch (1998), Globalization and European Labor Markets, CEPR Discussion Paper No. 1992, London.

Burtless, G. et al. (1998), Globaphobia, Washington, D.C.

Caballero, R. and M. Hammour (1997), Jobless Growth: Appropriability, Factor Substitution, and Unemployment, NBER Working Paper 6221, Cambridge, Mass.

Cline, W. (1997), Trade and Income Distribution, Washington, D.C.

Collins, S. (1998), Imports, Exports, and the American Worker, Washington, D.C.

Corrado, C. and L. Slifman (1999), Decomposition of Productivity and Unit Costs, *American Economic Review* 89(2), P. a. P., 328-332.

Deardorff, A. (1998), Fragmentation in Simple Trade Models, mimeo, University of Michigan.

Drèze, J. and H. Sneesens (1997), Technological Development, Competition from Low-Wage Economies, and Low-Skilled Unemployment, in: Snower, D. and G. de la Dehesa (eds.), Unemployment Policy, Cambridge, 250-277.

Feenstra, R. (1998), Integration of Trade and Disintegration of Production in the Global Economy, *Journal of Economic Perspectives* 12(4), 31-50.

Freeman, R. and L. Katz (1995), Differences and Changes in Wage Structures, Chicago.

Gordon, R. J. (1997), Is There a Trade-Off Between Unemployment and Productivity Growth, in: Snower, D. and G. de la Dehesa (eds.), Unemployment Policy, Cambridge, 433-463.

Hesse, H. (1998), Comment on Landmann and Pflüger, in: Gahlen, B. et al. (eds.), Verteilungsprobleme der Gegenwart, Tübingen, 159-167.

IMF (1995), World Economic Outlook, May.

IMF (1997), World Economic Outlook, May.

Krugman, P. (1994), Past and Prospective Causes of High Unemployment, in: A Symposium Sponsored by The Federal Reserve Bank of Kansas City (ed.), Reducing Unemployment: Current Issues and Policy Options, Jackson Hole, 49-98.

Krugman, P. (1995), Growing World Trade: Causes and Consequences, *Brookings Papers on Economic Activity* 1, 327-362.

Krugman, P. and R. Lawrence (1994), Trade, Jobs and Wages, *Scientific American*, April, 44-49.

Landmann, O. and J. Jerger (1993), Unemployment and the Real Wage Gap: A Reappraisal of the German Experience, *Weltwirtschaftliches Archiv* 129, 689-717.

Landmann, O. and J. Jerger (1999), Beschäftigungstheorie, Heidelberg-Berlin.

Landmann, O. and M. Pflüger (1996), Arbeitsmärkte im Spannungsfeld von Globalisierung und technologischem Wandel, in: Külp, B. (ed.), Arbeitsmarkt und Arbeitslosigkeit, Freiburg, 173-230.

Landmann, O. and M. Pflüger (1998), Verteilungswirkungen der Globalisierung, in Gahlen, B. et al. (eds.), Verteilungsprobleme der Gegenwart, 127-157.

Lucas, R. E. (1988), On the Mechanics of Economic Development, *Journal of Monetary Economics* 22, 3-42.

Mankiw, N. G., D. Romer, and D. Weil (1992), A Contribution to the Empirics of Growth, *Quarterly Journal of Economics* 107, 407-437.

Malinvaud, E. (1977), The Theory of Unemployment Reconsidered, Oxford.

Nickell, S. and B. Bell (1995), The Collapse in Demand for the Unskilled and Unemployment Across the OECD, *Oxford Review of Economic Policy* 11, 40-62.

Ochel, W. (1998), Mehr Beschäftigung und weniger Arbeitslosigkeit – Amerika, hast du es besser?, *Mitteilungen aus der Arbeitsmarkt- und Berufsforschung* 2, 262-276.

Phelps, E. S. (1994), Structural Slumps, Cambridge.

Phelps, E. S. (1997), Quids in if you work, *Financial Times*, October 31.

Sachs, J. (1979), Wages, Profits, and Macroeconomic Activity: A Comparative Study, *Brookings Papers on Economic Activity* 2, 269-319.

Siebert, H. (1999), (ed.), Globalization and Labor, Tübingen.

Srinivasan, T.N. (1995), Comment on Krugman, *Brookings Papers on Economic Activity* 1, 368-373.

Slaughter, M. and Ph. Swagel (1997), The Effect of Globalization on Wages in the Advanced Economies, IMF Working Paper 97/43, Washington, D.C..

Williamson, J. (1998), Globalization, Labor Markets and Policy Backlash in the Past, *Journal of Economic Perspectives* 12(4), 51-72.

Wood, A. (1991), Give Heckscher and Ohlin a Chance!, *Weltwirtschaftliches Archiv* 127, 20-49.

Wood, A. (1995), How Trade Hurt Unskilled Workers, *Journal of Economic Perspectives* 9(3), 57-80.

World Bank (1997), Global Economic Prospects and the Developing Countries, Washington, D.C.

Comment on Landmann : "Wages, Unemployment, and Globalization: a Tale of Conventional Wisdoms"

Arne Heise

WSI, Hans-Böckler-Stiftung,
Bertha-von-Suttner-Platz 1, 40476 Düsseldorf, Germany

It always arouses my curiosity when a paper engages in a critical inquiry of 'conventional wisdoms'. In case the author succeeds - as Oliver Landmann does - in generating clear, distinct, yet surprising and provocating insights on a well founded analytical basis adhering to the traditional paradigm which creates the very conventional wisdom under discussion, my esteem is even bigger.

I want to divide my comment into two parts: first, I would like to repeat, reemphasize and comment on some of Landmann's arguments which I found most interesting. Secondly, I will discuss some issues - and, I am afraid, here I will raise questions rather than provide answers - which I believe have been left out of consideration by Landmann.

Landmann's Arguments

With only few, yet precise and convincing statements, Oliver Landmann rejects one of the most common misunderstandings in the ongoing discussion on employment policy issues: *there is no trade-off between the level of real wages and the level of employment*. In a long run general equilibrium, Landmann argues on the basis of traditional employment theory, given technology and capital costs determine the capital-labor ratio and, as a result, the real wage rate independent of the level of employment. The wage formation process, often regarded as being able to choose freely between higher wages or higher employment, simply does not serve the purpose to exogenously set real wages - the system would be over-determined. This insight seems to be a severe blow for all insider-outsider theorists who maintain that the trade union monopolist purposefully reduces the quantity (employment) in order to increase the price (real wages). They simply have no means to do so.

For a post-Keynesian such as me, the endogeneity of real wages is common knowledge - yet, I would be glad if this insight could become part of mainstream 'conventional wisdoms'. However, this is also the point where I have to part company with Landmann: he argues that the wage setting behavior is the main determinant of the level of employment and, hence, the optimal stock of capital. If the wage setters (i.e. the trade unions) are seriously taken as quantity adjustors (for the real wage is given), we have to answer the puzzling question of why they would choose a position lower than full employment? The answer suggested by Landmann - wage setters play a noncooperative game and they benefit from lags - seem rather clumsy to me: the first argument cannot hold in an economy with centralized or corporatist trade unions (such as the German), the second would be a short run version of the insider-outsider model - what trade unions cannot get in the long run they try to achieve in the short run. This does not sound convincing to me. From a theoretical point of view, the problem lies, of course, in the adaptation of the standard textbook model. In a post-Keynesian model, given technology and capital costs not only determine the capital-labor ratio, but also the desired capital stock (i.e. necessary investment outlays), income and, as a derivative, employment. Not only the real wage rate, but also the level of employment becomes an endogenous variable. The wage-setting process is left to determine the price level (in equilibrium). Now, unemployment can be better understood as an ordinary feature of decentralized market (or better: private ownership) economies (equilibirum unemployment) or a clash of wage (and, thus, price) setters and price watchers (the central bank). Of ourse, this is a completely different story from the one told by Landmann.

We do not have to dwell any longer on these differences as the process of globalization - the topic of this conference - anyway plays a more central role when it comes to wage differentiation instead of wage levels. The risks of globalization have been nicely described recently by Dani Rodrik (1998, p. 4): „In a fully integrated economy, wages would be set in Shenzen, the price of capital determined in New York, and tax rates legislated in the Cayman Islands.“ Herbert Giersch puts the idea more bluntly: „In the extreme, simple (i.e. un- or low skilled, A.H.) work cannot be paid higher in Germany than in the Czech Republic, in the long run not even better than on the Indian sub-continent“ (Giersch (1994, p. 158)); my own translation). The Heckscher-Ohlin-Samuelson model (HOS) and the Stolper-Samuelson theorem - both being put forward by Landmann at some length - provide the theoretical underpinning of such an uncomfortable outlook for the low skilled workers in all highly-developed economies. Both, the increasing qualificatory wage (and income) dispersion in the 'flexi economies' of Anglo-american style as well as growing unemployment in the more regulated economies of the 'Rheinisch model' in continental Europe (see Albert (1991)) seem to fit the predictions of the HOS-theory. Nevertheless, although not much can be put forward against the fundamental idea of HOS-theory and the Stopler-Samuelson theorem, crucial assumptions - such as the ignorance of transaction costs and uniform technological conditions in all trading economies - have raised serious criticism and its empirical relevance has been questioned (see Lindlar and Trabold (1998)). Landmann mentions most of such criticisms and questions to which I want to add a few: the stylized facts connecting high wage dispersion with low unemployment particularly among the low-skilled and a compressed wage schedule with high(er) unemployment did not meet with empirical support until the end of the 1980s - after more than a decade of growing globalization. Despite higher and quickly increasing wage dispersion, unemployment - particularly among the low-skilled - was high in the UK and the USA, despite a stable wage dispersion it was low(er) in the so-called 'Rheinisch capitalism' countries - e.g. Germany and France. At that time, there was no mention of an unemployment-inequality trade-off but labor economists where asking themselves whether the 'flexi economies' of Anglo-american style were caught in the 'worst of both worlds' as they got both: inequality and unemployment (see Blanchflower and Freeman (1994); Gregg (1997)). What happened during the 1990s which caused a breakthrough of the HOS world only that late? Or are there better explanations which need not resort to the process of globalization? Institutional change could be a first guess for an explanation of what happened to inequality, the willingness to conduct expansionary macroeconomic policy a first guess for an explanation of what happened to unemployment (see Heise (1998), Heise (1999)). For whatever reason - ongoing globalization or skill-biased technological progress -, there is no doubt that the demand for low skill labor has continually declined. Yet, so has the supply of low skills due to higher investment in human capital (see Heise (1996)). Therefore, the rise of low-skilled unemployment must not necessarily be the result of changing demand-supply-conditions on the labor market but may also be due to a process of selection on a labor market which knows unemployment as an equilibrium phenomenon.

Further Questions

The quantitative dimensions may be disputed, however, there is large scale agreement among the economic profession such that the HOS model can explain only a small fraction of cross-border transactions. But if this is true, one must be puzzled by the fact that - almost as a reflex - the HOS model is so commonly used for an explanation of a phenomenon to which it can contribute only marginally. The overwhelming part of international trade and capital transactions seems to be caused by completely different determinants - such as e.g. subjective non-availabilities or regional economies of scope - other than the relative scarcity of factors of production. In international business studies, the ecclectical OLI paradigm (see Dunning (1981)) serves as a good substitute - although less consistent than the HOS model. Using this foundation, or probably the model of Krugman and Venables (1995), in which transaction costs and regional economies of scale feature prominantly, enriched by new approaches to post-Keynesian currency theories (see Schelkle (1990), Lüken-Klaßen and Betz (1989)), globalization may be seen in a completely different light once tendencies to push certain economies to the periphery become apparent and can be explained convincingly. Under such circumstances, the idea of global welfare gains - the final result of HOS reasoning - becomes meaningless and distributional issues arise.

Additionally, I want to raise a point which has completely been neglected by Landmann: the impact of globalization on economic policy and, in particular, employment policy. I consider myself an economist who still believes in the possibility (and necessity) of policy intervention in order to stabilize an economy and, particularly, to safeguard full employment (or, to put it less ambitiously, to secure a high level of employment). Therefore I am most interested in what globalization does to the capability of economic policy. Quite regularly, the 'end of macro policies' is called for: in a global economy where national states are mere regions, it is argued, only micro or supply-side policies (*Standortpolitik*) hold. At a closer look, the 'end of macro policies' simply means a priority for price stability (monetary policy) and consolidation of public budgets (fiscal policy). Growing capital mobility - i.e. the credible 'exit-threat' - requires this type of policy - this seems to be common knowledge among economists from all different schools, yet there is disaggreement as to whether to applaud or bemoan this development.

In this context, I want to emphasize two aspects: after the emergence of the European Monetary Union (EMU) on the 1st of January 1999 and the creation of the new common currency EURO, the global financial markets face a completely new situation. For the first time since 1944, the US dollar is seriously challenged as hegemonial or key currency of the international currency hierarchy. To lead the pack gives some advantages: (1) the central bank issuing the hegemonial currency - the ECB or the US Fed - is the only one being able to conduct a monetary policy somewhat independently (and this is not only true in the case of a fixed exchange rate system; see Thomasberger (1993)). (2) Economic agents contract cross-border activities in national currency what renders them independent of currency volatility and allows the central bank to pursue a policy of 'benign neglect' more easily. The attempt of the US Fed to stay on top of the hierarchy and the attempt of the ECB to reach that very top may lead both actors into the classical situation of a 'prisoner's dilemma': uncoordinated behavior may lead to an overly restrictive monetary policy, yet the pareto-superior attempt of mutual cooperation may fail due to the opportunity of defection. Without a credible international currency coordination - i.e. a new international currency architecture - the global economy may well face a period of worldwide monetary restriction and - as a result of the so-called 'inconsistent trinity' - heavy currency volatility - both of which are detrimental to the stability of national economies and the employment situation (see Bergsten (1999)).

Finally, I should like to make some remarks to fiscal policy: globalization impacts as much on the revenue side of fiscal activities as on the expenditure side. Although new studies (see Obstfeld (1998)) question the high degree of mobility of financial capital (not to mention real capital, see de Ménil (1999)), growing pressure on national taxation of mobile factors of production - particularly capital - cannot be denied (see Rodrik (1997)). This is the case because we do not even need a credible 'exit option' as long as there are possibilities of shifting profits within multinational corporations to locations with lowest tax rates. Once the locational link between the creation and the declaration of profits is cut, 'tax dumping' becomes a serious threat and the counter-argument that corporations are willing to pay taxes as long as they are rewarded with an equivalent in public goods (e.g. infrastructure) no longer holds. In effect, there may be a shortage of public goods - e.g. infrastructure or social security and stability or both - or a tax burden on less mobile factors which is felt as unfair and may lead to mass tax evasion or a reduced sense of solidarity (or both). On the expenditure side, fiscal policy is ever more losing its effectiveness because of spill-over effects due to a growing integration of commodity markets or because of the growing capital mobility forcing national governments to pay risk premia in case of extreme public deficits. Although these problems seem to be more severe for small, open economies at the bottom of the currency hierarchy than for a big, closed economy at the top of the currency hierarchy, only international coordination can still achieve predictable outcomes. Due to the high degree of integration within the EU - particularly after EMU - international coordination of fiscal policies may be effectively restricted to coordination within the EU. And as the coordination of fiscal policies represents a 'Chicken Game' rather than a 'prisoner's dilemma', the outlook - at least on paper and particularly on the expenditure side- seems to be quite good.

Oliver Landmann rightly mentions the recent article by Jeffrey Williamson (1998), in which he points to the fact that growing inequality in the historical process of globalization at the beginning of this century led to political 'backlashes'. Although Williamson denies simple historical parallels because the effects of globalization today are minor compared to those at the turn of the century, we should be aware that inequality in the countries of the 'flexi' mode has long reached the magnitude of those earlier days ('Victorian times' in the case of the United Kingdom). This may not be due to the process of globalization, as we have argued, but as long as inequality is seen as the price for globalization by many economists and politicians alike and as long as the possible and necessary compensation of such a development comes under strain because of the very process of globalization, we still have reason to fear that 'globaphobia' (see Burtless et al. (1998)) will be rampant after all.

References

Albert, M. (1991), Capitalisme contre Capitalisme, Paris.

Bergsten, C.F. (1999), America and Europe: Clash of the Titans?, *Foreign Affairs March/April*, 21-34.

Blanchflower, D. and R. Freman (1993), Did the Thatcher Reforms Change British Labour Market Performance?, in: Barrell, R. (ed.), The UK Labour Market: Comparative Aspects and Institutional Developments, Cambridge, 51-92.

Burtless, G.T. et al. (1998), Globaphobia - Confronting Fears about Open Trade, Washington, D.C.

de Ménil, G. (1999), Real Capital Market Integration in the EU: How Far Has It Gone? What Will the Effect of the Euro Be?, *Economic Policy*, 167-189.

Dunning, J.H. (1981), International Production and the Multinational Enterprise, London.

Giersch, H. (1994), Die Industrie und das Beschäftigungssystem im weltweiten Strukturwandel, in: Alfred Herrhausen Gesellschaft für internationalen Dialog (ed.), Arbeit der Zukunft - Zukunft der Arbeit, Stuttgart, 151-178.

Gregg, P.(1997), Was geschah eigentlich auf dem britischen Arbeitsmarkt?, in: Heise, A. (ed.), Beschäftigungskrise in Europa - Erfahrungsaustausch für eine bessere Politik, Marburg, 53-84.

Heise, A. (1996), Ist die Massenarbeitslosigkeit Begleiterscheinung des Strukturwandels? *List Forum* 22, 196-205.

Heise, A. (1998), The Political Economy of Meritocracy - Unemployment, Globalisation and Inequality, WSI Discussion Paper 50, Düsseldorf.

Heise, A. (1999), Unemployment in Germany and Britain - A Question of Micro-Rigidities or Macro-Obstruction?, in: Filc, W. and C. Köhler (eds.), Macroeconomic Cause of Unemployment: Diagnosis and Policy Recommendations, Berlin, 245-269.

Krugman, P. and A. Venables (1995), Globalization and the Inequality of Nations, *Quarterly Journal of Economics* 90, 857-880.

Lindlar, L. and H. Trabold (1998), Globalisation, Unemployment and Social Inequality: A Farewell to Welfare?, *Konjunkturpolitik* 44, 1-30.

Lüken-Klaßen, W. and K. Betz (1989), Weltmarkt und Abhängigkeit, in: Riese, H. and H.-P. Spahn (eds.), Internationale Geldwirtschaft, Regensburg, 217-265.

Obstfeld, M. (1998), The Global Capital Market: Benefactor or Menace?, *Journal of Economic Perspectives* 12, 9-30.

Rodrik, D. (1997), Has Globalization Gone Too Far?, Washington, D.C.

Rodrik, D. (1998), Symposium on Globalization in Perspective: An Introduction, *Journal of Economic Perspectives* 12, 3-8.

Schelkle, W. (1990), Peripherisierung in Binnen- und Weltmarkt, in: H.-P. Spahn, (ed.), Wirtschaftspolitische Strategien, Regensburg, 284-304.

Thomasberger, C. (1993), Europäische Währungsintegration und globale Währungskonkurrenz, Tübingen.

Williamson, J. C. (1998), Globalization, Labor Market and Policy Backlash in the Past, *Journal of Economic Perspectives* 12, 51-72.

II. Effects of European Monetary Integration on Unemployment

Effects of European Monetary Integration on Unemployment: How Costly Was (Intra-European) Exchange Rate Variability?*

Ansgar Belke

University of Bochum,
Universitätsstr. 150, 44780 Bochum, Germany

Daniel Gros

Centre for European Policy Studies,
1, Place du Congrès, B-1000 Brussels, Belgium

1 Introduction: Why Care About Exchange Rate Variability?

Eliminating intra-European exchange rate variability is often portrayed as one major advantage of EMU (reducing it was already a goal of the creation of the EMS in 1979). But why should politicians and economists care about exchange rate variability? Up to now the answer has usually been that exchange rate variability discourages trade. Unfortunately, a large empirical literature on this issue has not been able to document a strong link between exchange rate variability and the volume of trade. However, we would argue that the absence of a strong impact of exchange rate variability on the volume of trade does not imply that there should be no link between exchange rate variability and (un-) employment and investment. This becomes clear once one asks the question: why would an increase in exchange rate volatility lead quickly to a lower volume (flow) of trade? The theoretical models that are used in this context start typically from the idea that in order to export one needs to sustain a sunk cost. This sunk cost is meant to represent the need to build up a distribution system in foreign

* Thanks for valuable comments to participants in the 1997 International Seminar on Macroeconomics (NBER inc. EEA) Gerzensee/Switzerland, in the IMF Staff Seminar August 1998, Washington/DC, in the 'Jahrestagung des Vereins für Socialpolitik', September 1998, Rostock, in seminars at the universities of Antwerp, Birmingham, Dresden, Essen, Frankfurt and Hamburg, and at the ZEI Bonn, the ZEW Mannheim and the Ifo-Institute, Munich.

markets. But within Europe most firms already have a very elaborate distribution network in all member countries. A German automobile manufacturer will typically not have to build up a new distribution system in order to increase sales in other European countries. Hence we would argue that certainly for intra-European trade (the focus of our empirical work) market access costs cannot be the main reason why exchange rate volatility should affect trade.

Of course, an increase in volatility will lead firms to discount future profits from exports more heavily (as often assumed in the literature and also in the model used by us, see below). But this implies only that firms will invest less in export- (or in general in trade-) oriented activities. This might depress future export (trade) volumes but firms will not necessarily export less in the short run just because exchange rate variability has increased. The long run response will be much more difficult to isolate in empirical work because there are other long run trends that influence trade volumes (e.g., reduction in transport costs, shifts in tastes, etc.) and because variability changes so much over time. Trade volumes today might be influenced by some average of the variability experienced over a number of years but this would be difficult to measure even with the annual data on volatility that is often used.

The recent experience with large exchange rate swings in Europe has once again shown that there is a lot of 'pricing to market' (Dornbusch (1987), and Krugman (1989); the CEC (1995) documents the more recent European data), i.e., firms keep local prices fixed even in the face of large exchange rate changes. This implies that quantities react little to exchange rates, but profits by much more. Firms just keep producing and export more or less the same amount, but their domestic currency earnings become variable whereas their domestic cost remain stable. Exchange rate variability can thus certainly influence the variability of profits. If firms react to an increase in exchange rate (and hence profit) variability in the first instance by reducing investment in trade related activities, one would expect little impact on trade flows in the short run, but, potentially at least, a significant short run impact on investment (as we find) and on (un-)employment because investment is an important component of demand. Moreover, in most continental European countries (and even in the UK until the 1980s) hiring workers represents also an investment in the sense that there are high costs to reversing this decision. This is an additional reason (independent of the demand effect) why exchange rate variability should affect (un-)employment. Moreover, if labor is *de facto* a semi-fixed factor of production, short run marginal costs of changing the volume of production must be very high. This fits well with the observed sluggishness of reaction of the volumes of trade to exchange rate changes mentioned above.[1] We would therefore argue that exchange rate

---

[1] If consumers have adjustment costs in switching between products one could also explain why arbitrage across markets does not take place instantaneously and hence why local currency prices react so little to exchange rate changes.

variability should have little impact on production and export sales in the short run.[2] Firms will typically be reluctant to engage new labor (which involves a heavy sunk cost in most European countries) if the variability of the exchange rate is high so that the probability that this labor will not be used after all is also high. The model in the next section formalizes these ideas.

Our emphasis is on intra-European exchange rates because only their variability could be suppressed by EMU. In principle we should have used only the exchange rates of the 10 currencies that merged in the euro in 1999. But this group is very heterogeneous. The Austrian schilling was for about twenty years already in a de-facto monetary union with the DM whereas the Portuguese escudo was not so long ago not fully convertible and the Portuguese economy was affected by the aftermath of a revolution. We therefore preferred to work with a more homogenous group of currencies, namely the seven that were for a long time members of the Exchange Rate Mechanism (ERM). This group comprises anyway over 90% of the euro-area. We therefore measured variability against the currencies of the seven other original members of the ERM: Germany, Benelux, Denmark, France, Ireland, Italy, and the Netherlands. The ERM countries also represent the most likely early candidates for membership in EMU. A further reason why these initial ERM countries constitute a useful sample is that when the EMS was created, politicians used to emphasize the gains from exchange rate stability. However, we also tested whether the variability of the dollar exchange rate had a similar influence (and found in general weaker results). In this paper we consider the influence of this measure of intra-European exchange rate variability on two key labor market indicators as well as one other indicator linked to popular explanations of the impact of financial volatility on the real sector (Dixit (1989), Aizenman, Marion (1996), Ramey, Ramey (1995)). The three indicators of the real sector we used were: i) (changes in) unemployment, ii) manufacturing employment growth, and iii) (growth of) investment.

The outline of the paper is as follows: section 2 presents a simple model of investment and uncertainty. It discusses a possible transmission channel that could account for a negative relationship between uncertainty and investment even if the increase in uncertainty is not permanent. The next parts of the paper contain the empirical results. Section 3.1 explains our measure of exchange rate variability. Section 3.2 then starts with the results by presenting some simple causality tests for all 12 EC members as of 1994. Section 4 checks whether these results are robust to some alternative explanations and to an alternative estimation procedure. It is tested in particular whether the results hold up in the presence of cyclical variables (e.g., GDP growth) that might have also an impact on exchange rate

---

[2] In a previous version of this paper we also investigated the impact of exchange rate variability on industrial production. We dropped this variable in the light of the arguments discussed here.

variability.[3] Section 5 concludes and discusses the implications of the results for the EMU debate.

2 Investment and Uncertainty: The Option Value of Waiting

The following crude model is designed to illustrate the basic idea underlying the 'option value of waiting' a la Dixit (1989)[4]. The model does not pretend to be close to reality. It was designed to convey the basic idea in a simple way. Moreover, we wanted to present a model that allows us to ask whether even a *temporary, short-run* increase in uncertainty can have a strong impact on investment.

Consider a set-up in which there are three periods. During the first two periods (called zero and one) a single investment project can be undertaken that will bear fruit during the following periods. If this project is undertaken during period zero, it yields a return during periods one and two. If it is undertaken during period one, it yields a return only during period two. The investment project starts with a unitary cost that is sunk and its return is uncertain because it depends on the exchange rate (e.g., because costs are in domestic currency but the price is determined by the exchange rate). The return to the investment in period one (i.e., if the set-up cost is undertaken during period zero) has a certain component, denoted by r, and a stochastic element, e, which is uniformly distributed between $+\sigma_1$ and $-\sigma_1$. An increase in σ_1 means an increase in uncertainty, or an increase in the mean preserving spread (σ_1 is the standard deviation). The return in period two has also a non-stochastic part, denoted by r_2, and it also depends on the exchange rate. The exchange rate is assumed to follow a random walk. The expected exchange rate for period two is therefore equal to the exchange rate realized during period one, denoted by e_1. But the uncertainty can persist, hence it is assumed that the exchange rate during period two is distributed uniformly around $e_1 + \sigma_2$ and $e_1 - \sigma_2$. As will become apparent soon the variability of the exchange rate during the second period has no influence on the result. The nonstochastic parts of the returns can differ for many reasons that are not essential to the model

---

[3] At the conference in Hagen we presented an additional section which summarizes the results from a cointegration application of recent Autoregressive Distributed Lag (ARDL) techniques to the German labor market, using a slightly different data set and definition of exchange rate variability, which confirms the results found in the preceding sections. For details see Belke (1998a).

[4] See also lecture two in Krugman (1989). We do not pretend to add substantially to the large literature on the real effects of uncertainty. The literature on the importance of uncertainty distinguishes between an output and an investment channel. See Aizenman, Marion (1996), Bernanke (1983), Kulatilaka, Kogut (1996), Pindyck (1991) and Ramey, Ramey (1995).

and the same applies to the variances.[5] The (unconditional) expected value of the return from the project, if it is undertaken in period zero, is therefore equal to:

(1) $E_0(I_0) = -1 + r_1 + r_2 > 0$, with $r_1, r_2 > 0$.

For simplicity discounting issues and risk aversion are not taken into account here (but see Belke, Gros (1998)) so that ad decisions can be based only on expected values (the same assumption is used also by Dixit (1989)). To make the problem non-trivial the expected return from investing must be nonnegative.

If the firm waits until period one, it keeps the option whether or not to invest. It will invest only if the exchange rate realized during period one (and hence expected for period two) is above a certain threshold level, or barrier, denoted by b. Given that an investment in period one yields a return only during period two, this barrier to make the investment just worthwhile is given by the condition that the expected period two return equals at least the set-up cost:

(2) $-1 + r_2 + b = 0$ or $b = 1 - r_2$.

The decision whether or not to wait will be based on the expected value of that strategy, which is given by:

(3) $E_0(I_1) = 0\,[(\sigma_1+b)/2\sigma_1] + [(\sigma_1-b)/2\sigma_1]\,[-1 + r_2 + (\sigma_1+b)/2]$,

where the first element is the probability that it will not be worthwhile to invest (in this case the return is zero). The second term represents the product of the probability that it will be worthwhile to invest (because the exchange rate is above the threshold) and the average expected value of the return under this outcome. Given condition (2) this can be rewritten as:

(4) $E_0(I_1) = (\sigma_1-b)\,[-b + (\sigma_1+b)/2] / 2\sigma_1$,

simplifying and collecting terms yields:

(5) $E_0(I_1) = (\sigma_1-b)^2 / 4\sigma_1$.

This is the key result since it implies that an increase in uncertainty *increases* the value of the waiting strategy. Formally this results from the fact that in this model σ_1 must exceed b (otherwise the exchange rate could never reach the threshold).

---

[5] An interesting aspect of this crude model is that it does not contain an often used assumption, namely that the uncertainty is resolved at the end of the first period. In reality uncertainty is usually not resolved, but persists. In a model with an infinite horizon this could imply that the same decision represents itself every period in the same way. EMU constitutes an exception to the rule that uncertainty just continues in the sense that the start of EMU should definitely eliminate uncertainties about the economic environment. In this sense, the start of EMU might boost investment.

Equation (5) is then an increasing function of σ_1. As σ_1 increases it becomes more likely that it is worthwhile to wait until more information is available about the expected return during period two. At that point the firm can avoid the losses that arise if the exchange rate is unfavourable by not investing. This option not to invest becomes *more valuable* with *more uncertainty*. The intuitive explanation is that waiting implies that the firm foregoes the expected return during period one, but it keeps the option not to invest which is valuable if the exchange rate turns out to be unfavourable. The higher the variance the higher the potential losses the firm can avoid and the higher the potential for a very favorable realization of the exchange rate, with consequently very high profits. The difference between the two expected returns is equal to:

(6) $E_0(I_1) - E_0(I_0) = (\sigma_1 - b)^2 / 4\sigma_1 - (r_1 - b).$

An increase in the expected return to period one (r_1) makes it obviously less likely that it will pay to wait. An interesting special case is that of $b = 0$ (the non-stochastic component of the second period return equals the set-up cost; in this case the unconditional expectation of the overall return to the project (if undertaken immediately) is equal to r_1). In this case expression (6) collapses to:

(7) $E_0(I_1) - E_0(I_0) = \sigma_1/4 - r_1.$

The standard deviation of the exchange rate (or rather of the impact of the exchange rate on the return) would have to be four times as large as the non-stochastic part of the return in period one to make waiting the better choice.

An important implication of the model is that *only the current*, short-term uncertainty c, has an impact on the decision to wait. Future uncertainty, represented here by σ_2, does not enter in the decision under risk neutrality. If one takes a fixed period, e.g., one year, the likelihood that investment will be postponed to the end of that period depends only on the uncertainty during that period and not on future uncertainty. This implies that *even short spikes* in uncertainty can have a strong impact on investment.

This crude model has abstracted from risk aversion. However, we would argue that the basic conclusion that even a temporary increase in uncertainty can make a postponement of investment optimal does not change is robust because a prolonged period of high uncertainty means that expected returns beyond the next period would be discounted more heavily. In Belke, Gros (1998) the model is extended to prove this point formally in the presence of risk aversion.

What does this little model show? We retain two conclusions: i) Even a *temporary* 'spike' in exchange rate variability can induce firms to wait with their investment. ii) The relationship between exchange rate variability and (unemployment should go partially *via investment demand*. A direct impact of exchange rate variability on employment can arise if one considers that the investment project (that is at the core of the simple model presented here) could also just stand for training a new shift in the use of existing machinery. Even if it were possible to fire these workers rapidly, the investment in training would still be lost if the firm does not decide to export after all. The sunk cost aspect of hiring a new group of workers would be even stronger if they could then not be fired. In this interpretation the model would imply that an increase in uncertainty, even if only in the short run, could have a direct and immediate impact on employment, that is independent of the channel via investment demand.[6]

Our model is not detailed enough to have implications in terms of persistence. A simplistic interpretation in which the set-up cost consists just of the construction of a factory would imply that a short term increase in exchange rate uncertainty should increase unemployment in the short run, but should not have long run effects. However, it has often been argued that in Europe there is hysteresis; i.e., even *temporary* shocks can have *permanent* effects on unemployment. One channel through which hysteresis can arise is that the human capital of workers that have been fired depreciates rapidly so that they will not be able to find a new job at the old wage because they will have become less productive (see, e.g., Blanchard, Diamond (1994)). If one interprets the set-up cost as relating to human capital, this view could also be compatible with the model presented here. Hence even in our set-up there could be *strong hysteresis* (Belke, Goecke (1994, 1998)). However, some readers might have a strong prior that temporary shocks cannot have permanent effects. We do not want to take a stance on this issue here because it is not central to our analysis. Moreover, the results we present below are compatible with both views.

3 Empirical Evidence

3.1 The Operational Definition of Exchange Rate Variability

The variability of the currency of each country is measured by taking for each year the standard deviation of the 12 month-to-month changes in the logarithm of its nominal exchange rate against the currencies of the 7 ERM countries mentioned above. We use *nominal* exchange rates although one could argue that real exchange rates are more important for trade and other real variables. However, as is well known, over a monthly horizon real and nominal exchange rate changes are

---

[6] Though our model is mainly micro-founded, it could be aggregated to the macro-level along the lines of the Belke, Goecke (1994) model of micro- and macro-hysteresis in employment. In that model, a short-term increase in exchange rate uncertainty would lead to an increase in the width of the micro- and the macro-hysteresis loop and, thus, to significant real effects of short-term spikes in uncertainty. See also Belke, Goecke (1998).

practically indistinguishable. The 7 standard deviations based on bilateral rates are then aggregated in one composite measure of exchange rate variability (denoted by "EXV" below) weighting them by the shares of these currencies in the ECU (as defined in 1994). These official ecu weight are supposed to approximate to the importance of these currencies in trade and finance and they should thus be close to the importance the private sector attaches to each currency. We prefer these fixed weights to weights in terms of GDP which one could have re-calculated every year because variable weights would have introduced by definition a link between the level of exchange rates and our measure of variability. One could then have objected to our results that they do not represent the impact of variability, but of the level of the exchange rate.

We prefer *to aggregate the individual standard deviations* instead of using the standard deviation of some average or effective exchange rate because there is extensive evidence that exporters price to market.[7] The effective exchange rate of the lire could remain constant because it depreciates against the DM, but appreciates against the French Franc. If these are two separate markets Italian firms will not be indifferent between a situation in which the effective rate is constant because the ITL/DM and the ITL/FF are constant, or because the swings in these two bilateral rates just happen to cancel each other out. Dollar volatility is defined simply as the standard deviation of the 12 changes in the logarithm of the national exchange rate against the US dollar.

We use *monthly* exchange rates to calculate volatility instead of daily volatility because the required data were easier to obtain on a consistent basis for the entire sample period and all the countries we looked at. Another reason to prefer this measure over more short-term alternatives (e.g., daily variability) was that we are convinced that while the latter might be important for financial actors it is less relevant for decisions whether *to export or to invest*, which have a longer time horizon. The drawback of this decision was that we had to use annual data in order to have a meaningful measure of variability. We thus had only about 20-25 observations for each country, but this turned out to be sufficient.

In principle one could have used option prices to extract implicit forward looking volatilities, but options prices are generally available only for the US dollar and sometimes against the DM, and even then only for limited periods. Hence it would not have been possible to construct a measure of intra-European volatility on a consistent basis using option prices. We used *actual* exchange rate changes instead of only unanticipated ones, but at the monthly horizon the anticipated change is

[7] See Burgess, Knetter (1996) and Dornbusch (1987). For ERM members exchange rate variability is calculated only against the 6 remaining ERM partners, for non-ERM members against 7 currencies.

usually close to zero given the small interest rate differentials in Europe.[8] Hence actual and unanticipated changes should give the same results (see also Bundesbank (1996), pp. 67 , Gros, Thygesen (1992), p. 102, and Peeters (1997), pp. 5). The average of intra-ERM exchange rate variability for Germany was 0.64 (percent per month), with a peak of 1.5 and a low value of 0.25. For the UK variability is much higher, with a peak of 3.9 (again percent per month) and an average of 2.25 (Belke, Gros (1998), Annex).

Estimates of the standardized spectral density of the variability measures for some countries are finite or a kind of borderline at the zero frequency and the results of unit root tests, both from the Dickey-Fuller and the Phillips-Perron type are sometimes borderline. We therefore felt justified to use *both levels and changes* of our variability measure. As additional tests on the basis of necessarily modified critical values show that these tests indicate stationarity as soon as structural breaks are implemented in the test equations (Perron (1989), Belke (1996)). Though it cannot take the place of a formal time series test, already a visual inspection of the variability series (Figures 1 and 2) reveals that variability is much higher in the seventies than in the following period. The results of stationarity tests (McKinnon (1991), Phillips, Perron (1988)) for exchange rate variability and all the other variables used below are available on request. We generally differenced the data until it was stationary. This led us to use the first difference in unemployment rates, the first difference in the index of manufacturing employment, and percentage changes in investment at constant prices.

[8] For Europe, an interest rate differential of 6% p.a. would already be large. This corresponds to an expected rate of depreciation of 0.5% per month. The latter is lower than the standard deviation actually observed.

Figure 1: *Nominal exchange rate variability against 8 ERM-currencies: examples*

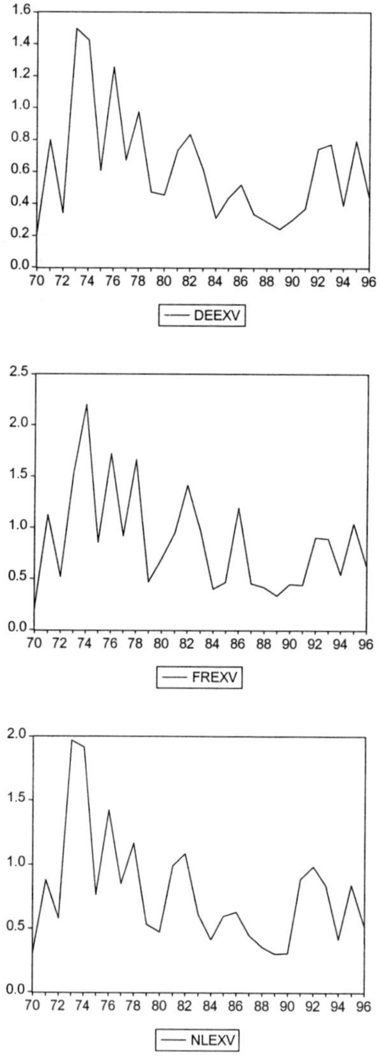

Note: ERM-8: Belgium, Denmark, France, Germany, Ireland, Italy, Netherlands. Variability is defined as the weighted sum of the standard deviation of changes in the logarithm of monthly nominal bilateral exchange rates (times 100). The weights are the implicit ECU-weights derived from average exchange rates 1991.

Source: International Financial Statistics, line ae (end-of-month).

Figure 2 : *Nominal exchange rate variability against the U.S. dollar: examples*

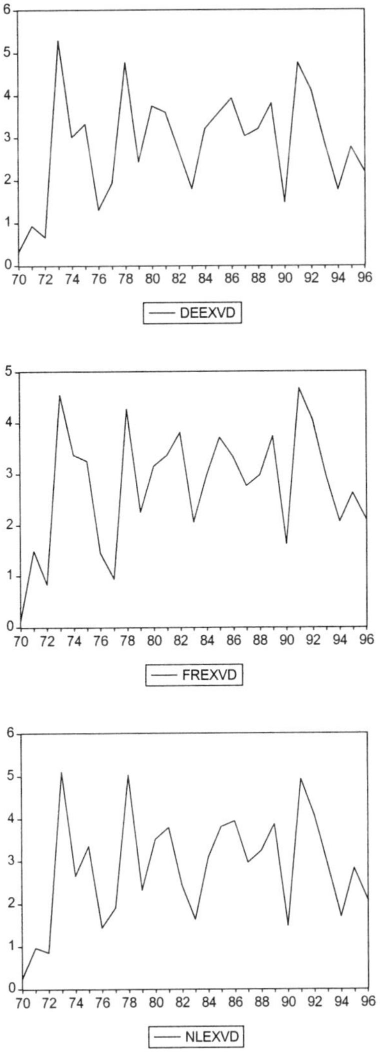

Note: Variability is defined as the weighted sum of the standard deviation of changes in the logarithm of monthly nominal bilateral exchange rates (times 100).

Source: International Financial Statistics, line ae (end-of-month).

In cases of doubt we always preferred *taking differences* since the disadvantages of differencing when it is not needed appear to us much less severe than those of failing to difference when it is appropriate. In the first case the worst outcome would be that the disturbances are moving average, but the estimators would still be consistent, whereas in the second case the usual properties of the OLS test statistics would be invalidated. Another reason for generally differencing was that this allows us to use the same approach for all countries. However, we generally repeated our test also in levels and found in most cases that the results were even stronger than the ones reported here for the first differences. All series were taken from the Ameco data set of the EC Commission.

3.2 Simple Tests: First Results

As a first step we present the results of some simple tests. The latter lead to a surprisingly unequivocal negative impact of our exchange rate variability measure on the three different variables for the real sector. We explain the first difference in unemployment rates, the first difference in the index of manufacturing employment and the percentage changes in investment at constant prices by their own past and lags of our measure of exchange rate variability. The results reported below in tables 1 and 2 are thus standard causality tests on the annual data used throughout this paper. The tables summarise results from bivariate VARs on annual data (1973-1996). The hypothesis tested is, as usual, that exchange rate variability does not have an influence on the three variables investigated here.[9] Table 1 shows the results using the level of exchange rate variability and table 2 the ones for the first difference in exchange rate variability.

The three variables mentioned at the head of each column are explained by their own past and lags of exchange rate variability. For each country the coefficient estimate, its significance level and the lag order of intra-ERM exchange rate variability are displayed in the tables. Only significant entries are tabulated. The numbers in parentheses correspond to the lag order of exchange rate variability. If the impact effect is for example estimated to be lagged two years, this might indicate inflexibilities in the respective national labor market. The expected sign of the (change in) exchange rate variability is positive for (the changes in) the unemployment rate and negative for (the changes in) manufacturing employment and investment (INV).

[9] We thus use VARs in first differences of the respective real variables. Since we classify all real variables as integrated of order one we feel justified to deviate from the usual specification of an Augmented Dickey-Fuller test (including a drift term) only by neglecting the (insignificant) lagged endogenous level variable. The significance of the coefficient estimates of the lags of the changes in the real variables and of the indicator of exchange rate variability can then be judged on the basis of the usual standard normal resp. the asymptotic values of the student-t-distribution. Cf. Haldrup (1990), 31 f.

The specification of the underlying equations is based on the usual diagnostics combined with the *Schwarz Bayesian Information Criterion (SCH)*. The latter is chosen as our primary model selection criterion since it asymptotically leads to the correct model choice (if the true model is among the models under investigation, Lütkepohl (1991)). The regression which reveals the lowest SCH-value and at the same time fulfills the usual diagnostic residual criteria is chosen. However, one important precondition for their application is the same number of observations for the alternative specifications (Banerjee et al. (1993, p. 286), Mills (1990, p. 139), Schwarz (1978)). The sample has been chosen to be 1973 to 1996 in order to exclude the Bretton Woods period of fixed exchange rates. The procedure is exactly the same for each country such that we never intervene to exercise a discretionary judgment. As usual, we add country specific dummies from time to time in order to account for possible breaks in the VAR relations. Significant dummies are added only if they are economically meaningful, if they improve the SCH statistics (higher informational contents even if a penalty for the extra dummy is taken into account) and lead to a non-rejection of the normality assumption of the residuals (Jarque, Bera (1987)). At the same time they should contribute to fulfill the criteria on the residuals, especially those on normality. However, none of our results is due to the implementation of these dummies.

Table 1 : *Level of exchange rate variability and the real sector (OLS)*

Country	*Change in Unemployment Rate*	*Change in Manufacturing Employment*	*Change in Investment*
BE	(0) 0.52*		
DK	(-1) 0.83**		
ES	(-1) 0.28*		
FR	(-1) 0.42**	(-1) -1.60***	(-1) -4.97***
			(-2) 5.71***
GR	(0) 0.10**	n.a.	(-1) -2.07**
	(-1) -0.10**		(-2) 1.74*
IR	(-2) 0.55***	(-1) 1.14**	(0) 2.95*
IT	(-2) 0.16*		
NL	(-1) 1.07***	(-1) -1.57**	(-1) -3.40**
PO	(-1) 0.14**	(0) -0.81**	
UK	(-2) 0.43**	(0) -1.08*	(0) -2.66*
WD	(-1) 0.67**	(-1) -3.33***	(0) -7.53***

The table summarizes results from bivariate VARs on annual data (1973-1996). The four variables mentioned at the head of each column are explained by their own past and lags of exchange rate variability. */**/*** indicates significance of the coefficient of exchange rate variability at α=0.1/0.05/0.01. Additional country-specific dummies were included when necessary. Numbers in parentheses correspond to the lag order of exchange rate variability. n.a.: not available. BE: Belgium; DK: Denmark; ES: Spain; FR: France; GR: Greece; IR: Ireland; IT: Italy; NL: Netherlands; PO: Portugal; UK: United Kingdom; WD: West Germany.

Table 2 : *Change in exchange rate variability and the real sector (OLS)*

Country	*Change in Unemployment Rate*	*Change in Manufacturing Employment*	*Change in Investment*
BE			
DK	(-1) 0.73**		
ES			
FR	(-1) 0.44***	(-1) -0.84*	(-1) -5.93***
GR	(-0) 0.10***		(-1) -1.91**
IR	(-2) 0.37*	(-1) 1.01*	
IT		(0) -0.46*	(-2) -1.28*
NL	(-2) 0.94***	(-2) -1.56***	(-1) -2.76*
PO	(-1) 0.12**	(0) -0.82**	(-2) -1.56*
UK			(0) -1.66*
WD	(-1) 0.56**	(-1) -1.99**	(0) -6.67*** (-1) -6.69***

For notes see table 1.

The results have to be read off the tables 1 and 2 as follows. With respect for example to the French case, a decrease of one percentage point in intra-ERM exchange rate variability leads to a decrease in the unemployment rate of 0.52 percentage points in the next year (impact effect). The first column of Table 1 contains a rather strong result: all 11 countries considered here show a statistically significant influence of (the level of) exchange rate variability on the unemployment rate. We are surprised to find that there are *more entries for the unemployment rate* than for manufacturing employment as can be seen by comparing columns one and two. This is not the case for changes in variability considered in Table 2. One possible explanation for this might be that the transmission of exchange rate variability effects to the labor market does not primarily work via the export channel.[10] Not surprisingly, there are fewer significant entries when we work with changes in exchange rate variability, but there is clear pattern across countries. Most countries show either no entry at all, or three or more. We are surprised to find that Belgium, the most open economy in our sample, has few significant entries, but this country is often a borderline case, moreover, a lot of the trade that appears in Belgium statistics is really transit trade and does not affect the Belgian economy. The positive coefficient of IREXV with respect to changes in investment (wrong sign) becomes clearly insignificant if one takes into account that there have been de facto fixed exchange rates to the British pound until 1979 and corrects the sample for this (1980-1996).[11]

[10] Correspondingly, Belke, Gros (1999) find that shocks to intra-EU export demand were less relevant for the EU labor market performance than previously expected.

[11] This is not valid for Ireland with respect to changes in growth of industrial production. With respect to changes in unemployment/employment the significance level shrinks from 0.99 to 0.95/0.95 to 0.90. The results are available on request.

We will comment only briefly on the impact coefficients because the longer run effects depend of course on whether one focuses on the level or the first difference of exchange rate variability and whether one considers temporary or permanent changes. The different implications of the two dynamic specifications that are admissible given the uncertainty about the stationarity of the exchange rate variability series can best be seen through *dynamic simulations*. We therefore perform three simulations with the estimated unemployment rate equations for West Germany:

I) The D(DEEXV) variable (first difference in the variability of the DM) is given the value 1 for 1975 and zero otherwise. This corresponds to a permanent shock to exchange rate variability. The result is a permanent increase in the unemployment rate whose size stabilizes quite rapidly.

II) The DEEXV variable (level of the variability of the DM) is given the value 1 for all the years from 1975 to the end of the sample; this represents a permanent shock as well. The result is that the unemployment rate now increases continuously. The long run implications of this specification are thus awkward from a theoretical, but not from an empirical perspective (a continuous increase in unemployment is indeed *the* stylized fact of the German labor-market in the last two and a half decades). The equation performs well in statistical terms because it is actually a good representation of the sample: exchange rate variability increases during the 1970s and the unemployment rate increases trendwise throughout the following decades.

III) The DEEXV (level of the variability of the DM) variable is again shocked, but this time giving it the value 1 only in 1975 (zero all other years). The result of this temporary shock is again a permanent increase in the unemployment rate. This permanent effect from a temporary shock could be understood as the implication of strong hysteresis (Belke, Goecke (1997)).

The level specification for exchange rate variability is thus acceptable for temporary shocks, but awkward for permanent shocks. Hence we would *emphasize* the results in *first differences* of exchange rate variability. Although they are somewhat weaker they still confirm that eliminating intra-European exchange rate variability could have substantial positive effects on its own. In the robustness test below we will also concentrate on the formulation in first differences.[12]

Regressions covering *the whole available* time span from 1960 to 1996 gave rather similar results. One justification for an inclusion of the Bretton Woods period might be that our indicator of exchange rate variability points to significant

---

[12] In order to convey a deeper impression of the order of magnitude of the regression results in Table 1 we give examples for West-Germany in Belke, Gros (1998), Annex 2 (Tables A4-A7).

spikes of volatility during that period. But these were usually discrete devaluations during a period that was otherwise characterized by stable rates. The chief value of tables 1 and 2 is that they give a broad brush visual impression of the importance of exchange rate variability for the four real variables considered here. Let us now turn to a more specific interpretation of the results, starting with a key policy variable.

i) Unemployment Rate

Since the unemployment rates of all countries in the sample have been found to be non-stationary, the analysis is performed using the changes ("D") in the unemployment rate ("UE"), called "DUE". The nature of the results can be seen by looking at one specific result, e.g. that for Germany. Our procedure based on the SCH criterion leads to the simple OLS regression of "DWDUE" on its own past (two lags, DWDUE(-1) and DWDUE(-2)) and the measure of the change in exchange rate variability during the previous year (DDEEXV(-1)) over the period 1973-96. According to these estimations, exchange rate variability had clearly a significant impact on unemployment in Germany. Given that only one lag of exchange rate variability turns out to be important, one can directly use the t-statistic on the coefficient for (the change in) exchange rate variability to check for the significance of the effect. The value of 2.19 is highly significant in the sense that the probability to find this effect if it does not exist in reality is lower than the usual α=0.05. The result is statistically significant. But is it also economically important? We would argue it is. The point estimate implies that a reduction in the variability measure "DEEXV" by one percentage point, i.e. DDEEXV=1, reduces unemployment after one year by 0.56 % (given a German workforce of about 30 million this amounts to about 168 thousand unemployed less).

If one wants to translate the result into an estimate of the gain from EMU one has to specify the counterfactual. We would argue that in the absence of EMU (intra-European) exchange rate variability could easily exceed the level of the early 1995 when EMU was already somewhat anticipated and the important FF/DM rate never moved much. (Despite this "DEEXV" was 0.8 (% per month) in 1995) Assuming as the counterfactual a jump in exchange rate variability of 1 percentage point, EMU could be said to reduce German unemployment on impact by about one half of one percentage point. Compared to the German unemployment rate of 9% reached in 1995, this is a small, but still non-negligible contribution. The effect would actually be somewhat stronger during the next period given the relatively high coefficient on the lag of the dependent variable. The simulation with this equation mentioned above show that the permanent gain in terms of the level of the unemployment rate for Germany would be around one percentage point.

We have concentrated on the results for Germany because it has often been argued that this country did not have an interest in EMU. But the results for most of the other EU countries are similar. The point estimates are actually somewhat higher for the Netherlands and Denmark and very similar for France. Portugal shows a much lower point estimate, but given that it had a much higher exchange rate variability its gain from EMU would also be large in economic terms.

ii) Employment in Manufacturing

A similar story emerges when one does the same test on the rate of employment growth in manufacturing (for West-Germany called D(EMPLMANWD)), defined as the first difference in the index of employment in manufacturing, i.e. roughly speaking the percentage change in the number of employed persons in manufacturing). For Germany our automatic procedure leads to the simple OLS regression of this variable on its own past and on the first difference of intra-ERM exchange rate volatility of the DM during the previous years.

Exchange rate variability had a significant impact on the German labor market from this angle as well (the t-statistic on DDEEXV(-1) is -2.20, implying that the likelihood of obtaining this result by chance is less than five in 100). The point estimate implies that eliminating the exchange rate variability of 1995, should increase, ceteris paribus, the rate of employment growth by about 1.99 percentage points (1.99*1.0). The estimate for manufacturing employment translates into an employment impact of EMU about two percentage points, assuming as the counterfactual a jump in exchange rate variability of again 1 percentage point. This would be equivalent to about 150 thousands of jobs in manufacturing gained (based on 7.5 million employed persons in the West German manufacturing sector as of 1995). This is very close to the impact on unemployment mentioned above, suggesting that most of the impact of exchange rate variability is in the tradables sector, as one would expect.[13]

The results for other countries show somewhat smaller impact multipliers, but are otherwise similar to the ones for Germany. The impact multipliers might appear to be rather small in some cases. But as the effects are permanent (no wonder given the well known persistence or hysteresis in West European (un-) employment, Belke, Goecke (1994)) the gain in present value terms is considerable.

---

13 Additional investigations reveal that the impact multiplier for manufacturing employment is nearly three times higher than that for the annual percentage change in the total occupied population. See also Belke (1998) and Gros (1996), p. 20. Given that manufacturing accounts for about a third of total employment this also suggests that most of the effect is in the tradable sector.

iii) Investment

Again, the results are similar (across countries) in the sense that countries that show an impact of exchange rate variability on employment or unemployment also show one for (the growth rate of) investment. Somewhat surprisingly two large countries (France and West Germany) show the largest coefficients. The point estimates for the coefficients on intra-ERM exchange rate volatility of -6.67*** (for the contemporary realization of DDEEXV) and -6.87*** for the one year lag of the same variable) mean that the elimination of 1995 exchange rate variability by EMU (the counterfactual again assumed to be a jump in intra-ERM-volatility of one percentage point) should boost investment in West Germany by between 6.5 to 7 percent. This would be equivalent to a demand shock of about 1.4 to 1.6 % of GDP. With a standard Okun coefficient of 3, this effect would be equivalent to a fall in unemployment of about 0.53 percentage points. This estimate is only slightly smaller than the direct impact on unemployment calculated above. Thus, our results are also consistent across equations.

The general impression one has from this rapid review of the first simple results is that it is difficult to maintain the hypothesis that there was no link between the levels and (also) the changes in exchange rate variability and the real variables we have looked at. All in all, the results of this section thus suggest that eliminating exchange rate variability could have substantial positive effects since it should reduce unemployment and increase employment in manufacturing and investment. We *emphasize* the results in *first differences* of exchange rate variability, although they are somewhat weaker they still confirm that eliminating intra-European exchange rate variability could have substantial positive effects on its own since it should reduce unemployment and increase industrial production and investment.

4 Robustness

4.1 Robustness I: The Impact of Potential Shock-Absorbers

The purpose of this section is to report the results of some tests for the robustness of the relationships found so far. We try to take into account the three most plausible ways in which exchange rate variability could stand for some other variable. For each hypothesis we then implement the same procedure based on the SCH criterion explained above. We do this only *for the first difference* in exchange rate variability since that variable gave the weaker results so far.

The three hypotheses we consider are:

i) Exchange rate variability was just a sign of a mis-alignment (i.e. a wrong level of the exchange rate)

ii) Exchange rate variability was just a sign of stress in the ERM caused by a tight German monetary policy.

iii) Exchange rate variability was just a sign of global uncertainty i.e. a proxy for dollar variability.

ad i) A first possible reason for the significant negative (positive) correlation of exchange rate variability with (un-) employment might be that this volatility just stands for misalignments of the real exchange rate. This aspect is often stressed for Germany (by German unions and industrialists). The basic argument is simple: the DM was strong when it was also variable. During the 1980s and early 1990s portfolio shifts out of the dollar went often into the DM whose ensuing strength caused tensions in the ERM (see Gros, Thygesen (1992)). This argument cannot be made with reference to the other ERM currencies because for them a variable exchange rate should have been associated with a weak currency which should favour exports. But it needs to be addressed because it represents a popular explanation for the results for Germany. In order to take this hypothesis into account we additionally implement the real effective exchange rate (REER) in the regressions displayed in table 2 for (economy-wide) unemployment and manufacturing employment. We do not repeat the procedure for industrial production and investment since we find so far that there is a close correspondence of the results concerning these latter two indicators and the first two. This leads to results shown in tables 3 (for unemployment) and 6 (for manufacturing employment). An unchanged positive (negative) sign of the change in intra-ERM exchange rate volatility (DEXV) and of the change in the real effective exchange rate (DREER) is expected in both tables under the hypothesis that variability is not just a proxy for the level.

Table 3 with the results for unemployment suggests that this alternative hypothesis might have some value for Germany as the significance level of the parameter for exchange rate variability falls. However, there seems to be just some collinearity as the parameter on the real exchange rate is not significant. For the other countries the addition of the exchange rate level did not affect the significance of the estimated effect of exchange rate variability on unemployment in a systematic way. The results with employment as the dependent variable in table 6 yield a similar picture for most countries, except Germany. In this case adding (the first difference) in the level of the exchange rate to the (first difference) of the indicator of exchange rate variability actually increases the statistical significance of the latter. Hence we would conclude that the argument that our results are just due to the fact that the DM was volatile when it was strong is not borne out by our investigations. It should go the other way for the other ERM countries and, except for one indicator for Germany, adding the level of the exchange rate does not have a discernible impact on the importance of exchange rate variability.

Table 3 : *Change in unemployment as a function of its own history, the change in intra-ERM exchange rate variability, and the change in the real exchange rate (OLS)*

Country	*Change in Unemployment Rate*	*Change in Intra-ERM Exchange Rate Variability*	*Change in Real Effective Exchange Rate*
BE	(-1)***	(0) 0.29 (↓)	(-1) 0.18
DK	(-1)***	(-1) 0.92*** (↑)	(-2) 0.07***
ES	(-1)***	(-1) 0.16 (↑)	(-1) 0.09* (-2) 0.07*
FR	(-1)*** (-2)	(-1) 0.44*** (→)	(0) 0.04**
GR	(-1)*** (-3)***	(0) 0.11*** (→)	(0) -0.01
IR	(-1)***	(-2) 0.44* (↓)	(-2) -0.04
IT		(-1) -0.02 (↓)	(-1) -0.03**
NL		(-2) 1.00*** (→)	(-3) 0.05*
PO	(-1)*** (-2)**	(-1) 0.12** (→)	(-1) -0.01
UK	(-1)***	(-2) 0.24* (↑)	(-1) 0.10***
WD	(-1)*** (-2)	(-1) 0.51* (↓)	(-2) 0.00

Notes: The table summarizes results from from trivariate VARs on annual data (1973-1996). The real variable mentioned at the head of this table is explained by its own past, lags of exchange rate variability and lags of an additional variable. */**/*** indicates significance at α=0.1/0.05/0.01. ↑ (↓) means that the coefficient of exchange rate variability becomes more (less) significant than in the respective equation without the additional regressor, here: the real effective exchange rate. Additional country-specific dummies were included when necessary. Numbers in parentheses refer to lags of variables at the head of columns. BE: Belgium; DK: Denmark; ES: Spain; FR: France; GR: Greece; IR: Ireland; IT: Italy; NL: Netherlands; PO: Portugal; UK: United Kingdom; WD: West Germany.

Table 4 : *Change in unemployment as a function of its own history, the change in intra-ERM exchange rate variability and monetary policy (OLS)*

Country	*Change in Unemployment Rate*	*Change in Intra-ERM Exchange Rate Variability*	*Monetary Policy (SPREAD)*
BE	(-1)***	(0) 0.37* (↑)	(-1) -0.11
DK	(-1)*	(-1) 0.68** (↓)	(-2) 0.06
ES	(-1)*** (-2)***	(0) 0.48* (↑)	(-2) 0.53**
FR	(-1)*** (-2)	(-1) 0.37** (↓)	(-1) -0.06
GR	n.a.	n.a.	n.a.
IR	(-1)***	(-1) -0.33**(↑)	(-1) -0.12*
IT	(-1)*	(-1) -0.08 (↑)	(-1) -0.10*
NL	(-1)*** (-2)***	(-2) 0.49*** (↓)	(-1) -0.18***
PO	n.a.	n.a.	n.a.
UK	(-1)*** (-2)**	(-1) -0.24*(↑)	(-1) -0.07
WD	(-1)* (-2)**	(-1) 0.60** (↑)	(-2) -0.15*

For notes see table 3.

Table 5 : *Change in unemployment as a function of its own history, the change in intra-ERM exchange rate variability and the change in $-exchange rate variability (OLS)*

Country	*Change in Unemployment Rate*	*Change in Intra-ERM Exchange Rate Variability*	*Change in $-Exchange Rate Variability*
BE	(-1)***	(0) 0.39* (↑)	(0) -0.05
DK	(-1)***	(-1) 0.86*** (↑)	(-3) 0.24***
ES	(-1)*** (-2)***	(-1) 0.13 (↑)	(-3) -0.35***
FR	(-1)*** (-2)*	(-1) 0.41*** (→)	(-2) 0.09*
GR	n.a.	n.a.	n.a.
IR	(-1)***	(-2) 0.35* (↓)	(0) 0.14
IT	(-1)	(-1) -0.15* (↑)	(-1) 0.11
NL	(-1)**	(-2) 0.62** (↓)	(-2) 0.16**
PO	(-1)*** (-2)*	(0) 0.02 (↓)	(-1) 0.14***
UK	(-1)*** (-2)***	(0) -0.20 (↑)	(0) 0.36**
WD	(-1)*** (-2)**	(-1) 0.74** (↑)	(0) 0.08

For notes see table 3.

Table 6 : *Change in employment as a function of its own history, the change in intra-ERM exchange rate variability and the change in the real exchange rate (OLS)*

Country	*Change in Manufacturing Employment*	*Change in Intra-ERM Exchange Rate Variability*	*Change in Real Effective Exchange Rate*
BE	(-1)***	(-2) 0.69 (↓)	(0) -0.04
DK	(-2)***	(-1) -0.89* (↑)	(0) 0.15***
ES		(0) -0.97** (↑)	(0) 0.49***
FR	(-1)***	(-1) -0.76* (↑)	(0) -0.12**
GR	n.a.	n.a.	n.a.
IR	(-1)**	(0) -1.02* (↑)	(-1) -0.22* (-2) -0.26**
IT	(-1)***	(0) -0.76** (↑)	(0) -0.21**
NL	(-1)***	(-2) -1.53*** (→)	(-1) -0.10
PO	(-1)***	(0) -0.67** (↓)	(-1) -0.12**
UK	(-1)***	(-1) 0.11 (↓)	(-1) 0.16
WD	(-1)*** (-2)***	(-1) -2.90*** (↑)	(-1) -0.05

For notes see table 3.

Table 7 : *Change in employment as a function of its own history,the change in intra-ERM exchange rate variability and monetary policy (OLS)*

Country	*Change in Manufacturing Employment*	*Change in Intra-ERM Exchange Rate Variability*	*Monetary Policy (SPREAD)*
BE	(-1)***	(0) 0.43 (↓)	(-1) 0.20
DK	(-2)***	(-1) -0.63 (↓)	(-2) -0.24*
ES	(-1)**	(-1) -2.05** (↑)	(-2) 0.63
FR	(-1)*** (-2)	(-1) -1.47** (↑) (-2) -0.97*	(-1) 0.44**
GR	n.a.	n.a.	n.a.
IR	(-1)*** (-2)	(0) -1.00* (↓)	(-1) 0.24
IT	(-1)***	(0) -0.62** (↑)	(-2) -0.28
NL	(-1)***	(-2) -1.65*** (→)	(-1) 0.53***
PO	n.a.	n.a.	n.a.
UK	(-1)***	(0) -0.39 (↑)	(-1) 0.31
WD	(-1)***	(-1) -1.61* (-2) -2.61*** (↑)	(-1) 0.66***

For notes see table 3.

Table 8 : *Change in employment as a function of its own history, the change in intra-ERM exchange rate variability and change in $-exchange rate variability (OLS)*

Country	*Change in Manufacturing Employment*	*Change in Intra-ERM Exchange Rate Variability*	*Change in $-Exchange Rate Variability*
BE	(-1)***	(-2) 1.01* (↑)	(-1) 0.17
DK	(-2)***	(-1) -1.31** (↑)	(-2) -0.13
ES	(-1)***	(-2) 0.63* (↑)	(0) -0.91***
FR	(-1)*** (-2)	(-1) -1.06** (↑)	(-1) 0.20
GR	n.a.	n.a.	n.a.
IR	(-1)**	(0) -0.53 (↓)	(0) -0.56
IT	(-1)*	(0) -0.57** (↑)	(-3) 0.14
NL	(-1)***	(-2) -2.99*** (→)	(0) 0.51***
PO	(-1)***	(0) -0.77*** (↑)	(-3) 0.50***
UK	(-1)***	(0) -0.36 (↑)	(-1) 0.29
WD	(-1)*** (-2)***	(-1) -3.08***(↑)	(-2) -0.24

For notes see table 3.

ad ii) A second argument can be made for the case of Germany, namely that exchange rate variability could be increased by the difficulties EMS-countries had often in following increases of short-term interest rates by the Bundesbank. Again this effect could not really appear for other countries, except if they followed German monetary policy. If they did so fully (e.g. Holland) then the DM exchange rate should be stable. The hypothesis is that a restrictive monetary policy leads to employment losses in the short-term, and that this is exclusively assigned to exchange rate variability in tables 1 and 2. However, this problem of identification can be reduced by explicitly adding a variable that indicates the tightness of the national monetary policy to the equation. We use the *spread* (long minus short term interest rates) as the main indicator. Adding only the short term rate to the equation leads to similar results. Again, this argument applies mainly to Germany, but it could also apply to the followers in the EMS. But we therefore check it for all countries in the sample.

The results for unemployment are shown in table 4. Here we expect an unchanged sign of the change in intra-ERM exchange rate volatility DEXV (if exchange rate variability does not just proxy and negative sign of the interest rate spread SPREAD (but this is secondary for us)). Revised estimations for (manufacturing) employment can be found in table 7 where an unchanged negative sign of the change in intra-ERM exchange rate volatility (DEXV) and positive sign of the spread (SPREAD) makes sense from a theoretical point of view. For Germany we find that the monetary policy variable does indeed have the expected sign in both tables, but this does not diminish the importance of exchange rate variability, which remain very high for both unemployment and employment. For most of the other countries the same applies: the spread is often important for (un-) employment, but the introduction of this additional variable does not have a systematic impact on the importance of exchange rate variability.

ad iii) Finally, a third argument is that EMS-dollar (or DEM/$) exchange rate volatility (Figure A2) influenced labor markets in EMS-countries either directly or indirectly via its influence on intra-ERM-volatility. This alternative hypothesis is more vague and could be put in the general idea that ERM volatility just represented general uncertainty in the world. As one cannot test such a vague hypothesis we prefer to check whether a concrete manifestation of this general idea could have influenced our results. The initial equations in table 2 are therefore augmented by the $-exchange rate variabilities D(EXVD). Results of the regressions that try to take this last argument into account are tabulated in tables 5 and 8 respectively. In this case we have some interest in the sign and significance of the additional variable. In contrast to tables 3,4 and 6,7 where we concentrate on any changes that might have occurred with respect to the exchange rate variability measure.

We find that dollar variability was in general less important than intra-European variability. To our surprise this is the case even for Germany. The coefficient on dollar variability is not significant and the coefficients on ERM variability are not affected. This suggests, contrary to what is often assumed, that there can be little collinearity between dollar and exchange rate variability. Spain (and to some extent Portugal) seems to represent the opposite of Germany: dollar variability is more important than intra-European variability. This is probably due to the fact that these two countries entered the ERM much later. In the case of the Netherlands the strong impact of dollar variability did not diminish the importance of intra-European variability and might be due to the importance of natural gas.

The broad result that emerges from the robustness tests of tables 3 to 8 is that the inclusion of additional variables does not really affect the role of exchange rate variability. There are about as many arrows pointing up (indicating that the inclusion of the control variable increases the significance of exchange rate variability) as there are arrows pointing down (indicating the opposite).

The results in tables 4 and 7 are corroborated by regressions using the change of the interest-rate spread (D(SPREAD)) instead of its level (SPREAD). This is motivated by the impression that the results of the unit root tests in some cases appear to be borderline though intuition and priors from economic theory tell us that the long- and the short-term interest rate should be cointegrated. The supplementary results are available on request.[14] We also find that the realization of the Schwarz-criterion could in most of the cases not be decreased by the inclusion of the different robustness indicators. I.e., the latter do not statistically contribute to an increasing fit after correcting for the gain reached solely by an increasing number of regressors. Moreover, intra-ERM exchange rate variability stays as significant as before or even becomes more significant.[15] A well-known prior -the significance of the interest rate spread in forecasting equations for real activity- is empirically accepted in an impressive manner. The sign is in most cases conforming to economic theory. But despite the inclusion of the important indicator of the stance of monetary policy the coefficient on exchange rate variability stays significant (wherever it was from the start).

4.2 Robustness II: Symmetric Shocks?

We have so far estimated all equations independently for each country. However, given that the business cycle is highly synchronized within the ERM countries the disturbance in the regression equation for one country should be correlated with the residuals other countries. In this case, the seemingly unrelated regression SUR estimator is more efficient, because it explicitly takes account of the entire matrix of correlations of all of the equations.[16]

---

[14] In addition, we complementarily conducted estimations including the *lowest* number of dummies necessary to fulfill the usual residual diagnostics. While ignoring the SCH-criterion in this case, which in our case recommendates the implementation of more highly significant dummies, the results nearly stay the same and are also available from the authors on request.

[15] Note, however, that there are a few ↑ which are accompanied by a change in sign. If the sign moves into the theoretically 'wrong' direction ↑ cannot be interpreted as evidence for our hypothesis.

[16] The SUR estimator minimizes the determinant of the covariance matrix of the disturbances. Each iteration of SUR reestimates the parameters after transforming the equations to remove the correlation across the residuals. We take only one iteration since the asymptotic statistical properties of these SURs are identical to iterating to convergence. Though the SUR method assumes nonstochastic regressors, the presence of lagged

Table 1a : *Level of exchange rate variability and the real sector (SUR)*

Country	*Change in Unemployment Rate*	*Change in Manufacturing Employment*	*Change in Investment*
BE	(0) 0.54***	(0) 0.95**	
DK	(-1) 0.97***	(-2) 1.09*	(-1) -5.71*
ES	(-1) 0.26***		(-2) 0.91*
FR	(-1) 0.41***	(-1) -1.15***	(-1) -5.49*** (-2) 5.16***
GR	(0) 0.11*** (-1) -0.08***	n.a.	(-1) -2.30*** (-2) 1.99***
IR	(-2) 0.39***	(-1) 1.05***	(0) 2.48**
IT		(-1) 0.56**	
NL	(-1) 1.07***	(-1) -1.39***	(-1) -2.36**
PO	(-1) 0.12***	(0) -0.52*	
UK	(-2) 0.36***	(0) -1.28***	(0) -2.99***
WD	(-1) 0.56***	(-1) -3.21***	(0) -8.21***

The table summarizes results from seemingly unrelated regressions on annual data (1973-1996); */**/*** indicates significance at α=0.1/0.05/0.01. Specification of the equations as in Table 1. Lag order of exchange rate variability in brackets. n.a.: not available.

Table 2a : *Change in exchange rate variability and the real sector (SUR)*

Country	*Change in Unemployment Rate*	*Change in Manufacturing Employment*	*Change in Investment*
BE	(0) 0.37***	(-2) 0.94***	(-1) -1.82*
DK	(-1) 0.87***		
ES		(-2) 0.67**	(-2) -0.94**
FR	(-1) 0.26***	(-1) -0.64**	(-1) -5.74***
GR	(-0) 0.11***	n.a.	(-1) -1.98***
IR	(-2) 0.24**	(-1) 0.66*	
IT	(-1) -0.16**	(0) -0.41**	(-1) -0.70* (-2) -1.30***
NL	(-2) 0.84***	(-2) -1.46***	(-1) -2.68**
PO	(-1) 0.11***	(0) -0.64***	(-2) -1.84***
UK			(0) -1.08**
WD	(-1) 0.57***	(-1) -1.80***	(0) -6.20*** (-1) -6.61***

For notes see table 1.

dependent variables creates no problem, if the residuals in each equation satisfy the classical assumptions. The reason is that in this case the asymptotic properties of the two-stage Aitken estimator are not affected (Kmenta (1990), Pindyck, Rubinfeld (1991), Zellner (1962)). The correct specification with respect to the residuals has been tested among others on the basis of the Breusch-Godfrey LM-test for residual correlation (instead of the DW-test!) and could not be rejected for every regression.

As tables la and 2a reveal, using a SUR system instead of single equation OLS did affect the results. The gain in efficiency shows up in the fact that (compared to single equation OLS) there are now even *more* significant relationships. At the same time, the significance level increases noticeably on average with respect to all real variables. The model outlined in section 2 implies that even temporary spikes in exchange rate variability can have a strong impact on (un-) employment and investment. This impact might even be stronger in the case of a *temporary* increase in uncertainty than in cases of a persistent increase. But the prior of most readers is likely to be that only a permanent rather than a temporary change in exchange rate variability can permanently affect (un-) employment or investment. We will therefore focus our further interpretation on table 2a.

In the case of investment all countries, except Denmark and Ireland, show a significant impact with the expected sign. Similarly, for the unemployment variable we find a significant relationship in 9 out of 11 countries. For employment we are able to identify 8 out of 10 countries in that respect. But this time there are a few (instead of one for Ireland in the OLS case) wrong signs for Belgium, Ireland and Spain. Seen on the whole, however, the results corroborate our findings shown in tables 1 and 2.[17] The strong results for investment (all coefficients of the correct sign, most significant at the 0.05 level) confirms that at least part of the influence of exchange rate volatility came via this channel.

We performed the same robustness tests as in tables 3 to 8 using the SUR method (see Belke, Gros (1998), Annex 5). We find, as in tables la and 2a, that after accounting for a common European element the results become even stronger. In all tables except one we find that exchange rate variability enters almost always significantly. For employment there is now, however, one country (Belgium) that shows consistently a wrong sign. Using SUR more countries show a significant impact of dollar volatility (with the right sign except one case) and the real exchange rate becomes also significant; albeit sometimes with an unexpected sign.

4.3 Robustness III: Simultaneity of Regressors and the Missing Variable Problem

Among the many possible objections against the simple test results presented so far is the argument that (un-) employment could have an impact on exchange rate variability or that the two are caused by a missing third variable. In Belke, Gros

[17] We find significant results both for 'soft-currency' and 'hard-currency' countries. One initial interpretation of our results has been that they are spurious because tensions in foreign exchange markets tended to come during the ERM period when prolonged periods of tranquility (i.e. without realignments) led to large misalignments of real exchange rates because inflation did not converge. We do not agree with this interpretation, which should lead to opposite results for 'hard' and 'soft' currency countries. Moreover, we show below that including the level of the real exchange rate does not affect our results.

(1998) we tried several candidates for the missing variable, including interest rates, variability of the dollar exchange rate and others, but the inclusion of these additional variables did not affect the results concerning (intra-ERM) exchange rate variability. We also tried to apply a TSLS-procedure to get around the simultaneity problem. Unfortunately, all efforts in this direction (including various measures of export demand used in Belke, Gros (1999)) were impeded by our inability to find a suitable instrument for exchange rate variability. None of the instruments we tried (inter alla current accounts, U.S. short- and long-term interest rates) did work to get significant and plausible results. In other words, there is no reason to interpret the latter series as endogenous. Moreover, exchange rate variability in most cases does not influence real variables contemporaneously but with a lag. From this point of view, reverse causation is less plausible as mirrored at least for Germany, France, the Netherlands and Greece by additional pairwise Granger causality tests displayed in table 9.

Table 9 : *Exchange rate variability and the real sector: pairwise Granger-causality tests*

a) *Impact of the level of intra-ERM exchange rate variability on the real sector*

EXV→DUE	EXV→D(EMPLMAN)	EXV→D(INDPROD)	EXV→D(INV)
FR*, WD*	FR*, GR***, NL***, WD***	FR***, GR**, NL*, WD*	FR***, GR***

Note: The table summarizes results from bivariate Granger-causality tests. It displays countries for which H0: D(real variable) does not cause EXV cannot be rejected but at the same time H0: EXV does not cause D(real variable) can be rejected. */**/*** indicates significance at a=0.1/0.05/0.01. Sample is 1973-1996, 2 lags in test equations. FR: France; GR: Greece; NL: Netherlands; WD: West Germany.

b) *Impact of the change in intra-ERM exchange rate variability on the real sector*

DEXV→DUE	DEXVD→(EMPLMAN)	DEXV→D(INDPROD)	DEXV→D(INV)
WD*	FR*, NL*, WD***	FR***, GR***, NL**, WD**	FR***, GR***, PO**

Note: The table summarizes results from bivariate Granger-causality tests. It displays countries for which H0: D(real variable) does not cause DEXV cannot be rejected but at the same time H0: DEXV does not cause D(real variable) can be rejected. */**/*** indicates significance at a=0.1/0.05/0.01. Sample is 1973-1996, 2 lags in test equations. FR: France; GR: Greece; NL: Netherlands; PO: Portugal; WD: West Germany.

c) *Impact of the level of intra-ERM exchange rate variability on the real sector*

DUE→EXV	D(EMPLMAN)→EXV	D(INDPROD)→EXV	D(INV)→EXV
BE***, PO**, UK*	BE**	ES**, PO**	BE**, PO*

Note: The table summarizes results from bivariate Granger-causality tests. It displays countries for which H0: D(real variable) does not cause EXV can be rejected but at the same time H0: EXV does not cause D(real variable) cannot be rejected. */**/*** indicates significance at a=0.1/0.05/0.01. Sample is 1973-1996, 2 lags in test equations. BE: Belgium; ES: Spain; PO: Portugal; UK: United Kingdom.

d) *Impact of the change in intra-ERM exchange rate variability on the real sector*

DUE→DEXV	D(EMPLMAN)→DEXV	D(INDPROD)→DEXV	D(INV)→DEXV
BE**, IT**	BE*	ES**, PO**	BE**

Note: The table summarizes results from bivariate Granger-causality tests. It displays countries for which H0: D(real variable) does not cause DEXV can be rejected but at the same time H0: DEXV does not cause D(real variable) cannot be rejected. */**/*** indicates significance at a=0.1/0.05/0.01. Sample is 1973-1996, 2 lags in test equations. BE: Belgium; ES: Spain; IT: Italy; PO: Portugal.

We are skeptical in general about the possibility that exchange rate variability at our high frequency was caused by *slow moving* variables such as labor market rigidities or unemployment. Indeed, all our attempts to use a two-stage procedure failed because we were not able to find satisfactory instruments for exchange rate variability. Most of the fundamentals in question, with the possible exception of monetary policy, are much less variable in the short run. A further argument validating our proceedings and our results is that of Canzoneri, Valles and Vinals (1996) who show that intra-EU exchange rates reacted mainly to *financial* shocks rather than real fundamentals. Rose (1995) and Flood and Rose (1995) also emphasize that exchange rate volatility is apparently to a large extent noise (as opposed to being caused by fundamental variability). It does not make much sense to treat a noise series as endogenous. Finally, in an earlier version of this paper we were not able to reject the hypothesis of (weak) *exogeneity* of our proxy for intra-ERM exchange rate variability in a cointegration framework.

Moreover, variability is a key element of an asset price, i.e., the price of currency options. If it were possible to forecast variability one could forecast option prices. Could exchange rate variability be caused by shocks? This is also rather unlikely since it has been difficult in general to document any link between exchange rate volatility and fundamentals.[18] Furthermore, it is a priori unlikely that the kind of shock that requires a substantial exchange rate adjustment (a fall in export demand) occurs with a monthly frequency. We would therefore agree that 'relative velocity shifts, misguided national monetary policy innovations, time varying risk premia and speculative currency attacks ... would go away once a monetary union is formed',[19] thus, allowing a reduction in exchange rate variability without more offsetting variability in other areas.

However, one might argue that the issue of reverse causation (from real variables to exchange rate variability) addressed in our additional Granger-Causality tests appears to be less of a problem than the possibility that exchange rate volatility might itself be affected by the additional regressors mentioned above. The literature on exchange rate volatility being caused by financial shocks provides support on the first count, but does not mean that these financial shocks could not have an impact on employment rather than exchange rate volatility itself. To check for robustness we therefore applied pairwise Granger-Causality tests to intra-ERM exchange rate volatility and the additional explanatory variables. Otherwise, the regression results presented might risk being spurious. That is, we checked the potential correlation of the change in intra-ERM exchange rate variability with the changes in the real effective exchange rate, the interest rate spread and the change in the $-exchange rate variability. Table 10 displays the results of pairwise tests (2 Lags, Sample 1973-1996) for five pairs (11 tests each). The tables have to be interpreted along the lines already described for Tab. 9.

Table 10 : *Exchange rate variability and additional regressors: pairwise Granger-causality tests*

a) *Change in intra-ERM exchange rate variability and the change in the real exchange rate*

DEXV→DREER	DREER→DEXV
ES*, UK borderline	PO***, UK borderline

b) *Change in intra-ERM Exchange rate variability and the interest rate spread*

DEXV→SPREAD	SPREAD→DEXV
/	/

18 Cf. Canzoneri, Vallés and Viñals (1996), 2 ff. and 11 ff., Gros (1996a), 14, Mélitz (1995), 496, and Rose (1994).

19 Canzoneri, Vallés and Viñals (1996), 3.

c) *Change in intra-ERM exchange rate variability and the $-exchange rate-variability*

DEXV→DEXVD	DEXVD→DEXV
IR borderline, UK***	/

d) *Change in intra-ERM exchange rate variability and the change in the real short-term interest rate*

DEXV→D(INTSR)	D(INTSR)→DEXV
BE**, FR**	/

e) *Change in intra-ERM exchange rate variability and the growth in real GDP*

DEXV→DGDP	DGDP→DEXV
FR*, GR*,IT*, WD**	BE*

Taken on the whole, table 10 clearly conveys the impression that our regression results are not spurious. In only two cases (out of 55) is one forced to reject the hypothesis that one of the five chosen variables does not influence intra-ERM exchange rate variability. For Belgium the rejection is only marginal (α=10%), for Portugal the extreme macroeconomic instability following the revolution might be one reason. Another mechanism that might have operated is that the exchange rate was kept constant for some time despite very high inflation rates. Strong capital controls allowed the government to delay the necessary adjustment. Thus, the hypothesis that intra-ERM exchange rate variability represents a factor of uncertainty on its own, i.e. is to a certain extent (strongly) exogenous, is not rejected by the data for the broad majority of EU countries and five (!) different potentially variability driving variables. The evidence is only slightly different with respect to the null hypothesis that intra-ERM exchange rate variability does not influence one of the five variables considered here. The latter is rejected in only 4 out of 55 cases at the five percent level. Moreover, the fact that exchange rate variability also influences real GDP growth is compatible with our theoretical model, but we show in this paper that there is also a direct channel through which exchange rate variability influences (un-) employment.

There is an additional reason why the role of missing variables should be studied in more detail. The results of the introductory regressions shown in Tab. 1, la and 2, 2a refer to bivariate VARs. However, it is well known in the literature that inference from such VARs is tricky, and that adding more variables can often dramatically change the results. This appears to be particularly important as the variables chosen are more or less cyclical, and *no additional* cyclical variables were included in the VARs so far. We therefore checked whether the results are robust to adding the *growth in real GDP* (and the change in the real short-term interest rate) to the VARs.[20] For this purpose, we extended the pairwise Granger causality tests to both time series again without any indication of spurious results (see table 10). In addition, we used OLS and a SUR system to check whether the results of tables 1 and 2 (resp. 1 a, 2a) are robust to the inclusion of the growth variable.

Unemployment is a typical cyclical variable whereas exchange rate variability is not. This already suggests that the link between these two is not the typical spurious correlation between two cyclical variables. Moreover, introducing GDP growth besides exchange rate variability implies that the RHS contains the most important contemporaneous determinant of unemployment. This greatly reduces the likelihood of finding any impact of exchange rate variability as a large part of the variability of unemployment is already explained by GDP growth. Moreover, any spurious correlation which could arise if there were any variables that influence at the same time aggregate demand and exchange rate variability would also be eliminated. For example, if higher interest rates were associated with higher exchange rate variability (although there is little statistical evidence for this as mentioned above) our results could be due to the negative impact of interest rates on demand. Conversely, if exchange rate variability had an impact on demand and thus GDP growth, for example, through its impact on investment demand as suggested by our other results, the equations including GDP growth would actually under-estimate the importance of exchange rate variability.

We finish our robustness tests by displaying the results from bivariate regressions (specified again according to tables 1 and 2, 1a and 2a respectively) augmented by the growth in real GDP.[21]

---

[20] In Belke, Gros (1998) we do the following extensive regression analysis also with the *change in the short-term real interest rate*, which could be viewed as a potential shock-absorber or perhaps even a determinant of exchange rate variability. But introducing this variable in the regressions did not affect the results concerning exchange rate variability.

[21] Corresponding regressions for *levels* of exchange rate variability and the growth in real GDP in (un-) employment equations can be found in Annex 3 in Belke, Gros (1998).

Table 11 : *Change in unemployment as a function of its own history, the change in intra-ERM exchange rate variability and the growth in real GDP (OLS)*

Country	*Change in Unemployment*	*Change in Intra-ERM Exchange Rate Variability*	*Growth in Real GDP (DGDP)*
BE	(-1)***	(0) 0.47** (↑)	(0) -0.24***
DK	(-1)***	(0) 0.39** (→)	(0) -0.57***
ES	(-1)**	(-1) 0.31** (↑)	(0) -0.48***
FR	(-1)***	(-1) 0.20* (↓)	(0) -0.19***
GR	(-1)*** (-3)**	(0) 0.09*** (→)	(0) -0.04*
IR	(-1)***	(-2) 0.40** (↑)	(0) -0.17*
IT	(-1)**	(-1) 0.07 (→)	(0) -0.09** (-1) -0.08**
NL	(-1)**	(-2) 0.63*** (→)	(0) -0.23**
PO	(-1)***	(-1) 0.12** (→)	(-1) -0.08***
UK	(-1)***	(0) 0.48*** (↑)	(0) -0.38***
WD	(-1)***	(0) 0.50*** (-1) 0.33** (↑)	(0) -0.26***

For notes see tables 2 and 3.

Table 12 : *Change in employment as a function of its own history, the change in intra-ERM exchange rate variability and the growth in real GDP (OLS)*

Country	*Change in Employment*	*Change in Intra-ERM Exchange Rate Variability*	*Growth in Real GDP (DGDP)*
BE	(-1)***	(-1) 0.29 (→)	(0) 0.55***
DK	(-1)***	(0) -1.35** (-1) -1.51** (↑)	(0) 1.07***
ES	(-1)	(0) -0.24 (→)	(0) 1.51***
FR	(-1)***	(-1) -0.04 (↓)	(0) 0.73***
GR	n.a.		
IR	(-1)***	(-1) 1.01** (→)	(0) 0.88***
IT	(-1)***	(0) -0.38** (↑)	(0) 0.68***
NL	(-1)***	(-1) -0.73* (-2) -1.16*** (→)	(0) 0.64***
PO	(-1)	(0) 0.01 (↓)	(0) 0.57***
UK	(-1)	(0) 0.22 (→)	(-1) 0.88***
WD	(-1)***	(-1) -1.78**(-2) -1.35** (→)	(0) 0.63***

For notes see tables 2 and 3.

Table 11a : *Change in unemployment as a function of its own history, the change in intra-ERM exchange rate variability and the growth in real GDP (SUR)*

Country	*Change in Unemployment*	*Change in Intra-ERM Exchange Rate Variability*	*Growth in Real GDP (DGDP)*
BE	(-1)***	(0) 0.31** (↓)	(0) -0.20***
DK	(-1)***	(0) 0.39*** (→)	(0) -0.56***
ES	(-1)***	(-1) 0.30*** (↑)	(0) -0.39***
FR	(-1)***	(-1) 0.24*** (→)	(0) -0.14***
GR	(-1)*** (-3)***	(0) 0.08*** (→)	(0) -0.04**
IR	(-1)***	(-2) 0.52*** (↑)	(0) -0.16**
IT	(-1)***	(-1) 0.06* (↓)	(0) -0.07*** (-1) -0.08***
NL	(-1)***	(-2) 0.55*** (→)	(0) -0.22***
PO	(-1)***	(-1) 0.13*** (→)	(-1) -0.07***
UK	(-1)***	(0) 0.40*** (↑)	(0) -0.35***
WD	(-1)***	(0) 0.44*** (-1) 0.35*** (→)	(0) -0.24***

For notes see table 3. The results have been compared to Tab. 2a, first column, (original SUR regressions).

Table 12a : *Change in employment as a function of its own history, the change in intra-ERM exchange rate variability and the growth in real GDP (SUR)*

Country	*Change in Employment*	*Change in Intra-ERM Exchange Rate Variability*	*Growth in Real GDP (DGDP)*
BE	(-1)***	(-1) 0.19 (↓)	(0) 0.44***
DK	(-1)***	(0) -1.58*** (-1) -1.59*** (↑)	(0) 0.98***
ES	(-1)**	(0) -0.53** (→)	(0) 1.51***
FR	(-1)***	(-1) -0.09 (↓)	(0) 0.73***
GR	n.a.		
IR	(-1)***	(-1) 0.90*** (↑)	(0) 0.74***
IT	(-1)***	(0) -0.33*** (↑)	(0) 0.67***
NL	(-1)***	(-1) -0.63** (-2) -1.08*** (→)	(0) 0.61***
PO	(-1)***	(0) -0.00 (↓)	(0) 0.55***
UK	(-1)	(0) 0.26 (→)	(-1) 0.82***
WD	(-1)*** (-2)***	(-1) -2.23*** (-2) -1.60*** (→)	(0) 0.55***

For notes see table 3. The results have been compared to Tab. 2a, second column, (original SUR regressions).

As one can see from the tables 11, 11a and 12, 12a the introduction of the growth in real GDP does not substantially affect our results (many arrows again point sideways, the ups and downs are on average at least balanced, in the case of unemployment the ups even exceed the downs independent of the estimation method chosen). As expected, the coefficient on growth in real GDP is often highly significant, with the right sign in both the OLS and the SUR estimations and enters throughout as a contemporary variable. If one takes the estimated unemployment equations as a basis, five highly significant new entries with the expected sign of the variability coefficient, estimate can be registered. With respect to employment, the patterns of tables 2, 2a are reproduced independent of the estimation method. We therefore conclude that adding the cyclical variable 'growth in real GDP' *does not change the results* of the bivariate VARs summarized in tables 1, la and 2, 2a at all. On the contrary, the evidence in favour of a negative impact of intra-ERM exchange rate variability on real variables even becomes *more impressive*.

We have attempted in the last two sections to see whether the results from the simple tests are robust. We have used GDP growth, which on its own explains a lot of the variability of employment and have found that its presence does not diminish the strength of the results. In previous work we already checked out a number of other policy instruments as potential control variables but, again with the results unaffected. We therefore believe that it is difficult to argue that the relationship between exchange rate variability and unemployment is spurious.

5 Conclusions and Implications for the EMU Debate

Our main policy conclusion is that (whatever its cost) EMU should bring substantial benefits by suppressing exchange rate variability in Europe. The data from the past suggest that intra-European exchange rate variability had a statistically significant (and economically small, but non-negligible) negative impact on employment, and investment for a number of countries. We would argue that this result is due to the fact that all employment and investment decisions have some degree of irreversibility. They are discouraged by exchange rate variability as shown in a simple model. Our model of the 'option value of waiting' also suggests that temporary *short run* increases in variability could have a stronger impact on investment than permanent ones.

Could the gains from suppressing exchange rate variability that are suggested by our results be lost if the volatility reappear elsewhere, for example in a higher dollar variability or higher interest rate variability? This is possible since dollar volatility had a significant impact in a number of cases (especially in the SUR estimates). But we would argue that it is simply not possible at present to show whether dollar variability will go up or down with EMU. Over the last 20 years there was also no clear association between intra-ERM and dollar variability. The same holds for other financial variables. Recent research (see e.g., Rose (1995)) shows that official action can reduce exchange rate variability even holding constant the variability of fundamentals such as interest rates and money. Coordination between the Fed and the ECB could thus keep the dollar-euro volatility under control.

We realize that our results are preliminary, not least because the questions posed in this paper *have not been posed* in this way in the literature so far. The limited number of observations we have, given the annual data we use, are a further reason to be cautious. But we are encouraged by the extent to which the results have been able to withstand the numerous robustness tests conducted by ourselves in this contribution and by a recent study (Müller, Buscher (1999)) focusing on exactly the results presented in this paper. Moreover, using more sophisticated techniques data and quarterly data (as detailedly documented in Belke (1998a)), we were able to confirm the result in an impressive way for Germany.[22] Our results are consistent across countries in the sense that most of the countries that are affected by exchange rate variability show this in more than one variable. Therefore, we consider the biggest challenge for future research to identify the details of the transmission channel.

The simple argument that exchange rate variability is just an expression of general uncertainty, and that it is this general uncertainty that drives unemployment and investment, is not compatible with the observation that the variability of the dollar rate does not have the same impact. General uncertainty, especially if it is uncertainty about the country concerned, should also have been reflected in the dollar rate, not only in intra-European rates. The fact that the measure of intra-European exchange rate variability remains significant even when dollar variability is introduced suggests that there is an *independent component* of intra-European variability that had effects on its own. This part of our results fits nicely with the finding that it is mainly for intra-European relations that one does find an impact of exchange rate variability on trade (de Grauwe (1987), and Sapir, Sekkat (1995)). However, we would argue that one should actually expect that exchange rate variability should have a stronger impact on investment and employment than on current production and exports, because the latter can be adjusted with the existing labor through variations in the intensity of labor use. Irreversibility of set-up costs is thus not an important consideration for production that can be sold within weeks or days, but it is a crucial aspect for decisions of a more long run character, e.g., to invest or hire additional workers.

It will never be possible to establish beyond any doubt that exchange variability does not stand for some other macroeconomic variable, such as the level of the

---

22 We found consistently that Germany (followed by the Netherlands and France) showed the strongest impact of exchange rate variability. In a previous version of Belke, Gros (1998) we therefore investigated the long term determinants of employment more deeply for Germany and confirmed the importance of exchange rate variability in a cointegration framework, i.e. in a more structural model of the labor market. This approach could be followed only for one country since replicating it for many others would simply have taken too much space. We leave this task for future research.

exchange rate, the interest rate, etc. We have tried to take some of the more obvious possibilities into account here and found that they did not affect the results. These results can certainly be disputed on technical grounds, e.g., that the level and variability of exchange rates are related. But our main counter-argument would anyway be that this argument presumably differs from country to country. For Germany one could argue that the DM was volatile against other European currencies when it was strong and the Bundesbank followed a high interest rate policy. But what about France or Italy? Would the argument not be the other way round: the lira (or the Franc) were volatile when they were weak? If this type of argument were true the bias should be in opposite directions and could thus not explain why one finds a strong effect of exchange rate volatility both for hard currency countries (Germany and the Netherlands) as well as weak currency countries (France, Italy, Greece).[23]

We readily admit that some aspects of the results remain unsatisfactory. For example, one would expect that more open countries show a stronger impact of exchange rate variability. But this was only partially confirmed by the data. We found a significant impact for such relatively open economies as France, Germany and the Netherlands. But Belgium, which is the most open economy in the EU, did sometimes not show significant effects. Moreover, one would have expected that the impact of exchange rate variability on manufacturing employment (or industrial production) is much stronger than that on economy-wide variables such as unemployment and investment. We found that this is true in terms of the magnitude of the coefficient, but not in terms of the statistical significance levels.

[23] Our results corroborate findings by Aizenman, Marion (1996) who find a significant negative relationship between private investment shares in GDP and the volatility of the real exchange rate (measured as the standard deviation from the average change in the effective real rate at annual frequency) for a cross section of 43 developing countries. Their result is also robust to the inclusion of measures of nominal variability, such as money supply or fiscal policy variability. Thus, one could conclude that in their context exchange rate variability has an impact even if one does not assume that it is mainly noise, but dependent e.g. on money supply variability.

References

Aizenman, J. and N. P. Marion (1996), Volatility and the Investment Response, NBER Working Paper 5841, Cambridge, Mass.

Andersen, T. and J. Sørensen (1988), Exchange Rate Variability and Wage Formation in Open Economies, *Economics Letters* 28, 263-268.

Banerjee, A., J. J. Dolado and R. Mestre (1992), On Some Simple Tests for Cointegration, The Cost of Simplicity, mimeo, Institute of Economics, Aarhus/Denmark.

Banerjee, A. et al. (1993), Co-Integration, Error Correction, and the Econometric Analysis of Non-Stationary Data, Oxford.

Bayoumi, T. and E. Prasad (I995), Currency Unions, Economic Fluctuations and Adjustment: Some Empirical Evidence, CEPR Discussion Paper 1727, London .

Bayoumi, T. and B. Eichengreen (1994), Shocking Aspects of European Monetary Integration, in: Giavazzi, F. and F. Torres (eds.), Adjustment and Growth in the European Monetary Union, Center for Economic Policy Research (CEPR).

Belke, A. (1996a), Testing for Unit Roots in West German and U.S. Unemployment Rates: Do 'Great Crashes' Cause Trend Breaks? *Konjunkturpolitik - Applied Economics Quarterly* 42, 327-360.

Belke, A. (1998b), Political Business Cycles in the German Labor Market? Empirical Tests in the Light of the Lucas Critique, forthcoming in: *Public Choice.*

Belke, A. (1998a), Exchange Rate Uncertainty and the German Labor Market: A Cointegration Application of the Autoregressive Distributed Lag Approach, Volkswirtschaftliche Beiträge, Discussion Papers 06/98, Ruhr-Universität Bochum.

Belke, A. and M. Goecke (1994), Starke Hysteresis auf dem Arbeitsmarkt, in: *ZWS - Zeitschrift fur Wirtschafts- und Sozialwissenschaften* 114, 345-377.

Belke, A. and M. Goecke (1997), Cointegration and Structural Breaks in German Employment – An Error Correction Interpretation, *Jahrbücher für Nationalökonomie und Statistik* 216, 129-152.

Belke, A. and M. Goecke (1998), A Simple Model of Hysteresis in Employment under Exchange Rate Uncertainty, Paper presented at the Econometric Society European Meeting (ESEM), Economic Theory Sessions, Berlin/Germany, September, forthcoming in: *Scottish Journal of Political Economy.*

Belke, A. and M. Goecke (1999), Aggregation of Employment Hysteresis: Does Exchange Rate Uncertainty Matter?, Paper to be Presented at the 1999 EEA Conference, 'Real Options' Session, Santiago de Compostela/Spain, and invited Paper prepared for the Fifth International Conference of the Society for Computational Economics 'Computing in Economics and Finance', Organized Session 'Hysteresis in Models of Economic Analysis', June 24-26, Boston College, Chestnut Hill, Massachusetts, U.S.A.

Belke, A. and D. Gros (1998), Evidence on the Costs of Intra-European Exchange Rate Variability, Paper presented at the 1997 International Seminar on Macroeconomics (NBER and EEA), Gerzensee /Switzerland, CentER for Economic Research Discussion Paper 9814, Tilburg/Netherlands.

Belke, A. and D. Gros (1999), Estimating the Costs and Benefits of EMU: The Impact of External Shocks on Labor Markets, *Weltwirtschaftliches Archiv* 135, 1-48 (also appeared as CentER for Economic Research Discussion Paper 9795, Tilburg /Netherlands).

Bernanke, B.S. (1983), Irreversibility, Uncertainty, and Cyclical Investment, *Quarterly Journal of Economics* 98, 85-106.

Blanchard, O.J. and P. A. Diamond (1994), Ranking, Unemployment Duration and Wages, *Review of Economic Studies* 57, 417-434.

Brunello, G. (1990), Real Exchange Rate Variability and Japanese Industrial Employment, *Journal of the Japanese and International Economies* 4, 121-138.

Burgess, S. and M. Knetter (1996), An International Comparison of Employment Adjustment to Exchange Rate Fluctuations, NBER Working Paper 5861 Cambridge, Mass.

Canzoneri, M., J. Valles and J. Vinals (1996), Do Exchange Rates Move to Address National Imbalances? CEPR Discussion Paper 1498, London.

Commission of the European Communities (1995), The Impact of Currency Fluctuations on the Internal Market, Brussels.

Darby, J. et al. (1998), The Impact of Exchange Rate Uncertainty on the Level of Investment, CEPR Discussion Paper 1896, London.

De Grauwe, P. (1987), International Trade and Economic Growth in the European Monetary System, *European Economic Review* 31, 389-398.

Deutsche Bundesbank (1996), Finanzmarktvolatilität und ihre Auswirkungen auf die Geldpolitik in: Monatsberichte der Deutschen Bundesbank, April, 53-70.

Dixit, A. (1989), Entry and Exit Decisions under Uncertainty, *Journal of Political Economy* 97, 620-638.

Dornbusch, R. (1987), Exchange Rates and Prices, *American Economic Review* 77, 93-107.

Flood, R, and A. Rose (1995), Fixing Exchange Rates: A Virtual Quest for Fundamentals, *Journal of Monetary Economics* 36, 3-37.

Frankel, J. A. and A. K. Rose (1996a), Economic Structure and the Decision to Adopt a Common Currency, Institute for International Economic Studies, Seminar Paper 611, Stockholm.

Gros, D. (1996), A Reconsideration of the Optimum Currency Area Approach: The Role of External Shocks and Labor Mobility, CEPS Working Document 101, Brussels.

Gros, D. (1996a), Towards Economic and Monetary Union: Problems and Prospects, CEPS Paper 65, January, Brussels.

Gros, D. and N. Thygesen (1992), European Monetary Integration, Harlow, New York.

Haldrup, N. (1990), Testing for Unit Roots with a Maintained Trend When the True Data Generating Process Is a Random Walk with Drift, Institute of Economics, Memo 1990-22, University of Aarhus.

Hannan, E. J. and B. G. Quinn (1979), The Determination of the Order of an Auto-regression, *Journal of the Royal Statistical Society* 41, 190-195.

Jarque, C. M. and A. K. Bera (1987), A Test for Normality of Observations and Regression Residuals, *International Statistical Review* 55, 163-172.

Kmenta, J. (1990), Elements of Econometrics, 2nd ed., New York, 635-648.

Kremers, J. J. M., N. E. Ericsson and J. J. Dolado (1992), The Power of Cointegration Tests, *Oxford Bulletin of Economics and Statistics* 54, 325-348.

Krugman, P. (l989), Exchange Rate Instability, Cambridge, Mass.

Kulatilaka, N., and B. Kogut (1996), Direct Investment, Hysteresis, and Real Exchange Rate Volatility, *Journal of the Japanese and International Economies* 10, 12-36.

Lütkepohl, H. (1991), Introduction to Multiple Time Series Analysis, New York.

McKinnon, D. G. et al. (1991), Critical Values for Cointegration Tests, in: Engle, R. F., C. W. J. Granger (eds.), Long-Run Economic Relationships - Readings in Cointegration, Oxford, 267-276.

Mélitz, J. (1995), The Current Impasse in Research on Optimum Currency Areas, *European Economic Review* 39, 492-500.

Mills, T.C. et al. (1990), Time Series Techniques for Economists, Cambridge.

Müller, C. and H. S. Buscher (1999), Exchange Rate Volatility Effects on the German Labor Market: A Survey of Recent Results and Extensions, Zentrum für Europäische Wirtschaftsforschung (ZEW), Mannheim, Paper prepared for the Workshop 'Arbeitsmarkteffekte der Europäischen Währungsunion', 24. März, IZA - Forschungsinstitut zur Zukunft der Arbeit, Bonn.

Peeters, M. (1997), Does Demand and Price Uncertainty Affect Belgian and Spanish Corporate Investment?, Dutch National Bank-Staff Reports 13, Amsterdam.

Perron, P. (1989), The Great Crash, the Oil Price Shock, and the Unit Root Hypothesis, *Econometrica* 57, 1361-1401.

Pesaran, M. H. and B. Pesaran (1997), Working with Microfit 4.0 - Interactive Econometric Analysis, Oxford .

Phillips, P. C. B. and B. Hansen (1990), Statistical Inference in Instrumental Variables Regression with I(1) Processes, *Review of Economic Studies* 53, 473-496.

Phillips, P. C. B. and P. Perron (1988), Testing for a Unit Root in Time Series Regression, *Biometrika* 75, 335-346.

Pindyck, R. S. and D. L. Rubinfeld et al. (1991), Economic Models and Economic Forecasts, 3rd ed., New York, 308-311.

Pindyck, R. S. (1991), Irreversibility, Uncertainty, and Investment, *Journal of Economic Literature* 29, 1110-1148.

Ramey, G. and V. A. Ramey (1995), Cross-Country Evidence on the Link Between Volatility and Growth, *American Economic Review* 85, 1138-1151.

Rose, A.K. (1994), Exchange Rate Volatility, Monetary Policy and Capital Mobility: Empirical Evidence on the Holy Trinity, NBER Working Paper 4630, Cambridge, Mass.

Rose, A.K. (1995), After the Deluge: Do Fixed Exchange Rates Allow Inter-Temporal Volatility Trade-Offs?, CEPR Discussion Paper 1240, London.

Sapir, A. and K. Sekkat (1990), Exchange Rate Volatility and International Trade, in: de Grauwe, P., and L. Papademos (eds.), The European Monetary System in the 1990s, London, 182-198.

Savvides, A. (1992), Unanticipated Exchange Rate Variability and the Growth of International Trade, *Weltwirtschaftliches Archiv* 128, 446-463.

Schwarz, G. (1978), Estimating the Dimension of a Model, *Annals of Statistics* 6, 461-464.

Theil, H. (1971), Principles of Econometrics, Wiley, New York.

Zellner, A. (1962), An Efficient Method of Estimating Seemingly Unrelated Regressions and Tests for Aggregation Bias, *Journal of the American Statistical Association* 57, 348-368.

Comment on Belke and Gros : "Effects of European Monetary Integration on Unemployment"

Carsten Hefeker

WWZ, University of Basel,
Petersgraben 51, 4003 Basel, Switzerland

This nice paper by Ansgar Belke and Daniel Gros presents a result that might be new to some economists but certainly not to businessmen. Indeed, I was always amazed by the fact how economists would argue that exchange rate variability has no effect on real variables like trade or employment while the financial press and public statements by corporate leaders would lament about the detrimental effects of exchange rate variability. For this reason, I have a lot of sympathy with the aim (and result) of the authors that fits well into a rapidly growing literature that has begun to bridge the gap between observation and economists' writings. It seems that there is a consensus emerging that real exchange rate changes have an effect on investment (Goldberg (1993), Campa and Goldberg (1995)), trade (Peree and Steinherr (1989)), and on employment (Burgess and Knetter (1996), Goldberg and Tracy (1999), Gourinchas (1998)).[1] The paper is particularly welcome because most of the existing literature is concerned with the US and relatively little is said about other countries or on a comparative basis (see, however, Burgess and Knetter (1996)). It departs from the literature in two more aspects. First, it looks at exchange rate variability instead of exchange rate levels, as most other papers do. And, while the literature generally looks at real exchange rates, the present paper looks at nominal exchange rates, arguing that this is justified because nominal exchange rates are highly correlated with real exchange rates.

The evidence by Belke and Gros is even more convincing as the authors have been very careful to test the robustness of their results. (I will not go into the technical details here.) It is indeed advisable to do that as, apparently, earlier versions have come under pressure from those who still do not like the idea of the connection between exchange rate variability and employment. (I will not speculate why that

---

[1] See, however, also Sapir and Sekkat (1995) who argue that misalignment is much more important than the exchange rate regime.

is so but some private interests may also play a role here, as the reaction by the Bundesbank to an early paper would suggest.)[2]

The theoretical reason for this influence is also well-known and summarized by the authors. Even if floating exchange rates have no direct influence on the volume of trade, they should have negative implications on investment and profits of firms and presumably thus on employment as well. These effects basically fall into three broad categories: pricing to market requirements for firms, which leads to unpredictable changes in profits (see Betts and Devereux (1996) for a survey), excess capacities of firms in different locations (Krugman (1989)) and hysteresis (Dixit (1989) and argued by Belke and Gros). And there is probably another argument, having simply to do with risk aversion which is supposedly the main reason for businessmen's interest in fixed exchange rates.

In addition, there can be little doubt, as experiences after the EMS crises in the first half of the nineties demonstrated, that there is a strong politically economic link between pressure for protectionism and exchange rate movements. It has, therefore, even been argued that a truly unified market needs a monetary union on political grounds (Eichengreen (1996)). Take all these arguments into account and you will actually be surprised that there is so much doubt in the profession that EMU will have a positive effect on real integration.

Belke and Gros' paper is also welcome because it contributes to fill another gap in the literature, namely that of trying to estimate the benefits of monetary union in Europe (and maybe more generally as well). Again, it is amazing how most of the literature on EMU, in particular that concerned with the celebrated optimum currency area theory, has almost exclusively focused on the costs of EMU (see Viñals (1996) for a similar argument). Gros is among the few who have aimed to provide estimates of the benefits of EMU, being one of the principal authors of the famous (though not undisputed) "One Market, One Money" study by the EC-Commission (1990). That study provided the main official justification for EMU by attempting to estimate the positive effects of EMU on investment, growth and hence on employment. The present paper continues that research by a direct estimation of the influence of exchange rate variability on employment in a major European country. It will be interesting to see more of that for other countries in the future.

Having said that all that, it should be clear that the paper is really an important piece of work. Nevertheless, I am skeptical as to the conclusion Belke and Gros draw from their evidence. Having shown that exchange rate variability has (had) a negative impact on employment in the past is much a different thing from saying the EMU will actually increase employment in Europe (as they do). This is so for several reasons: first of all it is not clear that hysteresis, which is named as the main reason for the connection the paper finds, works indeed symmetrically.

[2] See the article by Gros (1996) and the response by Jung (1996).

Secondly, it is simply assumed that EMU will have no impact on the working of the labor market. Instead, Belke and Gros focus only on the impact EMU might have on firms' decisions to invest etc. which is of course related to employment but they do not look at other variables that also influence the rate of employment such as wage setting and labor market regulation. To draw a conclusion about the evolution of employment under EMU one needs to look at these other variables as well, I believe. And here optimism is less justified, as I will argue in the rest of this comment. I begin with a few words on the argument that less exchange rate variability will directly reduce unemployment.

Will Reduced Exchange Rate Variability Reduce Unemployment?

Belke and Gros make a strong case that hysteresis is important for European markets, not only in trade and investment but also in labor markets. There is a lot of evidence that this is indeed so, in particular in labor markets. Thus, the authors argue that exchange variability has persistent effects on labor markets because firms that shed labor when being hit by negative exchange rate shocks do not rehire immediately when the situation improves, or that firms unwillingness to invest because of fluctuations might lower the rate of employment. But is it really certain that getting rid of nominal exchange rate fluctuations has employment improving effects? I am less certain than the authors. To begin with, it is important to realize that real exchange rates are important for competitiveness and investment and that these are not per se stabilized through the elimination of nominal exchange rate changes, although I would agree with Belke and Gros that there is a strong link between the two. Still, one should be clear about the potential difference between the two.

If we believe that trade expands because of reduced uncertainty of real exchange rates, this might indeed lead to a reallocation of resources into the tradable sector. But that this increases overall employment or reduces unemployment is not obvious. It could be that producing tradable goods is less labor intensive than the production of non-tradables, so under wage rigidity, it is not clear that unemployment falls. The authors' partial perspective does not allow such general conclusions. Also, one strong argument for EMU is that it should lead to more integration and competition. But that higher competition, going hand in hand with more integration of product markets, will have a strong positive effect on unemployment is not clear either — at least in the short-run. Instead it might very well even increase unemployment in the short-run. Higher competition and reduced uncertainty might also prompt some firms to reconsider their choice of location, leading to some movements in investment across Europe. Although investment in different locations might no longer be necessary, investments could also flow from Germany into other European countries. Hence, that this channel will reduce unemployment in a given country is not clear either.

Finally, it is argued quite often that one reason for hysteresis is the separation of the labor force into insiders and outsiders (Blanchard and Summers (1986)). And if the employment situation should improve because of EMU this would presumably also increase the market power of the insiders. This, in turn, would push up their wages without having necessarily a positive effect on unemployment. Instead, insider-outsider theories would suggest that unions aim to stabilize unemployment rather than to reduce it. To achieve this, a reduction in the insiders' power would be needed. In other words to achieve an improvement on European labor market, it might be more important to look into other directions, as very strongly argued by international organizations and professional economists (see, e.g., OECD (1994), Siebert (1997)). Therefore, EMU might not bring much improvement if not other overdue reforms are undertaken. This leads me to my second argument. To assess the impact of EMU on unemployment it hence necessary to have a look at other determinants of unemployment. I will thus ask next how EMU is to influence wage setting and how it might interact with deregulation of labor markets in general.

What does EMU do to Wages and Labor Market Regulation?

To explore the impact of (monetary) integration it is useful to take a familiar model as the starting point. The much cited Calmfors and Driffill (1988) model posits that the organization of national labor markets is a pivotal factor for the performance of labor markets. When wage setting concerns a whole industry, so that wages rise simultaneously across all firms producing similar products, the possibilities for firms to pass wage rises on to consumers via an increase of the relative output price are relatively large. In this situation unions have little incentive for wage restraint because part of the negative employment effect can be externalized. Thus, intermediate level bargaining gives rise to a prisoners' dilemma situation where each single union exploits the trade off between market power and employment. This is different with completely decentralized wage bargaining where every single firm is a price-taker. The single firm has no opportunity to increase its relative price when real consumption wages increase, so there is no relative price increase to offset a wage increase. Exactly the same is true for complete centralization because a uniform wage and price increase across all industries leaves relative amounts unchanged. Unions' incentives to push wages beyond the market clearing level are reduced with equally positive employment effects. An extension of this idea to the case of European goods market integration predicts that employment will increase or decrease depending upon the degree of wage centralization before integration. If there has been country wide bargaining before employment would be reduced because centralization decreases. If, however, bargaining has been sectoral integration could lead to more decentralization and more employment.

But this simple prediction fails to take into account some strategic aspects from integration that might actually lead to worse results. Focusing on imperfect substitutability between home and foreign goods, Corneo (1995) has established a positive wage externality among national labor unions in integrated product markets because wage increases in one country increase competitiveness of the other country. This will induce labor unions there to demand higher wages too, increasing thus overall unemployment as unions push up each others' wage demands. Driffill and van der Ploeg (1993) and Rama (1994) as well have noticed that wages might indeed increase under trade liberalization, because they improve a country's terms-of-trade, if labor is willing to trade off unemployment against real wage increases. This indicates that integration might change wage setting behavior and that it should be taken into account when making predictions.

Speculating about the effects of a monetary union should as well consider changes in wage setting. It has been suggested that EMU might actually discipline labor unions because it would a clear signal to labor market participants that excessive wages could no longer be compensated through monetary expansion (Eichengreen (1996)). Proponents of this view argue that countries that pegged their exchange rate to the DM have seen a change in the wage setting behavior in the past (see Hochreiter and Winkler (1995) on Austria; Kremers (1990) on Ireland, Gressani et al. (1998) on Italy and Blanchard and Muet (1995) on France). The positive evidence is not undisputed however (Viñals and Jimeno (1998), Calmfors (1998)). And it has in several cases been accompanied by severe adjustment costs (Ball (1996)).

In any case, comparability of pre-EMU developments in countries entering the ERM have only restricted predictive value for developments under EMU. Not only is EMU a stronger commitment to fixed exchange rates but in addition a common central bank is created, changing thus profoundly the interaction between labor and the monetary authority. Like indicated above for the case of goods market integration, a strategic interaction among national labor unions arises that is neglected in the discipline assumption. So far, however, only very few and theoretical papers exist that try to analyze the interaction between wage setting and the European Central Bank (ECB).

Like in the Calmfors and Driffill model introduced above, one can argue that EMU creates a strategic interaction among different national labor unions (Grüner and Hefeker (1999)).[3] The strategic interaction arises from the assumption that

[3] The same argument is made by Cukierman and Lippi (1999) who allow for several national labor unions. This does not change the result derived in a simpler setting.

labor unions care about inflation as well, an idea that has only recently emerged in the literature. In most cases, utility functions of labor unions are formulated with a real wage aim only — and that is per se compatible with any given rate of inflation. In this case, EMU has no influence on real variables like employment. However, it seems logical to assume inflation aversion of labor unions as well, at least when, as is usually done, a social welfare function a la Barro-Gordon is used. Under this assumption, the argument runs as follows.

Before EMU national labor unions face a trade off between real wages, unemployment and inflation. In setting their nominal wage demands they take the reaction of the central bank into account (which differs according to the inflation aversion of the central bank) and that inflation will increase in response to nominal wage demands. Assuming that, to some degree, unions oppose inflation as well, this should discipline them because too high nominal wages prompt higher inflation. Note that this is different for the core EMS countries because the followers of the German monetary policy know that the Bundesbank will not react to their demands and thus accordingly choose their point between real wages and employment directly and unilaterally without any reaction from the central bank.

The move to EMU, however, will change the situation. The ECB will set its monetary policy with regard to every country that is a member of the monetary union. Thus, the followers will now be taken into account, as will be those countries that had an independent monetary policy before. Therefore, even the unions in the core EMS can now expect that the ECB will react expansionary in response to excessive wage claims. This, comparable to the argument made above, should discipline each of the member unions in their wage setting behavior. However, all of them will only have a small influence on the overall policy of the ECB. This creates an incentive for national labor unions to demand higher nominal wages, because they perceive a possibility to achieve higher utility because real wages can be increased without prompting higher inflation. In other words, national labor unions have a looser disciplinary constraint from knowing that their wage demands create inflation. Obviously, since all unions increase their wage demands, the ECB will set higher inflation in response to Europe wide wage increases. This will not be enough to ensure the same employment level, however. Inflation and unemployment will increase from moving to EMU.[4]

Two conclusion emerge from this consideration. On the one hand, it would imply that many labor unions are detrimental to employment and monetary stability because then the neglect of external effects is strongest. This would suggest that labor unions across European countries coordinate their wage setting behavior, but this is difficult to achieve and not very likely to find much support among economist and politicians for other reasons. On the other hand, the theory would

---

[4] This is only different for the followers of Germany because they are taken into account by the ECB, in contrast to what the Bundesbank did earlier.

imply that a very stability oriented central bank would only worsen this situation. As Velasco and Guzzo (1999) show, a central bank that is very much concerned with stabilizing employment by using monetary policy (what they call a *populist* central bank) could be even welfare improving. This is because given that the reaction function of the central bank is known, the inflation aversion of labor unions kicks in again. But making the ECB more populist does not sound very tempting either.

Clearly, these theoretic papers do not fully reflect reality. However, the effect that each labor union is confronted with a different central bank than before is clearly relevant. And this does imply that the effect on one's own action on overall outcome are less internalized because the impact (and thus feedback) is reduced. In this respect, EMU does indeed suggest caution. Yet, these papers of course only ask what happens if nothing changes. As already said, one possibility to avoid this unfavorable result could be that unions coordinate their wage setting behavior to internalize the negative externalities of their behavior. But it is almost impossible to coordinate wages of dozens of labor unions in an expanding EMU. So the real question is whether other instruments aiming at employment improvement than wage setting can be used. This leads directly to the question of labor market deregulation.

Here as well, researchers have begun to discuss not only the level of wages in its impact on employment but also the question of labor market regulation. In its relation to EMU, the discussion has been on the incentives of governments and labor unions to change the level of regulation. The fact that EMU no longer allows to offset asymmetric shocks by monetary policy should provide an incentive to more reform. But this is not necessarily true if one views deregulation as a substitute for monetary expansion in lowering unemployment at the national level (Calmfors (1998), Sibert and Sutherland (1997)). Since regulation increases the rate of unemployment there is an incentive for the central bank to set a higher rate of inflation to compensate. If governments oppose inflation they should therefore push for deregulation because this lowers the inflationary incentives for central banks. When moving to EMU, however, the central bank's response to unemployment in every single country is automatically reduced, as argued above. The ECB reacts less to any country's unemployment problem which in turn lowers inflationary expectations in the member countries. Governments in these countries have therefore less incentive to use labor market deregulation to solve their monetary time-consistency problem. The conclusion is that EMU lowers governments' interest in labor market reform. Complementing the considerations of governments by those of labor unions, by asking in how far labor unions might themselves be induced to accept more deregulation in EMU, one can show that from this side neither deregulation would increase (Hefeker (1998)).

In conclusion, the theoretical arguments are not unambiguous as to how labor markets might react to the introduction of the euro. Some observers argue that monetary union hardens the antiinflationary stance of monetary policy and should therefore bring more discipline in the wage settings of labor unions. But his seems too simple if one takes account of strategic aspects. A less employment responsive monetary policy then leads to the opposite result. Inflation averse labor unions will use the reduced responsiveness to achieve a higher real wage at lower inflation, thus increasing unemployment. The simple but plausible assumption that labor is concerned with monetary stability as well produces this quite striking result. Which of the two views will prove to be correct is still open. But it suffices to be more cautious concerning the employment consequences of EMU.

So while I follow Belke and Gros in their analysis and its results, I feel somewhat uneasy with their conclusion. Although it seems straightforward to conclude that employment will increase from moving to EMU on the basis of the effects of exchange rate variability on employment, other changes brought about by EMU might very well lead to adverse affects on unemployment. Which of these effects are stronger is not clear yet.

References

Ball, L. (1996), Disinflation and the NAIRU, NBER Working Paper 5520, Cambridge, Mass.

Betts, C. and M. Devereux (1996), The Exchange Rate in a Model of Pricing-to-Market, *European Economic Review* 40, 1007-1021.

Blanchard, O. and P.-A. Muet (1993), Competitiveness through Disinflation: An Assessment of the French Macroeconomic Strategy, *Economic Policy* 16, 12-56.

Blanchard, O. and L. Summers (1986), Hysteresis and the European Unemployment Problem, NBER Macroeconomics Annual 1, 15-78.

Burgess, S. and M. M. Knetter (1996), An International Comparison of Employment Adjustment to Exchange Rate Fluctuations, NBER Working Paper 5861.

Calmfors, L. (1998), Unemployment, Labor-Market Reform and Monetary Union, Institute for International Economics Studies, Seminar Paper 639.

Calmfors, L. and J. Driffill (1988), Bargaining Structure, Corporatism and Macroeconomic Performance, *Economic Policy* 6, 13-62.

Campa, J. and L. Goldberg (1995), Investment, Pass-Through and Exchange Rates: A Cross-Country Comparison, NBER Working Paper 5139.

Corneo, G. (1995), National Wage Bargaining in an Internationally Integrated Product Market, *European Journal of Political Economy* 11, 503-520.

Cukierman, A. and F. Lippi (1999), Central Bank Independence, Centralization of Wage Bargaining, Inflation and Unemployment-Theory and Evidence, *European Economic Review*, forthcoming.

Dixit, A (1989), Hysteresis, Imports Penetration, and Exchange Rate Pass-Through, *Quarterly Journal of Economics* 104, 205-227.

Driffill, J. and F. van der Ploeg (1993), Monopoly Union and the Liberalisation of International Trade, *Economic Journal* 103, 379-385.

European Commission (1990), One Market, One Money, *European Economy* 44, October.

Eichengreen, B. (1996), A More Perfect Union? The Logic of Economic Integration, *Princeton Essays in International Finance* 198, Princeton University.

Goldberg, L. (1993), Exchange Rates and Investment in United States Industry, *Review of Economics and Statistics* 75, 575-589.

Goldberg, L. and J. Tracy (1999), Exchange Rates and Local Labor Markets, NBER Working Paper 6985, Cambridge, Mass.

Gros, D. (1996), Germany's Stake in Exchange Rate Stability, *Intereconomics* 31, 236-240.

Gressani, D., L. Guiso and I. Visco (1988), Disinflation in Italy: An Analysis with the Econometric Model of the Baca d' Italia, *Journal of Policy Modeling* 8, 163-203.

Gourinchas, P.-O. (1998), Exchange Rates and Jobs: What Do We Learn from Job Flows?, NBER Macroeconomics Annual, forthcoming.

Grüner, H. P. and C. Hefeker (1999), How Will EMU Affect Unemployment and Inflation?, *Scandinavian Journal of Economics* 101, 1-15.

Hefeker, C. (1998), Labor Market Rigidities, Unions and Monetary Union, WWZ-Discussion Paper 9801, Basle.

Hochreiter, E. and G. Winckler (1995), The Advantages of Tying Austria's Hands: The Success of the Hard Currency Strategy, *European Journal of Political Economy* 11, 83-111.

Jung, A. (1996), Is There a Causal Relationship Betwen Exchange Rate Volatility and Unemployment?, *Intereconomics* 31, 281-282.

Kremers, J. (1990), Gaining Policy Credibility for a Disinflation, *IMF Staff Papers* 37, 116-145.

Krugman, P. (1989), The Case for Stabilizing Exchange Rates, *Oxford Review of Economic Policy* 5, 61-72.

OECD (1994), The OECD Job Study: Evidence and Explanations, Paris.

Perée, E. and A. Steinherr (1989), Exchange Rate Uncertainty and Foreign Trade, *European Economic Review* 33, 1241-1264.

Rama, M. (1994), Bargaining Structure and Economic Performance in the Open Economy, *European Economic Review* 38, 403-415.

Sapir, A. and K. Sekkat (1995), Exchange Rate Regimes and Trade Prices: Does the EMS Matter?, *Journal of International Economics* 38, 75-94.

Sibert, A. and A. Sutherland (1997), Monetary Regimes and Labor Market Reform, CEPR Discussion Paper 1731, London.

Siebert, H. (1997), Labor Market Rigidities: At the Root of Unemployment in Europe, *Journal of Economic Perspectives* 11, 37-54.

Velasco, A. and V. Guzzo (1999), The Case for a Populist Central Banker, *European Economic Review*, forthcoming.

Viñals, J. (1996), European Monetary Integration: A Narrow or a Wider EMU?, *European Economic Review* 40, 1103-1109.

Viñals, J. and J. Jimeno (1998), The Impact of EMU on European Unemployment, Austrian Nationalbank, Working Paper 34, Vienna.

Part 4 :

Globalization, Unemployment and Economic Policies

I. Labor Market Policy

Labor Market Policy in a Global Economy

Norbert Berthold, Rainer Fehn

University of Würzburg,
Sanderring 2, 97070 Würzburg, Germany

1 Introduction

This paper deals with the much discussed question how to design labor market policy in a global economy. Mass unemployment is clearly the principal economic policy problem in most continental European countries nowadays and rising unemployment is often associated with more open goods and factor markets which are labeled with the catchword "globalization". Patience of the public diminishes in expecting governments to offer and successfully execute remedies to this grossly inefficient and unjust state of affairs on labor markets. The liberalization of trade and of capital flows is in acute danger of being reverted if the perception becomes even more widespread that growing unemployment is the inevitable consequence of globalization. Governments which fail or are too slow in reducing unemployment are relentlessly voted out of office these days. The German case is only one example in kind. However, lasting success in the fight against unemployment can only be expected if a correct diagnosis precedes the design and implementation of policy measures. Quixotic policies such as a move towards protectionism, which governments are all too tempted to undertake, are in general at best successful in the very short run while often exacerbating the unemployment problem in the longer run.

Hence, even a policy-oriented paper such as this one must in a first step outline the principal causes of rising unemployment. Economists have by now written extensively on European unemployment. It is generally recognized that unemployment in Europe is predominantly structural, i. e. a quasi-equilibrium phenomenon with only a minor cyclical component.[1] Hence, expansionary demand policies cannot be the main tool in fighting unemployment. Most of the burden must be shouldered by supply-side policies which above all have to improve the functioning of labor markets. However, there is much less agreement on which shocks and which transmission mechanisms cause unemployment to grow inexorably in some countries while returning to and apparently staying at

---

[1] See Feldstein (1997), Krugman (1994), Lindbeck (1996), van der Willigen (1995), and Viñals and Jimeno (1996). The OECD estimates that 85% of German unemployment in 1997 were of the structural type.

moderate levels in other countries. Yet, a precise understanding of these shocks and of the relevant transmission mechanisms is crucial for selecting the most effective institutional reforms and labor market policies. The observable great differences in national unemployment rates point to country-specific institutional factors as being important in explaining unemployment performances. Hence, identifying institutional setups which promote employment growth in a global economy is a prerequisite for successfully fighting unemployment.

To this end the paper is divided into three main sections. The first section provides a non-technical synopsis of the main causes of persistently high unemployment which can in particular be observed in continental Europe. Special emphasis is put on the question how the ongoing process of globalization of goods and factor markets conflicts with the institutional setup of these economies in general, but in particular of the labor market in continental Europe thus producing rising unemployment. The second section discusses how labor market institutions and labor market policy should be reformed in order to achieve better employment results. Building on the results of the first section, two areas are put under particular scrutiny: the system of transfer payments to the unemployed and the design of active labor market policies. The third section elaborates on how labor market reforms can be made viable in the politico-economic decision-making process.

2 A Synopsis of the Principal Causes of Unemployment in Europe

Unemployment has not always been higher in continental Europe compared to the U.S. Starting in the early seventies and taking in particular France and Germany as the two largest continental European countries for comparison, figure 1 shows that unemployment was at that time considerably lower than in the U.S. So the question really is what has happened in the meantime to reverse the picture in such a dramatic way. Of course, since the early seventies were almost thirty years ago, a lot of things influencing the situation on labor markets have happened. In order to gain a broad picture it is useful to briefly highlight the main elements, which are crucial for a coherent explanation of rising unemployment in continental Europe.

Figure 1: *An International Comparison of Unemployment Rates*

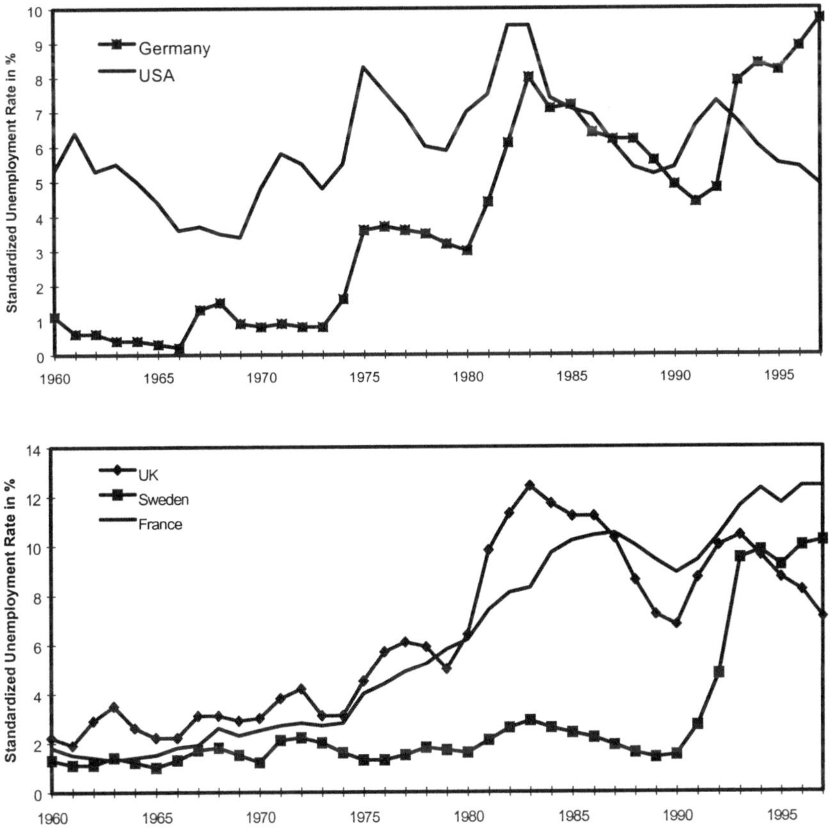

Source: OECD Employment Outlook.

2.1 Shifts in Relative Labor Demand

The by now standard explanation of rising unemployment is a change in the structure of labor demand towards higher skill requirements of firms, either caused by growing inter-industry trade or skill-biased technical progress or sector-specific technical progress, which conflicts with rigid wage structures in continental Europe. At first sight, this approach fits nicely with the facts that unemployment in continental Europe predominantly afflicts low-skilled workers, while this group faces a growing working-poor problem in the U.S., where wage structures are more flexible due to a less generous welfare state, weaker unions and less union coverage. Thus, in the words of Krugman (1994), the unemployment problem in continental Europe and the working poor problem in the U.S. are in a sense two sides of the same coin. If based on the trade argument or on the faster diffusion of knowledge, this approach has also got the appealing property of linking the much discussed process of globalization to the unemployment issue.

However, a number of points have to be raised before precipitately accepting this reasoning as the major explanation for the rise of unemployment in continental Europe. First, it has been increasingly recognized by now that inter-industry trade, and this is the one that only counts here, cannot have contributed much in the way of changing the structure of labor demand with respect to skills. Second, it is by no means clear, whether the world-wide speed of skill-biased technical progress, which is undoubtedly accelerated by growing trade, has grown sufficiently in recent years.[2] A high but constant speed of technical progress does not suffice to explain rising unemployment, if wage structures have not become more rigid and if the qualification spectrum of workers has not deteriorated. Yet, there is no convincing evidence for either one of these two possibilities. Third, unemployment among low-skilled workers is as much a problem in the U.S. as it is in Europe (table 1). Unskilled unemployment in the U.S. has in fact risen by more than 100% since the early seventies despite of the substantial fall in unskilled wages. Yet, in contrast to continental Europe, the more flexible wage structure allowed substantial employment growth even among low-earning workers (Ochel (1998)).

---

[2] Technical progress is usually measured as a residual so that its high explanatory power could also be interpreted as a lack of concrete knowledge.

Table 1: *Male Unemployment Rates by Educational Attainment*

	Time	Total unemploy-ment rate	Lower secondary education or below	Higher secondary education or above	Ratio
USA	1979-82	5,7	9,4	2,1	4,5
	1983-86	7,3	12,8	2,7	4,7
	1987-90	5,1	9,8	2,1	4,7
	1991-93	6,0	11,0	3,0	3,7
	1994	6,2	12,8	4,8	2,7
	1995	5,6	10,9	4,1	2,7
Germany	1979-82	3,4	7,6	2,0	3,8
	1983-86	6,3	13,9	3,3	4,2
	1987-90	4,9	12,1	2,9	4,2
	1991-93	4,1	10,7	2,2	4,9
	1994	7,3	14,8	5,8	2,6
	1995	7,2	13,5	5,4	2,5
France	1979-82	5,2	6,5	2,1	3,1
	1983-86	6,7	9,0	2,5	3,6
	1987-90	7,2	10,8	2,6	4,1
	1991-93	8,1	12,1	4,2	2,9
	1994	10,9	13,5	7,6	1,8
	1995	9,8	12,8	7,1	1,8
UK	1979-82	7,7	12,2	3,9	3,1
	1983-86	10,5	18,2	4,7	3,9
	1987-90	7,5	13,5	4,0	3,4
	1991-93	10,8	17,1	6,2	2,8
	1994	11,5	18,8	7,1	2,6
	1995	10,2	17,2	6,3	2,7
Sweden	1979-82	2,4	3,1	0,9	3,4
	1983-86	3,1	4,1	1,1	3,7
	1987-90	1,8	2,4	1,0	2,4
	1991-93	5,8	6,9	2,8	2,5
	1994	9,1	9,6	6,5	1,5
	1995	8,5	10,6	7,4	1,4

Sources: Nickell (1996, p. 26 f.) and OECD Employment Outlook.

The distinguishing features between unemployment in the U.S. and Europe are nonetheless the better performance in the overall unemployment rate and the much lower rate of long-term unemployment (table 2). This alludes to the two probably most important caveats concerning this approach: its validity requires that there has only been a change in the structure of labor demand towards higher skill requirements of firms and not an overall reduction of labor demand at given real wages. Hence, the increase in unemployment must essentially be a mismatch phenomenon with unemployment among low-skilled workers rising and among high-skilled workers falling. This cannot be the whole story as becomes immediately clear upon closer inspection of table 1. Unemployment among high-skilled workers has also risen in most OECD countries and in particular in France, Germany and the U.S. In fact, assuming an isoelastic wage-setting curve as in Blanchflower and Oswald (1994), the relative sizes of the increases in unemployment in the different skill groups point more to macroeconomic shocks than to changes in the structure of labor demand. A greater percentage point increase in unemployment among low-skilled workers is perfectly compatible with macroeconomic shocks as real wages are more rigid at the lower end of the wage distribution and as sorting effects induce firms to keep preferably higher skilled persons in case of crisis, e.g. due to higher investments in their firm-specific human capital (Nickell and Bell (1995) and Blanchard (1995)).

Table 2: *The Share of Long-Term Unemployment*

Year	USA	Germany	France	UK	Sweden
1983	13,3	41,6	42,2	45,6	10,3
1989	5,7	49,0	43,9	40,8	6,3
1990	5,5	46,8	38,0	34,4	4,7
1991	6,3	31,5	37,2	28,8	4,2
1992	11,1	33,5	36,1	35,4	8,3
1993	11,5	40,0	34,2	42,5	10,9
1994	12,2	44,3	38,3	45,4	17,3
1995	9,7	48,7	42,3	43,6	15,8
1996	9,5	47,8	39,5	39,8	17,1

Source: OECD Employment Outlook.

This assessment is also confirmed by empirical analyses of the relationship between the rate of vacancies and the rate of unemployment over time. They show, e.g. for Germany, that the Beveridge curve has moved outwards but that the increase in unemployment is not accompanied by an equal rise in the rate of vacancies. Persistently high unemployment in continental Europe can therefore not be a pure mismatch phenomenon based on a changing structure of labor demand in combination with rigid relative wages. More flexible wage structures would certainly help in reducing unemployment, but a thorough explanation for the dismal situation on labor markets in continental Europe must rather move on and also look for macroeconomic problems.[3]

2.1 Appropriation, Capital Formation and Technological Sclerosis

A general and ongoing increase in the aggressiveness of wage setting in continental Europe could of course in principle account for rising unemployment. However, while there is some evidence in this direction based on rising labor shares and mounting wage gaps in the seventies and early eighties, this conjecture is less convincing for the late eighties and early nineties. This should not be surprising. The late sixties and early seventies were characterized by a strengthening of unions and by an expansion of welfare states in continental Europe. This development of strengthening workers' bargaining position culminated and ended in Germany with the introduction of extensive codetermination rights in the mid seventies. The power of unions, e.g. in terms of union coverage and membership, has, if anything, decreased since then and it is fair to say that the generosity of welfare states has by and large been kept unchanged, albeit at a high level. Hence, changes in the aggressiveness of wage setting and for that matter also changes in the incentive structure of the unemployed to stay idle are hardly promising avenues for explaining further rising unemployment in continental Europe in the eighties and nineties. It rather appears that labor demand has undergone additional transformations beyond a move towards higher skill requirements of firms which undoubtedly has occurred to some extent. It is noteworthy that labor shares have by now dropped in France and Germany below the level in the U.S.

To make some leeway in analyzing in an admittedly highly stylized form the evolution of labor demand in continental Europe, the following standard description of the labor market is useful. Labor supply LS is for simplicity assumed to be infinitely elastic with respect to the real wage in efficiency units w up to full employment and completely inelastic beyond. The wage-setting curve WS, which reflects union wage bargaining and/or efficiency wage considerations, is as usual upward sloped so that increasing employment L leads to higher real wage settlements. The key to understanding the evolution of unemployment in continental Europe seems to be adjustments of labor demand LD. The reaction of labor demand to wage-setting shocks depends very much on the time span which is considered. Firing costs, putty-clay production technology, convex costs of changing factor proportions, delivery contracts etc. make labor demand highly inelastic in the short run as depicted by the vertical instantaneous labor demand

[3] Nickell (1997) points out that the skill shift accounts for at most 20 percent of the rise in unemployment in Europe, and that supposedly flexible Britain did not fare better in this respect than the rigid continental European countries.

curve LD^{SR}. Hence, capital is exposed to appropriation by myopic insiders. If a wage shock occurs, e.g. due to higher firing costs, the wage-setting curve moves from WS to WS'. Employment does in this extreme case not change at all in the short run and the economy is simply moved from point A to point B.[4] However, there is of course some substitutability between labor and capital over time as is reflected by the medium-run labor demand curve $LD_{\overline{K}}^{MR}$, so that employment will decrease to a point like C where the size of the capital stock is still unchanged. This is by no means the end of the story, though. The return to capital in point C is still lower than in the initial point A. Assuming that capital received in A just the internationally required rate of return and furthermore assuming that this world-wide interest rate has not changed in the meantime, capital clearly has an incentive to move out of the country concerned until the rate of return on capital rises back to its original level. Hence, a further reduction in employment is effectuated until point D is realized. Point D lies on the long-run labor demand curve LD_{ET}^{LR} with a perfectly variable size of the capital stock and an efficient choice of technology (Blanchard (1997) and (1998)).

[4] It is noteworthy that the speed in the reaction of labor demand to wage-push shocks is about four times higher in the U.S. than in Europe (Siebert (1997)), so that capital is more exposed to appropriation in Europe.

Figure 2: *The Long-Run Effects of Appropriation Problems*

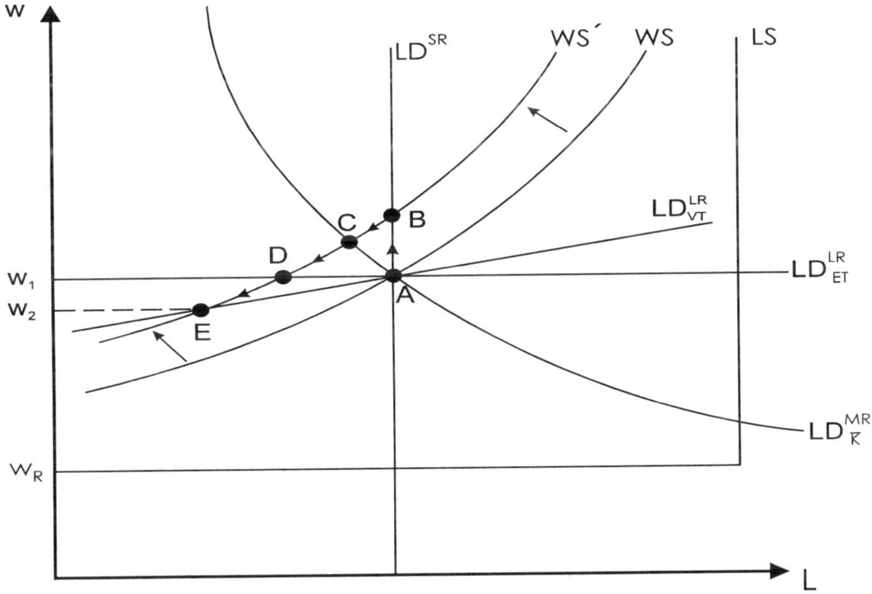

The analysis has hitherto abstracted from repercussions of the original wage-setting shock on the efficiency properties of the process of creative destruction. This is of course not innocuous once the analysis is extended to the long-run. A wage-push shock due to higher firing costs derails the process of creative destruction and moves the economy on a sclerotic time path. It artificially induces firms to invest less and when investing new vintages of capital to select production technologies which rely more on the use of capital in the production process. In other words, such an economy embarks on a different time path concerning the evolution of the production technology: firms will switch to more capital intensive production technologies in order to become less open to appropriation by insiders. The appropriability problem arises due to the existence of specific quasi-rents in the production process which cannot be contracted away. Such specific quasi-rents can be due to technological reasons such as firm-specific knowledge of workers and firm-financed training of workers or they can also be due to political reasons such as high firing costs possibly reinforced by generous unemployment benefits and a high level of unionization. Strong legal protection of management in publicly traded firms against close control by firm-owners is another politically induced and possibly important appropriation problem causing technological sclerosis (Caballero and Hammour (1997) and (1998a)).

The late sixties and early seventies clearly witnessed politically induced appropriation shocks. Firing costs were raised, unions gained in power and the welfare state in general expanded. Such an appropriation shock has negative long-run effects on the process of creative destruction and thus on employment. Not only was job creation unequivocally reduced, but rising unemployment depressed in addition shadow wages, i.e. earning opportunities of workers when they are laid off, thus reducing their appropriation potential and pressure to scrap old vintages of capital. The resulting increase in the average scrapping age of the existing capital stock causes a slowdown in the rate of technological progress thus diminishing productivity growth and equilibrium wages. Once these long-run processes of technological adjustment are taken into account in our simple diagram, the effective long-run elasticity of substitution between capital and labor increases and may well grow above one, thus giving rise to a slightly positively-sloped long-run labor demand curve with variable production technology LD_{VT}^{LR}.[5] Hence, this additional long-run labor demand curve with a counterintuitive positive slope incorporates the negative repercussions of an appropriation shock on the process of creative destruction. Unemployment therefore increases even further to a point like E as long as WS' remains the relevant wage-setting curve. The problem of microeconomic specificities, which is aggravated by political institutions in particular in continental Europe, experiences a highly inefficient macroeconomic solution.

Hence, there are long-run consequences on unemployment of the appropriation shocks which occurred in continental Europe in the late sixties and early seventies which are usually neglected. Three interesting implications emerge. First, similar to the Krugman (1994) approach, appropriation problems also lead to a substitution of labor in the production process, albeit not only by human capital but rather also by real capital. Second, the resulting long-run increase in unemployment is related to insider power and wage setting, but the trade-off between real wage and employment growth not only disappears, but there is actually a positive long-run relationship because the average worker is at any given rate of unemployment eventually paid more money in real terms in high-employment countries where the appropriation threat to capital by insiders is less of a problem and where the process of creative destruction therefore works more smoothly thus inducing a better allocation of resources. Third, the labor share must by implication also be greater in the long run in such countries, so that demands to increase the labor share via an aggressive wage policy are from a long-run perspective completely mistaken.

The ongoing process of globalization is closely linked to this appropriation issue. The greater mobility of capital causes faster downward adjustments of the capital stock in response to an appropriation shock. Furthermore, factor-substitution possibilities have been enhanced by globalization, as not only the speed of

[5] Stability of the system requires that the wage setting curve must be steeper than this long-run labor demand curve.

technological progress but also the potential for specialization has been increased. The broadened technological menu which firms have nowadays at their disposal promotes investment and growth, but workers may not share in the benefits if labor markets are heavily regulated and therefore malfunctioning. Finally, globalization accelerates the ongoing fundamental transformation of production structures from Fordism to holistic organizations. The implied changes in the organization of production, which essentially take place in all highly developed countries, magnify appropriation problems as the importance of microeconomic specificities, e.g. in terms of firm-specific knowledge is increased. Yet, this development has a particularly severe effect on employment in countries where politically induced appropriation problems are already large, i.e. political and technological appropriation problems are not substitutes but they rather reinforce each other.

2.2 Rising Volatilities

However, there is another important macroeconomic channel via which globalization raises quasi-equilibrium unemployment specifically in continental Europe. The level of volatilities, i.e. the size and frequency of shocks which firms have to cope with, has increased significantly in recent years. This is above all the result of more globalized goods and capital markets, which give rise to the observable rapid restructuring from manufacturing to the service industry, the already mentioned fundamental reorganization of production and firms, "footloose" industries, "caleidoscopic" comparative advantages, shorter product life cycles, unstable portfolio choices of foreign investors, and more pronounced fluctuations of stock market prices.[6] The ability of economies to absorb such greater volatilities without rising unemployment depends decisively on their institutional characteristics. Continental Europe is in a number of ways not well prepared for this task. First, the above-mentioned appropriability problem, which is particularly severe in continental Europe exacerbates in an asymmetric way the susceptibility of economies to shocks. The employment effects of adverse shocks are greater than those of positive shocks in economies which exhibit appropriability problems. Hence, recessions become deeper and booms more shallow so that an overall increase in volatility causes average unemployment to rise (Caballero and Hammour (1998b)).

---

[6] See Bhagwati and Dehejia (1994), Bertola and Ichino (1995a), Lindbeck and Snower (1996), Ljungqvist and Sargent (1998), Rodrik (1997), and Calvo and Mendoza (1997). The latter authors show in particular that more globalized capital markets make herd behavior of investors more likely because of fixed information costs concerning the fundamentals of countries and firms, and because they widen the band of multiple equilibria due to reputational effects. Gottschalk and Moffitt (1994) provide empirical evidence for the U.S. that not only the dispersion of earnings between individuals but also the volatility of an individual's earnings has increased since the early 1980s.

Second, greater volatilities entail the need for larger fluctuations on labor markets as firms have to adjust more often to changing economic circumstances. Yet, each layoff is coupled with an immediate loss of firm- or sector-specific human capital which, through the existence of rent sharing, is part of the remuneration package of workers. If unemployment benefits are tied as in continental Europe to last earnings and long-lasting, it is clear that a larger percentage of workers will stay (voluntarily) unemployed compared to a very harsh unemployment benefit system like in the U.S. where receipt of unemployment benefits is strictly limited to up to six months. Job offers in new firms or sectors will usually carry lower wages as they do not include the previously earned rent-sharing component, making them rather unattractive compared to remaining unemployed and still benefiting at least partially from the already depreciated specific human capital. Hence, unemployment rates are going to exhibit greater persistence in countries where welfare benefits are long-lasting and closely tied to last earnings. Sorting and discouragement effects furthermore contribute to the asymmetric persistence of unemployment rates which can be in particular observed in continental European countries and which are especially detrimental under rising volatilities.[7]

Third, high firing costs raise the level and the persistence of unemployment in a less stable economic environment. Rising volatilities in combination with high firing costs increase total expected labor costs as the probability rises that any particular worker becomes redundant at a given point in time so that firms have to bear large firing costs. Hence, firms turn more reluctant to use the quasi-specific production factor labor in the production process leading to an overall reduction in labor demand. Rising volatilities therefore unambiguously have a greater negative effect on labor demand in a rigid economy with high firing costs than in a flexible economy with low firing costs. Furthermore, high firing costs increase the bargaining power of insiders, because it becomes even more costly to replace insiders by outsiders. Wage pressure is as a consequence mainly contained by rising unemployment and less so by a high but stable level of unemployment. High firing costs therefore reinforce the asymmetric persistence of unemployment rates which is in particular a problem when shocks occur more frequently.[8]

Fourth, a more volatile economic environment reduces in particular labor demand in countries where firms have weak balance-sheet positions and are mainly financed by credits. A greater volatility of shocks causes the risky rate of interest which firms are charged by banks to rise as banks must counterbalance a higher default risk. This reduces investments so that labor demand of firms shrinks in

[7] See Ljungqvist and Sargent (1998), Elmeskov (1993), Layard (1996) and Lindbeck (1996).

[8] See Bertola and Ichino (1995a) and Fehn (1997). This result stays in contrast to the findings of Bentilola and Bertola (1990), where the effects of an increase in firing costs on labor demand at a constant level of volatilities were found to be ambiguous.

turn in the long run.[9] The ensuing larger marginal productivity of employed labor is needed to compensate firms for their greater obligations concerning interest payments and for the larger expected value of bankruptcy costs. The last two problems, high firing costs and reliance on credit finance, in relation with greater volatilities, could in principle be offset by more moderate wage agreements. However, high firing costs by themselves reduce the willingness of workers to react to greater volatilities with wage moderation. Furthermore, if such shocks are largely firm-specific, strong and central unions are unlikely to cut wage demands in reaction (Aizenman and Powell (1997) and Fehn (1998)).

In sum, the ongoing process of globalization entails significant changes concerning labor demand which conflict with important institutional characteristics of the continental European economies. In particular, the following institutions appear to be highly detrimental to employment growth in the era of globalization: generous and indefinite transfer payments to the unemployed, large firing costs, strong and relatively centralized unions, a predominance of credit financing of firms and a strong position of management vis-à-vis firm owners. The last two points make clear that insider-oriented systems, be they on labor or on capital markets, as a rule raise unemployment. However, reflecting the title of the paper the following sections only deal with labor market policy. It should nonetheless be kept in mind that reforms in other areas such as capital markets are highly complementary to labor market reforms, in the sense that they increase the achievable positive employment effects (Coe and Snower (1996)).

3 Designing an Efficient Labor Market Policy

Efforts to mitigate the negative employment effects of globalization in continental Europe should concentrate on redesigning labor market policy in order to help workers to cope with the consequences of globalization rather than on the futile attempt of restricting the process of globalization itself. The latter would in fact also reduce the opportunities to reap the benefits of globalization. Policies to increase employment must aim at raising the capacity of labor markets to adjust to negative shocks and at avoiding policy-induced shocks rather than on shielding labor markets from non policy-induced shocks. Although a multitude of shocks have led to rising unemployment in continental Europe, the number of institutional variables which act as negative transmission mechanisms is far more limited. The task of an efficiency-oriented labor market policy can be boiled down even further: it must concentrate on breaking the dichotomy between insiders and

[9] Empirical evidence for the negative effect of weak balance sheet positions on labor demand is provided inter alia by Funke et al. (1998), Nickell and Nicolitsas (1997) and Winker (1998).

outsiders on labor markets by promoting the reintegration of outsiders into the regular labor market. This can inter alia be achieved by an appropriate design of passive and active labor market policies, which will be the topic of the following sections. However, one must be circumspect in designing passive and active labor market policies in such way that negative repercussions on wage-setting behavior of insiders are avoided. These tasks are in principle not different compared to the era before globalization, but fulfilling them has become far more urgent because the welfare losses associated with inefficient institutional settings have increased dramatically.

The principal question is how outsiders, in particular the long-term unemployed, can be reintegrated into the regular labor market. It is important to recognize in this context that the ultimate goal must always be reemployment in the regular labor market as second or third labor markets tend to become a drag on the regular economy eventually, thus further reducing regular employment and entering into a vicious circle of rising taxes and government employment (Berthold and Fehn (1997)). Policies will only be successful in enfranchising outsiders if they either alter their incentive structure towards actively seeking jobs or enhance the incentives of firms to hire outsiders. The unemployment benefit system and the design of active labor market policy are of particular importance in this respect. They therefore deserve to be discussed in some detail.

3.1 Reforming Unemployment Benefit Systems

There can be no doubt that high levels of unemployment and especially of long-term unemployment are related to the generosity of the unemployment benefit system. Even without invoking Say's Law, it is immediately clear that if people are offered high and long-lasting pay for staying idle with little pressure to accept available jobs, a lot of them will of course stay idle. High benefits create high overall unemployment and long-term benefits generate lots of long-term unemployment. The detrimental effects of lavish unemployment benefit systems are among the best-documented and least controversial facts in labor economics. The negative employment effects arise not only due to a lower search intensity of the unemployed but also because the fallback position of insiders is improved thus making wage setting more aggressive. Empirical studies are almost unanimous in confirming this conjecture. Hence, reforming unemployment insurance must aim at reversing these effects, which is intricate as it involves difficult political choices.[10]

---

[10] See e.g. Layard et al. (1991), Nickell (1997) and Scarpetta (1996). Hunt (1995) has shown that prolonging unemployment benefits to the elderly in the 1980s in Germany significantly increased their unemployment spells. A more ambiguous assessment of the effects of unemployment insurance on the level and duration of unemployment can be found in Atkinson and Micklewright (1991).

3.1.1 Privatizing Unemployment Insurance?

A radical market-oriented reformer might suggest that government-run unemployment benefit systems should be completely abolished, thus letting private insurances take care of the different moral hazard effects concerning job search, wage setting and layoff patterns of firms, which are caused by unemployment benefits. Private insurances are able to cope with moral hazard problems on other markets, like e.g. car insurance, so that they should in principle also be able to do so on the labor market. However, the analogy is not quite that simple. As long as the government guarantees a minimum level of income to those citizens who cannot support themselves, as is the case in continental Europe, people clearly lack incentive to sufficiently insure themselves. They can always count on the government to step in if they are in need. Hence, to avoid free-rider behavior of its citizens, the government must at least force those who have a job to underwrite unemployment insurance contracts covering this guaranteed minimum standard of living for a certain time period.

Yet, there are furthermore doubts as to the viability of such a private unemployment insurance system. Not only is the probability distribution of becoming unemployed largely unknown, but this risk is also highly correlated in the case of macroeconomic shocks, so that private insurances might quickly go bankrupt if large macroeconomic shocks occur. Both factors make unemployment a risk that is difficult to insure on private markets. Considering that macroeconomic shocks, such as a large and sudden fall in stock prices, often hit several countries simultaneously, it would not even help much if private unemployment insurances tried to diversify internationally their portfolio of insured risks. A completely privatized system of unemployment insurance is therefore problematic as long as efficient diversification is impossible. It is from this perspective no coincidence that unemployment insurance is in all highly developed countries run by the government.[11]

3.1.2 Reforms within the Current Unemployment-Benefit System

However, there is considerable scope for efficiency-enhancing reforms concerning unemployment insurance which fall short of completely privatizing the system. Taking Germany as the institutional benchmark, the following

[11] See e.g. Anderson and Meyer (1993). One could however conceive of a mixed system where unemployment insurance is offered competitively by private insurance companies which are subjected to close government surveillance and which are bailed out by tax money in case of large macroeconomic shocks.

characteristics of the current unemployment benefit system are noteworthy: registered unemployed persons receive benefits for an extremely long time by international comparison (table 3). Unemployment benefits last up to 32 months depending on age and on the time contributions were previously made. Furthermore, unemployment benefits are followed by unemployment assistance, which is granted without time limit. Though unemployment assistance is means-tested, the amount paid in both types of benefits depends on previous net income as well as on family status. In each case this amount remains in principle unchanged until payments are terminated. Pressure exerted on registered unemployed persons to accept offered jobs has been increased in recent years but must still be considered to be low. In particular, the unemployed are rarely forced to move to another region if jobs are available there but not in her hometown and not within a 180 minutes per day commuting distance. It is even currently planned to cut this maximum commuting time per day to 150 minutes which would clearly be a step in the wrong direction. Unemployment insurance is organized on the national level and is mainly financed by a flat rate social security tax on gross wages which is levied in equal parts on workers and firms. There is no differentiation according to risk class of workers or firms or according to region. Unemployment assistance is exclusively financed by federal tax money.

Table 3: *An International Comparison of Unemployment Insurance*

	U.S.	Germany	France	UK	Sweden
Benefit Replacement Rate (%)	50	63	57	38	80
Benefit Duration (years)	0.5	unlimited (unemployment assistance)	3	unlimited (unemployment assistance)	1.2

Source: Nickell (1997, p. 61).

Considering the well-established negative effects of the German unemployment insurance system on the functioning of the labor market, a number of reforms need to be undertaken. The time span for which unemployment benefits can be received is empirically the most significant factor in explaining country-specific differences in unemployment and especially in long-term unemployment. Hence, cutting this maximum time span should get first priority. The unemployment benefit system must furthermore entice people to actively seek jobs even if available jobs differ concerning pay, qualification, region etc. from the previous one. This is the only way of avoiding persistent unemployment in times of high volatilities and rapid structural change. The longer an individual is unemployed, the greater must be the pressure on her in this respect. Having held a well-paid job in a certain region for some time cannot constitute a reason that the rest of society guarantees a related income position in this region for the rest of one's life.

These considerations first and foremost suggest that the design of unemployment assistance is fundamentally flawed. Unemployment assistance is not part of the insurance system but benefits are nonetheless linked to previous net income and they are granted without time limit. However, if somebody has not been successful in finding a job until unemployment benefits have expired, she should in case of need receive welfare benefits which have nothing to do with previous net income. Hence, unemployment assistance should simply be abolished. Recipients should be made aware of the fact that they are no longer part of the insurance system. The maximum time span for receiving unemployment benefits should in addition be reduced to say something like one year from where on the person concerned is usually considered to be long-term unemployed. Countries with flexible labor markets and a far better unemployment performance such as the U.S. even limit the receipt of unemployment benefits to six months.[12]

It must furthermore be remembered that unemployment insurance involves severe principal-agent problems as it is impossible to even come close to identifying the causes why a worker was laid off and to perfectly monitoring the search efforts of the unemployed. Yet, workers and firms have plenty of room for discretionary maneuver concerning whether and why a work contract is actually terminated. The reemployment probability depends in addition in large part on search effort. Experiments in the U.S. have demonstrated that economic incentives greatly affect the speed with which people leave the unemployment insurance rolls. Hence, unemployment insurance is not a benign transfer, it rather has repercussions on claimants' behavior. Moral-hazard and free-rider problems can be contained by introducing the right incentives. Models based on intertemporal utility maximization and on these moral hazard considerations suggest that there should be a punishment for terminating work contracts and a reward for finding regular employment again. Concerning the size of benefits this translates into a large drop in income in the first period of unemployment, with benefits then increasing up to a peak from where they decrease again all the way down to the level of welfare benefits. Finding a job again should in contrast be rewarded in the early periods of reemployment possibly by only slowly phasing in social security contributions. The total reward for reemployment must be the greater, the longer was the previous unemployment spell in order to contain the risk of fraud. This approach to installing a reemployment bonus is preferable to a cash handout. A cash handout would rather raise the incentive to file for unemployment insurance even though a job might be available immediately and even though the laid-off

---

[12] In particular the U.S. has a much more restrictive system of unemployment insurance. Unemployment rates were about the same in West-Germany and the U.S. in 1990, but Germany spent in that year 0.23% of GDP on unemployment benefits whereas the U.S. only spent about 0.09% of GDP on unemployment benefits; see Schmid (1995, 93).

person would currently not believe that filing for unemployment insurance is worth the trouble. Benefits should finally be terminated after a certain spell of unemployment, e.g. six months, if the unemployed person received suitable job offers, but at locations which are further away than 180 minutes per day commuting distance.[13]

However, it might also be useful to introduce a strictly rule-bound system of automatically punishing firms for terminating work contracts. This alludes to the issue of experience rating firms' contributions to unemployment insurance. Making the size of firms' contributions to unemployment insurance depend on their layoff behavior would help to internalize the social costs of layoffs. The U.S. is the only OECD country with experience rating. Based on its beneficial effects there, U.S. researchers mostly suggest to expand the present system of experience rating in unemployment insurance rather than to abolish it. Hence, it should be considered to include elements of experience rating in a comprehensive reform of unemployment insurance in Germany. Unemployment would then be taxed thus providing an incentive for firms to engage in stable activities and to smooth production over seasons and cycles. Experience rating would furthermore reduce cross subsidies from stable sectors, such as the service sector, to unstable sectors, such as construction. Hence, the overall stability of the economy would be promoted. Such a system of experience rating would have an additional advantage. It would protect workers against arbitrary layoffs thus reducing the case for government-imposed firing costs (Baicker et al. (1997, p. 23) and Card and Levine (1994)).

However, experience rating would further strengthen the position of insiders in wage negotiations. Hence, introducing a comprehensive system of experience rating would only make sense if government-imposed firing costs are simultaneously reduced. Firing costs e.g. in the form of severance payments are not only large in the German case, but they are also hard to calculate ex ante as their actual size mostly depends on rather discretionary decisions of labor courts. German labor courts usually give priority to the interests of the worker concerned with little consideration of the macroeconomic consequences. This has highly negative repercussions on the hiring decisions of firms and thus on long-run employment growth. The detrimental effects not only rise with the volatility of the

---

[13] See Wang and Williamson (1996). Hopenhayn and Nicolini (1997) suggest that optimal unemployment insurance consists of decreasing benefits coupled with a wage tax levied on workers that increases with the length of the previous unemployment spell to punish workers for continued unemployment by reducing their claims to all kinds of future consumption in unemployment and in employment. However, in the continental European setting, where welfare benefits constitute a minimum net wage, this appears to aggravate sorting effects among the unemployed as the incentive to reenter the regular labor market decreases with an increasing unemployment spell. Meyer (1995) provides a thorough discussion concerning the results of experiments with reemployment bonuses in the U.S.

economic environment, but they also increase the potential of insiders to appropriate firms by improving the fallback position of insiders.

Firing costs are only justified as they force firms to carry part of the mobility costs which are otherwise exclusively borne by workers in case of layoff and by protecting workers against short-term and maybe arbitrary dismissals. However, both goals would already be achieved by experience rating in combination with sufficiently long notification periods so that severance payments become in fact superfluous. Labor law should furthermore state very clearly under which circumstances it is legal to fire a worker in order to reduce insecurity in this field. The rule-bound element in labor relations would be promoted by substituting experience rating in unemployment insurance for the current system of large and hard-to-calculate government-imposed firing costs. The tendency that labor is becoming more and more a quasi-fixed factor would be reversed. Firms could react more quickly to greater volatilities so that employment growth would be promoted. However, unemployment insurance must be reformed in tandem with abolishing government-imposed firing costs. The increase in volatilities would otherwise induce a much greater rate of lay-offs, and this would cause an even further rise in long-term unemployment as long as unemployment insurance is not reformed in the outlined direction.

Returning to the issue of transfer payments to the unemployed, unemployment insurance should rely as much as possible on insurance principles. It is therefore not justified to differentiate payments according to family status. Income redistribution in favor of families should be completely detached from unemployment insurance (Snower (1995)). Unemployed parents who receive unemployment benefits which are below their claims to welfare benefits are entitled anyway to receive the difference in the form of supplementary welfare benefits. If a needy person has not found a job after one year of unemployment, she has access to welfare benefits. However, to again contain moral hazard problems, the full amount of welfare benefits should only be granted if at least one of the two following conditions is satisfied. First, the unemployed person is not able to work, e.g. due to having small dependent children or due to being severely handicapped. Second, she does not refuse training or jobs offered by the local authorities even though these might be of menial character and involve no or only very little additional pay. Her level of welfare benefits should be reduced and in severe cases completely terminated if a long-term unemployed person who is able to work rejects such job offers or training. Confronting the unemployed with such a choice is the only effective way of dismantling their advantage concerning leisure time. The opportunities of the unemployed to work on the black market would be curtailed and envy effects of people holding a job would be kept in check. Such envy effects arise especially in case of families because a working spouse with children often earns a net wage which is only marginally above the level of welfare benefits. The fairness and reciprocity principles of the welfare state would be strengthened by strictly enforcing these conditions.

3.1.3 Opening Unemployment Insurance for Institutional Competition

However, society as a whole might not yet be willing to go down this road of reforming transfer payments to the unemployed. Confidence in market mechanisms is scarce and many people will therefore doubt whether positive employment effects will materialize. Yet, the support for such reforms hinges on the size of the perceived positive employment effects because the unemployed are obviously treated more harshly. Considering the widespread but completely misguided thinking in given amounts of labor demand as the limiting factor for employment suggests that this support will be rather limited. The unemployment benefit system should therefore simply be opened for the concept of institutional competition between regions. The above proposals can then be taken as an institutional benchmark for an efficiency-oriented system but each region would be free in deciding about the precise design of its unemployment benefit system. Each region should be allowed to give individuals considerable choice concerning their unemployment insurance package such as the level and contour of benefits and the eligibility criteria. The contributions of the insured would then depend on how encompassing the chosen package is. Reductions of firms' contributions due to a worker choosing a package which is less generous than a predefined standard package would have to be paid out to the worker to set her incentives right (Snower (1995)).

Some regions are likely to choose stricter and more elaborate systems than the inefficient current system. The positive employment effects of more efficient setups in these regions will over time become evident to other regions as well. Pressure will therefore increase to undertake reforms in the same direction. Such an institutional competition approach requires of course that the financing of unemployment benefits must then also be organized on the regional level so that regions along with their firms and workers benefit more directly from efficient solutions. Yet, insurance principles demand that the organization and financing of unemployment benefits only be delegated to the level of large states such as Bavaria or North-Rhine-Westfalia. Smaller states with few dominant sectors such as Saarlouis would have to join with others such as Hesse and Palatine. Looking again across the Atlantic shows that unemployment insurance in the U.S. is organized at the state level, and that the experience of the U.S. with institutional competition in this field is encouraging.

Opening unemployment insurance for institutional competition would also allow even bolder reforms in certain front-runner regions. Individuals could be allowed to leave unemployment insurance altogether if they do not depend on welfare benefits for the standard duration of unemployment insurance, e.g. one year, in case they become unemployed. Free rider behavior could be excluded very simply by requiring individuals to keep savings amounting to at least their claim to welfare benefits for one year in a separate Individual Unemployment Account (IUA).[14] This IUA would have to be inaccessible for its owner while holding a job and before retirement, but it could substitute completely for contributions to unemployment insurance. Individuals would in case of unemployment simply draw on this IUA. If the person concerned found a job again, her choice of opting out of unemployment insurance would only be available again once the IUA is refilled up to her specific minimum amount. Positive balances on the IUA would have to earn interest payments approximately equal to those on government bonds. Any positive balance that would still remain at retirement age would be paid out to the individual. Such an IUA would have great advantages: individuals would draw on their own wealth to finance limited periods of unemployment rather than immediately collecting checks from the state. Consequently, they would tend to be more diligent in searching for work and they would also have a stronger incentive to explore alternatives to layoffs with employers. Furthermore, it would no longer matter why an individual had become unemployed so that there would be savings in terms of costs for bureaucracy. In sum, there is plenty of room for efficiency-enhancing reforms of unemployment insurance and it is time something is done about it.

3.2 Redesigning Active Labor Market Policy

Active labor market policy (ALMP) is often celebrated as a panacea for fighting unemployment. Politicians and international organizations alike are almost unanimous in their confidence in the efficacy of ALMP. This broad consensus is reflected in the fact that the massive use of ALMP in the eastern part of Germany is largely uncontroversial. ALMP are essentially measures which do not passively finance unemployment but which are rather expected to pave the way for the unemployed back into the regular labor market. There are three avenues via which ALMP can in principle increase employment. ALMP can reduce asymmetries of information between labor demand and labor supply. This is a rather uncontroversial task, which can be fulfilled both by a government agency and by private organizations. ALMP can furthermore contribute to qualifying the unemployed so that their qualification profile fits better with labor demand. These two strategies are essentially aimed at reducing mismatch unemployment. The

[14] See Orszag and Snower (1997) and Snower (1995); Feldstein (1998) makes a similar proposal in which workers would be required to save up to 4 percent of wages in special accounts and to draw unemployment compensation from these accounts instead of taking state unemployment insurance benefits. This proposal has the advantage of avoiding adverse selection effects as everybody would stay within the same system. The big disadvantage, though, is that the balance on the IUA could in such a setup be insufficient to cover the insurance period thus forcing the government to systematically step in with additional payments.

government can finally attempt to increase aggregate employment directly via work creation schemes or via wage subsidies (Calmfors (1994)).

Expenditures for ALMP in Germany increased massively in the late 1980s and the early 1990s, i.e. from 0.8% of GDP in 1985 to about 1.6% of GDP in 1993. This development is obviously related to reunification. Outlays for ALMP have been slightly reduced since then amounting to 1.3% of GDP in 1995. These numbers put Germany in a little bit above average position concerning expenditure for ALMP in OECD countries. Especially the Scandinavian countries spend far more on ALMP. Sweden for example used a whopping 3.0% of GDP for this purpose in 1995. These non-negligible sums reflect the widespread trust of policymakers in the efficacy of current ALMP in fighting unemployment. However, the efficiency of ALMP in raising employment cannot be taken for granted and rather depends upon its institutional design.

3.2.1 Can ALMP Raise Regular Employment?

ALMP is a useful instrument for fighting unemployment if it addresses the causes of rising unemployment and if possible negative side effects are not too large. It must in particular contribute to increasing the adjustment capacity to shocks and to raising regular employment. If successful, ALMP acts as a trampoline for laid-off workers, helping them to return into the regular labor market. This is in sharp contrast to simply handing out transfer payments to the unemployed, where the welfare state degenerates into a hammock for the unemployed, in which they can rest without time limit and be a burden for the rest of society. It should be noted that the impact of ALMP on regular employment must be the criterion of judgment and not official unemployment. The government could otherwise simply declare all the unemployed to be state employees or students, who are entitled to receiving tax money, and claim the unemployment problem to be solved.

The idea of financing work instead of unemployment and thereby upgrading workers' skills is appealing but in its very simple form misleading. Unemployment is of course a waste of resources but at least the short-term unemployed nonetheless fulfill an important macroeconomic function. They dampen wage demands of insiders thus producing macroeconomic stability in terms of constant inflation and in terms of guaranteeing capital its internationally required return. The stronger the position of insiders is, e.g. due to high union density, large firing costs and generous unemployment insurance, the more unemployment is needed to produce macroeconomic stability. Simply transferring the unemployed into state-organized ALMP schemes and paying them wages which are closely related to insider wages does therefore undermine macroeconomic stability. In terms of figure 2, such a measure would reduce effective labor supply thus moving the LS curve to the left and simultaneously pushing the WS curve upwards. The long-run consequences on employment would be even worse as such an inefficient ALMP would amount to another appropriation shock by improving the fall-back position of insiders. Hence, the economy would become even more sclerotic and long-run labor demand is further pushed downwards. Such an approach would end up in a government-guaranteed right to work, which is not compatible with a market economy. The failure of the Swedish model as well as the disastrous experience of the centrally planned economies of Eastern Europe should have completely discredited such an overambitious government employment policy.[15]

Repercussions on wage setting are therefore important and the total employment effects of any particular instrument of ALMP cannot be analyzed in isolation. A high reemployment quota of participants in an ALMP scheme is on the one hand not an unequivocal indicator that this scheme promotes employment at the macrolevel as reemployment might be at the expense of other workers and as the fallback position of insiders might be improved. The latter effect would lead to increased wage pressure and eventually to employment losses. On the other hand, ALMP schemes which appear useless on first sight might reduce the welfare level of participants. If insiders reckon that they would have to enroll into such a program in case of dismissal and bear the extra utility loss, this would reduce wage pressure thus raising total regular employment. Hence, a macroeconomic approach is called for evaluating ALMP.

In order to be successful, ALMP must therefore be organized in a more subtle way and especially avoid the fallacy of increasing appropriation problems and aggregate wage pressure. ALMP must improve the chances of the unemployed to return into the regular labor market and not simply hide unemployment. As wage pressure is mainly contained by the short-term unemployed, ALMP should concentrate on helping the long-term unemployed thus preventing a shrinkage of effective labor supply. The long-term unemployed suffer from a number of disadvantages concerning their prospects for reemployment. They not only lose work discipline and are stigmatized, but their skills are also often inappropriate for entering into expanding sectors such as the service sector. An efficient ALMP should counteract these effects thus increasing competitive pressure for insiders by raising effective labor supply. ALMP can also serve as a work-test device if those unemployed who refuse to participate in such schemes lose their claims to transfer payments. Hence, ALMP can in principle reduce mismatch unemployment as well as unemployment due to insider-outsider problems.

However, badly designed ALMP can also give rise to negative employment effects (Berthold and Fehn (1997)). First, ALMP may raise wage pressure if the government is perceived to become employer of last resort via this channel. This would further blur responsibility for persistently high unemployment. The public

[15] See Berthold (1994) and Sachverständigenrat (1995). Essentially the same reasoning is true for general wage subsidies which let gross wages inevitably rise by the amount of the subsidy thus producing a negative overall effect on employment if the subsidy is financed by distortionary taxes.

already tends to hold the government and not wage setters responsible for the dismal labor market situation. However, wage setters and not the government should mainly be held accountable in a market economy where wages should be the result of negotiations between workers and firms unfettered by government interference. Expanding ALMP supports this widespread misconception and thus even further reduces pressure on wage-bargaining parties to consider the employment effects of their wage settlements. Moral-hazard behavior of insiders is promoted, so that they will push for higher real wages and more rigid wage structures.

Second, ALMP can also lead to more wage pressure by increasing the utility level of outsiders, e.g. by raising their disposable income, by improving their chances to become employed again or by renewing their claims to receive unemployment insurance once participation in the particular program ends (revolving door effect). This is in particular a problem if the short-term unemployed, which is the reference group for insiders, are not excluded from participation in ALMP schemes. An increase in their utility level improves the fallback position of insiders and reduces pressure on insiders to display wage restraint.

Third, ALMP needs to be financed and it is usually more expensive to run ALMP schemes for the unemployed than to simply pay them benefits. Not only are wages in ALMP schemes often considerably above unemployment benefits but the organization of such programs is also costly. High capital mobility in a globalized economy largely protects mobile capital from having to finance ALMP. Hence, taxes on less mobile labor, i.e. on insiders, have to do the job. Yet, as this reduces the net income of insiders relative to their income when unemployed, the utility loss of being laid off is lower. This gives rise to increasing wage pressure. These three caveats show that one must be circumspect in designing ALMP in such a way that a vicious circle consisting of rising taxes and social security contributions, greater wage costs and shrinking regular employment is avoided.

Fourth, the positive effects on regular employment of ALMP must also be questioned as it is unavoidable that some participants gain employment at the expense of other unemployed or of insiders or that they would have been hired anyway. Such substitution, displacement and deadweight effects reduce potential positive employment effects of ALMP. However, it can be shown that there remains in any such case a positive net employment effect if ALMP programs are exclusively targeted at the long-term unemployed (Richardson (1997)).

Fifth, it must in a similar vein be questioned whether programs run by the government can qualify the unemployed according to market needs. General skills, which become more important due to the described changes in the organization of production, should be acquired at school age. As ALMP schemes are almost by definition targeted at adults, they should primarily convey firm- or sector-specific skills. Yet, firms have an inherent advantage over the government in teaching these types of skills, so that ALMP should as a rule be organized on the job and not off the job (Alogoskoufis et al. (1995)).

Assessing the overall employment effect of current ALMPs is by no means an easy task since intricate empirical questions are involved. However, it should be clear by now that the widespread enthusiasm about ALMP being a highly effective instrument for fighting unemployment is hardly justified. Whether ALMP in its present form really helps to raise regular employment is not clear at all, the results are rather ambiguous. Some studies show that countries with a higher degree of activity concerning ALMP tend to have lower unemployment rates, though this is as mentioned above a dubious criterion for judging ALMP. Others end up with a negligible or even negative effect on regular employment which is the criterion that should be applied. There exists in particular the problem that the wage-raising effects of expanding ALMP sometimes turn out to be greater than if regular employment grows by the same amount. This underlines the importance of the argument that governments which expand ALMP exonerate wage setters from their responsibility for the employment situation. There is very little evidence that ALMP helps substantially in reintegrating the long-term unemployed into the regular labor market. It rather seems that ALMP mainly serves to transform open into hidden unemployment thus putting a lid on the boiling pot of unemployment.16 Although ALMP is a favorite solution of all political camps to labor market problems, it has at best modest positive overall effects on regular employment. In particular, government training tends to have lower returns than private training. The case in point are Sweden's ALMPs which were for quite some time heralded as a razor-blade sharp weapon against unemployment, but put to the test in the 1990s they were found wanting (Freeman (1998) and Calmfors and Lang (1995)).

3.2.2 What Should an Efficient ALMP Look Like?

ALMP is therefore only able to raise regular employment if it is targeted at the long-term unemployed, if it contributes in particular to providing the long-term unemployed with marketable skills on the job and if support for any specific individual has a strict upper time limit (Robinson (1995) and Richardson (1997)). Such design features not only help to keep wage-raising effects and the financial burden to the government in check but they are also important in the sense that only well-qualified workers will in the longer run be employed on the regular labor market without falling into the working-poor category. The Benefit Transfer Program, which has been proposed in recent years by Dennis Snower incorporates by and large these criteria for an employment-oriented reform of ALMP (Snower

[16] See Calmfors (1994), Calmfors and Skedinger (1995), Jackman (1994), Nickell (1997), Robinson (1995), Walter (1995) and Scarpetta (1996).

(1994) and Orszag and Snower (1996)). It suggests that the unemployed should receive after a certain time spent in unemployment a hiring voucher which is worth a specific amount of money in addition to their regular unemployment benefits. The unemployed are entitled to hand these vouchers over to firms which are willing to hire them. The hiring firms can transform these vouchers into cash by handing them over to the government agency which is in charge, e.g. the labor office. Hence, these vouchers are essentially a wage subsidy which is directly linked to the claims of the unemployed to government benefits. There is no extra financial burden to the government as long as deadweight, substitution and displacement effects are not too large, because unemployment benefits are of course terminated once such a person finds a job (Fehn (1997)). The vouchers raise the critical wage level at which firms are willing to hire the respective unemployed. Thus, the number of mutually beneficial work contracts rises. To promote especially human capital formation, the cash value of any voucher should be higher if the firm proves that it provides the hired unemployed person with training schemes.

In order to prevent wage pressure from rising, receipt of such vouchers must be restricted to persons who have been unemployed for a longer time span. Two countervailing effects must be taken into account in this respect. The longer the unemployed must wait before they receive vouchers, the more difficult it is to reintegrate them into the regular labor market. This speaks in favor of handing out vouchers in addition to regular unemployment benefits early on. However, if short-term unemployed persons also obtain vouchers, wage pressure inevitably rises. Hence, in determining the time span after which an unemployed person receives a voucher, there is always a trade off between achieving a high reintegration quota into the regular labor market and avoiding negative repercussions on wage setting. In light of these opposing effects, it might be reasonable to deliver the first voucher after about six months of unemployment. Since chances for reemployment shrink with the length of the unemployment spell, the size of the monthly voucher should rise with each further month in unemployment to a maximum, say, after about two and a half years. If an unemployed person entitled to monthly vouchers receives a job, the size of the monthly voucher she continues to obtain is consecutively reduced. This is economically justified because the formerly unemployed person should build up new human capital with growing time back in employment thus being less dependent on wage subsidies. The size of the voucher must furthermore never exceed the claim of the unemployed person to unemployment benefits in order to not create an incentive for firms and unemployed persons to agree on fake work contracts paid for by the government. This condition must always be satisfied even when the size of the monthly voucher including the qualification premium reaches its maximum after say about two years of unemployment.

Such a system of vouchers which is directly linked to the unemployment benefit system exhibits a number of advantages. Above all, the twofold negative effect of the current unemployment benefit system is mitigated. The current system subsidizes unemployment while it punishes employment by financing benefits via taxes on the employed. Establishing such a voucher system lets the formerly unemployed persons indirectly uphold their claims to government transfers for a while even after they are again employed. This reduces the marginal tax rate between unemployment and regular employment significantly below hundred percent thus opening up the current unemployment trap. Consequently, search efforts of the unemployed along with effective labor supply will rise. Furthermore, those subsidies are directly financed out of the unemployment insurance system which is clearly superior to a tax-financed system because wage setters are then held to a greater extent accountable for the unemployment they helped to produce via inadequate wage settlements. Skills are in addition conveyed on the job rather than off the job which is an important advantage relative to government-run ALMP-schemes. Finally, such a voucher system enables outsiders to effectively undercut insider wages thus at least temporarily enhancing competitive pressure for them. Such targeted subsidies are therefore unlikely to lead to growing wage pressure.

However, it might be objected that such a voucher system stigmatizes those unemployed persons which offer firms vouchers in addition to their work input. Vouchers could signal firms that the unemployed person is regarded by the government as having low chances of encountering reemployment if left on her own. This negative signaling effect could just cancel out the positive monetary incentive of hiring such an unemployed person. Yet, since it is in general not difficult at all for firms to find out how long a job applicant has been unemployed before applying, this is not an objection carrying significant weight. It could furthermore be objected that persons will then prefer to stay unemployed for a longer time span in order to be entitled to receiving higher vouchers. Yet, such a behavior is not optimal as long as the size of the initial voucher is not too large and as long as the increase in the monthly voucher is at most sufficient to make up for the loss in skills which has occurred in the meantime. Such an obstructive behavior on the part of the unemployed can furthermore be contained by implementing strict rules which jobs have to be accepted for unemployment benefits not to be canceled.

The last point shows that any reform of labor market policies for reducing persistent structural unemployment will be found unsatisfactory if left on its own. As long as entrepreneurs do not have a significantly larger incentive to invest and to create new firms and jobs, obtaining sizeable reductions of unemployment will be nothing but a chimera. In order to achieve significant employment gains, reforming passive and active labor market policies must be embedded in a large package for creating a more employment oriented institutional framework. This means above all that wage setting must become more flexible, less aggressive and more differentiated. The most direct way of enacting such a change in wage setting is largely abolishing government-imposed firing costs and a bold and determined move towards decentralized wage setting. A further key factor in achieving more employment-oriented wage setting along with a greater level of investments and openings of new firms is a large reduction in the level of taxation that is levied on the private sector. The government must cut back on its grip on the economy in order to yield more freedom for entrepreneurial activities of the private sector. It is finally of utmost importance to tear down all barriers to the establishment of new firms such as excessive goods market regulations and badly functioning venture capital markets.[17]

4 The Political Economy of Reforming Labor Market Policy

Calls for reforming the institutional framework of labor markets in the above indicated direction have been widespread in the economics literature in recent years. However, what appears paradoxical is the lack of determined and comprehensive reform packages in particular in the two most important continental European countries, namely France and Germany, which could lead to a breakthrough on the respective labor markets. The hitherto prevalent scenario may be termed the "Franco-German nightmare", as those two countries are the most prominent, but by no means only European countries to have exhibited the following economic symptoms: unemployment along with unemployment benefits and taxes are undesirably high, but the government finds it politically infeasible to do anything decisive about it. To be sure, policy was by no means completely inactive in recent years in a country like Germany. Rather, the reforms undertaken were part of a piecemeal approach with only small isolated steps at a time, each of which met with considerable political resistance and did therefore not lead to a mounting wave of reforms. Two questions arise. First, why is it apparently so difficult to politically enforce employment stimulating reforms of the institutional framework of labor markets? Second, is it possible to break the stalemate on labor markets?

4.1 Why is it Politically So Difficult to Reform Labor Markets?

The first question has already received considerable attention in the literature in recent years.[18] It is rather obvious that the actual implementation of far-reaching reforms and the deregulation of labor markets are not particularly desirable from a political economy point of view. Labor markets are not rigid by accident, but

---

[17] See Coe and Snower (1996), Berthold and Fehn (1996a) and (1998) and Fehn (1999).

[18] See Saint-Paul (1995) and (1996), Bertola and Ichino (1995b) and Berthold and Fehn (1996b).

rather because rigid labor markets indirectly serve the interests of politicians. Politicians are not well informed, benevolent social dictators who maximize aggregate welfare. A realistic way of portraying political behavior should in contrast start with the assumption that they pursue mainly their own self-interest. As their primary objective is to win elections, they have a different way of accounting from economists: While economists add up welfare gains and losses, politicians rather count votes. Politicians are therefore highly reluctant to pursue policies which are economically efficient but which hurt at least in the short run the majority of voters and/or influential special interest groups. The support of special interest groups in the form of voting recommendations to their members and in the form of campaign contributions is often a key factor in winning elections.

It is quite clear from this political economy perspective that policies to liberalize labor markets and to strengthen the price mechanism on labor markets are difficult to enforce politically. Albeit high and especially rising unemployment reduces the reelection probability of an incumbent government, most policy recommendations to reduce structural unemployment get nonetheless trapped in the pitfall of political infeasibility since a large part of the electorate will lose at least in the short run and/or losses are concentrated on influential special-interest groups like unions. Rigid labor markets let insiders gain at the expense of outsiders and at the expense of highly qualified workers as long as those are rather immobile. They create a larger core of society which is interested in political stability by narrowing the income differential not only between employed workers and human capitalists, but also between employed workers and firm-owners. Protests by outsiders are kept under control by generous welfare-state provisions and ALMPs. Politicians will therefore be very cautious in adopting tough policy recommendations for deregulating labor markets, especially if none of the political parties is ideologically committed to liberalizing the labor market. This appears to be the case in most continental European countries because there exists a broad christian-social-democratic consensus that the labor market is to be sheltered as much as possible from market forces.

In sum, reforming the labor market is not in the interest of governments as long as influential interest groups like unions and the majority of voters along with the median voter prefer a rigid labor market. The ongoing stalemate concerning labor market reforms should therefore be regarded as the rational choice of political decision-makers. This does not mean, though, that rigid labor markets are there to stay forever. As the literature on the positive economics of labor market rigidities has shown, labor market reform is characterized by multiple political economy equilibria. Reforms are feasible under certain circumstances, such as in times of rapidly increasing unemployment and immediately after elections, in particular if the electorate enacted a switch in government. In addition, a higher real-wage elasticity of labor demand will promote labor market reforms since excessive wage increases become less attractive to insiders due to the ensuing large employment losses. With a close to horizontal labor demand curve most of the losses are carried by the insiders themselves via lay-offs. Hence, more open goods and factor markets, as described by the catchword globalization, promote labor market reforms in the long run as they increase the real-wage elasticity of labor demand (Fehn (1997)).

4.2 Can Comprehensive Reforms Break the Political Deadlock?

However, waiting for such fortuitous circumstances is a rather unsatisfying policy recommendation. Coming therefore to the second question, it might be asked whether anything can be done before globalization makes even short-run labor demand sufficiently elastic so that major reforms become finally politically feasible. An important recent idea in this respect is related to the complementarity of reforms (Coe and Snower (1996) and Orszag and Snower (1998)). Policy measures such as a cut in unemployment benefits have a much larger positive employment effect if the resulting greater intensity of job search is met by growing labor demand, e.g. due to greater restraint in wage setting or due to a reduction in the level of taxation. Especially the level of taxation is directly related to the generosity of the unemployment insurance. Generous unemployment benefits clearly require a large level of taxation for financing them. Both policy variables can also be set by the government. So why not enact a reform that reduces unemployment benefits and the level of taxation simultaneously in order to embark on an upward spiral concerning employment, both via rising labor demand and via greater effective labor supply?

This particular problem can be analyzed by means of figure 3. The tax rate is denoted by t while the level of unemployment benefits is b. It is assumed that taxes are exclusively levied on workers and firms for financing unemployment benefits. Hence, if $b = 0$, $t = 0$ as well. Increasing unemployment benefits gradually from zero has a twofold effect. First, unemployment rises so that total government layouts for unemployment benefits rise faster than the level of benefits. Second, the tax base shrinks as employment falls, inducing a rise in the tax rate to finance a fixed amount of government expenditure. However, rising taxes reduce the reward to work and to invest, thus further diminishing employment. Hence, taking all effects together shows unambiguously that, starting from the origin, a given increase in the level of unemployment benefits leads to a more than proportionate rise in the level of taxation. This overproportionality rises with the level of benefits and taxation because the negative effect of further increases in taxation and unemployment benefits grow with their level. Hence, the government budget constraint GBC becomes progressively flatter. Eventually, unemployment benefits reach a maximum beyond which further rises in the tax rate reduce employment and thus the tax base by so much that tax revenues shrink as a result. Thus, unemployment benefits must decline in order to balance the government budget. This is the well-known "Laffer effect" which is depicted by the downward sloping portion of the GBC.

Figure 3: *Political Hysteresis Concerning Unemployment Benefits and Taxation*

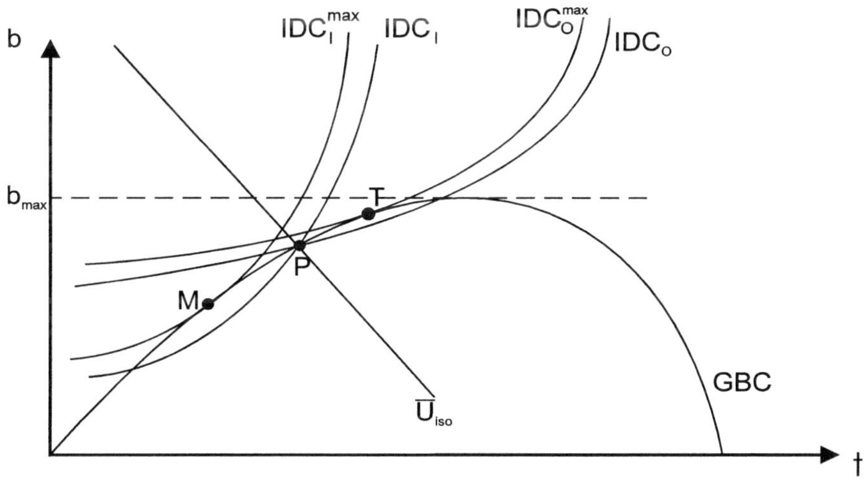

Source: Orszag and Snower (1998).

Analyzing the feasibility of a reform package which would simultaneously reduce the level of benefits and of taxation in order to stimulate employment requires introducing indifference curves of insiders and outsiders. Both sets of indifference curves are upward sloped because unemployment benefits are a good whereas taxes are a bad to both groups. The same utility level can therefore only be attained if higher taxes are balanced by a higher level of unemployment benefits. However, insider indifference curves are steeper than outsider indifference curves because insiders are more directly affected by the level of taxation whereas outsiders care more about the level of unemployment benefits. Insiders currently pay taxes while they are only affected by the level of unemployment benefits in case they are laid off. In contrast, outsiders currently receive unemployment benefits whereas they only pay taxes if they find a job. Hence, a given increase in the tax rate must be balanced by a higher increase in unemployment benefits for insiders than for outsiders in order to keep the utility level constant and to stay on the same indifference curve. The diagram is completed by isounemployment curves which are downward sloped because unemployment benefits as well as the level of taxation are both positively related to the rate of unemployment.

The equilibrium in this scenario with just two policy variables depends on the functioning of the political process. Assuming that only the median voter counts in political decision making and also assuming that the median voter is an insider produces an equilibrium at point M where the relevant insider indifference curve is just tangent to the GBC and where the utility of insiders is maximized. However, it is quite unlikely that governments of advanced, democratic countries, which are committed to the concept of "social market economy", will not take at all into account the interests of outsiders which are by now a sizeable part of the population. Such behavior would offend against the widely respected principle of liberal democracy, namely that the majority is only allowed to enforce particular decisions if it does not involve sacrifices by a significant minority. Thus, simply abolishing privileges of substantial minorities by majority vote without paying any attention to their interests is in general impossible in advanced democracies. However, interestingly and, at first glance somewhat paradoxically, taking also the interests of outsiders into account in political decision making leads to an equilibrium which involves a higher level of unemployment benefits and of tax rates. This is the case because outsider indifference curves are flatter than insider indifference curves and their optimum point T therefore lies to the right of the optimum for insiders. Intuitively, outsiders value unemployment benefits higher than insiders and their relative aversion against high tax rates is smaller compared to insiders so that the overall equilibrium is even less geared towards achieving a high level of employment than under pure majority voting.

Elaborating further on this assumption that no reform against the interests of outsiders is possible also shows that problems of political hysteresis arise. If only Pareto-improving reforms are politically feasible, any point on the upward sloped portion of the GBC and between points M and T is a political equilibrium. Taking e.g. point P, it is straightforward to realize that there is no feasible combination of changes in unemployment benefits and in tax rates which is welfare improving to insiders and to outsiders alike. The set of Pareto-improving policies is empty. Hence, under such conditions the economy is stuck at whatever political equilibrium it happens to find itself initially. Calls by economists for lower unemployment benefits and lower tax rates for stimulating employment, which are inspired by normative considerations, are in such situations useless from a political-economy point of view (Orszag and Snower (1998)).

Large-scale reforms become possible, however, if the economy happens to be to the right of point T and even more so if it is on the downward-sloped portion of the GBC as in figure 4. Such a situation can occur e.g. after large adverse shocks or after a tax and spend government has been in office for some while. A particularly interesting example is globalization itself, which reduces the tax revenues earned at any given tax rate by giving mobile capital and workers greater exit possibilities. Hence, the GBC moves downwards and to the left. If the tax rate was already relatively large initially and if the tax rate is not immediately adjusted after the shock, globalization might displace the economy from point P to a point like P', which is to the right of the maximum of GBC'. Yet, there is now a large set of possible Pareto-improving reforms. Unemployment benefits as well as taxes can in principle now be lowered all the way down to the point where the relevant outsider indifference curve intersects with the upward sloped section of the GBC' in point Q. Hence, this is an example where globalization is a blessing because it can enlargen the politically feasible set of reforms by initially worsening the situation. Both policy variables need to be changed simultaneously, though, with the explicit purpose of exploiting the arising economic and political complementarities. Piecemeal, uncoordinated reform, in which one policy variable is adjusted at a time, runs the risk of getting stuck early on in the reform process because after the first policy instrument has been adjusted, the economy may arrive at a political equilibrium involving political hysteresis, preventing the second policy instrument from being changed as well.

Figure 4: *Large-Scale Reforms under "Laffer" Conditions*

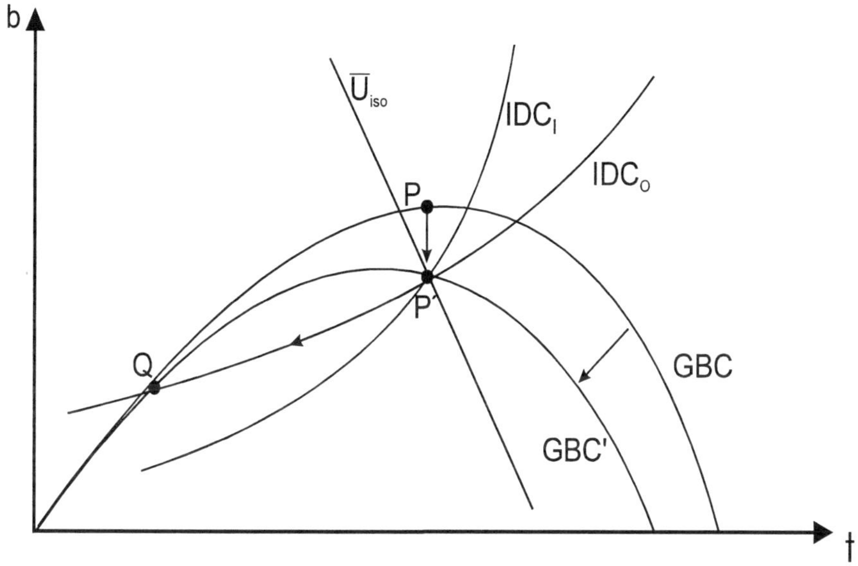

But what if a country does not find itself under Laffer conditions? Is such a country then doomed to stay in the status quo position such as point P in figure 3 which is not only inefficient due to high unemployment, but also inequitable, because insiders are much better off than outsiders? The political deadlock can be broken by broad-based reforms, i.e. by enlarging the set of available policy variables. Including further complementary policy measures in a package approach enables the government to compensate the losers of reforms without sacrificing efficiency gains. In the specific case considered, political hysteresis arises out of a simple conflict of interests: the government is unable to achieve simultaneous reductions in tax rates and in unemployment benefits, which are desirable from a normative point of view, because this would hurt the unemployed.

However, the stalemate can be overcome by including other instruments in the package, e.g. the afore-described hiring vouchers and/or a reduction of firing costs. Introducing a voucher system by itself clearly raises the welfare of outsiders because their reemployment chances rise. This occurs at the expense of insiders because competitive pressure for insiders would rise, in particular, because firms would have an incentive to replace some of their insiders by subsidized new recruits. Yet, insiders could be compensated for this loss by an adequate reduction in tax rates, for which they are particularly susceptible, financed by a reduction in unemployment benefits. The same effect can in principle be achieved by reducing government-imposed firing costs which increase the hiring chances of outsiders but increase the probability of current insiders that they will be laid off sometimes in the future. The political feasibility could be further promoted by also including measures to alleviate imperfections in capital and goods markets, which especially hinder the creation of new firms and employment growth. Hence, a circumspect and balanced combination of all five policy instruments in a package - reduction of tax rates, of unemployment benefits and of government-imposed firing costs along with a simultaneous introduction of hiring vouchers and with efficiency-enhancing reforms of capital and goods markets - can lead to a Pareto improvement and should thus be politically feasible. The failure of governments to implement such broad-based packages of complementary reform measures may be a key reason for why unemployment is so persistent in continental Europe and for why the "Franco-German nightmare" endures. Interestingly in this respect, the only two European countries which have significantly improved their employment performance in recent years, namely the UK and the Netherlands, have precisely relied on such a package approach by implementing a large set of complementary reform measures close to simultaneously.

5 Concluding Remarks

Mass unemployment is the major challenge to capitalist societies in the post-communist era. The ongoing process of globalization is in particular often blamed for the dismal situation on continental European labor markets. However, as has been shown, whether globalization leads to rising unemployment depends crucially on the institutional setup of the economy under investigation. Globalization first and foremost raises global welfare. It does furthermore not increase unemployment in countries where markets are well functioning and where governments by and large restrict themselves to efficiency-enhancing activities. However, the more governments interfere with the functioning of markets, in particular of labor markets, often motivated by distributional objectives, the more globalization exposes the drawbacks of such efficiency-reducing activities. Globalization raises rather dramatically the costs of regulations which distort the allocation of resources. Hence, deregulating especially labor markets and gearing labor market policy more towards effectively fighting unemployment must remain high up on the agenda for economic policy.

Yet, any policy analysis which does not take into account the politico-economic objectives for installing rigid labor markets remains incomplete. Overcoming the politico-economic hurdles is the major obstacle against implementing labor market reforms. In particular, any government which adopts a piecemeal approach in reforming labor markets and labor market policy is likely to get stuck early on in the reform process without having achieved much. The analysis revealed that only large scale reforms which include a multitude of complementary reform measures can be expected to produce major employment gains and at the same time be politically viable. Hence, concerning labor markets, installing a much more restrictive unemployment benefit system, reducing government-imposed firing restrictions, decentralizing wage bargaining down to the firm or individual level, introducing a comprehensive system of hiring vouchers and reducing tax wedges should be combined in an encompassing supply-side package for more growth and employment. The current reemergence of Keynesian thinking does in any case not address the major causes of European unemployment and is therefore highly likely to fail in the fight for lasting reductions of persistently high unemployment. The neglect of supply-side considerations associated with this renewed emphasis on Keynesian-type problems is likely to lead to another appropriation shock similar to those in the late sixties and early seventies with fatal long-run consequences for the employment situation.

References

Aizenman, J. and A. Powell (1997), Volatility and Financial Intermediation, NBER Working Paper 6320, Cambridge, Mass.

Alogoskoufis, G. et al. (1995), Unemployment: Choices for Europe, CEPR Report: Monitoring European Integration 5, London.

Anderson, P. and B. Meyer (1993), Unemployment Insurance in the United States: Layoff Incentives and Cross Subsidies, *Journal of Labor Economics* 11, 70-95.

Atkinson, A. and J. Micklewright (1991), Unemployment Compensation and Labor Market Transitions: A Critical Review, *Journal of Economic Literature* 24, 1679-1727.

Baicker, K. et al. (1997), A Distinctive System: Origins and Impact of U.S. Unemployment Compensation, NBER Working Paper 5889, Cambridge, Mass.

Bentilola, S. and G. Bertola (1990), Firing Costs and Labour Demand: How Bad is Eurosclerosis? *Review of Economic Studies* 57, 381-402.

Berthold, N. (1994), Arbeitsmarktpolitik in Schweden - Ende eines Mythos? *Ordo* 45, 17-49.

Berthold, N. and R. Fehn (1996a), Evolution von Lohnverhandlungssystemen - Macht oder ökonomisches Gesetz? in: Zohlnhöfer, W. (ed.), Die Tarifautonomie auf dem Prüfstand, Schriften des Vereins für Socialpolitik, N. F. Band 244, Berlin, 57-94.

Berthold, N. and R. Fehn (1996b), The Positive Economics of Unemployment and Labor Market Inflexibility, *Kyklos* 49, 583-613.

Berthold, N. and R. Fehn (1997), Aktive Arbeitsmarktpolitik - wirksames Instrument der Beschäftigungspolitik oder politische Beruhigungspille? *Ordo* 48, 411-435.

Berthold, N. and R. Fehn (1998), Die zehn Gebote für den Arbeitsmarkt, in: Klemmer, P. et al. (eds.), Liberale Grundrisse einer zukunftsfähigen Gesellschaft, Baden-Baden, 353-372.

Bertola, G. and A. Ichino (1995a), Wage Inequality and Unemployment: United States versus Europe, in: Bernanke, B. S. and J. J. Rotemberg (eds.), NBER Macroeconomics Annual 1995, Cambridge, Mass, 13-54.

Bertola, G. and A. Ichino (1995b), Crossing the River: A Comparative Perspective on Italian Employment Dynamics, *Economic Policy* 21, 361-420.

Bhagwati, J. and V. Dehejia, (1994), Freer Trade and Wages of the Unskilled - Is Marx Striking Again?, in: Bhagwati, J. and M. Kosters (eds.), Trade and Wages - Leveling Wages Down?, Washington D. C., 36-75.

Blanchard, O. (1995), Macroeconomic Implications of Shifts in the Relative Demand for Skills, Economic Policy Review of the Federal Reserve Bank of New York 1, 48-60.

Blanchard, O. (1997), The Medium Run, *Brookings Papers on Economic Activity*, 89-158.

Blanchard, O. (1998), Revisiting European Unemployment: Unemployment, Capital Accumulation and Factor Prices, NBER Working Paper 6566, Cambridge, Mass.

Caballero, R. and M. Hammour (1997), Jobless Growth: Appropriability, Factor Substitution, and Unemployment, NBER Working Paper 6221, Cambridge, Mass.

Caballero, R. and M. Hammour (1998a), Improper Churn: Social Costs and Macroeconomic Consequences, NBER Working Paper 6717, Cambridge, Mass.

Caballero, R. and M. Hammour (1998b), The Macroeconomics of Specificity, *Journal of Political Economy* 106, 724-767.

Calmfors, L. (1994), Active Labour Market Policy and Unemployment - A Framework for the Analysis of Crucial Design Features, Seminar Paper 563, Institute for International Economic Studies, Stockholm.

Calmfors, L. and H. Lang (1995), Macroeconomic Effects of Active Labour Market Programmes in a Union Wage-Setting Model, *The Economic Journal* 105, 601-619.

Calmfors, L. and P. Skedinger (1995), Does Active Labour Market Policy Increase Employment?, Seminar Paper 590, Institute for International Economic Studies, Stockholm.

Calvo, G. and E. Mendoza (1997), Rational Herd Behavior and the Globalization of Securities Markets, Discussion Paper 120, Federal Reserve Bank of Minneapolis.

Card, D. and P. Levine (1994), Unemployment Insurance Taxes and the Cyclical and Seasonal Properties of Unemployment, *Journal of Public Economics* 53, 1-29.

Coe, D. and D. Snower (1996), Policy Complementarities: The Case for Fundamental Labor Market Reform, IMF Working Paper, WP/96/93, Washington D. C.

Elmeskov, J. (1993), High and Persistent Unemployment: Assessment of the Problem and Its Causes, OECD Working Paper 132, Paris.

Fehn, R. (1997), Der strukturell bedingte Anstieg der Arbeitslosigkeit in Europa: Ursachen und Lösungsansätze, Baden-Baden.

Fehn, R. (1998), Capital Market Imperfections, Greater Volatilities, and Rising Unemployment: Does Venture Capital Help?, Discussion Paper 24, Lehrstuhl VWL 4, Economics Department, University of Würzburg.

Fehn, R. (1999), Schaffen Pensionsfonds über vollkommenere Kapitalmärkte mehr Beschäftigung?, in: Koslowski, P. (ed.), Shareholder Value und die Kriterien des Unternehmenserfolgs. Kapitalrechnung und gesellschaftliche Entwicklung, Heidelberg, 73-108.

Feldstein, M. (1997), The Political Economy of the European Economic and Monetary Union: Political Sources of an Economic Liability, NBER Working Paper 6150, Cambridge, Mass.

Feldstein, M. and D. Altman (1998), Unemployment Insurance Savings Accounts, NBER Working Paper 6860, Cambridge, Mass.

Freeman, R. B. (1998), War of the Models: Which Labour Market Institutions for the 21st century?, *Labour Economics* 5, 1-24.

Funke, M. et al. (1998), Capital Structure and Labour Demand: Investigations Using German Micro Data, forthcoming in: *Oxford Bulletin of Economics and Statistics.*

Gottschalk, P. and R. Moffitt (1994), The Growth of Earnings Instability in the U.S. Labor Market, *Brookings Papers on Economic Activity*, 217-254.

Hopenhayn, H. and J. Nicolini (1997), Optimal Unemployment Insurance, *Journal of Political Economy* 105, 412-438.

Hunt, J. (1995), The Effect of Unemployment Compensation on Unemployment Duration in Germany, *Journal of Labor Economics* 13, 88-120.

Jackman, R. (1994), What Can Active Labour Market Policy Do?, *Swedish Review of Economic Policy* 1, 221-257.

Jackman, R. (1995), Unemployment and Wage Inequality in OECD Countries, Centre for Economic Performance, Discussion Paper 235, LSE, London.

Krugman, P. (1994), Past and Prospective Causes of High Unemployment, in: Federal Reserve Bank of Kansas City (ed.), Reducing Unemployment: Current Issues and Policy Options, Jackson Hole, Wyoming, 49-80.

Layard, R. (1996), The Road Back to Full Employment, Centre for Economic Performance, Occasional Paper 10, LSE , London.

Layard, R. et al. (1991), Unemployment, Macroeconomic Performance and the Labour Market, Oxford.

Lindbeck, A. (1996), The West European Unemployment Problem, *Weltwirtschaftliches Archiv* 132, 609-637.

Lindbeck, A. and D. Snower (1996), Reorganization of Firms and Labour Market Inequality. CEPR Discussion Paper 1375, London.

Ljungqvist, L. and T. Sargent (1998), The European Unemployment Dilemma, *Journal of Political Economy* 106, 514-550.

Meyer, B. (1995), Lessons from the U.S. Unemployment Insurance Experiments, *Journal of Economic Literature* 33, 91-131.

Nickell, S. (1996), Unemployment and Wages in Europe and North America, Centre for Economic Performance, Discussion Paper 6, LSE, London.

Nickell, S. (1997), Unemployment and Labour Market Rigidities: Europe versus North America, *Journal of Economic Perspectives* 11, 55-74.

Nickell, S. and B. Bell (1995), The Collapse in Demand for the Unskilled and Unemployment Across OECD Countries, *Oxford Review of Economic Policy* 11, 40-62.

Nickell, S. and D. Nicolitsas (1995), How Does Financial Pressure Affect Firms?, Applied Economics Discussion Paper 170, University of Oxford.

Ochel, W. (1998), Mehr Beschäftigung und weniger Arbeitslosigkeit - Amerika, hast du es besser?, Mitteilungen aus Arbeitsmarkt- und Berufsforschung, 262-276.

OECD Employment Outlook, Various Issues, Paris.

Orszag, M. and D. Snower (1996), A Macro Theory of Employment Vouchers, CEPR Discussion Paper 1367, London.

Orszag, M. and D. Snower (1997), Expanding the Welfare System: A Proposal for Reform, CEPR Discussion Paper 1674, London.

Orszag, M. and D. Snower (1998), Anatomy of Policy Complementarities, CEPR Discussion Paper 1963, London.

Richardson, J. (1997), Can Active Labour Market Policy Work?, Discussion Paper 331, Centre for Economic Performance, LSE, London.

Robinson, P. (1995), The Decline of the Swedish Model and the Limits to Active Labour Market Policy, Centre for Economic Performance, Discussion Paper, LSE, London.

Rodrik, D. (1997), Has Globalization Gone Too Far?, Institute for International Economics, Washington D. C.

Sachverständigenrat zur Begutachtung der gesamtwirtschaftlichen Entwicklung (1995), Jahresgutachten 1995/1996: Im Standortwettbewerb, Stuttgart.

Saint-Paul, G. (1995), A Framework for Analysing the Political Support for Active Labour Market Policy, CEPR Discussion Paper 1205, London.

Saint-Paul, G. (1996), Exploring the Political Economy of Labour Market Institutions, *Economic Policy* 23, 264-315.

Scarpetta, S. (1996), Assessing the Role of Labour Market Policies and Institutional Settings on Unemployment: A Cross-Country Study, OECD Economic Studies 26, Paris, 43-98.

Schmid, G. (1995), Institutional Incentives to Prevent Unemployment: Unemployment Insurance and Active Labor Market Policy in a Comparative Perspective, *The Journal of Socio-Economics* 24, 51-103.

Siebert, H. (1997), Labor Market Rigidities - At the Root of Unemployment in Europe, *Journal of Economic Perspectives* 11, 37-54.

Snower, D. (1994), The Simple Economics of Benefit Transfers, CEPR Discussion Paper 1086, London.

Snower, D. (1995), Unemployment Benefits: An Assessment of Proposals for Reform, *International Labour Review* 134, 625-647.

Van der Willigen, T. (1995), Unemployment, Wages, and the Wage Structure, in: Corker, R. et al., United Germany: The First Five Years - Performance and Policy Issues, IMF Occasional Paper 125, Washington D.C., 21-40.

Viñals, J. and J. Jimeno (1996), Monetary Union and European Unemployment, CEPR Discussion Paper 1485, London.

Walter, C. (1995), Wie effizient ist die Arbeitsmarktpolitik in der Bundesrepublik Deutschland?, *Die Weltwirtschaft*, 180-192.

Wang, C. and S. Williamson (1996), Unemployment Insurance with Moral Hazard in a Dynamic Economy, Carnegie Rochester Conference Series on Public Policy 44, 1-41.

Winker, P. (1998), Financing Constraints, Output and Employment, forthcoming in: Filc, W. (ed.), Macroeconomic Causes of Unemployment.

Labor Market Analysis and Labor Market Policy in a Global Economy - An Alternative View (Commentary Paper)

Jürgen Kromphardt

Technical University Berlin,
Uhlandstr. 4-5, 10623 Berlin, Germany

In their contribution to this volume Berthold/Fehn present an explanation of the causes of the high and persistent unemployment in Europe and especially in Germany and deduce some implications for labor market policy. According to their explanation the main influencing factors are real wage shocks and the wage bargaining results due to „myopic insiders“. In my paper I give an alternative explanation of the evolution of unemployment in Germany which takes the demand side of the product market duly into account.

1 Theoretical Foundation

Berthold/Fehn explain the unemployment in Europe using the by now „standard description“ of the labor market developed by Carlin/Soskice (1990) and used by Bean (1994) in his well-known survey article on "European Unemployment". This model takes into account the imperfect competition dominating the product markets. It goes far beyond the simple neoclassical model and produces much less clear-cut results. Berthold/Fehn use this model but partly in a misleading way. Therefore, it is necessary to describe its essential features here.

On the supply side, the sum of the aggregated individual labor supplies is taken to be independent of the real wage rate, in accordance with the results of empirical studies about individual labor supply. In addition to this vertical line of labor supply a wage setting-curve is introduced which represents the real wage levels the workers (via their unions) demand at different degrees of employment: The better the employment situation the higher is the real wage level - calculated on the basis of the expected price level - which results out of the bargains between employers and employees. Carlin/Soskice (1990, p. 138 f) have named this curve the „Bargained Real Wage-Curve“ (BRW). It is important to realize the arrow of causation: The degree of employment determines the bargained wage rate, contrary to the traditional labor supply curve where the wage rate determines the rate of employment.

The factual price level is determined on the product markets dominated by imperfect competition. Therefore, the traditional labor demand curve is replaced by a curve called by Bean (1994) the price setting curve (PS) and by Carlin/Soskice (1990, p. 140) the „Price Determined Real Wage Curve“ (PRW). The latter denomination describes the direction of causation, which was clearly defined by Carlin/Soskice (1990, p. 159): „In the imperfect competition model, output, *y*, is fixed by the *demand for output*. The level of output in the economy depends on the level of aggregate demand in the *IS/LM* diagram, and this, via the short-run production function, determines the level of employment.“

The slope of the PRW-curve depends on the price-setting behavior of the firms in markets with imperfect competition. On such markets profit maximizing firms will engage labor up to the point where the (given) wage rate equals the marginal revenue due to the use of an additional unit of labor. This condition can be written as:

(1) $w = p\,(1 - 1/\eta) \cdot \delta X/\delta E$,

where w indicates the wage rate, $\delta X/\delta E$ the marginal product of labor (MPL); η the absolute value of the price elasticity of demand.

Assuming for simplicity that labor is the only variable factor of production, the quotient of w to $\delta X/\delta E$ equals marginal costs (MC). From equation (1) thus follows:

(2) $$p = \frac{1}{1 - 1/\eta} \cdot MC\ .$$

By rearranging this price equation we obtain the mark-up of prices over marginal costs (MC):

(3) $$\frac{p - MC}{MC} = \frac{1}{\eta - 1}\ .$$

Retaining the assumption of a decreasing marginal product of labor (MPL), the slope of the PRW-curve is nevertheless undetermined. It depends on whether or not the elasticity of demand (and thus the mark up) remains constant when employment and output change. Carlin/Soskice (1990, p. 141) point to „empirical evidence suggesting that the elasticity of demand is not constant. Rather, it seems that the mark-up falls as employment and output rise, reflecting the fact that the elasticity of demand rises with employment.“

If the mark-up declines strongly, the PRW-curve might even be a horizontal line, as Carlin/Soskice (p. 141) demonstrate in the following figure:

Figure 1: *The Price-Determined Real Wage Curve (PRW)*

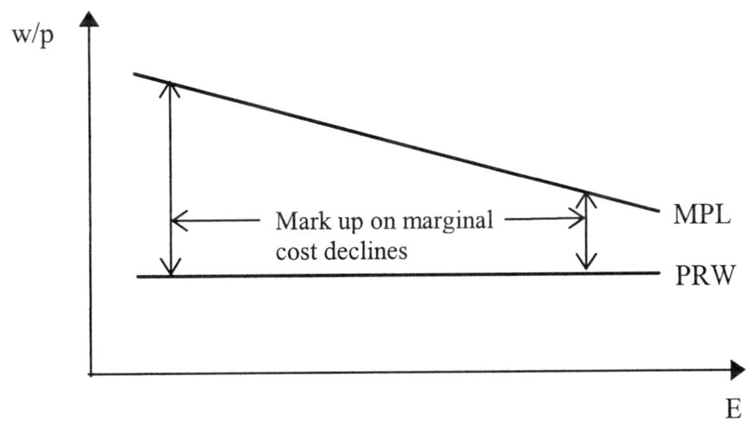

Two arguments are given by Carlin/Soskice for a declining mark-up (p. 141f):

„One argument that has been put forward to account for the pro-cyclical elasticity of demand (i.e. that elasticity rises with a rise in output) is based on the fact that customers develop a loyalty to a particular firm. In a boom firms face a rise in potential new customers, so it may be rational for them to invest in gaining the loyalty of these new customers by lowering their prices. In other words, the mark-up is reduced as the level of output (and employment) rises. A quite different explanation for the failure of prices to respond to changes in demand, and hence for the existence of a flat price-determined real wage curve, was accepted virtually universally in the 1970s. This is the view that prices are set by imperfectly competitive firms as a fixed mark-up over normal unit labor costs. It is known as *normal cost pricing*."

These arguments are supported by Bean (1994, p. 599): „Evidence from empirical studies of pricing behavior seem to suggest that the price-employment schedule is rather flat even in the short run."

Contrary to the simple neoclassical model the „standard labor market model" is consistent with the predominance of „classical unemployment" or of „Keynesian unemployment", since position and slope of the BRW-curve and the PRW-curve allow for different solutions (see figure 2). Whilst Berthold/Fehn restrict their analysis to a situation where the two curves intersect to the left of LD and the employment level is restricted by the real wage (BRW high), the following figure considers also a situation where employment is restricted by demand on the product market (BRW low). Both situations are possible in this model because position and slope of the PRW- and BRW-curves are not known exactly.

Figure 2 : *Labor Market with „Keynesian" or „Classical" Unemployment*

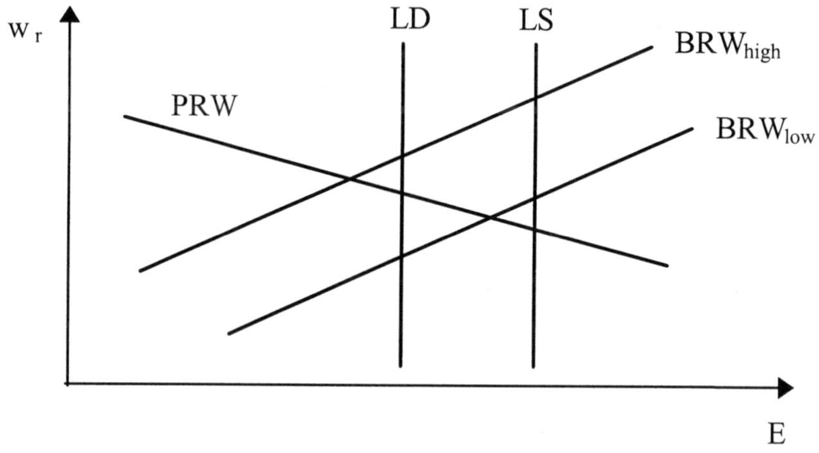

In figure 2, the position of the low BRW-curve is such that with sufficient demand in the product markets production near full employment would be possible (structural unemployment is left out of the picture in this discussion) and the firms would make enough profits to engage in this level of production.

Both BRW-curves are plotted such that employment at LD is accompanied by a divergence between the bargained real wage (based on the expected price level) and the real wage resulting from the price setting behavior of profit maximizing firms.

The consequences of this divergence are discussed by Carlin/Soskice only for the high BRW-curve. They indicate that if wages are set at the start of the period and prices only at its end, the actual real wage within the period will lie on the BRW-curve. At the end of the period prices will be increased, and the real wage rate will fall to the PRW-curve. If the workers react with higher wage claims, this will - as Carlin/Soskice show - lead to accelerating inflation. If the central bank intervenes by restrictive monetary policies, the employment at LD is not sustainable.

What is the result of the divergence of the bargained and profit maximizing real wage in the case of Keynesian unemployment? To answer this question (discussed neither by Bean nor by Carlin/Soskice) it is necessary to return to the micro-foundations given by equations (1) to (3) and to remember first that the profit maximum lies always in the region of an absolute value of the price elasticity of demand (η) above unity, and secondly, that η is the nearer to unity the more the profit maximum approaches the sales maximum.

Given these relations, it follows from equation (3): The lower marginal costs (MC) due to lower wages, the higher is the mark-up, because η declines and approaches unity. Therefore, there will be a tendency of prices to fall but, due to the difference in the slopes of the price curve and the marginal revenue curve, prices will fall less than the nominal wage rate, and the real wage rate will move upwards. If, contrary to these implications of the micro-economic theory on the pricing behavior of profit maximizing firms, the price level does not decline and firms will enjoy higher profits.

2 Wages and Employment in Germany

During the 60s and early 70s Western Germany was characterized by nearly full employment and a very low inflation rate. Unfortunately full employment disappeared after the first and second oil price shock. The question, therefore, arises: What happened to the German labor market after 1973? To answer this question, I shall first depict the evolution of real wages and employment in a graph corresponding to figure 2. However, in a growing economy with augmenting labor productivity the BRW-curve and the PRW-curve will both continuously shift upwards for any given employment level, because the employers can afford to pay higher wages and the workers will claim to participate in their augmented productivity.

These shifts can (geometrically) be avoided if one places on the vertical axis not the real wage, but the ratio of real wage to labor productivity, a ratio which is also called the real wage position. The relation of real wages to productivity is an indicator of real labor costs per unit of output. In calculating its development over time it must be taken into account that the part of dependent employees in the total working population is increasing. To this corresponds a decrease in the labor input of employers whose remuneration is not part of the wage bill but can be calculated as „imputed wage of the entrepreneur“. The rate of real wages to productivity must be calculated - and is calculated here - by taking this structural change into account.

The Commission of the European Union (1997) in Brussels has calculated the development of this relation for all 15 member countries from 1961 to 1997 showing that contrary to the preceding decades the relation declined in the decade of the 80s in all member countries except Greece and Luxembourg, whilst during the 90s the only exceptions are Great Britain and Portugal.

The necessary replacement of the wage rate by this real wage position introduces additional problems since the development of the labor productivity cannot be considered as an exogenous variable but is subject to short-term and medium-term influences which must be taken into account. In the medium-term it might depend on the evolution of the real wage: The higher the real wage and the faster its growth, the stronger the incentive for employers to substitute labor by capital, to produce in a more capital-intensive fashion and thus to enhance the productivity of labor. The size of this substitution is the object of much research but cannot be discussed here. However, this influence must be taken into account whenever policy implications are drawn.

In the short run, labor productivity is influenced by changes in the volume of production: It can be considered as a reliable result of many empirical studies that the volume of production and the labor productivity are positively correlated. Therefore, any sharp decline in the volume of production reduces the actual labor productivity, and the „real wage position" is augmented without any „excessive wage policy" in relation to the expected normal rate of productivity growth.

To judge the importance ascribed by Berthold/Fehn (section II.3) to wage shocks for the explanation of the high unemployment in Germany I present in figure 3 the development of the real wage position and the degree of employment in Germany. I chose the degree of employment instead of the number of employed persons to exclude the influence of the differences in population growth.

Figure 3 shows that the real wage position has augmented in the period from 1960 to 1974 and has decreased since 1982 with the exception of a short hike in the years 1992 and 1993. How can this historical development be described in terms of the model of the labor market presented in section I?

Up to 1973, the augmentation of the real wage position was not accompanied by a higher degree of unemployment. This is consistent with the position of the lower BRW curve as drawn in figure 2. The strong position of the wage earners during those years of full employment allowed them to push the real wage nearer to the maximum wage rate the employers were willing to pay. If one assumes that the workers refused afterwards to accept a reduction in their real wage level the BRW-curve has been shifting upwards during those years.

The oil price shock in the autumn of 1973 enhanced the cost of energy. To maintain their profits firms had to reduce the relation of real wages to labor productivity. Hence, the PRW-curve shifted downwards. At the same time, the German workers succeeded in the spring of 1974 to enforce very high wage increases in compensation for the higher energy prices. The influence of this „success" on the „real wage position" was reinforced by the slowdown of the

Figure 3: *The Real Wage Position (Real Wage/Labor Productivity) in Western Germany (1960 to 1994) and Germany (1991 to 1997)*

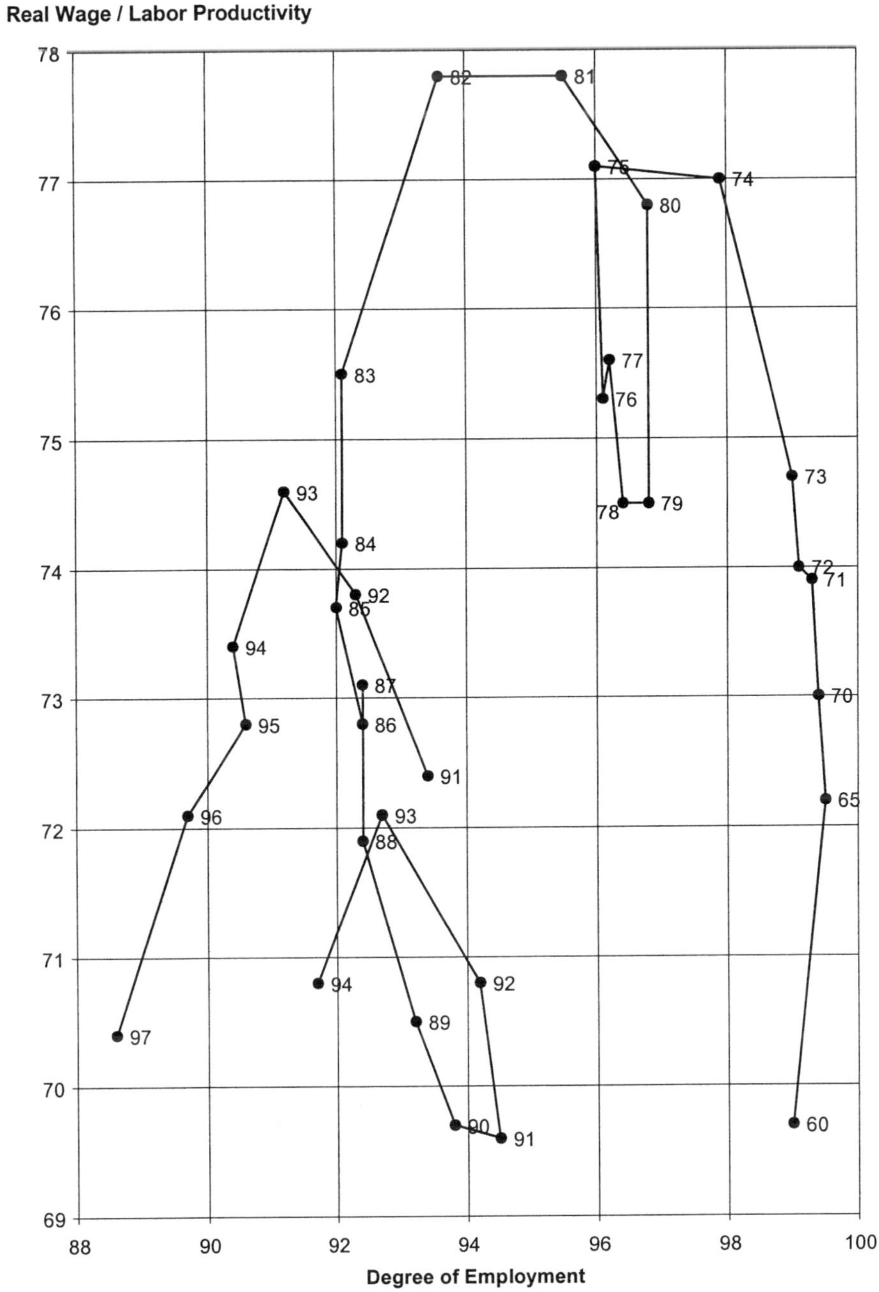

productivity growth due to the slowdown of production which occurred because most countries (and especially Germany) introduced simultaneously restrictive monetary policies to fight the outburst of inflation. Thus the demand for labor was reduced, and for both reasons the degree of employment diminished from 1973 to 1975. A comparable evolution happened after the second oil price hike; only the wage hike was less marked.

From 1974 to 1982, the evolution of wages and employment is consistent with the explanation given by Berthold/Fehn. These authors start their story with an (undated) wage shock which moved the BRW-curve upwards. (Its short term effect was augmented by the effect of the oil price shock in 1973 - not mentioned by Berthold/Fehn - which shifted the PRW-curve downwards). The wage shock reduced employment in the medium run to the new intersection of the BRW- and PRW-curve.

But contrary to the suggestions produced by Berthold/Fehn (see figure 2 in the contribution where the BRW-curve moves upwards and the PRW-curve becomes horizontal) the development in the years since 1982 did not lead to still higher unemployment; instead we observe (see my figure 3) a continuous reduction of the real wage position for nine years, which did not change significantly the degree of employment in Western Germany.

This decline of the real wage position can be easily explained by the „wage moderation" which was forced upon the workers due to their weak position during wage rate negotiations. Therefore, the evolution of the wage rate position was the result of the bad employment situation, and not the other way round.

Only during the unification boom in the years 1991/1992, the decline of the wage rate position was reversed. The recession in 1993 prolonged or even brought about by the restrictive monetary policy of the German Bundesbank (starting in that year in response to an increasing inflation rate) caused a decline in employment in Western Germany and in the total German economy (see Krupp/Cabos (1996) and Modigliani (1997, p. 248)). This decline was accompanied by renewed wage moderation, combined with further growth in unemployment. This combination may serve as an indication that wage moderation alone is no remedy for the unemployment problem.

It is difficult to avoid the conclusion that - contrary to the assertions of Berthold/Fehn - the real wage rate was not the cause of the persistent high unemployment in Germany, but its effect, even if these authors would be able to deliver the lacking empirical underpinning to their assertion of a „technological sclerosis" in Germany.

The tendency to „wage moderation" was enhanced by the very important consequence of the globalization and the growing weight of multinational, world-wide producing companies namely that in all countries the companies try to get the high rates of return to investment obtained in the USA and in Great Britain. Since in Germany the average rate of return seems to have been lower, firms investing and producing in Germany try to achieve higher rates of return by lowering wage costs. This contributes to the continuous decline of the real wage position in this country, a decline which is often accepted by workers to avoid the consequences of a possible departure of capital out of the country.

3 Implications for Labor Market Policy

3.1 Implications for the General Wage Level

The wage moderation since 1982 is quite contrary to the assertion of Berthold/Fehn (at the beginning of their section on labor market policy) that the „rising and persistent unemployment is largely due to rigid, undifferentiated and overly aggressive wage setting". Moreover this assertion is not supported by their own theoretical considerations.

Therefore, their claim that labor market policy should aim for a reduction of the wage level (relative to labor productivity) is not well founded. It might be added that in the US where the employment growth has been very high for many years, the real wage position has varied within a very small corridor: From 1981 to 1996 it varied between 76 and 72 % compared with a range from 78 to 69 % in Germany, no trend can be observed since 1984.

It can even be argued that the long lasting wage moderation in Germany has enhanced the employment difficulties in Germany (this argument applies also to France with a comparable evolution of the real wage position since the early eighties) because the corresponding relative decline in the purchasing power of the employees meant that their families were not able to expand their demand for commodities as fast as their production grew. This added to the weakness of demand which can be observed during most of the years since 1981, because the wage moderation did not produce higher demand for investment goods, contrary to the expectations of many partisans of wage moderation.

3.2 Measures to Fight Structural Unemployment

Undoubtedly, reforms of the labor market are necessary to fight structural unemployment in Germany especially with respect to long-term less qualified unemployed persons. They must be enabled to return to work and the conditions for enterprises must be improved to create working places for unqualified workers in spite of their low productivity.

3.2.1 Qualification Measures for the Long-term Employment

With respect to the long-term unemployed it is difficult to know which part of them is not really ready to accept a paid job if they receive an offer. It is often suggested that this part might be rather large. Contrary to these suggestions the number of long-term unemployed (> 2 years) declined before and during the unification boom in Western Germany from September 1988 to September 1992 from 347.000 to 235.000 (about 32 %) whilst the number of all other registered unemployed declined only by 12 % (see: ANBA, 1988, table 36).

This experience demonstrates that it is worthwhile to try to qualify these persons or at least to stop the deterioration of their qualifications, abilities and fitness.

3.2.2 Unemployment Benefits and the Duration of Unemployment

The influence of unemployment benefits on the willingness to accept job offers is much more restricted than is suggested by Berthold/Fehn. First, the benefits of the unemployment insurance system are limited generally to 12 months; only for employees older than 41 years (now 45 years) are they paid for a longer period of time, namely up to a maximum of 32 months for those older than 53 years (now 57 years) having worked at least 64 months during a reference period. Therefore, the unemployment insurance benefit system can have effects only on the behavior of the older long-term unemployed.

The situation is different for the unemployment assistance paid by the government: It is unlimited, but means-tested and the replacement rate is lower than with the insurance benefits and far from being generous or even lavish. The unemployment assistance can only be an obstacle to accept jobs if the jobs offered are much worse paid than the jobs held before, and if the person concerned has not accumulated enough wealth to be considered as not needy in the means-testing procedure. These conditions will only be met by young persons or by unqualified workers with low remuneration in the past who will be considered in the next section. Besides, the unemployment assistance has to be stopped if the unemployed refuses a job deemed to be acceptable for him by the legal prescriptions which have continuously been hardened during the last three decades.

Berthold/Fehn point to the investigation by Hunt (1995) who showed that extending the unemployment insurance benefits to the persons aged over 41 years during the second half of the 80s was accompanied by longer unemployment spells of these persons (other studies arrive at more ambiguous results - see Galler (1999)). But this result does not prove that the prolonged benefits were the cause of the longer spells. It might be the other way round. Given the high German unemployment level since the early eighties firms tried more and more to restructure their staff and to engage younger people who are more flexible, healthier, and often less expensive. Thus the chances of the elderly to get a new job declined, and the government took account of their economic difficulties by the prolongation of the benefit duration.

Beyond this, it is far from clear that the longer unemployment spells of the older unemployed lead to higher total unemployment. As long as there exists a shortage of work offers, their longer unemployment spells help younger people to get the jobs offered.

Thus there is no sufficient evidence to demand a general reduction of unemployment benefits and their duration. It is all the more necessary to introduce measures to improve the employment opportunities for less qualified persons.

3.2.3 Creation of Work Opportunities for the Less Qualified

The labor market conditions of workers with low or no qualification are most severely reduced by technical change and by the progressive international division of labor in the course of globalization. Both developments are favorable to people in the industrialized countries with high qualifications. Also, they reduce the number of jobs for the less qualified, because these jobs compete with those in low wage regions. Since it will not be possible to qualify all persons, structural changes are necessary to enhance the number of jobs for less qualified persons with low productivity: The tax system and/or the social security system have to be modified with the aim to reduce the wedge between take-home pay and the cost of labor to the employers. Such measures would make it more attractive to the employers to create such jobs and to the worker to accept them.

To cope with this problem Berthold/Fehn favor the „Benefit Transfer Program" proposed by Snower (1994); it suggests that persons who have spent a certain time in unemployment should receive from the government a hiring voucher which is worth a specific amount of money. The unemployed are entitled to give their voucher to the firm which is willing to hire them. These vouchers constitute a wage subsidy of limited duration. Whilst I support the idea of wage subsidies to the less qualified workers, I do not agree with their limitation. Since firms will only create jobs for less qualified persons with low productivity if the costs of their employment will be lowered permanently, it is necessary to reduce the wedge between the cost of labor and the take-home pay of these persons permanently, except if their productivity is raised strongly by training and learning on the job.

The German „Future Commission" (1998), installed by the Friedrich Ebert Foundation, has proposed to reduce this wedge by reducing progressively the burden of the contributions to the social security by employers and employees (which amount to more than 40 % of the negotiated wage and to about 50 % of the take-home pay): For a worker who accepts a job with an hourly wage of DM 8 (the lowest wage to find in any negotiated wage tariff in Germany) the contributions which he and his employers have to pay themselves are reduced to 0 %. The contributions are taken over by the „community of the participants in the social security system" or by the government, i.e. the tax payers. Therefore, the claims of the insured persons are not reduced. With growing hourly wage rates, the percentage to be paid by the employer and the employee is increasing too, arriving at 100 % of the contribution at an hourly wage rate of about DM 16. The slow growth of the percentage is necessary to leave enough incentives to the employed persons to deepen their qualification and to search for a better paid job.

The members of the „Future Commission" express the hope that the proposed reduction of the financial burden due to the contributions to the social security system will induce the creation of new jobs in the service sector which are not productive enough to support at the same time an acceptable level of take-home pay and the whole burden of the social security contributions.

In principle, the proposal of the „Future Commission" is comparable to the idea behind the US-American „Earned Income Tax Credits" which have become more and more important during the 90s. However, this measure is not connected to the social security system but to the tax system.

4 On the Political Economy of Labor Market Policy

Berthold/Fehn express (in part IV) their concern about the difficulties to implement their reform proposals for the labor market institutions. I believe that their proposals encounter these difficulties because they combine measures which might be helpful in the domain of structural unemployment and are directed to certain groups of the labor force (long-term unemployed, persons with low or no qualification) with proposals directed to a reduction of the general wage level which are ill-founded. This combination provokes the opposition of the dependent workers because they suspect an attack on their living standard.

Therefore, the chances of labor market reforms would be enhanced if the corresponding proposals would be restricted to structural reforms but try to leave the general wage level unaffected, and if they were combined with proposals which are aimed at demand-side, trying to enhance the demand for products and thus for labor.

Such a supply-side and demand-side package for more growth and employment - as it is, e.g., proposed in the „Manifesto on Unemployment in the European Union" signed by Modigliani, Snower, Solow et al. (1998) - would have much more chances to be acceptable to the majority of the participants in the political process. Contrary to the apprehensions expressed by Berthold/Fehn, such a „re-emergence of Keynesian thinking" will not lead to the „neglect of supply-side considerations", but to the implementation of those proposals derived from supply-side considerations which are directed to structural problems which need to be solved.

References

ANBA (1998), Arbeitsmarktstatistik 1997 - Jahreszahlen. *Amtliche Nachrichten der Bundesanstalt für Arbeit* 46, special edition.

Bean, Ch. (1994), European Unemployment: A Survey. *Journal of Economic Literature* 32, 573-619.

Carlin, W. and D. Soskice (1990), Macroeconomics and the Wage Bargain. A Modern Approach to Employment, Inflation and the Exchange Rate, Oxford.

Commission of the European Union (1997), *European Economy* 63, 140.

Future Commission of the Friedrich Ebert Foundation (1998), Economic Performance, Social Cohesion, Environmental Sustainability. Three Goals - One Path, Bonn.

Galler, H. (1999), Arbeitsmarkt und soziale Sicherungssysteme - Empirische Evidenz zu den Anreizwirkungen der sozialen Sicherung. *Allgemeines Statistisches Archiv* 83, 63-87.

Hunt, J. (1985), The Effect of Unemployment Compensation on Unemployment, Duration in Germany, *Journal of Labor Economics* 13, 88-120.

Krupp, H.J. and K. Cabos (1996), Geldpolitik und Beschäftigung in: Gahlen, Hesse, Ramser (eds.), Arbeitslosigkeit und Möglichkeiten ihrer Überwindung, Tübingen, 365-393.

Modigliani, F. (1997), The shameful rate of unemployment in the EMS: Causes and Curves, in: Collignon, S. (ed.), European Monetary Policy, London and Washington, 242-270.

II. Fiscal Policy

Fiscal Policy and Unemployment in a Global Economy

Clemens Fuest, Bernd Huber, Florian Wöhlbier

University of Munich,
Ludwigstr. 28/VG, 80539 München, Germany

1 Introduction

In most countries of Western Europe, the problem of finding ways to reduce unemployment is probably the most important policy issue. One of the reasons for the bad employment performance in Europe is the increasing tax burden on labor. Therefore, much of the current debate on tax policy centers around the question of how the tax system can be made more favorable for employment.[1] An important restriction on the scope of feasible tax reforms, however, is the impact of globalization. As goods and factors of production become increasingly mobile across borders, national governments have to take into account that their tax policy has implications for the country's competitiveness, for instance, as a location of investment and economic activity. This limits the extent to which the tax burden can be shifted from labor, which is relatively immobile, to other factors of production.

The present paper discusses the employment effects and, to a lesser extent, also some distributive implications of various tax reform strategies, taking into account the issue of globalization and labor market imperfections. Our analysis is based on a model of a small open economy with unemployment. Unemployment arises because wages are set via bargaining between trade unions and firms. In this framework, we essentially analyze three tax reform strategies. First, there is the idea of reducing labor taxes by raising more revenue via consumption taxes. Secondly, we consider the question of whether positive employment effects can be attained through labor tax cuts financed by higher taxes on internationally mobile factors of production. Thirdly, we develop a tax reform proposal that does not involve a shifting of the tax burden from the employed to other agents in the economy. Essentially, this proposal introduces an element of experience rating

[1] See, for instance, Bovenberg and Van der Ploeg (1994), Van der Ploeg (1995), Sorensen (1997a) and Pissarides (1998).

into the labor tax system. It turns out that this reform also has a positive employment effect.[2]

We proceed as follows. In section 2, we introduce the model underlying our analysis. In sections 3 and 4, we discuss consumption tax reforms and the introduction of taxes on internationally mobile factors of production. In section 5, we develop our concept of modified experience rating and discuss some problems of implementing this type of reform. Section 6 concludes.

2 The Model

2.1 Firms, Workers, and the Tax System

In this section, we develop a simple model of a small open economy with unemployment. Unemployment arises due to a wage rigidity which is a consequence of trade union power. The basic structure of the model is as follows. There is a large number of identical firms in the economy, each producing a composite consumption good Y. The producer price of Y is assumed to be determined by world market conditions and normalized to unity. For analytical convenience, the number of firms is also normalized to unity. There are two factors of production: Labor (L), which is internationally immobile, and an internationally mobile factor which we call energy (E). We assume that the production function is Cobb-Douglas, such that output is

$$(1) \quad Y = AL^{\alpha}E^{\beta} \quad ,$$

where A>0, α>0, ∃>0, ∀+∃<1. The profits of the representative firm are

$$(2) \quad \Pi = AL^{\alpha}E^{\beta} - wL - p(1+\tau)E \quad ,$$

where w is the wage rate, p is the price of energy and ϑ is the energy tax. In the following analysis, we will assume that the wage rate is subject to bargaining between unions and firms whereas employment is set unilaterally by the firms. Maximizing (2) over L and E yields the marginal productivity conditions

$$(3) \quad \alpha AL^{\alpha-1}E^{\beta} = w \quad ,$$

and

[2] Another important debate is that on the employment effects of labor tax progression. On this issue, which cannot be dealt with here, see Lockwood and Manning (1993), Sorensen (1997b) and Fuest and Huber (1997a,b).

$$(4) \quad \beta A L^{\alpha} E^{\beta-1} = p(1+\tau) \ ,$$

From (3) and (4), we can derive the factor demand functions L(w, p(1+ϑ)) and E(w, p(1+ϑ)), with $L_w, L_{p(1+\tau)}, E_w, E_{p(1+\tau)} < 0$, where subscripts denote partial derivatives. For later use, we define the wage elasticity of labor demand as

$$(5) \quad \varepsilon_{L,w} \equiv -L_w w / L = \frac{1-\beta}{1-\alpha-\beta} > 1 \, .$$

Consider next the tax system. Apart from the energy tax already introduced above, we assume that the government raises a labor income tax with rate t, a profit tax with rate T, and a consumption tax, which is levied according to the destination principle, with rate 2. There are two types of agents in the economy: Firstly, there are capitalists who own the firms and do not work. The number of capitalists is also normalized to unity. Their budget constraint is

$$(6) \quad \Pi(1-T) = C^{c}(1+\theta) \ ,$$

where C is private consumption and the superscript c indicates a capitalist. The second group consists of N workers. Each worker inelastically supplies one unit of labor. While all workers are identical ex ante, the existence of unemployment implies that, in the equilibrium, there are employed and unemployed workers. The budget constraint of an employed worker is

$$(7) \quad w(1-t) = C^{e}(1+\theta) \ ,$$

and that of an unemployed worker

$$(8) \quad b = C^{u}(1+\theta)$$

where b denotes a transfer from the government (unemployment benefits) which is assumed not to be taxed.

Finally, the government budget constraint is

$$(9) \quad \begin{aligned} G = R = T\Pi + wtL + \tau pE + \frac{\theta}{(1+\theta)}\big(\Pi(1-T) + w(1-t)L + (N-L)b\big) \\ -(N-L)b \end{aligned}$$

where G is general government expenditure, which is assumed to be exogenously given, (N-L)b is public expenditure on unemployment benefits and R is tax revenue net of expenditure on unemployment benefits.

2.2 Wage Setting

As mentioned above, we assume that wages are determined via union-firm bargaining. For given wages, employment is then set unilaterally by firms.[3] There are many unions and firms in the economy, such that each individual union or firm takes the structure and the level of taxes as given. We determine the outcome of the wage bargaining process using the Nash bargaining solution (Nash (1950)). For analytical convenience, we assume that all agents are risk neutral. It is the objective of the union to maximize the expected income of a representative worker, which is

$$(10) \quad \frac{L}{N}w(1-t)+(1-\frac{L}{N})b.$$

In the case of disagreement, all workers in the firm under consideration become unemployed and receive unemployment benefits, which means that the unions threat point is simply b. As no production takes place in the case of disagreement, the threat point of the firm is zero.

The Nash maximand can thus be written as

$$(11) \quad \Omega=\gamma \log\frac{L}{N}(w(1-t)-b)+(1-\gamma)\log\Pi(1-T) \quad ,$$

where γ denotes the unions' relative bargaining power. With γ=1, we have the case of a monopoly union; γ=0 describes the opposite polar case of competitive labor markets.

Maximizing (11) over w yields the first-order condition

$$(12) \quad \Omega_w=\gamma\frac{L_w(w(1-t)-b)+L(1-t)}{L(w(1-t)-b)}-(1-\gamma)\frac{L}{\Pi}=0 \quad .$$

Using (5) and $wL/A=\forall/(1-\forall-\exists)$, (12) can be rearranged to yield

$$(13) \quad w(1-t)=\phi b \quad ,$$

where

$$\phi\equiv\frac{(1-\beta)\gamma+(1-\gamma)\alpha}{\alpha}.$$

---

[3] For surveys on the theory of trade unions and wage bargaining see Oswald (1982, 1985) or Booth (1995). In this paper, we use the right-to-manage model of wage bargaining. For the efficient bargaining model, which is the most frequently used alternative set-up, see McDonald and Solow (1981).

Since 1-∀-∃>0, we have ∀<1-∃, which means that N>1 for (>0 and N=1 for (=0.

This result can be interpreted as follows. If the unions have any bargaining power ((>0), the outcome of the bargaining process is such that the after tax wage exceeds the income of the unemployed by a factor N>1, which means that wage bargaining then gives rise to involuntary unemployment. For the special case of a monopoly union ((=1), the net wage is simply

$$(14) \quad w(1-t) = \frac{(1-\beta)}{\alpha} b.$$

In the opposite polar case of competitive labor markets ((=0), we have N=1, which means that the net wage is equated to the level of unemployment benefits.[4] In the following, we will concentrate on the case with (>0, i.e. situations where unions do have some bargaining power such that there is some involuntary unemployment in the equilibrium. For the following analysis of policy reforms, one may note that an increase (reduction) in the labor tax leads to and increase (reduction) in the wage rate emerging from the bargaining process:

$$(15) \quad \frac{\partial w}{\partial t} = \frac{w}{(1-t)} > 0.$$

The effect of a change in unemployment benefits, holding constant the labor tax, is

$$(16) \quad \frac{\partial w}{\partial b} = \frac{\phi}{(1-t)} > 0.$$

It immediately follows from (15) and (16) that, holding all other policy instruments constant, employment can be raised by either i) cutting labor taxes or ii) reducing unemployment benefits.[5] A reduction in unemployment benefits, however, may not be an available policy option for most governments; it may be undesirable from a distributional point of view or may face political resistance. In the following analysis, we will therefore assume that the level of unemployment benefits (b) is exogenously fixed. We will therefore concentrate on reforms aiming at a reduction of the labor income tax. Of course, labor tax cuts have to be financed either by a reduction of public expenditure or by an increase in other taxes. In our model, we assume that the level of government expenditure is given (apart from expenditure on unemployment benefits, which is determined endogenously). This leaves us with the option of financing labor tax cuts with

---

[4] Of course, this requires N to be large enough that there is some voluntary unemployment in the equilibrium.

[5] For the effects of taxation on wage setting and employment in unionized labor markets see also Hersoug (1984).

increases in other taxes. In the debate on employment enhancing tax reforms, two types of proposals to restructure the tax system are especially important. Firstly, there is the idea of financing labor tax reductions by higher consumption taxes. Secondly, there is the idea to shift the tax burden from labor to other inputs, in particular polluting factors of production such as energy. We begin with the first type of tax reform.

3 Consumption Tax Reforms

There are at least two variants of the proposal to finance labor tax reductions by raising consumption taxes. Firstly, it has been suggested to raise taxes on specific consumption goods, in particular taxes on polluting consumption. Since we only consider one homogenous consumption good in our model, we do not explicitly analyze this type of tax reform in the following. However, the relevant economic effects are very similar to those of the second type of consumption tax reform, namely the financing of labor tax cuts by raising general consumption taxes. One example for this type of consumption taxes would be the value added tax. In our model, such a tax reform implies a reduction in t financed by an increase in 2.

Before we analyze the impact of such a simultaneous change in t and 2, it is helpful to consider how changes in each of these taxes affect the government budget constraint. To keep the analysis simple, we assume for this section that profit taxes and the energy tax are zero, i.e. $T=\vartheta=0$. Using (13), we can write tax revenue net of expenditure on unemployment benefits as

$$(17)\qquad R = \phi b L \frac{t}{(1-t)} + \frac{\theta}{(1+\theta)}\left(\Pi + (\phi-1)bL + Nb\right) - (N-L)b \ .$$

The effect of a change in t on R is

$$(18)\qquad \begin{aligned} R_t = {} & \frac{\phi b}{(1-t)^2}\left(L + tL_w w\right) + \frac{\theta}{(1+\theta)}\left(-L\frac{w}{(1-t)} + (\phi-1)bL_w\frac{w}{(1-t)}\right) \\ & + L_w \frac{w}{(1-t)} b \end{aligned}$$

Equation (18) shows that the impact of a change in the labor tax on the government budget can be decomposed into three effects which are captured by the three terms on the right-hand-side of (18). Firstly, there is the direct effect on labor tax revenue. If $L+tL_w w>0$, which we assume to be the case in what follows, an increase in the labor tax raises labor tax revenue. The second term in (18) captures the effect of the labor tax change on the consumption tax base and, hence, consumption tax revenue. As a labor tax increase triggers a wage increase, it gives rise to a decline in profit income. Moreover, some workers are dismissed following the wage increase, which means that their consumption level falls from Nb to b. The third term in (18) takes into account that the reduction in employment caused by a labor tax increase also raises expenditure on unemployment benefits.

In general, the effect of a labor tax change on overall tax revenue net of unemployment benefits is thus ambiguous. In the following analysis, however, we assume that a labor tax increase does raise overall tax revenue net of unemployment benefits, for a very simple reason. In the opposite case, the economy would be in a situation where the Laffer Curve (interpreting unemployment benefits as negative taxes) slopes downwards. This would imply that a labor tax reduction would not only reduce the cost of labor and, hence, raise employment, but also increase revenue. A labor tax reduction would then be a „free lunch", and there would be no need to search for ways of financing labor tax cuts.

Consider now the impact of a consumption tax change on the government budget.

$$(19) \quad R_\theta = \frac{1}{(1+\theta)^2}\left(\Pi + (\phi - 1)bL + Nb\right) \ .$$

A consumption tax increase unambiguously raises revenue. Note that consumption tax changes do not affect wage setting. The reason is that, in our model, consumption taxes cover all types of consumption. They cannot be evaded, for instance, by reducing employment since the unemployed also have to pay the consumption tax.[6]

What are the effects of a revenue-neutral reduction in the labor tax, financed by higher consumption taxes? Revenue neutrality implies

$$(20) \quad R_\theta d\theta = -R_t dt \ .$$

As has already been mentioned above, an increase in the consumption tax does not affect wage setting whereas a reduction of the labor tax reduces the wage rate. This directly leads to our first key result:

Result 1: A labor tax reduction, financed by an increase in consumption taxes, raises employment.

The economic explanation for the employment enhancing effect of a switch to consumption taxes is that the consumption tax base includes not only labor

---

[6] Things would be different if we included the utility of leisure in our model. In this case, a consumption tax increase would also trigger wage increases and reduce employment. The overall qualitative effects of consumption tax reforms, however, would be the same as in the model we use.

income but also profits and transfers to the unemployed. Its tax base is therefore broader than that of the labor tax. The consumption tax reform under consideration therefore shifts part of the tax burden from employed workers to firm owners who receive profit income, and the unemployed.

While a consumption tax reform thus seems attractive as a strategy to make the tax system more favorable for employment, one should also take into account that it implies an increase of the tax burden borne by the unemployed. To a certain degree, a consumption tax reform as described above is therefore equivalent to a labor tax cut financed by a reduction in unemployment benefits. For the reasons discussed above, such a reduction in unemployment benefits is usually dismissed as a major way of fighting unemployment.

One may therefore raise the question of whether a consumption tax reform would still raise employment if the unemployed are compensated for the additional consumption tax burden in such a way that their utility, i.e. their consumption remains constant. It is easy to check that, to keep the consumption level of the unemployed constant, unemployment benefits have to be raised by

$$(21) \quad db = \frac{b}{1+\theta} d\theta.$$

The increase in unemployment benefits, however, will trigger an increase in the wage rate that emerges from the bargaining process and thus counteract the labor cost reduction achieved by the labor tax cut. Formally, the change in the wage rate is

$$(22) \quad dw = \frac{\phi b}{(1-t)^2} dt + \frac{\phi}{(1-t)} db \quad .$$

For the employment effect of the consumption tax reform, it is now crucial which of the two effects dominates. Assume for simplicity that the reform departs from an equilibrium with 2=0. Revenue neutrality then implies

$$(23) \quad dR = wLdt + t(L + L_w w)dw + d\theta(\Pi + wL(1-t)) + L_w bdw = 0.$$

Using (21) and (22), this yields

$$(24) \quad \left.\frac{d\theta}{dt}\right|_{dR=0} = -\frac{1}{(1-t)}\left[\frac{wL + L_w w(wt+b)}{wL + L_w w(wt+b) + \Pi}\right] .$$

The effect on the wage rate then turns out to be

$$(25) \quad \left.\frac{dw}{dt}\right|_{dR=0} = \frac{\Pi}{(1-t)} \frac{w}{wL + L_w w(wt+b) + \Pi} ,$$

which is positive because $L + L_w b > 0$ holds if the slope of the Laffer curve is positive. A revenue neutral reduction of t will thus reduce the wage rate. This implies

Result 2: A labor tax rcduction, financed by an increase in consumption taxes and holding constant the utility of the unemployed by an increase in the unemployment benefits, raises employment.

A consumption tax reform thus also raises employment if the unemployed are compensated for the additional consumption tax burden. In this case, the consumption tax reform shifts part of the tax burden from employed workers to firm owners. It would thus be equivalent to a labor tax reduction, financed by a profit tax increase. Of course, this requires that profit income is consumed domestically. This may only partly be the case, given that people living on profit income are often internationally quite mobile. Essentially, what the analysis shows so far is that a switch from labor taxes to consumption taxes will have an employment enhancing effect only in so far as the base of the consumption tax is broader, such that part of the tax burden is shifted from labor income to other types of income, in particular profits and transfer income.

4 Financing Labor Tax Cuts by Higher Taxes on Internationally Mobile Factors of Production

The second widely discussed possibility of financing labor tax cuts is to raise taxes on other factors of production. One example for this type of tax reform is the concept of taxing energy, which is part of the discussion on environmental tax reforms.[7] In our model, such a tax reform would imply that we raise the tax ϑ, which is raised on the internationally tradeable factor E.

Before considering the employment effects of this tax reform, one should note that it is a benchmark result in Optimal Tax Theory that the optimal tax rate on internationally mobile factors of production in a small open economy is zero.[8] The reason is that the taxation of internationally mobile factors in a small open economy does not mean that the tax burden can be shifted to the suppliers of these factors. As a small economy has no significant influence on the factor price net of taxes, that is the world market price, the burden of this type of taxes has to be borne domestically. It is then more efficient to tax domestic factor incomes

[7] See, for instance, Bovenberg and van der Ploeg (1996, 1998), Schneider (1997) or Koskela et al. (1998). Of course, the factor E may also be interpreted as internationally mobile capital. The price p would then be the interest rate in the international capital market.

[8] See, for instance, Gordon (1986).

directly. Of course, this result is based on some critical assumptions: the first assumption is that labor markets are competitive; secondly, it is assumed that profits are fully taxed. In our model, labor markets are not competitive, such that the first assumption does not hold. In the following analysis, we will also assume that the profit tax rate is below 100%. The reason is that, with full profit taxation, an increase in the energy tax, holding constant all other taxes, will reduce tax revenue, such that it makes no sense to undertake the financing of labor tax cuts with higher energy taxes.[9]

In the following, we consider a labor tax cut financed by higher energy taxes, departing from a situation with a positive labor tax, a profit tax which is below 100% and a zero energy tax. In order to keep the analysis tractable, we further assume that the consumption tax rate is zero. Tax revenue net of unemployment benefits can then be written as

$$(26)\quad R = T\Pi + wtL + \tau pE - (N-L)b \quad .$$

Using (15), it is straightforward to show that revenue neutrality implies

$$(27)\quad \left.\frac{d\tau}{dt}\right|_{dR=0} = -\frac{wL(1-T) + L_w w(tw+b)}{(1-t)p(E(1-T) + L_{p(1+\tau)}(tw+b))} \quad .$$

We again assume that the Laffer curve has a positive slope for all taxes, such that $d\vartheta/dt<0$. As the wage rate in our model is independent of the energy tax rate, it is clear that the wage rate declines in response to the labor tax cut. For the employment effect, however, one has to take into account that labor demand not only depends on the wage rate but also on the energy price $p(1+\vartheta)$, which increases.

$$(28)\quad dL = L_w dw + L_{p(1+\tau)} p d\tau$$

Substituting (27) into (28), using $dw/dt=w/(1-t)$ and making some rearrangements yields

$$(29)\quad \left.\frac{dL}{dt}\right|_{dR=0} = \frac{w}{(1-t)R_\tau}\left[(EL_w - LL_{p(1+\tau)})(1-T)\right] \quad .$$

Since

$$(30)\quad EL_w - LL_{p(1+\tau)} = -\frac{LE}{w} < 0,$$

[9] The crucial role of profit taxation is also emphasized in Bovenberg and van der Ploeg (1996) and, in a contribution on environmental taxation in a small open economy with competitive labor markets, Bovenberg and de Mooij (1998).

we have

$$(31)\quad \left.\frac{dL}{dt}\right|_{dR=0} < 0 \ .$$

We may thus state

Result 3: Departing from an equilibrium with t>0 and ϑ=0, a labor tax reduction, financed by an increase in the energy tax, raises employment.[10]

This result can again be explained by the fact that the tax reform under consideration shifts part of the tax burden from the employed workers to other agents in the economy, namely the firm owners. This does not automatically imply, however, that the firm owners suffer a loss from the tax reform. While the energy tax increase reduces profits, the wage reduction induced by the tax reform has a positive effect on profits. The overall effect is

$$(32)\quad \left.\frac{d\Pi}{dt}\right|_{dR=0} = -Lw_t - pE\left.\frac{d\tau}{dt}\right|_{dR=0} \ .$$

Using (15) and (27), this can be written as

$$(33)\quad \left.\frac{d\Pi}{dt}\right|_{dR=0} = -L\frac{w}{(1-t)} + E\frac{wL(1-T) + L_w w(tw+b)}{(1-t)(E(1-T) + L_{p(1+\tau)}(tw+b))} \ ,$$

which yields, after some rearrangements

$$(34)\quad \left.\frac{d\Pi}{dt}\right|_{dR=0} = -\frac{EL(tw+b)}{(1-t)(E(1-T) + L_{p(1+\tau)}(tw+b))} < 0 \ ,$$

which is unambiguously negative. This means that a labor tax reduction, financed by a higher energy tax, not only raises employment but also profits, although the burden of the energy tax is borne by profit income. This can be stated as

Result 4: Departing from an equilibrium with t>0 and ϑ=0, a labor tax reduction, financed by an increase in the energy tax, raises profits.

To understand this result, one should note that taxes on factors of production which are completely elastic in supply are fully borne by other factors which are less elastic in supply. If there are no such factors, these taxes are borne by firm owners. In our model, the net wage rate is given, which means that labor is effectively completely elastic in supply. Therefore, both taxes on the

---

[10] In a framework that differs somewhat from the model used here, in particular by the fact that profit taxes are assumed to be zero, Koskela et al. (1998) derive similar results.

internationally mobile factor of production and taxes on labor are borne by firm owners, as are direct profit taxes. The difference between direct profit taxes and factor taxes is that the latter distort the factor input decision. In a situation where there are only labor taxes but no taxes on E, the employment of labor, given the net wage rate, is distorted while the input decision for E is efficient. The explanation for result 4 is that the marginal cost of introducing a small distortion for the input of E is much lower than the marginal gain from reducing the large distortion induced by the labor tax.

Of course a critical assumption underlying the analysis is that the after tax wage rate is fixed in our labor market model. This implies that the wage tax reduction does not give rise to net wage increases. Moreover, the wage rate is independent of changes in the price of energy. These are implications of the labor market model we use which may be criticized and have to be taken into account when interpreting the results. One may argue, for instance, that a more plausible labor market model would be one where the union captures part of the wage tax reduction by negotiating higher net wages.[11] It is also likely that the wage rate emerging from the bargaining process will change in response to changes in the energy tax rate, although the direction of this impact is not clear a priory. A more complex model that takes these effects into account may therefore well produce different results. Also, studies of optimal taxation in small open economies with imperfect labor markets offer little support to the view that internationally mobile factors of production should generally be taxed.[12] Finally, one should note that, in the simple model we have considered here, wage bargaining only distorts the demand for labor but not demand for the internationally mobile factor E. However, if E is interpreted as capital, and if there are sunk costs of investment, union bargaining power may also lead to a distortion of investment. In this case, Fuest and Huber (1998) show that it may even be desirable to subsidize capital.

Finally, one may also note that the revenue that can be raised via the energy tax is the smaller, the higher the profit tax rate because, as has already been mentioned above, the burden of the energy tax is borne by profit income. In the case of full profit taxation, an increase in the energy tax would even reduce overall tax revenue. The result that mobile factors should be taxed in the case of incomplete profit taxation, however, is known from the standard Theory of Optimal Taxation. In this respect, the result that all agents in the economy benefit from the energy tax reform is not too surprising.

Summarizing, the analysis in sections 3 and 4 has shown that tax reforms which finance labor tax cuts i) via higher consumption taxes or ii) via higher taxes on internationally mobile factors of production, provided that profit taxation is

[11] On the theory of tax incidence in unionized economies see Lockwood (1990). A brief survey of empirical studies of this issue can be found in Layard et al. (1991).

[12] See Richter and Schneider (1998) and Fuest and Huber (1999).

incomplete, may have beneficial effects on employment. One important assumption underlying these results, however, is that of a constant net wage, which implies that tax reductions will fully carry over to reductions in labor costs. Moreover, the consumption tax reform has the unsatisfactory property that it places a burden on recipients of transfer income. In most real world tax reforms, it is unlikely that these groups will effectively be compensated. In the following section, we will therefore discuss a reform of the system of labor taxation which raises employment but does not shift the tax burden to other groups in the population.

5 Raising Employment via Modified Experience Rating

In this section, we develop a reform which raises employment by changing the labor tax system itself in a revenue neutral way, without changing other taxes. As will become clear, our proposal may be understood as the introduction of a variant of experience rating in labor taxation. In general, an experience rated labor tax system denotes a tax system where the level of the tax is determined not only by today's tax base but also by the value of the tax base in the past or changes in the tax base. One example for such a system is the financing of unemployment insurance in the United States of America. In this system, unemployment benefits are financed via payroll taxes. The tax rate, however, may differ across firms, the reason being that its level depends on each firms layoff behavior in the past. The larger the number of workers that have been laid off in the past, the higher the tax rate and vice versa.

To make our point clear, we will first characterize the form of the tax function in our reform proposal. In the above analysis, we have only considered labor income taxes and abstracted from payroll taxes paid by the firm because the economic effects of the two taxes are equivalent. As will become clear below, we now have to introduce a payroll tax, in addition to the income tax that already exists. The payroll tax payment (T^P) is assumed to be

$$(35) \quad T^P = a(w_0 L_0 - wL) \ ,$$

where a is a positive parameter and w_0L_0 is the firms payroll at some point in time in the past, before the reform proposal is announced. The overall labor tax paid in the firm (T^L)(by workers and the firm) is then

$$(36) \quad T^L = twL + a(w_0 L_0 - wL) \ .$$

With a=0, we have the same tax system as that analyzed in the preceding sections. With a>0, however, we have a tax system that reduces the overall labor tax burden in firms that have raised the number of employed workers since the reference date where w_0L_0 is determined and vice versa. As the following analysis concentrates on labor taxation, we may now abstract from the internationally mobile factor E, which can be done by simply assuming ∃=0. With the tax schedule in equation (36), the profits of the representative firm in our model can then be written as

$$(37) \quad \Pi^* = AL^{\alpha} - (1-a)wL - aw_0L_0 \quad .$$

The labor demand function is now

$$(38) \quad L = [(1-a)w]^{-\varepsilon} \quad .$$

Of course, the new labor tax system will also affect the wage bargaining process. The Nash maximand can now be written as

$$(39) \quad \Omega = \gamma \log \frac{L}{N}(w(1-t)-b) - (1-\gamma)\log \Pi^* \quad .$$

The first order condition for the solution of the bargaining problem is

$$(40) \quad \Omega_w = \gamma \frac{L_w(w(1-t)-b) + L(1-t)}{L(w(1-t)-b)} - (1-\gamma)\frac{(1-a)L}{\Pi^*} = 0 \quad .$$

Equation (40) implicitly defines the wage rate emerging from the bargaining process as a function of t and a. Suppose now that a=0 and denote the wage rate emerging from the bargaining process according to equation (40) by $\hat{w}$. Assume further that

$$(41) \quad w_0L_0 = \hat{w}\hat{L} .$$

We can then rewrite (40) as

$$(42) \quad \Omega_w = \gamma\left(-\varepsilon + \frac{w(1-t)}{(w(1-t)-b)}\right) - (1-\gamma)\frac{(1-a)wL}{\Pi^*} = 0 \quad .$$

Totally differentiating (40) yields

$$(43) \quad \Omega_{ww}dw + \Omega_{wt}dt + \Omega_{wa}da = 0 \quad .$$

The second-order condition for the solution of the bargaining problem implies $\Omega_{ww} < 0$. In addition, we have

(44) $\Omega_{wt} = \gamma \frac{b}{(w(1-t)-b)^2} > 0$,

and, using $w_0 L_0 = \hat{w}\hat{L}$

(45) $\Omega_{wa} = -(1-\gamma)w \frac{(1-a)L_a - L}{\Pi^*} = -\frac{(1-\gamma)w(\varepsilon-1)L}{\Pi^*} < 0$.

We thus have w=w(a,t) with

(46) $w_t = -\frac{\Omega_{wt}}{\Omega_{ww}} > 0$,

and

(47) $w_a = -\frac{\Omega_{wa}}{\Omega_{ww}} < 0$.

We can now analyze the effect of a transition from a conventional labor tax system, with a=0, to an experience rated tax system with a>0. In order to concentrate on the labor tax system, we assume that the consumption tax rate and the profit tax rate are zero. The government budget constraint can then be written as

(48) $R = twL + a(w_0 L_0 - wL) - (N-L)b$.

Differentiating (48) and evaluating at a=0 yields the revenue neutrality condition

(49) $\left.\frac{dt}{da}\right|_{dR=0} = -\frac{R_a}{R_t} = -\frac{(tw+b)(L_a + L_w w_a) + tLw_a}{wL + L_w (tw+b) w_t}$,

With a positively sloped Laffer curve for both taxes, we have

(50) $\left.\frac{dt}{da}\right|_{dR=0} < 0.$

i.e. the introduction of the experience rated payroll tax allows a reduction of the labor tax rate t. The employment effect of such a reform would be

(51) $\left.\frac{dL}{da}\right|_{dR=0} = L_a + L_w\left(\frac{dw}{da} + \frac{dw}{dt}\frac{dt}{da}\right) = L_a - \frac{L_w}{\Omega_{ww}}\left(\Omega_{wa} + \Omega_{wt}\frac{dt}{da}\right) > 0$.

We can thus state

Result 5: The introduction of an experience rated payroll tax as defined by equation (35) unambiguously reduces wages and raises employment.

The economic explanation for result 5 is that the experience rated payroll tax reduces the marginal cost of employment. This raises labor demand for given net wages but also affects the wage bargaining process. The wage bargaining parties will take into account that, on the margin, the tax burden on employment is now lower. This induces the wage bargaining parties to agree on a lower wage rate.

While our payroll tax reform proposal has the advantage that the positive employment effect is not due to a redistribution of the tax burden to other agents in the economy, the disadvantage is that various difficulties arise with respect to the practical implementation of the proposal. These problems do not occur in our simple model because all firms are assumed to be equal. Firstly, the question arises whether declining firms, who reduce employment, will be taxed more heavily than growing firms, which may put firms at a competitive disadvantage which are struggling anyway. This may be avoided by applying our tax scheme asymmetrically. This would mean that one might, for instance, set $T^P=0$ if $w_0L_0 > wL$ and $T^P = a(w_0L_0 - wL)$ otherwise. Secondly, the question arises how to deal with new firms. Here a viable solution may be to give them average or somewhat above average tax rates.

A third and perhaps more important problem is that, as firms are different, they have different employment histories, which means that, under experience rating, the effective labor tax burden will differ across firms. This creates incentives to shift workers from firms with high taxes (due to a reduction or a relatively slow growth in employment in the past) to other firms with low taxes, while letting them do the same work as before. One way of limiting these arbitrage opportunities would be to have a maximum tax advantage due to employment history. Of course, this will also limit the employment effect of our proposal. In general, while it is clear that tax arbitrage is difficult to prevent administratively, it should be clear that the U.S. unemployment insurance system faces the same problems and seems to work satisfactorily.

6 Conclusions

In this paper, we have analyzed the employment effects of tax reforms in a small open economy where wage bargaining gives rise to unemployment. We have shown that, under certain assumptions on the wage bargaining structure, labor tax cuts financed by i) higher consumption taxes or ii) higher taxes on internationally mobile factors of production may raise employment. However, the discussion of the results has shown that in particular the positive employment effect of taxing internationally mobile factors of production may not hold if some of the simplifying assumptions usually made in the literature (and in our model) are relaxed. As a third reform possibility, we have discussed the introduction of a variant of an experience rated payroll tax system. We have shown that such a tax system reduces the marginal cost of labor and may therefore be a promising strategy of making the tax system more favorable for employment. We have also discussed some difficulties which may arise with the implementation of our proposal, the main problem being that differences in the effective labor tax burden across firms may create arbitrage possibilities. On the other hand, the existence of experience rating in the U.S. unemployment insurance system suggests that these practical problems can be solved.

References

Booth, A. L. (1995), The Economics of the Trade Union, Cambridge University Press, Cambridge (Mass.).

Bovenberg, L. A. and R. A. de Mooij (1998), Environmental Taxes, International Capital Mobility and Inefficient Tax Systems: Tax Burden vs. Tax Shifting, *International Tax and Public Finance* 5, 7-39.

Bovenberg, L. A. and F. van der Ploeg (1994), Effects of the Tax and Benefit System on Wage Formation and Unemployment, Working Paper, Tilburg University.

Bovenberg, L. A. and F. van der Ploeg (1996), Optimal Taxation, Public Goods, and Environmental Policy with Involuntary Unemployment, *Journal of Public Economics* 62, 59-83.

Bovenberg, L. A. and F. van der Ploeg (1998), Tax Reform, Structural Unemployment, and the Environment, *Scandinavian Journal of Economics* 100, 593-610.

Fuest, C. and B. Huber (1997a), Wage Bargaining, Labour Tax Progression, and Welfare, *Journal of Economics* 66, 127-150.

Fuest, C. and B. Huber (1997b), Steuerprogression und Arbeitslosigkeit, *Zeitschrift für Wirtschafts- und Sozialwissenschaften* 117/4, 567-584.

Fuest, C. and B. Huber (1998), Why do Countries Subside Investment and not Umployment? NBER Working Paper 6685, Cambridge, Mass.

Fuest, C. and B. Huber (1999), Tax Coordination and Unemployment, *International Tax and Public Finance* 6, 7-26.

Gordon, R. (1986), Taxation of Investment and Savings in a World Economy, *American Economic Review* 76, 1086-1102.

Hersoug, T. (1984), Union Wage Responses to Tax Changes, *Oxford Economic Papers* 36, 37-51

Koskela, E., R. Schöb and H.-W. Sinn (1998), Pollution, Factor Taxation and Unemployment, *International Tax and Public Finance* 5, 379-396.

Layard, R., S. J. Nickell and R. Jackman (1991), Unemployment: Macroeconomic Performance and the Labour Market, Oxford University Press, Oxford.

Lockwood, B. (1990), Tax Incidence, Market Power, and Bargaining Structure, *Oxford Economic Papers* 42, 187-209.

Lockwood, B. and A. Manning (1993), Wage Setting and the Tax System - Theory and Evidence for the United Kingdom, *Journal of Public Economics* 52, 1-29.

McDonald, I. M. and R. M. Solow (1981), Wage Bargaining and Employment, *American Economic Review* 71, 896-908.

Nash, J. (1950), The Bargaining Problem, *Econometrica* 18, 155-162.

Oswald, A. J. (1982), Wages, Trade Unions, and Unemployment: What can simple models tell us?, *Oxford Economic Papers* 34, 526-545.

Oswald, A. J. (1985), The Economic Theory of Trade Unions, *Scandinavian Journal of Economics* 87, 160-193.

Pissarides, C. A. (1998), The Impact of Employment Tax Cuts on Unemployment and Wages: The Role of Unemployment Benefits and Tax Structure, *European Economic Review* 42, 155-183.

Richter, W. F. and K. Schneider (1998), Taxing Mobile Capital with Labor Market Imperfections, Revised Version, University of Dortmund Discussion Paper 97-108.

Schneider, K. (1997), Involuntary Unemployment and Environmental Policy: The Double Dividend Hypothesis, *Scandinavian Journal of Economics* 99, 45-59.

Sorensen, P. B. (1997a), Public Finance Solutions to the European Unemployment Problem, *Economic Policy* 25, 221-251.

Sorensen, P. B. (1997b), Optimal Tax Progressivity in Imperfect Labour Markets, Paper prepared for the 53rd IIPF Congress, Kyoto.

Strand, J. (1998), Pollution Taxation and Revenue Recycling under Monopoly Unions, *Scandinavian Journal of Economics* 100, 765-780.

Van der Ploeg, F. (1995), Public Finance and Unemployment in Europe, Paper presented at the 51st Congress of the IIPF, Lisbon.

Comment on Fuest, Huber and Wöhlbier : "Fiscal Policy and Unemployment in a Global Economy"

Matthias Wrede

University of Bamberg and Technical University of Aachen, Germany

Introduction

Fuest, Huber and Wöhlbier tackle the still important question of whether fiscal policy can help to reduce unemployment when the imperfection of the labor market cannot be directly redressed. Therefore, they consider the employment effects of several changes in the tax and transfer system in a small open economy where the labor market is distorted. The paper assumes that wages do not automatically clear the labor market. Instead, they are determined by Nash bargaining between a trade union and a firm.

The main results are as follows: First, a labor tax reduction, financed either by an increase in consumption taxes or by an increase in an energy tax, raises employment, and second, introducing an experience rated payroll tax also raises employment.

Some features of the model and some assumptions are crucial to obtain the results. First, the Cobb-Douglas production function guarantees that the outcome of the Nash-bargaining game, the net wage, is only determined by the unemployment benefits and exogenously given parameters, and is, particularly, independent of the energy tax rate. Second, the focus is naturally on the upward sloping parts of the various Laffer curves. Third, to make the analysis interesting, it is assumed that unemployment benefits per person, which are mainly responsible for involuntary unemployment, are exogenously fixed.

The following sections of this comment will be restricted to the role of the energy tax and the analysis of the experience rated payroll tax.

Taxation of Internationally Mobile Energy

The seminal paper of Bovenberg and de Mooij (1994) started a discussion on the relationship between „green taxes" and employment. In their market clearing model a labor tax has a broader tax base than the green tax, and, therefore, the green tax exacerbates the labor supply distortions and reduces employment.

In the mid nineties the discussion switched to labor market imperfections. Using a model with taxes on output, Koskela and Schöb (1996) have shown that the results of Bovenberg and de Mooij (1994) do not generalize to an economy with involuntary unemployment.

Rather than discussing a green output tax, Fuest, Huber and Wöhlbier deal with an energy tax, and energy is considered as an internationally mobile factor of production. Hence, the paper is related to, e.g., Bovenberg and van der Ploeg (1996), and even more closely to Koskela, Schöb, and Sinn (1998a, 1998b).

Since the environmental aspect of energy is not explicitly dealt with, energy could also be interpreted as any other internationally mobile factor of production, for instance, as capital. Therefore, their result, namely that a (partial) replacement of the labor tax by an energy tax is advantageous, is in sharp contrast to well known results of optimum taxation theory. The non-optimality of taxes on internationally mobile factors has been shown in a simple partial equilibrium model (e.g. Sinn (1994)) and also in a general competitive equilibrium model (e.g. Bucovetsky and Wilson (1991)).[1]

Although the clearness of the positive impact of an energy tax on employment seems to be caused by the strictness of the assumptions, an economic explanation for the interesting result, which has also been derived by Koskela, Schöb, and Sinn (1998a, 1998b), is required. Fuest, Huber and Wöhlbier argue that due to the fixed net wage rate not only energy but also labor is effectively completely elastic in supply. An existing labor tax causes a large distortion. According to the second-best theorem, it is beneficial to create a small distortion through an energy tax, if, simultaneously, the large distortion of the labor tax can be reduced. However, this explanation is not completely satisfactory, since the result does not require a strictly positive wage tax rate (if employment benefits can be financed by a profit tax below 100%).

To shed additional light on role of wage and energy taxes, it is useful to consider the complete welfare effects of fiscal policy by incorporating leisure. The resource constraint of the entire economy is

---

[1] Richter and Schneider (1999) present a thorough analysis of optimum capital taxation with labor market imperfections. They show that the results are less clearcut than with competive markets and, furthermore, sensitive with respect to the type of labor markt imperfection.

$$C + G = f(L, E) - pE,$$

where C and G are private and public consumption, respectively, and L denotes labor, E indicates energy, p the world price of energy and f the production function with the usual properties and decreasing returns to scale. Welfare is measured by the quasi-linear function

$$w(L, E) = f(L, E) - pE - v(L),$$

where v is disutility of labor.

The labor tax rate is denoted by t, and the energy tax rate by τ. The wage-setting process generates a fixed net wage rate $w(1-t) = \overline{w}$, and profit maximization establishes $f_L = w$ and $f_E = (1+\tau)p$. Involuntary unemployment will occur if $w > v'$ which is assumed in the following analysis.

A change in welfare is given by

$$\begin{aligned}\Delta w &= w(L_1, E_1) - w(L_0, E_0)\\ &= \int_{L_0}^{L_1} (f_L(L, E_0) - v'(L))\, dL + \int_{E_0}^{E_1} (f_E(L_1, E) - p)\, dE\\ &= \int_{E_0}^{E_1} (f_E(L_0, E) - p)\, dE + \int_{L_0}^{L_1} (f_L(L, E_1) - v'(L))\, dL\end{aligned}$$

.

Figure 1: *Welfare effects of a labor subsidy*

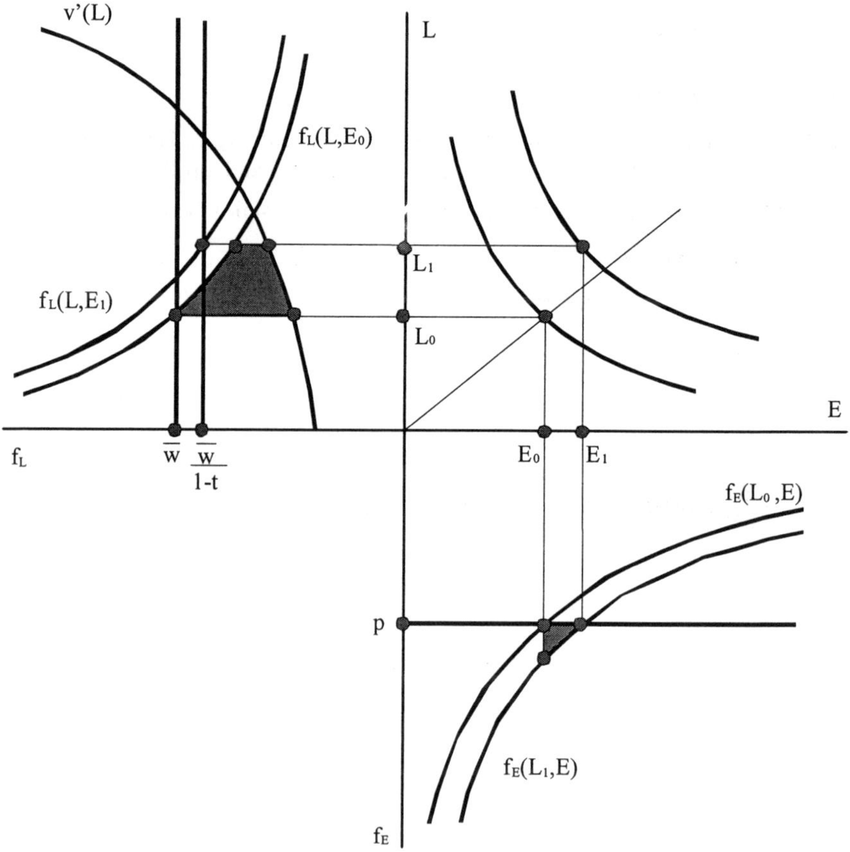

Figure 2: *Welfare effects of an energy subsidy*

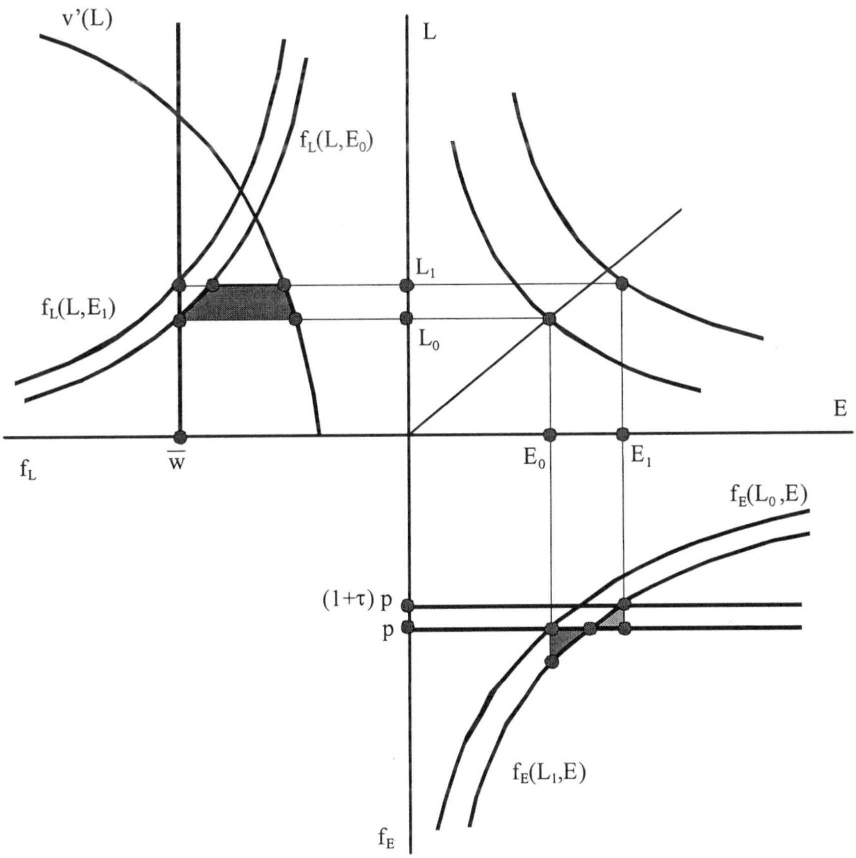

The shaded areas in the two figures show how the introduction of a labor subsidy ($t < 0$) and the introduction of a energy subsidy ($\tau < 0$) change welfare, where each starts in a situation without labor and energy taxation (E_0, L_0). Both welfare effects are unambiguously positive if the energy subsidy rate is sufficiently small. However, the labor subsidy has the advantage of a reduction in the labor market distortion without any additional distortion being established. An energy subsidy also reduces unemployment but at the expense of a distortion in the energy market. Both, a labor subsidy and an energy subsidy are useful instruments in fighting unemployment, but the former is a more purposeful one.

Analogously, the labor tax distortion is still larger than the energy tax distortion even if government expenditure cannot be financed solely by profit tax revenue.

Finally, it is worthwhile to ask whether an energy tax is a second-best tool or rather a third-best instrument (in comparison with, e.g., a consumption tax).

Experience Rating

Ignoring energy, Fuest, Huber and Wöhlbier discuss in the second part of the paper a modified experience rating model. They refer to the US unemployment insurance system where some states base unemployment payroll tax rates on layoff history. The more layoffs by a firm, the higher the payroll tax rate it must pay. The purpose of experience rating is to increase a firms costs of laying off workers and, at the same time, to reduce the subsidy of layoffs through unemployment compensation. As has been shown by Topel (1983), experience rating reduces layoffs.

Fuest, Huber and Wöhlbier show that the introduction of a payroll tax with a fixed tax rate, where the tax base is the difference between the firms payroll in a previous and a current period, reduces wages and raises employment if the wage tax rate is reduced simultaneously. The payroll tax affects the wage bargaining process and strengthens the bargaining position of the firm, such that the parties agree on a lower wage rate.

However, the suggested payroll tax is in fact a subsidy, since the introduction of the experience rating payroll „tax" raises the payroll of the firm, such that the overall payroll tax

$$T^P = a(w_0 L_0 - wL)$$

is negative (a is the payroll tax rate, and the subscript 0 indicates the period before the experience rating payroll tax was introduced). To see the impact of the tax reform, note that according to[2]

$$\frac{d\,wL}{d\,a} = w\left[L_a + L_w\left(w_a + w_t\frac{d\,t}{d\,a}\right)\right] + L\left(w_a + w_t\frac{d\,t}{d\,a}\right)$$
$$= wL_a + (wL_w + L)\left(w_a + w_t\frac{d\,t}{d\,a}\right) > 0,$$

the revenue neutral introduction of the experience rating payroll „tax" increases the payroll, such that $dT^P/da < 0$ if $w_0 L_0 = wL$ holds in the beginning.

Although experience rating increases employment within the model, in reality it also has some disadvantages. Some were discussed by Fuest, Huber and Wöhlbier. An adequate treatment of declining firms and tax arbitrage will limit the positive employment effects. One should take the destabilizing effects into account. Moreover, it is also worthwhile to stress that any instrument which penalizes layoffs also makes hiring labor less profitable.

---

[2] Using (5), this can easily be calculated from the analysis of Fuest, Huber and Wöhlbier (1999), p. 17.

The analysis of Fuest, Huber and Wöhlbier is an interesting first attempt in dealing with experience rating, but a complete analysis can be undertaken only in a multi-period-framework.

Concluding Remarks

The analysis of taxes and transfers in the presence of involuntary unemployment leads to interesting and insightful results. Political instruments, namely taxes on internationally mobile factors of production, which are not reliable in an economy with perfectly competitive labor markets, might be useful to reduce labor market distortions.

However, since the effects which those instruments have on employment, tax revenue and welfare heavily depend on the type of the labor market distortion (as shown by Richter and Schneider (1999)), one should be careful in drawing economic policy lessons from the theoretical analysis.

References

Bovenberg, A. L. and R. A. de Mooij (1994), Environmental Levies and Distortionary Taxation, *American Economic Review* 84, 1085-1089.

Bovenberg, A. L. and F. van der Ploeg (1996), Optimal Taxation, Public Goods and Environmental Policy with Involuntary Unemployment, *Journal of Public Economics* 62, 59-83.

Bucovetsky, S. and J. D. Wilson (1991), Tax Competition with Two Tax Instruments, *Regional Science and Urban Economics* 21, 333-350.

Fuest, C., B. Huber and F. Wöhlbier (1999), Fiscal Policy and Unemployment in a Global Economy, *contribution in this Volume.*

Koskela, E. and R. Schöb (1996), Alleviating Unemployment: The Case for Green Tax Reforms, CES Working paper 106, Munich.

Koskela, E., R. Schöb and H.-W. Sinn (1998a), Pollution, Factor Taxation and Unemployment, *International Tax and Public Finance* 5, 379-396.

Koskela, E., R. Schöb, and H.-W. Sinn (1998b), Green Tax Reform and Competitiveness, CES Working paper 176. Munich.

Richter, W. F. and K. Schneider (1999), Taxing Mobile Capital With Labor Market Imperfections, Working paper, University of Dortmund.

Sinn, H.-W. (1994), How much Europe? Subsidiarity, Centralization and Fiscal Competition, *Scottish Journal of Political Economy* 41, 85-107.

Topel, R. (1983), On Layoffs and Unemployment Insurance, *American Economic Review* 73, 541-559.

III. Stabilization Policy

Globalization and Inflation

Helmut Wagner

University of Hagen,
Feithstr. 140, 58084 Hagen, Germany

1 Introduction

Stabilization policy is often directed towards fighting or preventing both inflation and unemployment. The main problem for this, however, is the well-known short-run trade-off between inflation and unemployment and the phenomenon of an inflation bias which is based on the credibility problem of optimal monetary policy. The question posed in this paper is whether globalization is going to ease the task of stabilization policy, in particular of preventing inflation.

During the 1990s a world-wide decline in inflation started which had already started in industrialized countries in the early 1980s (see Figure 1). The popular press often connects this with the ongoing process of globalization which is said to be leading to a decline in inflation. (Bootle even titled his provocative best-seller on the effects of globalization (Bootle (1996)) "The Death of Inflation".) In academic publications, however, there are hardly any attempts to explain the observed decline in inflation by referring to the globalization process (a rare exception is Tootell (1998)). Academics often simply contend that the reasons for the decline in inflation and for low inflation at full employment levels are unknown. "It is not known why it (sc. the fact that inflation is so low given the full employment level in the US during the 90s) is so" (Dornbusch (1998), "Growth Forever", in: Wall Street Journal Europe, July 31-August 1). Others, like Tobin (1998), speak of a "mystery, fully understood by neither central bankers nor economists" (p. 19). In this paper I shall mainly consider the role of globalization. However in chapter 4.2, I will also analyze how the decline in inflation can be explained without referring to globalization. The central question raised in this paper, however, is whether the neglect of a relationship between inflation and globalization in the academic literature is well-founded because there is no causal relationship, or whether there is in fact such a relationship which has simply been overlooked or underestimated. If there is a (strong) relationship between globalization and inflation, this may have (enormous) future consequences for economic institutions and policy strategies provided that the globalization process is continuing[1].

Figure 1: *Inflation Rate in Industrial Countries and Median Inflation Rate in Developing Countries* (in percent)*

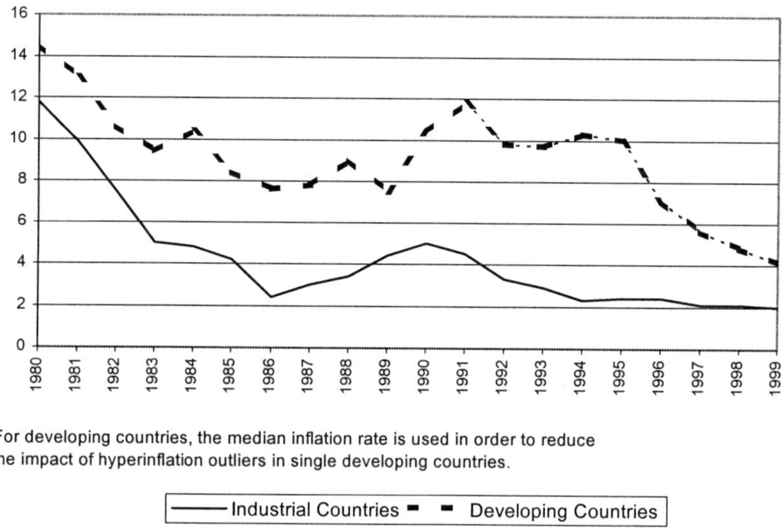

*For developing countries, the median inflation rate is used in order to reduce the impact of hyperinflation outliers in single developing countries.

Source: World Economic Outlook, IMF

Globalization is a widely used term, but is in fact rather vague. It refers to the growing economic interdependence of countries worldwide through the increasing volume and variety of cross-border transactions in goods and services and of international capital flows, and also through the more rapid and widespread diffusion of technology (e.g., IMF (1997, p. 45))[2].

---

[1] Political support for continuing globalization cannot be taken for granted. Economic integration among nations is not a new phenomenon. In many ways it can be regarded as a resumption of the intensive integration which began in the mid-1800s and ended with World War I (for this see IMF (1997, pp. 112-116); see also O'Rourke (1999)). "In some respects, however, the recent process of global integration is qualitatively different from that of the earlier period" (IMF (1997, p. 45)). In particular, the mass intercontinental migration which lowered New World living standards and therefore created a new wave of protectionism is absent today (for more details see ibd., Williamson (1998), O'Rourke/Williamson (1999) and O'Rourke (1999)).

[2] See also Rodrick (1997), idw (1998), Wagner (1991).

The main impetus for this globalization process has up to now been based on the increased integration and globalization of the financial markets (see Figure 2a and 2b; see also the tables and charts in Citrin/Fischer's contribution in this volume), favored in particular by the abolition of capital controls (or artificial barriers to the movements of capital) and by a drastic decrease of transaction costs thanks to new communication and information technologies (see Table 1). Another impetus has been the increase in international trade (see Figure 2c). These globalization processes, however, are still in the development stage (e.g., Shirakawa et al (1997), and IMF (1997)) so that it might be claimed that the real or decisive effects of globalization have not yet arrived and are under way (see also OECD (1998)). This means that our topic includes of necessity some speculation in that we argue "If globalization is continuing, then ...".

Table 1: *Costs of Air Transportation, Telephone Calls and Computer Price Deflator (in 1990 U.S. dollar unless otherwise indicated)*

Year	Average Air Transportation Revenue per Passenger Mile	Cost of a Three-Minute Call, New York To London	U.S. Department of Commerce Computer Price Deflator (1991 = 100)
1930	0.68	244.65	
1940	0.46	188.51	
1950	0.30	53.20	
1960	0.24	45.86	125,000
1970	0.16	31.58	19,474
1980	0.10	4.80	3,620
1990	0.11	3.32	1,000

Source: World Economic Outlook May 1997, IMF, p. 46
[Source: Richard J. Herring and Robert E. Litan, Financial Regulation in the Global Economy (Washington: Brookings Institution, 1995), p. 14]

Figure 2a: *Direct Investment (in billions of U.S. dollars)*

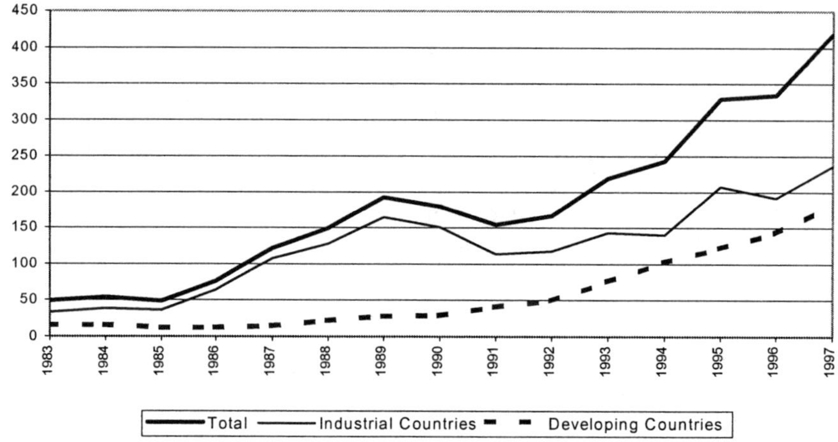

Source : Balance of payments statistics yearbook, IMF

Figure 2b: *Portfolio Investment (in billions of U.S. dollars)*

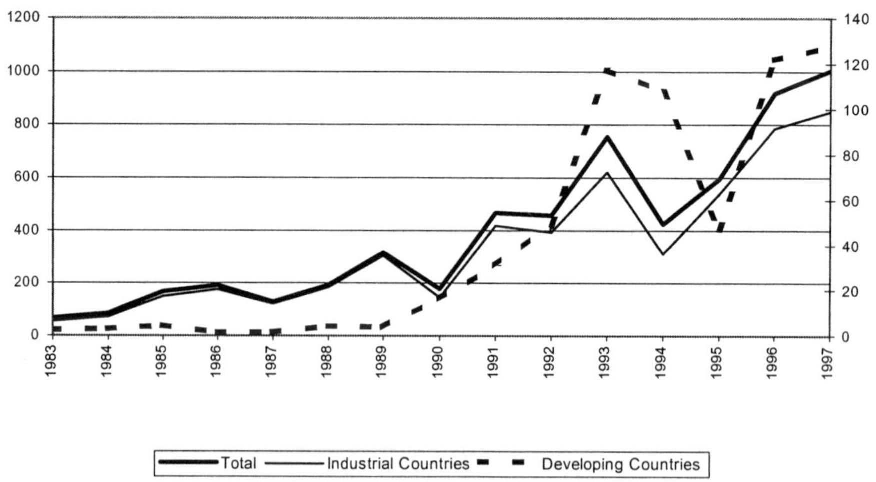

Source: Balance of payments statistics yearbook, IMF
Scale on right-hand side: Portfolio Investment in Developing Countries
Scale on left-hand side: Portfolio Investment in Industrial Countries and Total

Figure 2c: *Exports (in billions of U.S. dollars)*

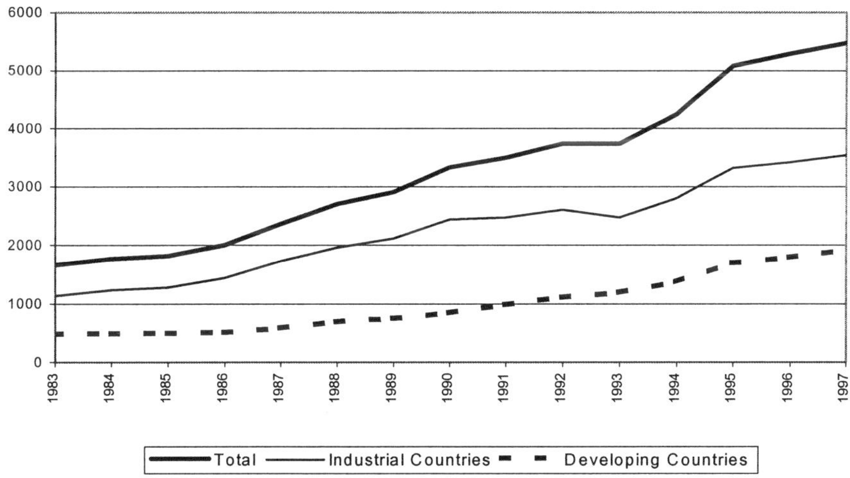

Source: Direction of trade statistics yearbook, IMF

Globalization here is understood as a development which increasingly exposes countries to international competition[3]. This process or competition is regarded as being effective not only in the goods market, but also in the markets for mobile production factors (human capital and, in particular, real capital). This exposure to international competition, which manifests itself in the movement of mobile production factors to countries which offer them the highest rate of return, increases a country's costs of maintaining inefficient and overly regulated market structures. The higher the mobility of these production factors the more their rates of return are determined on world markets. As different countries compete with their institutional facilities for attracting these mobile production factors, countries with inefficient facilities are forced to adjust. If they do not adjust, their living-standards will decline both in relative and in absolute terms (see, e.g., Siebert (1996))[4].

The existence of a high socially optimal inflation rate as well as the existence of an inflation bias[5] may be interpreted as the result of inefficient institutional

[3] Whether this is true, is open to question. Here I only describe a single possible scenario, however likely this is to appear.

[4] Competition among countries or governments may be interpreted in a manner similar to Tiebout (1956), as a market for institutional arrangements. According to this theory, national governments try to find even better institutional arrangements in order to keep mobile production factors at home or to attract them.

[5] An inflation bias is defined as the deviation of the inflation rate from the socially optimal inflation rate. In this paper, I shall focus special attention on the effects of globalization on

facilities based on nominal and institutional rigidities in the economic and political systems (see below). If globalization tends to erase or reduce these rigidities then we may expect that inflation is also going to be decreased. This, however, may have enormous consequences for economic and, in particular, monetary policy, although it cannot yet be clearly seen what these consequences would be, and/or which net effects on welfare this would have. This is the main topic of this article.

The paper is structured as follows. In section 2, I shall detail the inflation problem, point to the costs of inflation, analyze the current substantiation for an inflation bias, and give a brief overview of the main solutions proposed for an inflation bias. In section 3, I shall analyze the question of whether inflation may be reduced or even wiped out completely in a "globalized" economy, and through which channels. Section 4 contains an analysis of some alternative explanations of the recent decline in inflation within the context of a traditional positive model of monetary policy. Section 5 then discusses the institutional and policy consequences of such an inflation reduction. Section 6 provides a brief summary.

2 The Inflation Problem

There is a general consensus among economists today with respect to the following statements:

- inflation is costly, so that the optimal rate of inflation should be low,

- there is an inflation bias inherent in the existing (imperfect) market economies, therefore

- there should be an anticipatory anti-inflation policy with adequate institutions, such as central bank independence, for example.

2.1 Costs of Inflation

The actual rate of inflation is a function of the socially optimal (or of the desired) rate of inflation[6] and an inflation bias, apart from shocks. The socially optimal rate of inflation can be regarded as a function of the benefits and costs of inflation. Although the subject of inflation costs counts to the least solved questions in

---

the inflation bias which currently represents the main explanation in monetary economics of enduring or trend inflation in developed market economies.

[6] There is a difference between optimal and desired rate of inflation insofar as, even with given preferences, the optimal rate of inflation can change if the costs and benefits of inflation change. In principle, however, we can also argue that the desired rate of inflation, i.e. the preferences, may change with changing costs and benefits of inflation, at least in the long term.

macroeconomics, it may nonetheless be claimed that at least high inflation obviously is very costly. Most recent empirical studies show for instance that double-digit inflation is bad for economic growth. However, the results leave the nature of the relationship at lower rates uncertain. Bruno/Easterly (1998), for instance, show that 40 percent annual inflation is a threshold above which a country is likely to go into a high-inflation, low-growth crisis. Their results also show that high inflation is bad for growth, and that stabilization to below 40 percent is good for growth. However, they do not establish the nature of the ceteris-paribus relationship between inflation and growth at lower rates of inflation. Sarel (1996) finds a breakpoint in the estimated non-linear inflation-growth relationship at about 8 percent inflation. The relationship is found to be zero (or slightly positive) at lower rates of inflation, and negative at higher rates of inflation. See Gosh (1997) as well for transition countries.

This means, inflation in the one-digit percent range, is far more difficult to prove to be very costly than is high inflation (see also Barro (1995)). In some studies inflation even proves beneficial. Tobin (1965) for instance showed that a higher rate of inflation (by decreasing the real rate of return on money holding) shifts the structure of private sector's portfolio from money towards capital. Given the level of real wealth in the economy, this portfolio shift increases the capital stock. However, this Tobin effect is based on the assumption that money serves as a store of value. In contrast, cash-in-advance models have emphasized the transaction demand for money. If some market activities, such as the purchase of investment goods, are subject to cash-in-advance restrictions, high inflation means that these market activities are more inflation-taxed in comparison to a situation with low inflation rates. This complementarity of money and capital may then lead to an inverse relationship between inflation and economic growth (Stockman (1981)). However, in the most recent literature the growth effects of inflation are analyzed not only with regard to the long-term growth level but also with regard to the long-term rate of growth. These studies are based on the theory of endogenous growth. Some authors (e.g. De Gregorio (1993); Marquis/Reffett (1991)) show that inflation reduces the long-term growth rate. More recent empirical studies confirm qualitatively the inverse (but (not yet) the causal) relationship between inflation and economic growth, but the extent of growth losses remains controversial (Grimes (1991); Fischer (1993); Barro (1995, 1997); Bruno/Easterly (1998)).

There are even studies that come to the conclusion of very high costs of even very small rates of inflation (e.g. Feldstein (1997)). These studies emphasize in particular allocative costs of inflation such as the interactions of existing capital income tax rules and inflation. Most of these costs derive from the distortion of the intertemporal allocation of consumption caused by the inflation-induced reduction in the real rate of return on saving. The result eventually depends on the non-indexation of capital income taxation.

Other costs which refer to anticipated inflation (like most of the just mentioned costs as well) are the costs of suboptimally low real balances (so-called shoe-leather-costs), costs of price adjustment (so-called menu-costs) and costs arising from a tax system which does not (fully) take into account the effects of inflation (cold progression etc). Even more important, at least for the subject of an inflation bias, than these costs of anticipated inflation are the costs of non-anticipated inflation. These costs particularly refer to aspects of arbitrary re-distribution and allocation effects because of the distorted information content of prices (cf. Fischer/Modigliani (1978), Wagner (1985), Fischer (1994)). The main aspects are in brief (Romer (1996, pp. 431-432)): Firstly, unanticipated changes in inflation redistribute wealth because many assets are denominated in nominal terms. Secondly, increased uncertainty about inflation may make individuals and firms reluctant to undertake investment projects, particularly long-term ones, as long as contracts/debts are denominated in nominal terms. Thirdly, highly variable inflation may also discourage long-term investment since individuals and firms view it as a symptom of a government that is functioning badly and is therefore resorting to policies that are detrimental to capital-holders, such as confiscatory taxation.

In sum, there is currently a kind of wide consensus among the economics profession that it is worthwhile also to fight inflation in the one-digit range.

2.2 Substantiation of an Inflation Bias

Inflation is nowadays mainly regarded as a monetary phenomenon insofar as an accommodating monetary policy is the sine qua non condition for inflation (e.g., Wagner (1990)). An inflation bias is today usually explained in the context of game-theoretic considerations, referred to a view that monetary policy decisions are taken sequentially in a second-best world and therefore a socially desirable monetary policy may suffer from a lack of credibility caused by time inconsistency. A policy is considered to be *time-inconsistent* if the best plan which one of the players (here, the policymaker) in a dynamic game currently establishes for some future period is no longer optimal from his or her point of view when that period arrives. Hence there will be an incentive for the policymaker to deviate from the former plan (here, to stabilize the price level). The central idea of the time inconsistency theory is as follows: the private agents (knowing the objectives of the policymaker and understanding his/her mode of behavior) are aware of the incentive of the government to deviate/inflate and hence expect that rate of inflation which excludes for the government any systematic incentive to deviate from the expected rate of inflation.

In sum, because of time inconsistency of the (ex ante) optimal, however not enforceable, monetary policy any implementable credible policy leads to a suboptimal high inflation rate, i.e. an inflation bias.

In the literature one can find mainly three reasons for this credibility-based inflation bias referred to as employment, revenue and balance-of-payments motives (Cukierman (1992)):

i) employment motive

This is based on the hypothesis that monetary policy is willing and able to influence the level and variability of employment by means of unanticipated (surprise) inflation. It is supposed that distortions in labor markets induce policy-makers to prefer higher employment than it would be consistent with the natural rate of employment. Because of fixed nominal wage contracts, unanticipated inflation can decrease real wages. This expands output since firms increase labor demand. Therefore, policy-makers can increase output and employment by causing an unexpected increase in inflation, part of which is at the expense of other countries. The temptation of a policy-maker to inflate is, however, tempered by a dislike for inflation (induced mainly by the costs of inflation discussed in the foregoing section). This employment motive is seen to dominate monetary policy in developed countries with well-functioning capital markets. The higher the NAIRU (above the socially desired level) and the more significant are nominal rigidities (so that the output gain from an unanticipated monetary expansion is large), the greater is the incentive for the authorities to inflate the economy.[7]

ii) revenue motive

Monetary expansion may be a means of financing government expenditures. In many countries the government is entitled to borrow directly from the central bank and utilize this privilege to finance part of its budget. Besides this standard public finance aspect, the following argument is important for an inflation bias. In the presence of nominal debt the government has an incentive to generate an unexpected inflation by monetary expansion. Inflation surprises have the consequence that nominal interest rates on government bonds remain unchanged in spite of inflation, and therefore not only the real debt burden declines but also real balances as the basis of seigniorage revenues remain unchanged.

This revenue motive dominates in countries with thin capital markets and relatively inefficient tax systems, i.e. in developing and transition countries.

iii) balance-of-payments motive

Governments may be tempted to use an unexpected devaluation to solve their balance of payments problems. A nominal devaluation is expected to - at least temporarily - lower real wages and boost export supply. This motive is especially strong for countries with insufficient international reserves and limited access to international capital markets unable to borrow their way out of balance of payments difficulties. This comparatively less often cited motive can also be

---

[7] See the underlying model in more detail in chapter 4 below.

explained by referring to the argument that for small open economies with a fixed but adjustable peg governments may have an incentive to produce unanticipated inflation in order to improve the current account balance so that the stock of currency reserves does not fall to a suboptimally low level.

The theory of the inflation bias has originally been developed in the realm of a closed economy (for a survey see, e.g., Fischer (1990), Persson/Tabellini (1997), Illing (1998)). The influence of the process of globalization still needs to be integrated[8] although a completely globalized economy again could be treated/modeled like a closed economy.

2.3 Solution Concepts Proposed

2.3.1 Constitutional Rules

One possible way to deal with the credibility problem behind the inflation bias consists in removing all discretionary power from the government. This could for example happen by the government passing a law requiring itself to fix the growth of money supply at a steady rate.

This solution, however, has some disadvantages. Studies on the employment motive for monetary expansion show that when stochastic shocks are taken into account the optimal monetary policy does not conform to a simple ironclad rule but also includes an optimal shock absorption (Rogoff (1985a); King (1996)). By following a simple rule the government might be able to eliminate the inflation bias, but would produce suboptimally high output fluctuations. On the other hand, statutory entrenchment of the optimal state-contingent rule appears to be extremely difficult, because it is hard to imagine how all contingencies might be described ex ante and verified ex post. What remains is the choice between simple rules, which are inflexible, and discretionary policies which display an inflation bias.

2.3.2 Other, More Flexible Solutions

The above disadvantages have led many economists to search for other, institutional solutions of the credibility problem that show more flexibility and nevertheless reduce or even erase the incentive to renege and to produce

[8] Motive iii above, however, is embedded or can only be developed in an international context and has naturally been developed in such a context, see, e.g., Horn/Persson (1988) and Cukierman (1992). For the simplest presentation just interpret "y" in equation (1) of section 4 below as current account level. For other representations of inflation bias aspects in the context of open economies cf. Rogoff (1985b), Romer (1993), Persson/Tabellini (1995), Sachs/Tornell/Velasco (1996) and Levine/Pearlman (1998).

suboptimal high inflation rates. This research resulted in particular in the dominant proposal of central bank independence.

Theoretical approaches on central bank independence

The above trade-off between credibility and flexibility has induced a game-theoretic foundation of central bank independence. Here two approaches can be differentiated:[9] on the one hand, Rogoff's (1985a) proposal to delegate monetary policy to an independent "conservative" central banker and the contracting or targeting approach on the other hand. What the theories have in common is that they propose the establishment of central bank structures which permit monetary policy to react to economic disturbances independently without interference from the government. However, they differ in their policy advices regarding the determination of central bank's objectives.

Rogoff (1985a) deals with the employment motive in the framework of a Barro/Gordon model with stochastic supply shocks. Rogoff shows that social welfare can be improved if the government delegates monetary policy to a "conservative" central banker who agrees with the social preferences regarding the target values of inflation and output, but places a greater weight to the inflation target than the government (society). Once appointed, the "conservative" central banker operates under discretion and is independent to pursue an activist policy (Fischer (1994, p. 290)). By appropriate choice of the degree of conservativeness society realizes a better equilibrium position than the government itself can achieve following inflexible rules or discretionary policies. In comparison to the discretionary solution without delegation the inflation bias is reduced but not completely eliminated. In the presence of supply shocks, this welfare gain is reduced by higher output volatility. Because the solution is based on the assumption that the "conservative" central banker optimizes a preference function with, in comparison to the social welfare function, distorted (i.e. greater) inflation aversion, it presupposes central bank independence and the binding commitment of the government not to renege on delegation ex post.[10]

A more recent solution proposal, however, is based on the contracting or targeting approach. Starting from a principle-agent approach, Walsh (1995a) and Persson/Tabellini (1993) come to the conclusion that, even though the government should transfer control over monetary policy instruments to an independent central bank, the government should also provide the central bank with incentives to optimize the social welfare function. This will be done in the form of a (performance) contract between the government (as the principal) and the central bank (as the agent). Under the assumption that the preferences of the government and the central bank coincide, Walsh (1995a) shows that a simple contract which

---

[9] This subsection heavily draws on Kißmer/Wagner (1998).

[10] For extension of and further critical aspects on this and the following solution approach see for example Kißmer/Wagner (1998, pp. 9-13).

makes the central banker's remuneration linearly dependent on the realized rate of inflation eliminates the inflation bias without any sacrifice in stabilization efficacy. The trade-off between credibility and flexibility would be solved by this and the welfare properties of the ex ante optimal rule mimicked. In addition, it was shown that the incentive structures of optimal performance contracts can also be generated through the implementation of inflation-dependent dismissal rules (Walsh 1995b). Such dismissal rules come close to the corresponding rules of the Price Targeting Agreement in force in New Zealand (Walsh (1995b), Persson/Tabellini (1997, p. 42)).

As incentives in the standard approaches depend exclusively on deviations between realized inflation from the socially desirable rate of inflation, performance contracts are frequently interpreted in the sense of a direct inflation targeting as well. Svensson (1997) shows that, under conventional assumptions, the result of an optimal central bank contract can also be achieved when the government imposes an inflation target on the central bank which is below the socially desirable inflation target.

In sum, theoretical studies show that central bank independence by itself does not improve the social welfare in a discretionary regime. To do this, either the preferences of central bankers must differ from those of the government in an appropriate manner and/or the central bank must be provided with policy targets or incentive structures.

Empirical evidence on central bank independence

The empirical substantiation of central bank independence is based on studies which mainly refer to the pre-1990-period and see a "free lunch" in the existence of an independent central bank (e.g. Grilli/Masciandaro/Tabellini (1991, p. 375)): on average, countries with more independent central banks realize comparatively low inflation rates without real economic costs in terms of reduced economic growth or higher output volatility. In fact, many empirical studies on the relationship between central bank independence and inflation confirm a negative correlation between inflation and central bank independence. The derivation of these findings is based on the use of different measures for central bank independence. For industrial countries, legal indices are mainly used as proxies for central bank independence whereas for developing countries more behaviorally oriented indicators are used (e.g., Cukierman (1998); Eijffinger/De Haan (1996, p. 33)). In addition, there appears to be hardly any correlation between central bank independence and long-run growth or output volatility, but some studies come to the conclusion that the disinflation costs are related positively to central bank independence.

In the 1990s therefore numerous countries have provided their central banks with greater legal independence from the government. This trend to increased central bank independence has been witnessed in both industrialized and developing countries (in particular, Latin America). Within the former socialist countries of

Central and Eastern Europe, economic transition has also been accompanied by substantial central bank reforms granting greater 'goal' and 'instrument' independence. Now one could argue that this increase in central bank independence may explain the decline in inflation at that time. Inflation, however, has not only declined in countries that introduced central bank independence. Insofar such an explanation is not satisfactory or sufficient.

In addition, it is questionable whether the above-mentioned empirical findings regarding the relationships between central bank independence and inflation or output may be seen as stylized facts. More recent studies criticize not only the consistency of the indicators for central bank independence but also the robustness of the statistical associations as well as the causality. For an extensive survey see Eijffinger/De Haan (1996), Cukierman (1998) and Kißmer/Wagner (1998).

Instead of referring to central bank independence, the recent decline in inflation might also be alternatively explained, for example, by referring to supply shocks and different speeds of adjustment between the natural rate of output (or employment) and the target rate (see section 4.2.1). In the following chapters, however, I mainly want to analyze whether a permanent tendency towards an extinction of the inflation problem can be substantiated by working out the effects of present and future globalization on inflation and the possible reactions to these with respect to present institutional and policy arrangements.

3 The Effects of Globalization on Inflation

In this section I want to analyze the question of whether inflation is or will tend to be reduced or even eliminated in a "globalized" economy.

In subsection 3.1 I start by analyzing the effects of globalization on the inflation bias motives described in section 1.1 above. In subsection 3.2, I then describe the direct threat of losing capital and the resulting disciplinary mechanism induced by globalization (or international competition for portfolio capital and mobile production factors). Then, in subsection 3.3, I will take a more differentiated, critical view by considering politico-economic restrictions.

3.1 Weakening of the Inflation Bias Motives

Globalization may reduce the inflation bias by influencing/decreasing its various motives described above.

i) employment motive

The recent literature has identified openness as one of the countervailing forces that lessen the incentive to inflate. The argument which is originally due to Romer

(1993) is that, the more open the economy, the smaller the real benefits of higher output from surprise monetary expansion, and thus the lower the equilibrium rate of inflation. As domestic output increases, the terms of trade worsens: the more open the economy, the larger the fraction of foreign goods in domestic consumption, and the greater the welfare loss from the terms of trade loss. In short, more open economies may be blessed with a lower incentive to inflate.[11]

In addition, it may be argued that the process of globalization (international competition) enforces structural adjustments regarding the elimination of nominal and institutional rigidities, particularly on the labor market. Thus NAIRU will decline, hence the incentive to inflate will be diminished. (Indexation will be used in a less extent, distributional conflicts will decline, wage flexibilization and labor mobility will rise, and the welfare system will be reduced, etc. This also expresses the positive expectations or hopes regarding European Monetary Union.) The employment motive is greater, the more short-term the government's planning horizon is (depending above all on the chances of re-election), but this is lengthened by the pressure of international competition.

ii) revenue motive

The revenue motive, i.e. that the state rids itself of its debts by a temporarily higher rate of inflation, or squeezes its debt burden in the same way, is to be regarded as less expedient in view of open global money and financial markets, at least for developed industrial countries. Because large parts of government debt are continuously being prolonged, a government would in fact in real terms devalue its pending debt load through a surprise inflation, but at the same time it would be forced to provide an additional risk premium for all new debt agreements, and this premium is higher on the open global financial markets. The relief effect would therefore only be of a very short-term nature, and with a more long-term observation the disadvantageous effects on the government's overall debt would probably clearly outweigh this.

The above argument naturally also applies to closed national economies. However, it may be assumed that the risk premium in the situation of open global money and financial markets would be higher, because it can be presumed that international organizations will pay more attention to this. In addition, empiricism indicates a negative correlation between the openness of a national economy and the density of its regulations. Among other things, this means that in a closed

[11] Lane (1997) showed that the prediction that more open economies have lower equilibrium inflation rates is true independently of the terms of trade mechanism emphasized by Romer (1993). The mechanism linking the welfare effects of monetary surprises, and hence the incentives to inflate, to openness does not depend on a large-country terms of trade effect but rather is due to imperfect competition and nominal price rigidity in the non-traded sector.

economy interest rates tend to be regulated and interest payments kept artificially low in a greater extent, and this reduces the government's costs for seigniorage financing.

iii) balance-of-payments motive
The more open a currency area is, the greater is the effect of devaluation on domestic price level increases. The price index for imported goods increases through the devaluation, and the more open the economy, the greater the volume of imported goods in the basket of commodities. From this it may be concluded that the public in an open economy is more sensitive towards expansionary or inflationary monetary policy, and will resist this type of policy at a much earlier stage, because it will tend to see through the connection between inflation and expansionary monetary policy (i.e., the incentives to collect information, to learn, are greater), cf. Johnson (1972).

With the special case of a "fully" globalized world, with free substitutability of currencies, mobility of capital and flexible exchange rates, another argument may also be brought in which has been used in the public choice critique on monetary unions. This refers to competition between central banks as a countervailing force which lessens the incentive to inflate. In principal it reduces all three motives described above. In this world with its free substitutability of currencies, mobility of capital and flexible exchange rates, central banks are subjected to the pressure of international monetary policy competition. If a central bank is unsuccessful in holding national inflation rates at the level of those countries with which the state is in competition, private economic agents will be forced to hold assets in other, more stable currencies, and to restrict their use of the inflationary currency for transactions. As a consequence, the benefits of inflation, which consist of income from seigniorage and the possibility of carrying out employment programs, are reduced. On the other hand, a central bank which succeeds in holding the inflation rate down, or at a lower rate, will be rewarded by an increased use of its currency. The competition between national monetary policies accordingly exercises an important disciplinary function on the central bankers, and keeps them from generating too great a rate of inflation. The argument runs that in the competition between central banks the one which offers the most stable currency will prevail: those which refuse to take part will be faced with a flight of capital, and will either have to devalue and put up with a corresponding loss of face, or fulfil wide-ranging payment obligations later on in the framework of international balance of payments settlements (cf. Vaubel (1993)).

3.2 Disciplinary Mechanism: Threat of Losing Capital

The following argument not only refers to a decline in the inflation bias but also, and even more, to a decline in the optimal (or even the desired) inflation rate for a society[12]. As argued above, the socially optimal rate of inflation declines if the benefits of inflation decrease and/or its costs increase. We have just argued that globalization tends to reduce the inflation bias by inducing a decrease in the inflation motives. That is, the benefits of inflation decrease. On the other hand, we may claim that the costs of inflation increase as well, because globalization exerts a direct threat of losing capital. This creates a disciplinary mechanism against inflationary policy. The main hypothesis here is[13] : in a globalized economy, other things being equal, countries with greater price stability and fewer inflation surprises attract capital, or mobile production factors, from countries with less price stability and more inflation surprises[14]. The increase in the supply of capital lowers the rate of interest and thus may cause higher output and higher employment. Conversely, less capital increases the domestic interest rate and therefore may lead to lower output and employment and more unemployment which is usually undesired. This does not necessarily imply that decreasing or eliminating inflation is also an optimal strategy. It may just be the dominant strategy of a general prisoner's dilemma, caused by global competition for capital (see also Case 5 in section 4.2.3 below). The only way out of such a prisoners'' dilemma would be a world-wide coordination of economic policies, something which at present appears to be utopian.

The hypothesis here is not only that it is impossible for a single country to tolerate inflation when other countries adhere to a rigorous anti-inflationary policy. Each country has for itself an incentive to commit itself to an anti-inflationary policy because, for example, ceteris paribus, investors will prefer to invest in a country which they believe has adopted a more reliable anti-inflationary policy (i.e. one with fewer inflationary surprises) than other countries. In explaining this hypothesis we can differentiate here between two alternative lines of capital mobility arguments. The first refers to portfolio capital, the second to direct investments. The German "Monopolkommission" recently emphasized both aspects, in particular the portfolio capital aspect: "(...) The mobility of *portfolio capital* has above all consequences for national stability policy: monetary and fiscal policies are evaluated by the international financial markets. (...) A comparably less stability-oriented monetary policy with the consequence of risks

[12] As argued above, there are two effects of an increase in the costs of inflation, caused by globalization, which should be differentiated: one is that, with given preferences, the optimal rate of inflation is decreased; on the other hand, a permanent increase in the costs of inflation, caused by globlization, may also change preferences and therefore reduce the *desired* rate of inflation.

[13] See also Monopolkommission (1998, pp. 17-18) and Vogt (1999, pp. 32-33).

[14] The evidence of world-wide declining inflation rates in the 1990s may be interpreted in this way, i.e. by referring to this incentive. However, other factors (business cycle, energy prices, etc.) may also have played a role in the decline in the inflation rate in countries with and in those without independent central banks. On the other hand, we have to consider that globalization has just started (again) on a universal basis and will probably become much stronger during the next decades (cf. Rodrick (1998, pp. 4-5)).

of domestic inflation and exchange rate risks lead, as do excessive budget deficits, to a shift in the flows of money with undesirable domestic interest consequences.

In contrast to this, a high price level stability and a solid budgetary policy are honored by the financial markets through high flows of capital. *In this way, the international financial market creates additional leeway for the domestic economy*" (Monopolkommission (1998, pp. 17-18); here translated).

With regard to the attraction of real capital or direct investments, the respective statement of the Monopolkommission is as follows: "The increasing mobility of *real capital*, which is unable to migrate in the short term but can migrate in the long term with new investments or re-investments, has effects on a more broadly defined economic policy, including tax and duties policy, wage policy and the financing of social security, in other words the organization of the institutional regulatory framework for a location" (ibid. 17; here translated). In this sense, inflation may also be regarded as an obstruction in the path of direct investments. The attractiveness of a location (country) for direct investments, as I have just said, depends essentially on the design of the institutional framework as well. The inflation climate may be seen as an important element in the design of this framework. For example, there appears to be a correlation between inflation and political stability to the extent that countries with high inflation are comparatively less politically stable, and vice versa (for more details, cf. Wagner (1998b, pp. 126-128)). It can also be found that surprise inflation creates planning uncertainty that reduces the expected revenue of investments in general and of transnational enterprise (direct) investments in particular (cf. Wagner (1997a)). Here the problem is not so much the level of inflation but the existence of inflation surprises (as a proxy: the variance of inflation).[15]

In general, however, the level of inflation is also relevant for the expected revenue of investments if only because of distorted tax systems, such as the existence of taxation of paper profits (e.g., Desai/Hines Jr. (1997); Feldstein (1997)). Another

[15] With imperfect information in the sense of "genuine" or strategic uncertainty, there are increases in the amount of misinvestments in the case of inflation caused by expansionary macro policies. "'Real' (demand-led) price signals are namely then overlaid with purely inflation-related (cost-related) price changes, which, intensified by delays in price adjustments, can no longer be differentiated by economic agents from the former. Economic agents can no longer rely on the information function of market-price relations when making their plans. Misinterpretations and misinvestments based on this now occur (more frequently). This forces economic agents to use (more) scarce resources (working time and capital) to obtain the information which is no longer supplied, or no longer supplied sufficiently reliably, by market prices. If the gaps in information with regard to the signal function of price changes cannot be filled by this (...), these gaps will have to be accounted for in the investment account by means of a subjective 'uncertainty discount'. However, both will reduce the expected uncertainty-adjusted return on an investment (...) and thus tend to restrict the formation of real capital." (Wagner (1985, pp. 213-214); here translated).

argument for avoiding surprise inflation is based on the hypothesis that this type of inflation tends to go along with an increase in average cost (Vogt (1999, p. 32)) and therefore worsens the competitiveness of domestic production. Against the background of these arguments, it may be argued that a country that commits to an anti-inflationary policy may attract additional capital. The competition for international capital would change the optimal monetary and fiscal policy towards more price stability and a more solid budget (fiscal) policy[16], and, in addition, increases the costs of short-sighted economic policy. Even if all countries tolerate some unexpected inflation (for example, as I have mentioned above, by means of a world-wide coordination of economic policies in the hypothetical case that an uncoordinated universal strict anti-inflationary strategy is not optimal), each country has an incentive to adopt a rigorous anti-inflationary policy, because it can thereby attract foreign capital and thus eventually raise its living standard. To sum up, a rigorous anti-inflationary policy is borne out by the desire to defend a country's own capital and by the universal attempt to attract capital from abroad.

3.3 Discussion

The above hypothesis may be questioned in general (section 3.3.1) and in particular with respect to developing and transition countries (section 3.3.2).

3.3.1 Who is Threatened by Globalization?

It might be argued that the problem lies much deeper, or that the above hypothesis with respect to the explained globalization effect is based on a fallacy, which is induced by the oversimplified aggregation concept implied in the arguments of section 3.2 above. The above hypothesis is based on the idea that there is a credible and effective potential threat through international competition for a "country" which, because of the motives listed above (employment, revenue and balance-of-payments), flirts with inefficient inflation production. But who is the "country"? It is a fallacy to think that a "country" can be threatened. Only governments can be threatened, and then only if persons or groups representing homogenous preferences of persons, who also act as voters in elections, and/or government members themselves are hurt by the international competition effects analyzed above. And who may these threatened persons or groups be, apart from

[16] The evaluation of fiscal policy by the international financial markets results in location disadvantages for a country with excessive budget deficits. Increasing deficits cause higher interest payments on government debt, with the consequence of further increases in the deficit. In the end (with non-monetization), primary surpluses are required through increasing taxes or reducing government spending. This can lead to companies and labor emigrating because of rationally expected increases in taxation and/or an expected worsening of the infrastructure services. This itself results in a sinking tax base and the necessity of additional tax increases and reductions in government spending.

government members themselves? These are in particular on the one hand domestic companies which compete with foreign companies, and on the other hand those workers who are threatened by unemployment in consequence of the non-competitiveness of these companies[17]. Are these agents or groups really powerful enough (in the sense that they can coordinate or organize their interests and that there are enough of them, cf. Olson (1965)) to force the government to follow a suitable (i.e. here anti-inflationary) monetary policy course (avoiding surprise inflation)? (The logic behind this argument that there is a threat is that in addition to 'exit', i.e. capital flight, 'voice', i.e. protest of voters, is also and (particularly) effective as a corrective feedback mechanism against inflationary policy.) The more companies are involved and the more workers have to fear that they will lose their jobs through the non-competitiveness of the respective *companies* (not countries!) the greater is the pressure on the government to follow the preferences of these threatened groups or subjects and hence to liberalize the markets for goods, financial services and labor, and to reduce institutional restrictions (inefficient and overly regulated structures) in order to improve the competitiveness of domestic companies and to keep or steer the production activities of international companies into the home country. Merely to rely on the government's being concerned by tax losses as consequence of inefficient structures, however, is not enough, as the recent experience with enduring high unemployment in Europe has proved. As long as the pressure of globalization is not (yet) strong enough, i.e. companies and workers threatened by bankruptcy and unemployment are not sufficiently numerous and organized enough to reduce the election chances of governments, these anticipated tax losses may not outweigh the positive effects expected by government from, among other things, the inflation bias motives listed above.[18]

3.3.2 The Special Case of Developing and Transition Countries

Even if the number of companies and workers feeling threatened by an increasing non-competitiveness of domestic companies is very large, this may not be sufficient to force the government to react in an adequate way that increases competitiveness and thereby social wealth (living standards) as long as the political system itself is not competitive (democratic) enough. Only if governments or politicians have to fear a loss of power by not considering the fears and/or losses of these groups will they act in a socially rational (welfare-

---

[17] Besides these, other persons or groups may also feel themselves threatened since an economic recession or depression, caused by the non-competitiveness of these companies, leads to a decline in tax income and therefore a potential decline in the supply of public goods.

[18] As can easily be seen, I do not assume welfare-maximizing governments here but governments that try to maximize their own utility which must not (and usually does not) coincide with welfare maximization.

maximizing) manner. The preconditions for this are a functioning democracy including an enlightened, well-informed electorate. Considering this, there is an inclination to guess that the effects of globalization on monetary policy that we described above may be weaker in both developing countries and in transition countries than in highly industrialized countries of the Western Hemisphere. In many developing countries, for instance, the majority of the electorate, or the average voter, is relatively uninformed with regard to macroeconomic relationships or stylized facts and is therefore more easily seduced or cheated. (But even in so-called highly developed industrial countries there are still more or less considerable imperfections in the political systems. For example, there are apparent weaknesses of the political system in Japan and in some southern European countries.) Furthermore, democracy itself in these countries is often not developed or established enough to be as effective as in highly developed industrial countries with long traditions in democracy and a highly-developed infrastructure. Pressure from particular oligarchic interest groups trying to exploit the inflation bias motives described above can therefore be more steady and longer-lasting in developing countries, even in the light of world-wide globalization (see Figure 1). Thus the revenue motive in particular tends to be very strong in these countries even under globalization. Besides these and other political economy considerations (see, e.g., Cukierman/Edwards/Tabellini (1992), Alesina/Drazen (1991), and in particular Alesina/Roubini (1997), for an overview) there are also socio-cultural explanations (emphasizing the lack of institutional infrastructure, or heterogeneous preferences, or different structural model views) that may explain the special problems of implementing policy solutions in developing and transition countries which are economically apparently rational (cf. Wagner (1996, 1997b)).

4 Model Analysis

The aim here is not to give rise to the impression that globalization alone can be used to explain the reduction in inflation during the 1980s and 1990s. Certainly, institutional reforms such as making central banks independent, as mentioned above, played an important role in some countries (but only in some). Another possible explanation may be found in the different alteration speeds of employment aims and the so-called "natural" employment rate following supply shocks. This will be explained in greater detail in section 4.2.1. The consequence of an introduction of central bank independence (see section 4.2.2), can be shown more exactly in a simple macroeconomic model, which will be elaborated below in section 4.1. The role played by globalization can also be interpreted in the context of this model (see section 4.2.3). More or less direct conclusions for the institutional design of monetary policy and for stabilization policy in general may be derived from this (see section 5).[19]

4.1 The Model

I formulate a model of macroeconomic policy and inflation, which is in the spirit of Fischer (1977), Kydland and Prescott (1977) and Barro and Gordon (1983). This model has been the starting point for much of the recent literature.

I follow the rational expectations literature in thinking about policy as a rule. Policy is supposed to minimize the following quadratic loss function:

$$(1)\quad E[L'(\pi,y)] = L = E\{0{,}5[(\pi - \pi^*)^2 + b(y - y^*)^2]\}$$

where π and y denote inflation and employment (or output growth), respectively, π^* and y^* are society's most preferred values for inflation and employment (or output growth), and b is the relative weight on fluctuations in these two variables.

The loss function is minimized under the constraint (4) below which is derived from the modeled behavior of the private sector.

The relevant constraint can be derived from the supply side of the model which assumes that nominal wage-setting aims at implementing an exogenous real wage growth target w_r. Letting π^e denote rationally expected inflation, nominal wage growth w then becomes:

$$(2)\quad w = w_r + \pi^e\,.$$

Employment (or output growth) is given by:

$$(3)\quad y = a - c(w - \pi) - \varepsilon\,,$$

where c is assumed at first to be equal to 1 (for reasons of simplicity), and where ε is a supply shock (with mean 0 and variance σ_ε^2) and a is a parameter.

By combining (2) with (3), we get an expectations-augmented short-run Phillips curve[20]

[19] Another possible explanation for the decline in inflation, in particular in the USA, is the existence of global excess capacities. With globalization, these could, in certain circumstances, trigger inflation-curbing effects, even in a country such as the USA, which has tended to suffer from capacity shortages in the recent past.

[20] The constraint (4) can also be derived from a model of price-setting firms, or from a Lucas-style "island model".

(4) $y = y_n + (\pi - \pi^e) - \varepsilon$

where $y_n \equiv a - w_r$ can be interpreted as the natural rate of employment (output growth)[21].

It is assumed that $y_n < y^*$.

If we add the demand side of our model being represented by

(5) $\pi = m + v$

where m is the money growth rate and v is a velocity shock (with mean 0 and variance σ_v^2), and in addition assume rational expectations information so that

$\pi^e = E(\pi \mid y_n) = E(m \mid y_n)$

where E is the mathematical expectations operator, we obtain the famous neutrality result:

$y = y_n + m - E(m \mid y_n) + v - \varepsilon$.

This neutrality result says that only unanticipated aggregate demand policy affects real variables. Policy, however, can still stabilize employment if it responds to shocks.

Furthermore, the model assumes the following timing of events:

(1) The "institutional design stage": We assume first of all (see section 4.2.2 for another institutional design), that the government itself fixes monetary policy and does not delegate this to an autonomous instance.

(2) The private actors develop their inflation expectations with knowledge of the objective function and of the constraints (and on the basis of information on y_n) but without knowledge of shocks v and ε. Private inflation expectations are reflected in nominal wage increases.

(3) Finally, shocks v and ε are observable for the government.

(4) With knowledge of these shocks, the government realizes a defined monetary policy, i.e. it fixes m (which leads to a defined π and y). Given the existence of a binding commitment technology, the ex-post optimal policy selected in step (4) can only deviate stochastically from a policy which would be the optimum on the basis of information and conditions for action in step (1) (ex-ante optimal policy). However, if there is no such commitment technology,

---

21 "Natural rate" here denotes the equilibrium rate where is full anticipation of inflation and no shocks. In section 4.2.1, I shall deviate from this model structure and assume a stochastic natural rate of employment.

the ex-post optimal policy can also deviate systematically from the ex-ante optimal policy.

Optimal rule

First suppose the policy (rule) is credible and hence enforceable. That is, the policy maker(s) can make a binding commitment to an optimal state-contingent policy rule. The optimal rate of inflation can then be derived as being [22]:

(6) $\pi_O = \pi^* + [b/(1+b)]\, \varepsilon$.

Without a commitment technology, such a policy rule cannot be implemented.

Discretion

The adequate timing assumption here is the following: policy is chosen under "discretion" when the policy instruments are set at stage (4) above, i.e. after inflation expectations have been formed and wages have been set. To be credible, a policy now must simultaneously fulfil two conditions: the policy must be *ex post* optimal (i.e., $dL/d\pi = 0$, given π^e and ε); and expectations must be rational (i.e., $\pi^e = E(\pi \mid y_n)$).

The discretionary inflation rate can be derived as:

(7) $\pi_D = \pi^* + b(y^* - y_n) + [b/(1+b)]\, \varepsilon$.

When we compare (6) and (7), we see that there is an

inflation bias : $b(y^* - y_n)$

with discretionary policy (whereas the employment outcome remains the same as in the case of the optimal policy rule above, namely $y = y_n - [1/(1+b)]\, \varepsilon$ in both cases). The inflation bias is more pronounced the more valuable is employment on the margin (i.e. the higher is b), and the higher is preferred employment relative to the natural rate (i.e., the higher is y^* relative to y_n). Both factors lead to a greater "temptation" for the policymaker to exploit her short-run ability to raise employment by expansionary policy once wages are fixed.

This inflation bias is due to two key assumptions in our model: (i) the sequential timing of monetary policy decisions, and (ii) $y^* - y_n > 0$, i.e. the assumption that the employment target is higher than the natural rate. This latter assumption reflects a lack of policy instruments and hence that some distortion in the product or labor market keeps employment too low.

---

[22] For the derivation of the equations (6), (7) and (11) see, e.g., Wagner (1998a, pp. 138-143).

4.2 Alternative Explanations of the Decline in Inflation

Here I want to discuss three alternative explanations, namely what I call "return to normality", "implementation of central bank independence", and "globalization".

4.2.1 Return to Normality

I start with an interpretation which cannot be represented by the simple model structure above. To do this, I would have to reformulate the above model in a stochastic manner. However, because I want to concentrate on the subsequent interpretations, I shall not present this rather complex model structure here but only provide an explanation.

We could try to interpret the recent decline in inflation as return to the normality of the 50s and 60s when inflation was rather low even in periods of (nearly) full capacity. In the 70s, inflation rates rose to a relatively high level. During the last almost 20 years, inflation has once again declined to the low levels of the 50s and 60s (see Figure 3).

How can we explain this? One possible explanation refers to the exceptional situation during the 70s, which were characterized by an extraordinary wave of world-wide supply shocks. In addition, we can refer to different effects or speeds of adjustment of the natural rate and of the preferred employment rate to these supply shocks. We can presume that the natural rate y_n is random whereas the employment target y^* is either constant or at least more stable than y_n. Inflation is then not only more variable under discretionary policies than under the state-contingent policy rule, but also increases as a consequence of supply shocks. If, as in the 70s, there are severe supply shocks world-wide, the natural rate of employment decreases whereas the employment target at first remains nearly constant (this means, y^* stays constant or falls less than y_n, so that $y^* - y_n$ rises). This increases the inflation bias. (I assume here that the inflation bias is still positively correlated with the difference $y^* - y_n$ as in the simple model structure in section 4.1 above.) After a while, however, as in the 80s and 90s, when the structural problems on the labor market become more severe and tend to induce legitimization problems in the political and economic systems, the employment target is adapted or decreased gradually (so that $y^* - y_n$ decreased again). On the other hand, there were no more severe world-wide supply shocks during the last two decades, so that the natural rate rose again (hence $y^* - y_n$ decreased further).

Figure 3: *Inflation Rate in Industrial and in Developing Countries (in percent)*

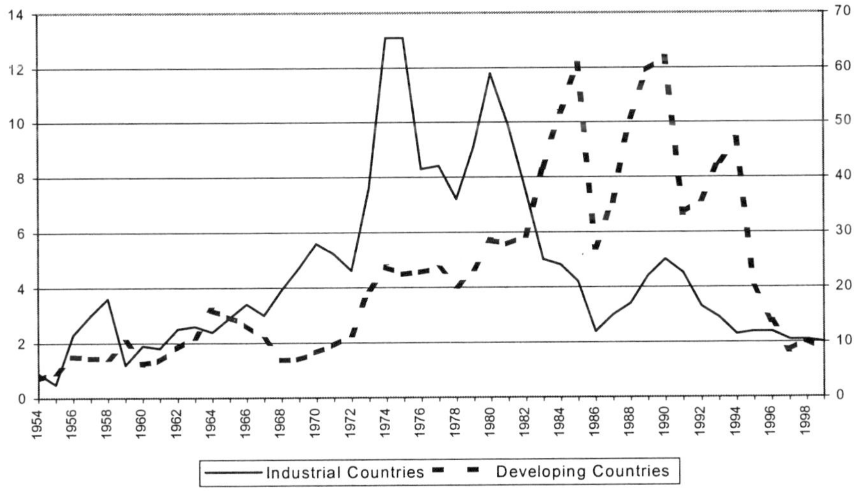

Source: 1954 - 1987: International Financial Statistics, IMF
1988 - 1999: World Economic Outlook, IMF
Scale on right-hand side: Inflation Rate in Developing Countries
Scale on left-hand side: Inflation Rate in Industrial Countries

As (long as) the preferred employment rate does not react to this latter tendency (at least not quickly enough), $y^* - y_n$, and thus the inflation bias, remains reduced, so that low inflation and high capacity utilization are possible simultaneously (as in the 50s and 60s when there were no severe world-wide supply shocks either). Changes in the gaps between preferred and natural employment (output growth), $y^* - y_n$, lead to shifts in the policymaker's desired level of surprise inflation, which lead to shifts in the equilibrium values of the inflation rate.

Such an asymmetric pattern of adjustment speed to supply shocks could explain the recent experience of inflation trends during the last decade. If this interpretation is correct, then the inflation bias will remain low, but only until the next wave of severe world-wide supply shocks occurs. In general, we can explain and forecast "long waves" of inflation cycles as the consequence of severe world-wide supply shocks. However we cannot substantiate a systematic long-run decline in inflation with this explanation. This can only be done by referring to permanent institutional reforms (such as the implementation of central bank independence, for instance) or to enduring "natural" or "socio-cultural" developments (such as perhaps "globalization"). Both factors will be analyzed in the following by using the above model structure again.

4.2.2 Implementation of Central Bank Independence (CBI)

In section 4.1, the inflation bias was expressed by the term $b(y^* - y_n)$. The explanation in the foregoing subsection 4.2.1 referred to a decline in $(y^* - y_n)$. In this subsection we regard the case of a declining b, given $y^* - y_n$. Suppose that society, whose true preferences take the form of (1), appoints a central banker. This central banker is attributed with independence; i.e., once appointed, society can no longer interfere with her decisions. Prospective central bankers have the same loss function as the society, but differ in their personal values of b.[23] The private sector, which observes the respective values, forms its inflationary expectations accordingly. The appointed central banker then sets monetary policy according to its own preferences. This gives the equilibrium outcome:

(8) $\pi_{CBI} = \pi^* + b'(y^* - y_n) + [b'/(1+b')]\,\varepsilon$.

This corresponds to the discretionary inflation rate (7) with the difference that b' now denotes the appointed central banker's personal value of b. Rogoff (1985a) has shown that society should appoint a central banker whose b' lies between 0 and b. Then the inflation bias will be lower than at discretion[24].

We could therefore conclude that the wave of central bank reforms in many countries during the last years that were described above, and that provided central banks with independence, has been the real cause for the world-wide decline in inflation during the 90s. As I emphasized above, however, this can only explain part of the story because the decline in inflation also happened in many countries where central bank reforms were not launched.

4.2.3 Globalization

In section 3, I interpreted globalization as a technological-institutional process that makes the production of inflation more costly for a society or country. This cost aspect can be modeled in several ways. I want to concentrate here on five possibilities that appear to me to be the most interesting alternatives. These imply that the cost-increasing effect of globalization can be modeled alternatively as

1) a lower preferred inflation rate π^*

2) a higher aversion to inflation, i.e. a lower b

---

[23] This suggests a heterogeneity in the society with respect to the relative weight put on inflation versus employment, which the above formal model abstracts from. See, however, Alesina/Grilli (1992). In their model, heterogeneous voters elect the central bankers directly.

[24] The disadvantage or cost, however, appears to be that output or employment variability is then higher (see below). This model-based result, however, could not be confirmed in many empirical studies (see in section 2.3.2 above).

3) a lower output effect of a surprise inflation, i.e. a lower c (see equation (3))
4) an additional cost factor in the loss function of the central bank or of the government
5) an additional cost factor in the loss function of the society.

We will see that inflation is reduced in all five cases, however the consequences in detail differ greatly, depending on the modeling assumption.

Case 1) a lower π^*

A lower preferred inflation rate $\pi^{*'} < \pi^*$ would decrease the inflation level, but would not change the inflation bias compared to the results in section 4.1.

(6') $\pi_O^{case\ 1} = \pi^{*'} + [b/(1+b)]\ \varepsilon$

(7') $\pi_D^{case\ 1} = \pi^{*'} + b(y^* - y_n) + [b/(1+b)]\ \varepsilon$, where $\pi^{*'} < \pi^*$.

Case 2) a lower b

Alternatively, we can assume that the cost of inflation caused by globalization, if it is understood and internalized by society, leads to a higher aversion to inflation, i.e. a lower b, let this be b''. This then corresponds to the above CBI case and also leads to the same inflation reduction effect in principle. That is, the inflation bias is reduced. The equilibrium inflation rate will be

(8') $\pi_D^{case\ 2} = \pi^* + b''(y^* - y_n) + [b''/(1+b'')]\ \varepsilon$, where $b'' < b$.

Case 3) a lower c

Alternatively, we may interpret the above cost aspect in such a way that it decreases the output effect of a surprise inflation, c. This would mean that the Phillips curve is steeper ($d\pi/dy = 1/c$ increases). This would again reduce the inflation bias:

(9) $\pi_D^{case\ 3} = \pi^* + cb(y^* - y_n) + [cb/(1+c^2b)]\ \varepsilon$, where $c < 1$.

Case 4) an additional cost factor in the loss function of the central bank or of the government

We may assume that the cost aspect enters into the loss function of the central bank or of the government, but not into that of society as a whole. For reasons of simplicity, I assume that the cost factor enters the loss function linearly. The loss function of the central bank (or government) would then change in the following way:

$$(10)\quad L_{CB} = E\{0,5[(\pi - \pi^*)^2 + b(y - y^*)^2] + f(\pi - \pi^*)\}$$

where f(.) expresses the cost of inflation when inflation is higher than the equilibrium world inflation rate; for reasons of simplicity, it is here assumed that this equilibrium world inflation rate corresponds to society's most preferred value for inflation.

The social loss function, however, would still be (1).

Globalization here punishes governments or central banks which create inflation above the equilibrium world inflation rate and thus forces or gives them incentives to move towards this level. As one easily can see, this resembles Walsh's performance contract model (1995a).

With (10), which assumes a linear cost on inflation, inflation may be reduced. If the cost f is equal to the inflation bias $b(y^* - y_n)$, we even obtain

$$(11)\quad \pi_D^{\text{case 4}} = \pi^* + [b/(1+b)]\,\varepsilon = \pi_O\,,$$

which is the same as the optimal inflation rate of equation (6). Here the inflation bias is wiped out by the cost threat imposed by globalization.

Case 5) an additional cost factor in the loss function of the society

Alternatively, we can assume that the cost of inflation caused by globalization is understood and internalized by society as a whole and thus leads to a change in the social loss function where the cost factor is added in the same way as in equation (10) above:

$$(12)\quad L = E\{0,5[(\pi - \pi^*)^2 + b(y - y^*)^2] + f(\pi - \pi^*)\}$$

In this case, the solution is quite surprising. The main aspect here is that the optimal rule now is different from the solution in equation (6). The optimal rule now is

$$(13)\quad \pi_O^{\text{case 5}} = \pi^* - f + [b/(1+b)]\,\varepsilon$$

(For the derivation see the appendix.)

The *optimal rule* (optimal here means the best of the alternative rules) consists in undercutting the socially desired rate of inflation because "globalization" rewards this to the extent of $f(\pi - \pi^*)$. The inclination here is perhaps to conclude that globalization leads to a *deflation bias* of the *optimal rule* because the expectations value of π_O lies systematically below π^*. By doing this, we would measure the systematic bias on the difference between $E(\pi_O)$ and π^*. Such a procedure, however, is not quite correct: Usually these two rates coincide on average, and therefore the inflation bias is normally calculated as the difference between the discretionary inflation rate and either π_O or π^*. In this model, however, the term bias should be rationally referred to as deviations from π_O. The discretionary solution is:

(14) $\pi_D^{\text{case 5}} = \pi^* - f + b(y^* - y_n) + [b/(1+b)]\,\varepsilon$

(For the derivation see again the appendix.)

Globalization does not reduce the difference from π_D and π_O. This difference still amounts to $b(y^* - y_n)$ and is independent of f.

This result can be interpreted as follows:

a) With a rule-based policy and globalization there is a systematic undercutting of the socially desired rate of inflation (which is here equal to the equilibrium world rate of inflation). This undercutting must not be interpreted in the sense of an incentive to depart from the rule solution, because the rule solution consists exactly of this.

b) The rule solution is not time-consistent ($E(\pi_D) > E(\pi_O)$).

c) The time-consistent solution consists of the discretionary policy, which on average leads to a rate of inflation which is above the rule solution. Whether the discretionary inflation is also greater than the socially desired inflation depends among other things on f. If the cost f (accidentally) is equal to the inflation bias $b(y^* - y_n)$, both inflation rates are equal.

d) The rule-based policy is superior to the discretionary policy from the aspect of welfare theory. If the difference from welfare losses with discretionary and rule-based policies is formed, then $L_D - L_O = 0{,}5[b(y^* - y_n)]^2$. This difference is positive and independent of f. Globalization in the sense of $f > 0$ reduces in the same manner the welfare losses of rule-based and discretionary policies.

A certain explosive charge in this interpretation of globalization is that rule-based policy with globalization in this sense implies a general incentive to undercut the socially desired rate of inflation. In our special case where the socially desired rate of inflation is equal to the equilibrium world inflation rate, there is also a general incentive to deviate downwards from the world rate of inflation, i.e. to undercut it. If all states attempted this, there would be a tendency towards deflation. This could possibly only be countered by (an appropriate or efficient) international policy coordination.

Table 2: *Inflation, output and loss with different regimes*[25]

	π^e	π	y	L
Optimal Rule	π^*	$\pi^* + \frac{b}{1+b}\varepsilon$	$y_n - \frac{1}{1+b}\varepsilon$	$0{,}5(bX^2 + \frac{b}{1+b}\sigma_\varepsilon^2)$
Discretion	$\pi^* + bX$	$\pi^* + bX + \frac{b}{1+b}\varepsilon$	$y_n - \frac{1}{1+b}\varepsilon$	$0{,}5[b(1+b)X^2 + \frac{b}{1+b}\sigma_\varepsilon^2]$
Central Bank Independence	$\pi^* + b`X$	$\pi^* + b`X + \frac{b`}{1+b`}\varepsilon$	$y_n - \frac{1}{1+b`}\varepsilon$	$0{,}5[(b + b`^2)X^2 + \frac{b`^2 + b}{(1+b`)^2}\sigma_\varepsilon^2]$

Continued on next page.

25 X is defined as X := y* - y_n. The term L_{opt}^G in the last column of the table indicates the optimal value of the relevant social loss function in the various globalization cases. As usual, it is derived under the assumption that the central bank can make a binding commitment to an optimal state-contingent policy rule.

	π^e	π	y	L	L_{opt}^G
Globalization Case 1	$\pi^{*`}+bX$	$\pi^{*`}+bX+\frac{b}{1+b}\varepsilon$	$y_n-\frac{1}{1+b}\varepsilon$	$0{,}5[b(1+b)X^2+\frac{b}{1+b}\sigma_\varepsilon^2]$	$0{,}5(bX^2+\frac{b}{1+b}\sigma_\varepsilon^2)$
Globalization Case 2	$\pi^*+b^{``}X$	$\pi^*+b^{``}X+\frac{b^{``}}{1+b^{``}}\varepsilon$	$y_n-\frac{1}{1+b^{``}}\varepsilon$	$0{,}5[(1+b^{``})b^{``}X^2+\frac{b^{``}}{1+b^{``}}\sigma_\varepsilon^2]$	$0{,}5(b^{`}X^2+\frac{b^{``}}{1+b^{``}}\sigma_\varepsilon^2)$
Globalization Case 3	π^*+bcX	$\pi^*+bcX+\frac{bc}{1+bc^2}\varepsilon$	$y_n-\frac{1}{1+bc^2}\varepsilon$	$0{,}5[b(1+bc^2)X^2+\frac{b}{1+bc^2}\sigma_\varepsilon^2]$	$0{,}5(bX^2+\frac{b}{1+bc^2}\sigma_\varepsilon^2)$
Globalization Case 4 (with f = bX)	π^*	$\pi^*+\frac{b}{1+b}\varepsilon$	$y_n-\frac{1}{1+b}\varepsilon$	$0{,}5(bX^2+\frac{b}{1+b}\sigma_\varepsilon^2)$	$0{,}5(bX^2+\frac{b}{1+b}\sigma_\varepsilon^2)$
Globalization Case 5 (with f = bX)	π^*	$\pi^*+\frac{b}{1+b}\varepsilon$	$y_n-\frac{1}{1+b}\varepsilon$	$0{,}5(bX^2+\frac{b}{1+b}\sigma_\varepsilon^2)$	$0{,}5[b(1-b)X^2+\frac{b}{1+b}\sigma_\varepsilon^2]$

Up to now we elaborated different models of the hypothesis developed in Section 3 that inflation will be more costly for a society (government, central bank) with globalization (or at least is felt to be more costly). In addition, it is often argued that more efficient communication and information technologies in combination with the introduction of financial innovations can lead among other things to greater uncertainties in the transmission process of monetary policy (cf. e.g. Taylor (1998)). Since Brainard (1967) these uncertainties are registered not only with the help of additive shocks, but above all by taking into account uncertainty about the multipliers. We can examine the effects of increased multiplier uncertainty in the framework of the model introduced here if we replace equation (5) by the following modified version[1]:

$$\text{(5a)} \quad \pi = \eta \cdot m + v \qquad \text{with } E(\eta) = 1,\ \sigma_\eta^2 = \text{const.},\ \sigma_{v\eta} = \sigma_{\varepsilon\eta} = \sigma_{v\varepsilon} = 0$$

I call this "Case 6" of globalization.

For inflation with an optimal (active) rule policy we find the solution:

$$\text{(15)} \quad \pi_O = \frac{\eta\pi^*}{1+(1+b)\sigma_\eta^2} + \frac{\eta b\varepsilon + (1+b)(1+\sigma_\eta^2 - \eta)v}{(1+b)(1+\sigma_\eta^2)}$$

With discretionary policy there follows for inflation:

$$\text{(16)} \quad \pi_D = \pi_O + \frac{\eta b(y^* - y_n)}{1+(1+b)\sigma_\eta^2}$$

The most interesting thing about Case 6 is on the one hand that, as in Case 5, if a rule policy is pursued, inflation on average falls below the socially desired (world) rate of inflation. However, this assumes that the socially desired rate of inflation (π^*) is greater than zero. The following namely applies:

---

[26] This model variation is also used by Letterie/Lippi (1999). However, these authors are primarily occupied with the welfare effects of instrument uncertainty with discretionary monetary policy. In contrast to this, I shall explicitly compare the rule-bound solution with the discretionary solution in the following. Moreover, contrary to Letterie/Lippi (1999), the existence of supply shocks is taken into account and it is also assumed that the socially desired rate of inflation (π^*) is not necessarily zero.
I would like to thank Friedrich Kißmer for suggesting this alternative Case 6 to me.

$$E(\pi_O) = \frac{\pi^*}{1+(1+b)\sigma_\eta^2} < \pi^*, \text{ with } \frac{d(E(\pi_0))}{d(\sigma_\eta^2)} < 0 \text{ when } \pi^* > 0$$

On the other hand, globalization (interpreted in Case 6 as an increase in σ_η^2) obviously leads here, in contrast to Case 5, to a reduction in the inflation bias. The following namely applies:

$$E(\pi_D) - E(\pi_0) = \frac{b(y^* - y_n)}{1+(1+b)\sigma_\eta^2} > 0 \text{, with } \frac{d[E(\pi_D) - E(\pi_0)]}{d(\sigma_\eta^2)} < 0$$

For the derivation of the above findings it is however decisive that the money supply is fixed by the monetary authority before η can be seen.
Globalization in the sense of increasing uncertainty in the transmission process leads here in Case 6 to lower additional costs with a discretionary policy,: compared to a rule-bound solution. The following namely applies

$$L_D - L_O = \frac{0{,}5b^2(y^* - y_n)^2}{1+(1+b)\sigma_\eta^2}$$

1 Stabilization Policy Consequences

In this section I shall be more or less speculating on the question what it would mean for stabilization policy if the above hypothesis of a systematic (significant) influence of globalization on inflation should prove true in the future. However, I shall only point out some selected stabilization-political subjects.

That is, here we accept the above hypothesis that, as a consequence of increasing globalization, the socially optimal rate of inflation declines and the credibility-based inflation bias is significantly diminished. In a "totally" globalized economy, it may even be eliminated completely. As I have argued above, for this to be the case, globalization or international competition would have to penetrate not only the economic but also the political system of a society. In reality, however, there are and always will be niches of formal and informal protectionism, or institutional restrictions, so that we can argue that inflation and the inflation bias will never be totally erased. The main point, however, is that they will be more or less drastically reduced by the globalization process.

We ask what effect would this have on the optimal institutional design of monetary policy, and on other stabilization policy aspects?

5.1 Effect on Optimal Central Bank Independence

If globalization leads to a higher aversion to inflation, and hence produces the inflation rate (8'), as argued above, as one possible interpretation of the effects of globalization, we may conclude that globalization creates the same disciplining effect as central bank independence. Therefore, against the background of the alleged costs of central bank independence,[27] we could also conclude that central bank independence is then not needed any more, at least not in its function as a shield against the time-inconsistency problem. It appears to become superfluous. Nevertheless, we could add, there would still then be a need for other institutional solutions, since the central bank independence solution referred to above is only second-best at most: one can show in the above formal model context that $E(\pi_O) = E(\pi_{CBI})$, and $var(y_O) < var(y_{CBI})$ (see below, see in more detail, e.g., Wagner 1998a, pp. 138 ff.).

However, this seems to be a wrong interpretation, at least if we stay within the above model world. As long as society has b'' ≠ 0 (i.e., has some aversion against inflation), the optimal b' (the appointed central banker's personal value of b) will always lie below b''. The solution can still be improved by central bank independence, because the optimal (central banker's) b' is a function of b''. Globalization in the sense of a reduction of b'' does not therefore replace central bank independence, but increases the degree of optimal inflation aversion of the central banker.

---

[27] It is often contended that central bank independence increases output or employment volatility: from the above model structure we can derive the following patterns of output or employment $y_D = y_O = y_n - [1/(1+b)]\ \varepsilon$ with discretion and with the optimal state-contingent policy rule, whereas with central bank independence $y_{CBI} = y_n - [1/(1+b')]\ \varepsilon$. This means that volatility of output or employment is greater with central bank independence. This could, however, be reduced by a partial reduction of central bank independence, for instance by implementing an overriding mechanism (cf. Lohmann (1992)). Here, the government appoints a conservative central banker but threatens to terminate his/her contract if deviations from the target inflation become too large. Moreover, central bank independence is found to reduce electorally-induced volatility of output or employment (cf. Alesina/Gatti (1995)); Lippi (1998) provides evidence that could support this proposition. This aspect of a reduction in the political economy cycle may also explain, why the above hypothesis of greater output or employment volatility with central bank independence has not been proved in many empirical studies.

On the other hand, if we depart from the above model and no longer measure central bank independence against b, but against the degree of self-assertion of the central bank, it may in fact be possible to establish the above hypothesis of a decline in the degree of optimal central bank independence with increasing globalization in the above meaning (8'). Up to now we have only differentiated between central bank dependence and central bank independence by means of two different relative degrees of inflation aversion "b". Of course (as in Eijffinger/Hoeberichts (1998)), we can also record central bank independence in accordance with the degree of the ability of the central bank to push through a course which is more averse to inflation, against the government. Suppose the following two loss functions:

Government's loss function: (17) $L^G = E\{0,5[(\pi - \pi^*)^2 + b(y - y^*)^2]\}$

Central bank's loss function: (18) $L^{CB} = E\{0,5[(1+k)(\pi - \pi^*)^2 + b(y - y^*)^2]\}$

The expression (1+k) before the term $(\pi - \pi^*)^2$ in (18) is supposed to denote the higher inflation aversion of the central bank (k > 0)[28].

The independence of a central bank can now be regarded as the extent to which it determines monetary policy without interference of the government. The loss function that determines monetary policy, L, is here a weighted average of the central bank's loss function L^{CB} and the government's (society's) loss function L^G where the weight $0 < q < 1$ is the degree of central bank independence:

(19) $L = q\,L^{CB} + (1-q)\,L^G$

Substituting government's loss function (17) and central bank's loss function (18) into (19) gives

(20) $L = E\{0,5[(1+kq)(\pi - \pi^*)^2 + b(y - y^*)^2]\}$

What matters for monetary policy is kq: the product of conservativeness and independence of the central bank. There is an optimal degree of conservativeness and independence (kq*) which minimizes society's loss L. Insofar, as Eijffinger/Hoeberichts (1998) have emphasized, there is a trade-off between central bank independence and conservativeness. The underlying intution is that, if politicians and citizens become more concerned with inflation (caused for instance by globalization, see case 2 above), the time-consistent inflation rate goes down. (This can be seen if we add the Phillips curve equation (4') $y = y_n + c(\pi - \pi^e) - \varepsilon$ to

[28] This formulation is only correct if one interpretes b as an *absolute* aversion parameter, not as a relative one, as we have done above. For the latter case, it would be necessary, however possible, to reformulate the approach.

the above model structure, substitute (4') in (20), take first order conditions with respect to π and solve for rational expectations.) Therefore, society's credibility problem becomes less pressing. With an unchanged weight placed on output stabilization, the balance between flexibility and credibility needs to be adjusted in favor of a reduced commitment of fighting inflation.

In the interpretations of cases 4) and 5) of globalization above as well, where globalization eliminates the inflation bias or tends to lead to a deflation bias respectively, central bank independence appears to become superfluous[4]. Then there is apparently no longer any institutional need to protect society against this now fictitious/no longer existent problem. Again, we might conclude that there is no longer any need for central bank independence, in particular if we bear in mind that central bank independence itself is not without costs (see above).

However, it may be argued that institutional competition, which was described above as a characteristic of globalization, tends to make institutions such as central bank independence into a "must" for a state to be able to sell bonds on the international financial markets, at least at a "reasonable" price. In other words, bond issues without a quality seal have practically no chances on the capital markets. For example, today investors in general demand a premium with issues of bonds without rating. Central bank independence may be understood as a sort of institutionalized rating, as a seal of quality for transparency and financial solidity. This increases the credibility of macroeconomic policies, thus facilitating the raising of capital on international capital markets and lowering its costs.

Up to now, central bank independence has solely been regarded as a strategic shield against an inflation bias. Central bank independence, however, may or must be maintained if its task consists not only of being a shield against time inconsistency of optimal monetary policy, but also serves other purposes. What might these purposes be? One example is the avoidance of political business cycles[5].

Furthermore, central banks usually perform a variety of functions. These include:

- determining market interest rates through their control over the monetary base
- managing the payments system
- managing the foreign exchange reserves

---

[29] Another interpretation, which tends towards the same conclusions, may be that there has never been a real time inconsistency problem, at least not in mature industrial countries such as the USA or Germany in the last decades (cf. Blinder (1997), Tobin (1998)). See also recent theoretical approaches which doubt the relevance of the time inconsistency problem (cf. Herrendorf/Neumann (1998)).

[30] Cf. Alesina/Roubini (1997).

- promoting the stability of the financial system, by supervising the banks and by serving as lender of last resort
- acting as the government's banker
- determining the exchange rate (in full or joint responsibility).

The relevant question which arises here, and which would have to be analyzed in detail, is which of these tasks require central bank independence, or would be better carried out with central bank independence.

5.2 Effects on Recessions and Policy Coordination Efforts

We may be inclined to draw conclusions from the inflation-suppressing effect of globalization on unemployment, which is the main topic of this volume. However, I hesitate to follow this inclination. The main reason for this is that globalization will only lead to an essential decline in unemployment if it succeeds in directly reducing labor market rigidities, which are mainly responsible for the high structural unemployment problem in Europe, by causing intensified competitive pressure[6]. A reduction in inflation and the inflation bias has only a very limited influence on this. However, it may alleviate the supplementation of this necessary structural adjustment policy by expansionary demand policy, if this appears to be necessary, too[7].[8]

The following two aspects support this view.

Firstly, it has been shown that US post-war recessions have mainly been triggered by restrictive monetary anti-inflationary policies (Romer/Romer (1994)). If we can now infer a lesser danger of inflation, as a result of globalization, it should also be possible to establish a reduction in the frequency and severity of recessions

---

[31] In addition, it must be taken into account that pressure to reform (to dissolve structural rigidities) based on economic rationality is not directly converted into political reform activities (because of politicians' own interests based on elections and ideology). For this reason, a necessary precondition for success, i.e. for a reduction in unemployment, is that the expected costs-savings arising from such changes to institutions must be greater than the expected costs of reform itself, which may be regarded as a politico-economic hurdle in the path of the required labor market reforms. For this purpose, suitable institutional reforms are necessary, for which the competitive pressure triggered by globalization has to rise above a certain critical level.

[32] Cf. Modigliani et al. (1998).

[33] On the other hand, we could refer to the danger of an increase in unemployment that could come from deflationary effects which have recently often been claimed to result from globalization (cf. Bootle (1996)). For an anlysis of this effect cf. Wagner (1990).

(mainly caused by monetary policy shocks)[9]. Since it can be established empirically and explained at least plausibly that recessions are linked with unemployment, and that the duration and severity of recessions correlate with the duration and extent of unemployment (possibly increased by hysteresis effects), it should be possible to deduce a decline in average unemployment or positive employment effects of globalization.

Secondly, the "lesser danger of inflation" derived above and explained by the increase in costs of inflationary policy caused by globalization, and the lesser benefits that lead to a decrease in inflation motives or incentives for governments, may produce an incentive for greater coordination of policies. On the one hand, it may force/induce fiscal policy in certain circumstances to greater coordination with monetary policy. This in turn may induce central banks rationally to behave less restrictively (or less "strictly cautiously") in their policy of controlling inflation.

On the other hand, globalization may give more room to international policy coordination. Implementing international policy coordination is usually criticized or prevented by reference to the expected costs of an international policy coordination set up to combat common recessions, namely the danger of an increase in inflation. These expected costs will probably be reduced by the inflation-suppressing effects of globalization, and international policy coordination may therefore increase.[10]

2 Resumée

The „increase“ in globalization is a clear stylized fact, as has been the decline in inflation in the last two decades in industrial countries. The question that was raised in this paper is whether this could theoretically be interpreted as a causal connection between these two facts which runs from globalization to a reduction in inflation. We analyzed the correlation between globalization and inflation in this paper, and came to the conclusion that there are significant indications that globalization does indeed exercise a suppressing effect on inflation. This is done not only by reducing the benefits of inflationary policy, thereby reducing the inflationary motives of governments, but also by increasing the expected costs of inflationary policy (triggered above all by the danger of capital flight), thereby

---

[34] The situation in the USA in the last five years, in which the Fed has not initiated a recession out of fear of inflation (as previously) in spite of increasing or sustained overheating trends in the labor market, may serve as a first example here.

[35] In addition, the result derived in globalization cases 6 and 5 in section 4.2.3 above of a systematic undercutting of the socially desired rate of inflation would further increase the incentive to intensify international policy coordination.

developing general disciplinary mechanisms against inflationary policy. Therefore, not only the inflation bias but also the optimal/desired rate of inflation tends to decline.

The extent to which past globalization has already contributed to the world-wide decline in inflation during the last decade is an open question, and one which has, to my knowledge, not yet been examined in detail. However, theoretical arguments support the view that it may have been an important factor. We have investigated this effect of an increase in the costs of inflationary policy caused by globalization in a model analysis in this paper. We examined several interpretations of this cost effect of globalization, and for each of these cases we were able to substantiate the hypothesis that globalization leads to a decline in inflation.

With respect to stabilization policy consequences we only raised some brief considerations about the effect of globalization on the optimal degree of central bank independence, on the frequency and severity of recessions (and hence unemployment), and on policy coordination. On the one hand, we found that globalization might reduce the optimal degree of central bank independence if we determine central bank independence as the extent to which it determines monetary policy without interference of the government. On the other hand, we argued that globalization, by its suppressing effect on inflation, tends to decrease the frequency and severity of recessions, and in addition, to produce an incentive for greater coordination of policies, on the national level and the international level as well.

Specific statements on the quantitative parameters of these effects were not intended to be made here, because the purpose of this paper was only to provide an initial qualitative-theoretical examination of the above correlation and its policy consequences, which is still largely terra incognita. To enable a discussion of quantitative results, separate empirical studies have to be set up. But even the theoretical considerations carried out here are still quite basic, so that there is still a demand for research in the theoretical field, if a definitive evaluation is to be provided for the above question regarding the effect of globalization on inflation and on stabilization policy consequences.

Appendix

Derivation of equation (13):

(12) $L = E\{0{,}5[(\pi - \pi^*)^2 + b(y - y^*)^2] + f(\pi - \pi^*)\}$

(4) $y = y_n + \pi - \pi^e - \varepsilon$

(5) $\pi = m + v$

The solution approach (with μ as Lagrange factor for the condition that expectations are rational) is:

$$\underset{\pi, \pi^e}{Min}: \quad L + E(\mu(\pi^e - E(\pi))) =$$

$$E\{0{,}5[(m + v - \pi^*)^2 + b(y_n + m - m^e + v - \varepsilon - y^*)^2] + f(m + v - \pi^*) + \mu(m^e - E(m)\}$$

Differentiation gives:

(i) $$\frac{\delta L}{\delta m}\bigg|_{m = E(m)} = (m + v - \pi^*) + b(y_n + m - m^e + v - \varepsilon - y^*) + f - \mu$$

(ii) $$\frac{\delta L}{\delta m^e} = - b(y_n + m - m^e + v - \varepsilon - y^*) + \mu \ .$$

To calculate the rationally expected money growth rate, first the expectation values of the first order conditions have to be constructed.

From $E(\frac{\delta L}{\delta m^e}) = 0$ one gets: $\mu = b(y_n - y^*)$. .

Inserting into the expectations value of $E(\frac{\delta L}{\delta m}) = 0$ then gives:

(iii) $E(m) = m^e = \pi^* - f$ and thus $\pi^e = \pi^* - f$.

Substituting (iii) back into (i) and calculating the ex post first order condition $(\frac{\delta L}{\delta m} = 0)$ then gives:

$m = \pi^* - f - v + [b/(1+b)]\,\varepsilon$ and thus

(13) $\pi_O = \pi^* - f + [b/(1+b)]\,\varepsilon$.

Derivation of equation (14):

One gets (14) by calculating the expectations value of equation (i) with considering that the last term μ is suppressed now.

Instead of (iii) one then gets

$E(m) = m^e = \pi^* - f + b(y_n - y^*)$ and thus

$\pi^e = \pi^* - f + b(y_n - y^*)$.

Substituting this back into (i) and calculating the ex post first order condition $(\frac{\delta L}{\delta m} = 0)$ then gives:

$m = \pi^* - f - v - b(y_n - y^*) + [b/(1+b)]\,\varepsilon$ and thus

(14) $\pi_D = \pi^* - f + b(y^* - y_n) + [b/(1+b)]\,\varepsilon$.

References

Alesina, A. and R. Gatti (1995), Independent Central Banks: Low Inflation at No Cost? *American Economic Review* 85, 196-200.

Alesina, A. and A. Drazen (1991), Why are Stabilizations Delayed? *American Economic Review* 81, 1170-1188.

Alesina, A. and V. Grilli (1992), The European Central Bank: Reshaping Monetary Politics in Europe, in: Canzoneri, M. B., Grilli, V. and P. R. Masson (eds.), Establishing a Central Bank: Issues in Europe and Lessons from the US, Cambridge and New York, 49-77.

Alesina, A. and N. Roubini (1997), Political Cycles and the Macroeconomy, Cambridge, Mass.

Barro, R. J. (1995), Inflation and Economic Growth, *Bank of England Quarterly Bulletin* 35, 166-176.

Barro, R. J. (1997), Determinants of Economic Growth. A Cross-Country Empirical Study, Cambridge, Mass.

Barro, R. J. and D. B. Gordon (1983), Rules, Discretion, and Reputation in a Model of Monetary Policy, *Journal of Monetary Economics* 12, 101-120.

Blinder, A. S. (1997), What Central Bankers Could Learn from Academics—and Vice Versa, *Journal of Economic Perspectives* 11, 3-19.

Bootle, R. (1996), The Death of Inflation. Surviving and Thriving in the Zero Era, London.

Brainard, W. (1967), Uncertainty and the Effectiveness of Policy, *American Economic Review* 57(2), P. a. P., 411-425.

Bruno, M. and W. Easterly (1998), Inflation Crises and Long-Run Growth, *Journal of Monetary Economics* 41, 3-26.

Cukierman, A. (1992), Central Bank Strategy, Credibility and Independence: Theory and Evidence, Cambridge, Mass.

Cukierman, A. (1998), The Economics of Central Banking, in: Wolf, H. C. (ed.), Contemporary Economic Issues: Proceedings of the Eleventh World Congress of the International Economic Association, Tunis, Volume 5, Macroeconomics and Finance, New York, 37-82.

Cukierman, A., S. Edwards and G. Tabellini (1992), Seignorage and Political Instability, *American Economic Review* 82, 537-555.

De Gregorio, J. (1993), Inflation, Taxation, and Long-run Growth, *Journal of Monetary Economics* 31, 271-298.

Debelle, G. and S. Fischer (1994), How Independent Should a Central Bank Be? in: Fuhrer, J. C. (ed.), Goals, Guidelines and Constraints Facing Monetary Policymakers, Boston, Federal Reserve Bank of Boston, Conference Series No. 38, 195-221.

Desai, M. A. and J. R. Hines Jr. (1997), Excess Capital Flows and the Burden of Inflation in Open Economies, NBER Working Paper 6064, Cambridge, Mass.

Eijffinger, S. C. W. and J. De Haan (1996), The Political Economy of Central-Bank Independence, *Special Papers in International Economics* 19, Princeton, New Jersey.

Eijffinger, S. C. W. and M. Hoeberichts (1998), The Trade off between Central Bank Independence and Conservativeness, *Oxford Economic Papers* 50, 397-411.

Feldstein, M. (1997), The Costs and Benefits of Going from Low Inflation to Price Stability, in: Romer, Ch. D. and D. H. Romer (eds.), Reducing Inflation. Motivation and Strategy, Chicago, 123-166.

Fischer, S. (1977), Long-term Contracts, Rational Expectations and the Optimal Money Supply Rule, *Journal of Political Economy* 85, 163-190.

Fischer, S. (1990), Rules versus Discretion, in: Friedman, B.M. and F.H. Hahn (eds.), Handbook of Monetary Economics, vol. II, Amsterdam, 1155-1184.

Fischer, S. (1993), The Role of Macroeconomic Factors in Economic Growth, *Journal of Monetary Economics* 32, 485-512.

Fischer, S. (1994), Modern Central Banking, in: Capie, F., C. Goodhart, S. Fischer and N. Schnadt (eds.), The Future of Central Banking, Cambridge, Mass., 262-308.

Fischer, S. and F. Modigliani (1978), Towards an Understanding of the Real Effects and Costs of Inflation, *Weltwirtschaftliches Archiv* 114, 810-833.

Gosh, A. R. (1997), Inflation in Transition Economies: How Much? And Why?, IMF Working Paper 97/80,Washington,D.C.

Grilli, V., D. Masciandaro and G. Tabellini (1991), Political and Monetary Institutions and Public Financial Policies in Industrialized Countries, *Economic Policy* 13, 341-392.

Grimes, A. (1991), The Effects of Inflation Growth: Some International Evidence; *Weltwirtschaftliches Archiv* 127, 631-644.

Herrendorf, B. and M. J. M. Neumann (1997), A Non-Normative Theory of Inflation and Central Bank Independence, mimeo.

Horn, H. and T. Persson (1988), Exchange Rate Policy, Wage Formation and Credibility, *European Economic Review* 32, 1621-1636.

idw (1998), Globalisierung. Bedrohung oder Chance? Köln.

Illing, G. (1998), Mechanism Design for Central Banks - Results and Unsolved Issues, in: Wagner, H. (ed.), Current Issues in Monetary Economics, Berlin, Heidelberg and New York, 29-54.

IMF (1997), World Economic Outlook, (May), Globalization - Opportunities and Challenges, Washington, D.C.

Johnson, H. (1972), cited in: Vaubel, R. (1993), p. 62.

King, M. (1996), Direct Inflation Targets, in: Deutsche Bundesbank (ed.), Monetary Policy Strategies in Europe, München, 45-74.

Kißmer, F. and H. Wagner (1998), Central Bank Independence and Macroeconomic Performance: A Survey of the Evidence, Diskussionsbeitrag Nr. 255, FB Wirtschaftswissenschaft der FernUniversität Hagen (forthcoming in: Healey, N. and P. Levine (eds. 1999), Central Banking in the Transition Economies of Eastern Europe, London).

Kydland, F. E. and E. C. Prescott (1977), Rules Rather than Discretion: The Inconsistency of Optimal Plans, *Journal of Political Economy* 85, 473-491.

Lane, P. R. (1997), Inflation in Open Economies, *Journal of International Economics* 42, 327-347

Letterie, W. and F. Lippi (1999), Credibility and Imperfect Monetary Control, Chapter 1.2 in: Lippi, F. (1999), Central Bank Independence, Targets and Credibility: Political and Economic Aspects of Delegation Arrangements for Monetary Policy, 23-39

Levine, P. and J. Pearlman (1997), Delegation and Fiscal Policy in the Open Economy: More Bad News for Rogoff's Delegation Game, mimeo.

Lippi. F. (1998), On Central Bank Independence and the Stability of Policy Targets, *Scandinavian Journal of Economics* 100, 495-512.

Lohmann, S. (1992), Optimal Commitment in Monetary Policy: Credibility versus Flexibility, *American Economic Review* 82, 273-286.

Marquis, M. H. and K. L. Reffet (1991), Real Interest Rates and Endogenous Growth in a Monetary Economy, *Economics Letters* 37, 105-109.

Modigliani, F. et al. (1998), An Economists' Manifesto on Unemployment in the European Union, *Banca Nazionale del Lavoro Quarterly Review* 51, 327- 361

Monopolkommission (1998), Systemwettbewerb, Sondergutachten der Monopolkommission gemäß § 24 b Abs. 5 Satz 4 GWB vom 30. Juni 1998, Köln.

OECD (1998), The World in 2020. Towards a New Global Age, Paris.

Olson, M. (1965), The Logic of Collective Action, Cambridge, Mass.

O'Rourke, K.H. (1999), Globalization in Historical Perspective, *contribution in this volume*.

O'Rourke, K. H. and J. G. Williamson (1998), Globalization and History: The Evolution of a 19th Century Atlantic Economy, Cambridge, Mass.

Persson, T. and G. Tabellini (1993), Designing Institutions for Monetary Stability, *Carnegie-Rochester Conference Series on Public Policy* 39, 53-84.

Persson, T. and G. Tabellini (1995), Double-edged Incentives: Institutions and Policy Coordination, in: Grossman, G. and K. Rogoff (eds.), Handbook of International Economics, Vol. III, Amsterdam, 1973 - 2030.

Persson, T. and G. Tabellini (1997), Political Economics and Macroeconomic Policy, CEPR Discussion Paper 1759, forthcoming in: Taylor, J. and M. Woodford, (eds.), Handbook of Macroeconomics, Amsterdam.

Rodrick, D. (1997), Has Globalization Gone too far? Washington, D.C.

Rodrick, D. (1998), Symposium on Globalization in Perspective: An Introduction, *Journal of Economic Perspectives* 12, 3-8.

Rogoff, K. (1985a), The Optimal Degree of Commitment to an Intermediate Monetary Target, *Quarterly Journal of Economics* 100, 1169-1190.

Rogoff, K. (1985b), Can International Monetary Policy Cooperation be Counterproductive? *Journal of International Economics* 18, 199-217.

Romer, Ch. and D. Romer (1994), Monetary Policy Matters, *Journal of Monetary Economics* 34, 75-88.

Romer, D. (1993), Openness and Inflation: Theory and Evidence, *Quarterly Journal of Economics* 108, 869-903.

Romer, D. (1996), Advanced Macroeconomics, New York.

Sachs, J., A. Tornell and A. Velasco (1996), The Mexican Peso Crisis: Sudden Death or Death Foretold? *Journal of International Economics* 41, 265-283.

Sarel, M. (1996), Nonlinear Effects of Inflation on Economic Growth, IMF Staff Papers 43, 199-215.

Shirakawa, M., K. Okina and S. Shiratsuka (1997), Financial Market Globalization: Present and Future, IMES Discussion Paper Series 97-E-11, Tokyo.

Siebert, H. (1996), On the Concept of Locational Competition. Kieler Arbeitspapiere 731, Kiel.

Stockman, A. C. (1981), Anticipated Inflation and the Capital Stock in a Cash-in-Advance Economy, *Journal of Monetary Economics* 8, 387-393.

Svensson, L. E. O. (1997), Optimal Inflation Targets, "Conservative" Central Banks and Linear Inflation Contracts, *American Economic Review* 87, 98-114.

Taylor, J. B. (1998), Information Technology and Monetary Policy, Institute for Monetary and Economic Studies, Bank of Japan, *Monetary and Economic Studies* 16, 19-28.

Tiebout, Ch. M. (1956), A Pure Theory of Local Expenditure, *Journal of Political Economy* 46, 416-424.

Tobin, J. (1965), Money and Economic Growth, *Econometrica* 33, 671-684.

Tobin, J. (1998), Monetary Policy: Recent Theory and Practice, in: Wagner, H. (ed.), Current Issues in Monetary Economics, Heidelberg and New York, 13-21.

Tootell, G. M. B. (1998), Globalization and U.S. Inflation, *New England Economic Review*, July/August, 21-33.

Vaubel, R. (1993), Die Politische Ökonomie einer Europäischen Zentralbank. Probleme und Lösungsvorschläge, in: Bofinger, P. et al (eds.), Währungsunion oder Währungschaos? Was kommt nach der D-Mark? Wiesbaden, 59-64.

Vogt, W. (1999), Inequality, Unemployment and Inflation, University of Regensburg, mimeo.

Wagner, H. (1985), Einfluß der Inflation auf die Realkapitalbildung, in: Ehrlicher, W. and D.B. Simmert (eds.), Der volkswirtschaftliche Sparprozeß, Beihefte zu *Kredit und Kapital*, 9, Berlin, 201-233.

Wagner, H. (1990), Can Purely Monetary Disinflation Policy Produce Long-Run Involuntary Unemployment? *Jahrbuch für Sozialwissenschaft* 41, 198-216.

Wagner, H. (1991), Einführung in die Weltwirtschaftspolitik. Internationale Wirtschaftsbeziehungen - Internationale Organisationen - Internationale Politikkoordinierung. München (4. ed. 1999).

Wagner, H. (1996), Conditionality in Development Aid. Is it Welfare-Enhancing in Developing Countries? in: Köhler, G. et al (eds.), Questioning Development - Essays on the Theory, Policies and Practice of Development Interventions, Marburg, 245-262.

Wagner, H. (1997a), Rechtsunsicherheit und Wirtschaftswachstum (Legal Uncertainty and Economic Growth), in: Behrends, S. (ed.), Ordnungskonforme Wirtschaftspolitik in der Marktwirtschaft, Berlin, 227-253.

Wagner, H. (1997b), Wachstum und Entwicklung. Theorie der Entwicklungspolitik, 2. ed., München.

Wagner, H. (1998a), Stabilitätspolitik. Theoretische Grundlagen und institutionelle Alternativen, 5. ed., München.

Wagner, H. (1998b), Europäische Wirtschaftspolitik. Perspektiven einer Europäischen Wirtschafts- und Währungsunion (EWWU), 2. ed., Berlin.

Walsh, C. E. (1995a), Optimal Contracts for Central Bankers, *American Economic Review* 85, 150-167.

Walsh, C. E. (1995b), Is New Zealand's Reserve Bank Act of 1989 an Optimal Central Bank Contract? *Journal of Money, Credit, and Banking* 27, 1179-1191.

Williamson, J. G. (1998), Globalization, Labor Markets and Policy Backlash in the Past, *Journal of Economic Perspectives* 12, 51-72.

Comment on Wagner : "Globalization and Inflation"

Paul J.J. Welfens

EIIW, University of Potsdam,
August-Bebel-Str. 89, 14482 Potsdam, Germany

Inflation has been dead in the 1990s in OECD countries, except for a few short periods which in all cases led to consistent disinflation policies thereafter. So the question emerges whether central bankers have become so much more efficient in controlling the money supply process or whether changes in the institutional setting or shifts in policy preferences in the era of globalization have contributed to the low inflation period of the 1990s. Some countries even witnessed temporary deflation, and some observers indeed raised the topic of the perils of global disinflation. Surprisingly, there have only been few thorough analyzes on the link between globalization and disinflation.

The analysis of Wagner (1999) is a timely and important contribution to the emerging literature on the new topic and it is an important contribution since it comes up with a clear analytical perspective of how to cover the problem of globalization and inflation, with some aspects of unemployment included. He starts out with the observation that inflation in the 1990s seems to have become a rare phenomenon whose nature, however, is not fully understood. Globalization is defined as a development which increasingly exposes countries to international competition, a concept which possibly does not emphasize enough the role of increasing foreign direct investment. The basic question which is raised is whether globalization tends to bring about institutional reforms or changes in goods and labor markets which reduce the moderate pro-inflation observed in most OECD countries in the 1970s and 1980s; and to which extent intensified locational competition for mobile capital puts pressure on formerly inflation-prone governments to follow the low inflation model of leading OECD countries. The main motivation for consistent anti-inflationary policy in Western market economies will stem from the social cost of inflation. So, have the private or social costs of inflation increased in the 1990s, namely in the context of globalization? Or have the three basic inflation motives cited by Wagner reduced: i.e. the employment motive, the revenue motive and the balance-of-payments motive? In the following I will pick up some arguments of Wagner and add some additional remarks which might shed some light on the critical issues.

Wagner points out that the cash-in-advance models employed in part of the literature lead to an inverse relation between inflation and economic activity, where the most recent models include endogenous growth aspects. According to some studies, even modest inflation can have considerable negative output and welfare effects. While anticipated inflation can have negative welfare effects in the context of non-neutral tax systems it must be emphasized that unanticipated inflation has much greater effects. Allocative inefficiencies as well as undesired redistribution effects play a role here. The level and – to some extent – the variability of the inflation rate negatively affect economic welfare. So does globalization help in reducing the global inflation rate and its variability? Wagner´s answer with respect to the inflation level clearly is yes, and he offers an approach which goes beyond the simple argument that globalization tends to favor politically independent central banks.

A major impulse for a low-inflation bias of central bank policy stems from the fact that a country with a proven track record of low inflation rates tends to attract more mobile capital than high inflation countries. Competition for mobile capital affects the choice of (optimal) monetary policy and increases the costs of a short-sighted policy which aims to generate temporary benefits from surprise inflation. Quite interesting is Wagner´s modeling of the inflation bias in the context of a modified Fischer-Barro-Gordon model which consists of a quadratic loss function (with inflation and employment), a wage setting equation, a supply-side equation and an expectation-augmented Phillips curve plus a simple demand side equation. One can derive the familiar optimal inflation rate result. Wagner translates globalization in adequate changes of the parameters in the model and can show that – with and without time-inconsistency problems – the globalization process tends to reduce equilibrium inflation. A rule-based policy is typically found to have more favorable welfare effects than discretionary policy strategies. One certainly would like to see some empirical flesh added to Wagner´s concise analysis in the future. In the following analysis I will add a few thoughts to the topic of globalization and inflation where the term globalization will emphasize the role of foreign direct investment (FDI) flows which increased so much after 1985 and have contributed to an acceleration of the innovation-diffusion cycle (Welfens (1999a); Moran (1998)).

One may note that globalization has reinforced opportunities of small open economies since (vertical) FDI goes along with intra-company trade which further raises overall trade. However, even a newly industrialized country with a currency board, namely Argentina which recorded 4% annual growth in the 1990s and low inflation rates, had problems with the interplay of domestic politico-economic forces and globalization. At the end of the Menem era the unemployment rate was up to 15% again.

International Organizations and Monitoring

It should be noted that the 1990s have witnessed an unprecedented number of countries becoming members of regional or global organizations (EU, Asean, Apec; IMF, WTO) so that monitoring of economic policies has reinforced. This international monitoring process and the application of traditional benchmarking approaches to economic policy performance has increased the external pressure on policymakers to pursue rational policies. Conditional loans offered by the IMF to many countries certainly gave a direct leverage to reduce inflation rates. Furthermore, the example of the Asian NICs made clear that even relatively fast growing developing countries can combine rising government revenues without much long-term inflation. This does, of course, not rule off problems with a spike in the inflation rate as a consequence of massive devaluations and "forced" monetary expansion resulting from the central bank's attempt to save otherwise illiquid banks. While globalization might reduce the level of inflation worldwide in an indirect manner, mainly by reinforcing locational competition and competition of alternative policy concepts, the volatility might increase in some countries. This holds in particular for countries subject to temporary high portfolio inflows; if there is a massive outflow in a period of a confidence crisis the central bank might be forced to adopt an accommodating monetary policy course which effectively creates an inflationary potential.

Optimal Taxation Issue and Resource Prices

There is one development in the context of globalization which could encourage a more pronounced pro-inflation bias. Globalization means that real capital is increasingly less taxed so that taxes on labor income – or on consumption - have to be increased or government services and the welfare state to be trimmed. From an optimal finance perspective it would be natural to raise inflation rates somewhat in order to avoid a nonoptimal increase in taxes on labor income.

The negative supply shocks of the 1970s, namely the OPEC price shocks, are gone. The OPEC price shocks have indeed shown that the real prices even of finite natural resources cannot increase strongly in the long term because a price increase fuels new exploration, a strong substitution move in the medium term and innovativc conservation strategies. As long as we have an innovative chemicals industry no natural resource price will be able to increase over several decades in real terms. Globalization in the energy industry occurred in the 1990s and indeed brought about more trade in energy, including electricity, and the creation of future markets for electricity trade. The overall consequence is less medium-term price uncertainty and an overall fall of real electricity prices. Generally, the fall of infrastructure service prices and the development of new service bundles (energy, telecomms and information) has been a positive international supply shock.

Foreign Direct Investment, Innovation and Inflation

In the following I will draw on some recent research (Welfens (1999b); Welfens, Breuss and Tanaka (2000)) which has an explicit focus on globalization and monetary integration. In the 1990s economic globalization has been reinforced by further acceleration of foreign direct investment (FDI) flows and the removal of investment and trade barriers on the one hand, on the other hand the technological innovation of the internet has raised the share of tradable goods and services in overall output (World Bank (1998); Welfens (1999c, d)). Higher FDI flows imply that locational competition has intensified worldwide where low-inflation countries benefit from a high share of mobile real capital. This higher real capital mobility – partly reinforced by deregulation and privatization of network industries (telecomms, energy, traffic) in many countries – should lead to lower inflation worldwide as high inflation countries face a penalty for insufficient anti-inflationary policies. Openness indeed could weaken the motivation for a surprise inflation in the sense that a rise of the inflation rate amount to a negative terms of trade effect which has a relatively high negative welfare effect in the case of a rather open economy (Romer (1993)).

According to Tcha (1999) Australian FDI outflows positively react to the frequency/length of strikes in Australia, and a similar pattern – with a negative sign - holds for FDI inflows. This link between FDI and strike activities also can be found in some other countries. An important aspect of FDI is (Welfens (1998)) that a high stock of outward FDI reinforces the credibility of employers to relocate production abroad, i.e. globalization makes the labor demand curve more elastic in the main source countries of FDI.

A rising share of tradables in overall output implies that aggressive wage pressure from the nontradables sector – a typical ingredient in so-called Scandinavian inflation models – should become less important. As a consequence the pressure on the central bank to allow accommodating inflationary monetary policies could be reduced. This also would result in lower inflation in OECD countries.

Shifting Preferences?

Globalization is likely to go along with a biased technological progress which favors skilled labor, i.e. the wage ratio of skilled to unskilled labor would increase. While this development might lead to more social conflicts which in turn could lead to an inflationary bias of monetary policy the counter-argument is the following: Skilled workers will be able to save more during the active working period, at the same time they (i.e. the pension funds) will be eager to benefit from the international increase in the marginal product of capital, i.e. there will be a portfolio shift in favor of real capital. To the extent that the skilled worker represents the median voter of the 21st century – rather than the unskilled worker in the 1970s and 1980s in Europe – there might thus be a shift in political preferences in favor of lower inflation rates.

Globalization could also undermine – outside Europe – the viability of fixed exchange rate regimes. With more global exchange rate flexibility we will have more visible independence and responsibility of national central bankers which in turn should lead to lower inflation rates. Even in a fixed exchange rate world there would be a reduced incentive for inflationary monetary policies if the world's leading economies, the US and Euroland (the latter due to the convergence criteria), have a stable or falling debt-GDP ratio. The incentive to inflate is lower than in a world of growing public debt-GDP ratios in which (surprise) inflation reduces the real burden of public debt.

The Euro itself is reinforcing the process of economic globalization as it intensifies the competition in world currency markets. Furthermore it gives incentives for both more intra-Euroland foreign investment and more FDI flows into Euroland (plus eastern Europe) which presents itself as a highly integrated economic area. The Euro reduces the information costs for all prospective outside investors. However, at the same time the Euro represents a complex signal problem in the field of fiscal policy as an outside investor reading newspapers on Euroland's fiscal policy stance might find 11 contradicting statements of national fiscal policymakers. To the extent that the currency competition works in the Euro introduction period in favor of the dollar – as the Euro is depreciating for various reasons (including lower growth rates of Euroland compared to the US) – it could be less globalization which matters for reduced international inflation rates but rather a more anti-inflationary monetary policy course of the US in the context of a more open economy.

Some issues here can, of course, only be clarified by empirical research. A crucial issue in this respect is whether the share of sunk costs is increasing from a long-term perspective - globalization stimulates the rise of R&D-GDP ratios (and R&D expenditures are sunk costs) - and whether this raises overall price flexibility. One should expect that strategic entry of newcomers will lead the incumbent to a pricing strategy which reduces prices down to a level which ignores all sunk costs.

Hence a higher share of sunk costs in the era of globalization could raise price flexibility temporarily. It is an open question whether most entry attempts would occur indeed in a period of a recession.

One should note, however, that to the extent that R&D intensive goods are also durable products which partly serve as a store of value efficient price setting of firms would rather discourage higher price flexibility. Which proud owner of a Porsche would like to see the price of his fast asset strongly depreciating in periods of excess supply in the market for newly produced Porsches?

References

Moran, T. H. (1998), Foreign Direct Investment and Development, Institute for International Economics, Washington D.C.

Romer, D. (1993), Openness and Inflation: Theory and Evidence, *Quarterly Journal of Economics* 435, 869-903.

Tcha, M. (1999), Labor Disputes and Direct Foreign Investment - the Experience of Korea in Transition, *Economic Development and Cultural Change* 46, 305-328.

Wagner, H. (1999), *contribution in this volume.*

Welfens, P. J. J. (1998), Towards Full Employment and Growth in the European Union, in: Addison, J. T. and P. J. J. Welfens (eds.), Labor Markets and Social Security, Heidelberg and New York, 251-309.

Welfens, P. J. J. (1999a), Globalization of the Economy, Unemployment and Innovation, Heidelberg and New York.

Welfens, P. J. J. (1999b), The Start of the Euro, International Monetary Relations and Inflation, EIIW Discussion Paper 62, European Institute for International Economics at the University of Potsdam.

Welfens, P. J. J. (1999c), Internet Market Dynamics in Germany: From a Small Market towards a Strategic Sector of the Economy, EIIW Discussion Paper 59, European Institute for International Economics at the University of Potsdam.

Welfens, P. J. J. (1999d), Market Deregulation and Internationalization of Telecommunications: Economic Growth, Service Expansion and Foreign Direct Investment in Europe and the US, Research Paper for the European Commission, mimeo, Potsdam.

Welfens, P. J. J., F. Breuss and D. Tanaka (2000), The Euro and International Monetary Relations in the Triad, Heidelberg and New York, forthcoming.

World Bank (1998), World Development Report. Knowledge Development, Washington, D.C.

Notes on Contributors

Thomas Beißinger

Thomas Beißinger is assistant at the Department of Economics of the University of Regensburg. He studied economics and received his doctorate in 1996 from the University of Regensburg.

Ansgar Belke

Angar Belke is assistant at the Department of Economics of the University of Bochum. He studied economics in Münster, Kiel and Paris and received his Ph.D. in 1995 from the University of Bochum. He was visitor at the Center for Economic Research (CentER) in Tilburg, Netherlands, and at the Center for European Policy Studies (CEPS) in Brussels and finished his Habilitation in 1999.

Norbert Berthold

Norbert Berthold is professor of economics at the University of Würzburg. He studied economics at the Albert-Ludwigs-University in Freiburg, from which he also received his doctorate and Habilitation. He was professor of economics at the University of Hamburg from 1987 to 1990. He has been a member of the council of advisers to the German Ministry of Economics since 1995.

Daniel A. Citrin

Daniel Citrin is Assistant Director at the Office of the First Deputy Managing Director of the International Monetary Fund and Adivsor to Mr. Stanley Fischer (First Deputy Managing Director). He received his Ph.D. from the University of Michigan in 1981. He has worked at IMF since 1984.

Rainer Fehn

Rainer Fehn is assistant at the Department of Economics of the University of Würzburg and currently spending the academic year 1999/2000 as a John F. Kennedy Fellow at Harvard University. He studied business administration at the University of Würzburg and Economic Policy Research at the Kiel Institute of World Economics. He received his doctorate from the University of Würzburg in 1997.

Stanley Fischer

Stanley Fischer is the First Deputy Managing Director of the International Monetary Fund. He received his Ph.D. in 1969 from MIT (Massachusetts Institute of Technology), where he has also been professor of economics since 1973 (on leave since 1994). From 1988 to 1990 he served as Vice President, Development Economics and Chief Economist at the World Bank. He has held visiting positions at the Hebrew University, Jerusalem, and at the Hoover Institution at Stanford. He has also held consulting appointments with the U.S. State Department, the U.S. Treasury, the World Bank, the International Monetary Fund, and the Bank of Israel.

Bernd Fitzenberger

Bernd Fitzenberger is professor of economics at Dresden University of Technology. He studied economics, mathematics, and statistics at the University of Constance and at Stanford University. He received his Ph.D. in economics from Stanford in 1993 and his Habilitation from Constance in 1998. He has been a research associate of the Institute for Fiscal Studies, London, since 1998 and of the Centre for European Economic Research, Mannheim, since 1999.

Clemens Fuest

Clemens Fuest is a senior lecturer at the University of Munich. He studied economics at the universities of Bochum and Mannheim. From 1991 to 1995, he was a junior lecturer at the University of Cologne and received his Ph.D. from this university in 1994.

Daniel Gros

Daniel Gros is the Deputy Director of the Centre for European Policy Studies (CEPS), in Brussels, where he has been employed 1986-88 and then since 1990. He holds a Ph.D from the University of Chicago. From 1983 to 1986, he worked at the International Monetary Fund, from 1988 to 1990 as an Economic Advisor at the Directorate General II of the European Commission. He has taught at various universities across Europe, including the Catholic University of Leuven, the University of Frankfurt, Bocconi University, the Kiel Institute of World Studies and the Central European University in Prague. He is advising the EU Commission, particularly on the process of enlargement of the EU.

Carsten Hefeker

Carsten Hefeker is a post-doctoral fellow at the University of Basle. He studied economics at the Universities of Hannover and Constance, He received his doctorate from the University of Constance in 1996. Before moving to Basle, he was with the Centre for European Policy Studies (CEPS) in Brussels.

Arne Heise

Arne Heise is Senior Researcher at the Economic and Social Research Institute within the Hans Böckler Foundation, Düsseldorf. He studied economics at the Universities of Manchester and Bremen, where he received his Ph.D. in 1990 and his Habilitation in 1998. He was visiting professor at the Manchester Metropolitan University in 1996, The University of Applied Science and Business, Berlin, in 1997 and is currently visiting professor at the University of Constance.

Bernd Huber

Bernd Huber is professor of economics at the University of Munich. He studied economics at the University of Giessen. From 1985 to 1994 he was a lecturer at the University of Würzburg. During that time, he also received his doctorate and Habilitation from this university. He was visiting professor at the Universities of Bochum, Dresden and Munich.

Jürgen Kromphardt

Jürgen Kromphardt is professor of economics at the Technical University Berlin. He studied economics at the Universities of Göttingen and Kiel and received his Ph.D. from the University of Kiel. He was professor of economics at the University of Gießen from 1968 to 1980. Before he worked about eight years at the Commision of the (then) European Community. Since March 1999 he has been a member of the German "Council of Economic Experts".

Oliver Landmann

Oliver Landmann has been professor of economics at the University of Freiburg since 1987. He received his doctorate in economics in 1976 and his Habilitation in 1984 from the University of Basle, Switzerland. From 1989 to 1996, he directed a National Research Program of the Swiss Science Foundation on the challenges posed to Switzerland by global economic change.

Joachim Möller

Joachim Möller is professor of economics at the University of Regensburg. He studied economics and philosophy at the Universities of Tübingen, Strasbourg and Constance. He received his doctorate and Habilitation in economics from the University of Constance.

Kevin O'Rourke

Kevin O'Rourke is a statutory lecturer in economics at University College, Dublin, and a research fellow at the CEPR in London. He was a college lecturer at UCD from 1992 to 1997, and an assistant professor at the Graduate School of Business, Columbia University, from 1989 to 1992. He was a visiting associate professor at Harvard University in 1999. He holds a Ph.D. from Harvard University (1989).

Ronald Schettkat

Ronald Schettkat is professor of economics at Utrecht University, Netherlands. He studied engineering and economics in Hamburg and Berlin. He was a Senior Research Fellow at the Wissenschaftszentrum Berlin and a guest professor in the United States (Stanford University, University of California at Berkeley), The Netherlands (Tinbergen Institute, Amsterdam, The Netherlands Institute for Advanced Studies, Wassenaar), and Italy (Universities of Bologna and Modena). He has done consultant work, among others, for OECD, the European Commission, the European Parliament, the Federal Government of Germany and the German Bundestag.

Marinus Verhagen

Marinus Verhagen is lecturer in economics in the Department of Economics and Policy Studies at Utrecht University. He studied economics at Tilburg University and received his Ph.D. from this university in 1993.

Winfried Vogt

Winfried Vogt has been professor of economics at the University of Regensburg since 1968. He studied economics and mathematics at the Universities of Munich and Kiel. He was professor of economics at the University of Kiel from 1964 to 1971, visiting fellow of All Souls College at the University of Oxford 1970, and guest professor at the Institute for Advanced Studies in Vienna and at the Universities of Vienna, Zürich, Basle and Linz.

Helmut Wagner

Helmut Wagner is professor of economics at the University of Hagen (FernUniversität). He received his Ph.D. from the University of Regensburg in 1976 and his Habilitation from the Technical University of Aachen in 1981. He was professor of economics at the University of Hamburg (HWP) from 1982 to 1995 and visiting professor/scholar at the University of California from 1982 to 1983, at MIT in 1987, at Princeton University from 1991 to 1992, at the Bank of Japan's Institute for Monetary and Economic Studies in Tokyo in 1988, at the IMF Research Department and at AICGS/The Johns Hopkins University in Washington DC in 1997.

Paul J.J. Welfens

Paul Welfens is professor of economics at the University of Potsdam. He studied economics at Universities of Duisburg and Paris Dauphine. He received his Ph.D. in 1985 and his Habilitation in 1989 from the University of Duisburg. He was professor of economics at the University of Münster from 1991 to 1994 and McCloy Distinguished Research Fellow in Residence at AICGS/The Johns Hopkins University in Washington DC from 1990 to 1991.

Florian Wöhlbier

Florian Wöhlbier is a junior lecturer at the Chair in Public Finance at the University of Munich. He studied economics at the University of Munich.

Matthias Wrede

Matthias Wrede has been visiting professor of economics and public finance at the Technical University of Aachen since April 1999. He studied economics at the University of Heidelberg and the University of Bamberg and received his Ph.D. in 1993. He was visiting scholar at the Oklahoma State University in 1998 and visiting professor of economics at the University of Essen from 1998 to 1999.